reporting on the courts

reporting on the courts:

how the mass media cover judicial actions

William Haltom

University of Puget Sound

Nelson-Hall Publishers / Chicago

Editor: Dorothy Anderson
Design: Jane Rae Brown
Cover painting: Betty Ann Mocek, "Late Times"
Typesetter: Skripps and Associates
Manufacturing: Bang Printing

Library of Congress Cataloging-in-Publication Data

Haltom, William
Reporting on the courts: how the mass media cover judicial actions / William Haltom
    p.   cm.
Includes biblioographical references and index.
ISBN 0-8304-1405-3 (alk. paper)
1. Journalism, Legal—United States   2. Mass media—United States
I. Title.
KF8725.H35   1998   98-7441
343.7309'9—dc21   CIP

Manufactured in the United States of America

1 0   9   8   7   6   5   4   3   2   1

The paper used in this book meets the minimum requirements of American National Standard for Information Sciences—Permanence of Paper for Printed Library Materials. ANSI Z39 48-1964

For Sister Joan Holliday

Lumen sine fuco

My parents saw me, and they believed in me.

Candace has seen me, yet she believes in me.

Sister Joan had not seen, but she believed.

contents

acknowledgments

Stephen L. Wasby had the idea for this book when he was a consulting editor with Nelson-Hall. I was flattered that he thought I might be able to write such a book. He apparently was correct; with his generous assistance and scholarly insistence that I get matters right, I could write such a book. I thank Steve for suffering through my drafts and for his acumen. He gave his best; what he got in return is a matter for him and for the reader to decide.

Other scholars helped me as well. Elliot Slotnick carefully critiqued my prospectus and straightened me out as much as he could. W. Lance Bennett slogged through some early chapters and devoted part of a New Mexican jaunt to clarifying for me what I was trying to say. Charles Sheldon took great pains to sort through my discussion of judicial elections, and Mark Silverstein suggested examples and data that made my case better than I was making it. Hans A. Ostrom read the manuscript for style, and finding little that could be called literary, suggested how I might attain prose. John Brigham, Sheldon Goldman, and Christine Harrington commented on some of my earliest ideas at a colloquium at the University of Massachusetts. Michael W. McCann waded through my chapter on civil courts and Regina Lawrence suggested how to improve the chapter on criminal courts. Finally, Martin Edelman and Michael Huspek attempted to tease out my most problematic assumptions at a colloquium at the State University of New York at Albany.

The University of Puget Sound contributed a John Lantz Fellowship to pay me to begin this book, and John Burke and Howard Ball at the University of Vermont made me visiting faculty so I could rummage about in their library. I thank both institutions and the decision makers involved.

Stephen Ferrara was patient with my geologic pace in writing this book, insisting that it was more important that the work be done well than that it be done quickly. I hope he finds his investment repaid.

Dorothy J. Anderson and my copy editor, Catherine Podojil, did the best they could with my rambunctious prose.

Candace L. Smith and Sarah V. Smith sacrificed hours and days so that I might have the opportunity to complete this manuscript. I owe them a trip to Europe.

INTRODUCTION

Getting Courts and Media in Perspective

On St. Patrick's Day of 1994, readers of the *Burlington Free Press* awakened to more snow and a large headline — "Tonya: I'm Guilty" — that seemed to resolve a story that had, like Vermont's snow, overstayed its welcome. In its entirety, that story read:

> Tonya Harding ended her competitive figure skating career but avoided jail Wednesday by pleading guilty to a conspiracy charge in the attack on Nancy Kerrigan and resigning from the U. S. Figure Skating Association.
>
> As part of a plea bargain, Harding was fined $100,000 and agreed to three years' probation. Withdrawing from the USFSA excluded her from all amateur competitions, including the world championships next week in Japan. She was to leave today for Japan.
>
> Harding has said she learned of the attack after she and her ex-husband, Jeff Gillooly, returned from the U. S. Figure Skating Championships in Detroit on Jan. 10. In her plea bargain, Harding admitted that she and Gillooly met with her bodyguard, Shawn Eckardt, in Portland on Jan. 10 and went over a cover story they had concocted.[1]

This brief (173 words) item, quite similar to coverage in small dailies across the nation, seems to me quite ordinary. Please reread the story, and then I shall show you why I find this ordinary story inaccurate and incomplete.

The story seems accurate at first because it sticks to facts that most readers would probably not dispute. However, the story incorporates judgments that critical readers must contest. The first sentence (the "lead paragraph") might have been correct if it had stated that Ms. Harding *probably* ended her amateur skating career by her plea. Since Ms. Harding's competitive skating career need not be over, the first clause of the story stated as fact what could only be speculation.

That first sentence could have stated with accuracy that Harding's plea bargain provided for no imprisonment. Instead, it stated that Harding avoided jail, from which the reader might infer that the reporter was insinuating that Harding was headed to jail if the legal process had gone forward. That presumption or inference was not a certainty in a year in which the Menendez brothers and Lorena Bobbitt all escaped criminal sanctions.

That first sentence has, in my reading, two more flaws. Ms. Harding—as the article later confirms—pleaded guilty to conspiracy to cover up the attack on Ms. Kerrigan and not, as the first sentence might be read to imply, to conspiracy in the attack itself. Finally, the structure of this first sentence does not state as clearly as it might that the resignation was part of the plea agreement, which leaves the lead paragraph incomplete and allows a reader sympathetic to Ms. Harding to infer that she resigned on her own.

The final paragraph of this story is also inaccurate. The first sentence of the final paragraph reiterates Harding's insistence that she had no knowledge of the assault before it was executed, but the second sentence calls her insistence into question by saying that Ms. Harding admitted that she and Mr. Gillooly met with Mr. Eckardt to go over a cover story that "they had concocted." Perhaps the reporter and editor did not see "they" as ambiguous, but the critical reader would demand the antecedent. If "they" means Mr. Gillooly and Mr. Eckardt, Ms. Harding's insistence might still be true, but if "they" includes Ms. Harding, the tense of the verb "had concocted" indicates that Ms. Harding must have known about the attack before January 10.

My point is *not* that the reporter and editor mangled the story. Rather, I want you to note how flimsy our grasp of our political world must be if we derive our knowledge from mass media (and perhaps flimsier yet if we do not!). By selecting certain "facts" to relay and then arraying those "facts" in the manner they chose, the reporter and editor encouraged their readers to view Harding's plea in one manner when an entirely different interpretation might follow.

Consider how a supporter of Harding might rearrange the "facts" of the wire report into a story with a slant very different from that chosen in the *Burlington Free Press*:

> Tonya Harding today pleaded guilty to conspiring to obstruct justice in the attack on Nancy Kerrigan and was fined $100,000 and placed on three years' probation. As part of a plea agreement, she agreed to resign from the United States Figure Skating Association. As a result, she will not skate in the 1994 World Championships and may never skate in competition again.

Ms. Harding had repeatedly expressed deep regret over trying to shield her ex-husband, Jeff Gillooly, and her bodyguard, Shawn Eckardt, from authorities and had noted her ex-husband's history of abuse as one reason that she did not betray him until the FBI forced her to do so. Mr. Gillooly pleaded guilty to racketeering in planning the attack. After their arrests, Mr. Gillooly and Mr. Eckardt implicated Ms. Harding in the plot to disable Ms. Kerrigan and when Mr. Gillooly pleaded guilty, his lawyer attacked Ms. Harding.

I do not endorse this slant any more than I approve the angle of the story in the *Burlington Free Press*. Still, this fanciful report is more concise and more precise than the story in the *Free Press*.

Where Are We Headed?

The *Burlington Free Press* versus Tonya Harding illustrates a point that I shall drive home throughout this book: we must learn to look at journalistic reports of the courts from more than one point of view. My modest goal is to review what scholars have learned and have yet to learn about interactions of mass media and courts. My more ambitious goal is to see relationships between journalism and adjudication from more than one perspective.

My modest goal—to review a body of literature that has yet to develop much in most areas—is a worthy objective because serious students of mass communication need to incorporate coverage of legal and judicial politics into their thinking about news and journalism. Progress in understanding how mass media interact with legal institutions and processes will require devotees of different disciplines to appreciate the work of others. Accordingly, I shall review studies from communication, law, sociology, and political science. I shall accomplish my modest goal if I induce you to enter an interesting, important interdisciplinary conversation. My review of the literature will reveal many gaps in knowledge about court coverage.

My more ambitious goal—theoretical synthesis—is to assemble the conclusions and conjectures in the literatures that we review into tentative, coherent generalizations. Insights from one study or discipline can inform other studies and disciplines only if the insights are fitted into somewhat general representations of the subject. If I cannot construct from studies of judicial and legal journalism any usual patterns, tendencies, or expectations, then the interdisciplinary conversation is impossible.

Both my synopsis of findings to date (goal 1) and my synthesis of generalizations that future findings will test (goal 2) will have to overcome an unevenness of study in this area. I have an abundance of good scholarship with which to work when we consider coverage of the Supreme Court of the United States and on some aspects of judicial selection. I shall have to expand on less bountiful studies of coverage of criminal trial courts. To discuss courts that try civil cases and most appeals courts, I shall have to speculate. Throughout the book, then, you must remember that both my review of the literature and my theoretic synthesis must be tentative and anticipatory.

The rest of this chapter shows that research findings may be synthesized into more than one perspective. I shall begin by defining two perhaps extreme views of court coverage. The first view, the naive "Inside-Out" Perspective, formulates assumptions commonly employed by defenders of law or journalism. In contrast, the more skeptical "Outside-In" Perspectives surface more often in literature critical of law or journalism to provide fascinating insights.

Once I have introduced these two views of court coverage, I argue throughout this book that the "Inside-Out" and "Outside-In" Perspectives are useful, independently and together, to understand how mass media cover courts. You may be inclined to discover which is the better perspective. I believe that such "either/or" thinking is misleading. These perspectives need *not* compete with one another; they often complement one another. They can make our vision of judicial journalism stereoscopic. Unsophisticated students of court coverage will too quickly embrace one point of view or the other. Those who would understand how the media portray the legal system will want to see matters from more than one point of view. Aim for "both/and" thinking.

Is This Trip Necessary?

Why formulate general perspectives to describe such common-sensical situations? Much criticism of court coverage is not very systematic. Instead, judges and lawyers complain that journalists' ignorance has led to specific distortions, reporters complain that judges' and lawyers' evasiveness and indifference have impaired reporting in some instances, and academics document both complaints. If journalists are doing their jobs, if judges and lawyers are doing their jobs, and if journalistic and jural duties lead to collisions, we should expect disagreements about court coverage. Why dress up common sense?

I address common sense because all or most common sense is based on perspectives, patent or latent. Many if not most critics of court coverage, I shall argue, tend to presume part or whole of *the* common perspective, which I shall label the Inside-Out Perspective. That they do not acknowledge their reliance on aspects of the mainstream perspective does not make the underlying perspective unreal— it simply makes it unacknowledged. I move that we acknowledge our latent assumptions so that we may assess our reasoning. I hope that motion strikes you as reasonable.

I insist on formulating perspectives, then, as a way of making explicit what is too often implicit in descriptions, analyses, and evaluations of judicial journalism. Consider a common evaluation. Suppose a citizen reads an account of a legal case with which she or he is familiar. This citizen is aghast to discover that the account is seriously deficient in some way. The citizen throws up his or her hands and exclaims, "Is it too much to ask that a newspaper get even the most obvious details right?"

If this exasperated citizen is not merely venting or displaying smug superiority, she or he has assumed that most reports of court activities are and ought to be accurate and complete. More, any fair critic must also assume that most reporters can easily acquire and assimilate legal details into a coherent story. In turn, the fair critic must assume that the astute, clever lawyers and judges have not undertaken to deceive reporters and, through reporters, ordinary readers and viewers. In sum, if the enraged reader is to be taken seriously, that reader must presume that legal practitioners are ordinarily candid and media personnel are usually accurate. Is that presuming too much?

With all due respect to the reader and to common sense, in some instances the reader *is* asking too much. First, if the reader expects an accurate, comprehensive, and coherent story to emerge from a convoluted and consequential contest, he or she will sometimes demand that reporters and editors create comprehensibility where lawyers and judges have been unable to do so. Not only does the reader demand that the reporter "make the news," but the reader expects the journalist to make the news accurate, intelligible, and credible while battling deadlines, editors, and legal jargon. Second, this demanding reader assumes that courts issue clear results that may be relayed to ordinary readers easily. If judges and lawyers are the least bit sophisticated, unclear, ambiguous, strategic, or deceptive, however, the demanding reader is expecting too much of courts.

Even if the legal process produced only simple, clear happenings that reporters could instantly render into succinct but complete accounts, the demanding reader may further presume that such accurate, complete coverage would be interesting to enough readers to pay the reporters' salary and expenses. To the degree that newspapers and other media must compete for consumers and to the degree that happenings and reports compete for scarce space in the paper or time on the air, the reader may expect too much from media that must struggle to remain profitable.

In sum, even the most elementary expectations of court coverage assume certain roles for press, courts, and citizens. Those assumptions may be usually true, occasionally justified, or utterly idealistic. Unless the citizen-reader thinks through her or his presumptions carefully, he or she cannot be certain whether her or his criticisms are well founded. Thus, systematic formulation of our expectations is necessary if we are to fathom and evaluate judicial journalism. The theoretical trip on which we now embark is, I hope I have convinced you, necessary.

Two Contrasting Perspectives

We have just seen that observers of and commentators on judicial journalism often explicitly or implicitly define courts and/or mass media idealistically. Even—perhaps I should say "especially"—experts on court coverage incorporate those idealistic definitions into the conventional view of courts, media, and the public. As a result, such experts may presume too much in some, most, or all cases. I shall label this common view the Inside-Out Perspective to denote the tendency of journalists, lawyers, and other observers who are caught up in views "inside" the courts and/or "inside" the press to use idealistic views to construct a coherent but partial representation of reality for those "outside" one or both.

Recall throughout our tour of the Inside-Out Perspective that most writers need not subscribe to this perspective completely. Some would disavow every part of this view if they were fully aware of it. Indeed, this perspective often serves as a source of common beliefs to be refuted by those who invoke it. Rather, the Inside-Out Perspective is important because it furnishes a commonly accepted, coherent representation of how media, elites, and mass audiences interact, a representation that many of you will have seen or heard.

Table I.1 Two Perspectives on Media, Politicians, and Citizens

	Inside-Out *The Conventional,* *Idealistic View*	Outside-In *An Unusual,* *Skeptical View*
Media Mission	Objective accuracy	Inexpensive hype
Court Mission	Craft and candor	Strategic imagery
Audience	Extensively attentive	Mostly inadvertent
Information Flow	Mediated two-step	Drama and spectacle
Stance	Primarily prescriptive	Primarily descriptive

The better to recognize and to understand the Inside-Out Perspective, I shall also define *an* (not *the* because one can imagine a host of alternatives) Outside-In Perspective. This contrasting, coherent, yet partial view begins outside the presumptions of the Inside-Out Perspective and then constructs a theory of journalistic and legal interests to suit such "external" presumptions. Table I.1 will help us to keep track of contrasts between these two extreme perspectives. I have defined this Outside-In Perspective to contradict the idealistic Inside-Out Perspective at every point to sharpen contrasts between the perspectives. The stark differences between these two perspectives should help us look for and find features in court coverage that we might miss if we relied on only one perspective or failed to see how we rely on one perspective.

The Inside-Out Perspective

Table I.1 shows how users of the Inside-Out Perspective—sometimes inadvertently, sometimes intentionally—invoke a coherent representation of the interactions of mass media, courts, and citizens. The coherence of the Inside-Out Perspective springs from two sources: professional ideals, both of journalists and of judges, and traditional prescriptions, for citizens in democracies as well as for judges and journalists. The professional ideals that insiders learn while training to be journalists or judges prescribe the missions of reporters and judges. Proponents of the Inside-Out Perspective take those prescriptions to be normal behavior for reporters and adjudicators. To explain why journalists and judges tend to live up to their professional ideals, Inside-Outers (as those who use the Inside-Out Perspective will be nicknamed) must presume that audiences for judicial journalism assume traditional roles. In sum, the Inside-Out Perspective follows from professional and traditional presumptions about judges, journalists, and the public.

First, Inside-Outers presume that media usually are and should be objective and accurate (refer to the intersection of the top row, Media Mission, and the left column, Inside-Out, in table I.1). If media do not at least approximate these ideals, Inside-Outers further presume, audiences will reject biased or inaccurate coverage and seek better news, while judges, lawyers, and other politicians will penalize media for unfairness or error. Please keep in mind that even devout Inside-Outers must be aware of obstacles to ideal objectivity and accuracy. However, in the very act of criticizing coverage that falls short of ideals, Inside-Outers reassert the canons of journalism—the standards and ideals prescribed by the profession. Insider-Outers' very criticisms of coverage, therefore, tend to reinforce this ideal view of what media should do and usually do.

Inside-Outers, second, tend to treat judicial accounts as well-crafted justifications of thoroughly legal decisions.[2] Now, we must not assume that insiders are fools. They do not expect legal actors to be utterly impartial or painstakingly candid. Rather, they adopt the common expectation that justifications that are mere tissues of rationalization will be shredded by the first puffs of response. They hold judges to the standards of acceptability expected by elite and mass audiences, and they assume that judges are willing and able to anticipate and to counter rhetoric from those disappointed with the decisions. Transparent falsehoods and specious arguments will elicit fierce criticisms and politicize decisions and decision makers who are supposed to be "above politics." As with mass media, criticisms of courts will tend to reinvoke and thus reinforce the internal standards for adjudication, so that even scathing denouncements of judges for lacking candor and abandoning craft will begin from the Inside-Out assumption about the mission of the court.[3]

Third, to make sense of these idealistic presumptions about the media and courts, Inside-Outers must posit a primary audience for court journalism that is informed, astute, interested, and thus attentive. Such an attentive audience unquestionably exists, but Inside-Outers must presume that this attentive audience is extensive enough to discipline errant reporters or judges who fail to meet standards.

Without realistic sanctions, Inside-Outers have trouble explaining why journalists and judges would not abuse their positions for political ends. Vigilant audiences for legal coverage provide a traditional, democratic, and edifying explanation for the willingness of reporters and judges to live up to their ideals. With this assumption, as with the previous two, Inside-Outers tend to presume an attentive audience because conventional understandings demand it and not because any data support it.

Inside-Outers, fourth, and as a consequence of the first three presumptions, tend to assume a *mediated* two-step flow of legal information.[4] In step one, decision makers announce their decisions before mass media. In step two, mass media relay decisions to an extensive and attentive public.[5] This two-step process assigns crucial roles to three principal sets of actors: attentive citizens, mass media, and decision makers. Since even attentive citizens need never see a judicial holding, opinion, or order, mass media are needed to link such citizens to judicial events. If any set of actors fails, the inside-out model of judicial coverage becomes incoherent and suspect.

Inside-Outers, fifth, and in sum, tend not just to evaluate but even to describe court coverage using the ideals, standards, and prescriptions of journalism and law. They also tend to match these criteria of journalism and adjudication to "civics textbook" prescriptions for democratic citizenship. The roles of courts (judges, lawyers, staff, and parties), reporters, and citizens must coordinate to confirm the relevance and realism of the ideals, missions, and standards that constitute the Inside-Out Perspective. The "stance" of the Inside-Out Perspective must be primarily prescriptive, then, because its idealistic presumptions imbue even its attempts to describe and explain.

Examples of the Inside-Out Perspective

Although articles and books on court coverage commonly invoke one or more elements of the Inside-Out Perspective, the view surfaces most pristinely and completely in only a few places, such as in practical primers on media coverage of legal matters. "How-to" articles and books, for example, tend to assume the professional ideals both of law and of journalism. From these jural and journalistic ideals, authors dispensing professional advice may construct the entire Inside-Out Perspective outlined earlier. However, readers should remember that at least some elements of the Inside-Out Perspective will remain implicit.

Reporter Lyle Denniston

For a first example, consider the paragraphs by which accomplished judicial journalist Lyle Denniston began his text on reporting legal news:

> Truth is the common pursuit of the professions of law and journalism. Each, of course, pursues it in its own way. But when either succeeds, the result is the same: a free and self-governing society's most basic interests are served.
>
> Indeed, the establishment of truth often is the very achievement of justice. When the law succeeds in finding the truth, it gratifies the community's sense of right. That is justice. When journalism succeeds in disclosing the truth, it informs the community's capacity to function. That, too, can produce justice.[6]

Clearly, Mr. Denniston expects law and journalism to pursue ideals much of the time or he would not bother to relate law and journalism to truth and justice. A cynical, irreverent reader might explain Denniston's idealism by noting that the American Bar Association and the American Newspaper Publishers Association Foundation co-sponsored the book. A more sensible explanation for this high-minded start would focus on Denniston's desire to inspire his readers with legal and journalistic idealism before describing the rigors of living up to the ideals.[7] This explanation conforms to Denniston's reputation as an experienced and critical observer of the Supreme Court.[8]

See how many elements of the Inside-Out Perspective you can spy in excerpts from the rest of Denniston's introduction. I have added emphasis where I find those elements.

> This common calling [i.e., of law and journalism to seek the truth] is a high one, and it has compelled the two professions to learn — slowly and still imperfectly, it is true, but *determinedly* — that they must approach each other with "the same turn of mind," as the Biblical injunction would have it. "There must be no room for rivalry and personal vanity among you. Look to each other's interest and not merely to your own."
>
> This publication originated in that spirit, seeking to reach across the separations in *habit and philosophy* between law and journalism. Out of a mutual appreciation that we must know each other in order to work together, as often we are obliged to do, *the professions are now committed to a process of reciprocal education.*[9]

As I read Denniston, he is arguing that both lawyers and journalists assiduously pursue truth and that each is committed to explaining to the other profession the distinctive methods (differences in "habit and philosophy") by which each pursues truth. Denniston's passage seems to me wholly consistent with the statements of missions that the Inside-Out Perspective assumes for media and courts.

After reviewing recent debates about how to preserve both the rights of the press to cover criminal trials and the rights of defendants, Denniston reprises the missions of journalists and lawyers:

> It is no longer accepted that there is an irreconcilable conflict between *the press' mandate to inform the people so that they may govern responsibly, and the mandate of the bench and bar to do justice.*
>
> The process of accommodation remains a difficult one, nonetheless. *Each profession, as much out of habit as out of purposeful intent, is enough absorbed in its own processes and ends* that it is less than fully aware of the methods and goals of the other. . . .
>
> This volume also proceeds on the assumption that much of the popular perception of law is fundamentally flawed, in considerable part because of the *inattention or the ineptness of the press as a chronicler of the legal process.* [10]

In my reading, Denniston claims that journalists are at fault for some public misunderstandings of the legal system because they are so imbued with their own mission and ideals that they do not or cannot fathom the mission and ideals of bench and bar. If I read Denniston as he intended to be read, substandard coverage results from excessive attention to missions and too little appreciation of the other profession's ideals.

Having stated in the passage just quoted "the press' mandate to inform the people so that they may govern responsibly," Denniston invokes a two-step information flow:

> . . . It is no exaggeration to suggest that *most citizens will be able to monitor the quality of justice only if the press does it for them. The average citizen* reads no court opinions, watches few proceedings in court, studies no law review articles, has no regular contacts with judges or attorneys, and handles no legal problems himself. *The press is his law reporter.* [11]

Most readers will readily grant Denniston that almost every citizen who is not a lawyer (and many lawyers, for that matter!) will only be able to monitor the legal system through mass media. In discussing the flow of outputs from legal institutions through reporters to citizens, however, Denniston writes of "most citizens" and "[t]he average citizen." I read these phrases as an implicit assumption of an extensive attentive audience for legal news.

My respect for Denniston requires me to reiterate that I do not argue that he or others who invoke—directly or indirectly, deliberately or inadvertently—the Inside-Out Perspective fully embrace the factuality or even the plausibility of that perspective's presumptions. Rather, I have chosen as an exemplar of the Inside-Out Perspective the dean of legal reporters. Because a reporter who has covered the courts for decades cannot be presumed to be ignorant of reporting and judging that fall far short of ideals, and because Denniston himself concedes such failings both in an inset quotation above and throughout his book, the Inside-Out Perspective must surface because it furnishes the most common set of assumptions from which analysis and criticism may proceed.

Professor J. Edward Gerald

I warned you that the Inside-Out Perspective is usually implicit and thus must be ferreted out through close reading and inference. Perhaps you are not convinced that Denniston intended any Inside-Out presumptions. Let us turn to a careful reading and interpretation of another introduction from another unlikely source to see if I can persuade you that the Inside-Out Perspective infuses much writing about judicial journalism.

You should be able to spy Inside-Out presumptions in the following excerpts from Professor J. Edward Gerald's *News of Crime*.[12] What makes Gerald's implicit use of the Inside-Out Perspective remarkable is that the preface from which I quote was intended to defend an unabashedly critical stance:

> Much of what the media and the judges communicate about themselves is refracted through the lens of self-interest. The court decisions [on how the press may cover criminal trials without compromising the rights of defendants], *while conforming to law*, are sometimes tilted because *some judges believe that publicity ordinarily enhances chances for fairness while others regard it as an impediment*. Some judges favor less governmental control than others.

The public must decide whether justice has been done. *The press is the medium by which the public becomes informed.* The public is equally entitled to truthful information about the press in order to decide whether and to what extent the messenger has been fair and equitable in reporting the facts.

The courts and the press alike are entitled to our respect. *The quality of their work* accounts for the satisfaction with which most of us view self-government in comparison with other kinds. At the same time, the work is done by human beings; friendly and helpful evaluation is always in order.

The main purpose of this book is to help dispel misconceptions based on irritation and anger and *to encourage peace between the courts and the press.* (Emphasis added)

Gerald makes it clear that judges and courts conform to law and only "tilt" decisions out of concern for constitutional values such as free press (guaranteed in the First Amendment) and fair trials (guaranteed in the Sixth Amendment). Gerald further presumes that "the public" judges the justice system, an implicit presumption of an attentive audience for judicial journalism that is more than minuscule. He then presumes a two-step flow of information in which this nonminuscule attentive public monitors judicial performance through the press (which I take to include broadcast media as well as newspapers).[13] After a salute to the fine performance of mass media and courts (and thus an assumption that the missions of courts and media generally describe their performance), Gerald undertakes to show how harmony between courts and the press ought to prevail if only "misconceptions" about their missions and performance be dispelled.

Professor Chester A. Newland

Having analyzed the presumptions of reporter Denniston and communication scholar Gerald, I now turn up similar views in the work of a fellow political scientist, Chester A. Newland. Professor Newland's pioneering study of press coverage of the United States Supreme Court suggests anew that the Inside-Out Perspective will appear whenever observers attempt to establish the importance of coverage of courts. Just as primers such as Denniston's and critical surveys such as Gerald's tend to invoke professional ideals, assessments of press coverage tend to invoke democratic ideals. Newland's work, then, affords us a third example of Inside-Out thinking, an example designed to advance presumptions about audiences and the flow of information.

Newland's article begins with a paragraph resplendent in Inside-Out premises:

> Public opinion of judicial behavior and law are of vital consequence in the American legal system as a critical aspect of a polity based upon principles of popular sovereignty and limited government. This is particularly true of the United States Supreme Court. With the spread of legal realism and social science criticism in this century, the Supreme Court has lost the somewhat protective cloak provided by past myths of mechanical judging, and its opinions and processes are subjected to increasingly broad public scrutiny. Consequently, respect for the Supreme Court and law in general depends increasingly upon popular appreciation of the inherent merits of the Court's work. At the same time legal concepts and institutions are subjected to an ever-diminishing time span of technical and social change which imposes heavy pressures upon the Court and upon the American people whose ultimate support the Court needs. Great obligations are placed upon the high court justices and media of mass communication by these circumstances. [14]

This opening paragraph asserts high stakes: the Supreme Court and such key beliefs as popular sovereignty and limited government depend, at least in great measure, on news coverage of the Supreme Court. Newland's subject is thus of great import. Press coverage of the Court matters because "increasingly broad public scrutiny" has followed hard on the demise of myths of mechanical judging.[15] Newland here seems to assert that some attentive public is extensive enough to be a threat to the Court. Newland reinforces this reading when he infers that "respect for the Supreme Court and law in general depends increasingly upon popular appreciation of the inherent merits of the Court's work." If popular respect for law depends on coverage that conveys the merits of the Court's decisions and opinions, then mass media are crucial to the two-step flow of "good news" about the justices.

Newland has stated explicitly the object of his analysis: "This analysis supports the conclusions that both the Court and the press need to improve their methods if essential public understanding and support of the Court and a dynamic legal system are to exist."[16] Here again Newland assumes that a broadly informed public that understands and supports the Court is *necessary*. He further maintains that justices and reporters alike must better approximate their norms in a democratic society if this necessary public support is to ensue. Although the virtues that the press and the Court must embrace are not explicit in this prescription, I hope you will agree that all five elements of the Inside-Out Perspective are at least implicit in these parts of the first two paragraphs of Newland's article.

A Conclusive Reminder

The point of reading Denniston, Gerald, and Newland carefully is *not* to excoriate their idealism but to expose a model of press, courts, and citizenry submerged in their own descriptions of their scholarship. Were I to attack that model, I should have to shoulder a tremendous burden of proof, for the Inside-Out presumptions are, by my own argument, the mainstream view. However, my purpose is not to attack the Inside-Out Perspective but to show how familiar and common that perspective is.[17] If I am correct, the Inside-Out Perspective provides most observers with commonsense expectations of courts, media, and citizens, and that conventional view is the one most familiar to you.

An Outside-In Perspective

The simplest way to contrast the Inside-Out Perspective with an Outside-In Perspective is to see how less optimistic assumptions might yield a different expectation for court coverage. Outside-Inners need not negate each element of the Inside-Out Perspective with diametrical opposites. All that is necessary is to relax the internal view, assumption by assumption. I shall start with assumptions about the audience because I find them the least plausible element of the Inside-Out Perspective defined earlier.[18]

From an Attentive to an Inadvertent Audience

Suppose an Outside-Inner were to assume that a majority of the audience for court coverage is an "inadvertent public," far less sophisticated, interested, aware, and attentive than the Inside-Out Perspective must presume. There is far more evidence suggesting widespread ignorance and apathy than there is for a very extensive attentive public for courts or any other political news.[19] As we saw earlier, the hopeful, "civics textbook" portrait of citizens is as crucial to the Inside-Out Perspective as any other presumption, so any relaxation of the presumption of an attentive public immediately threatens the coherence of the perspective. Having relaxed the mainstream presumption of an attentive audience that is not negligible, let us now see how easily the Inside-Out Perspective transmutes to an Outside-In Perspective.

An inadvertent public cannot punish journalists or judges for transgressions about which citizens neither know nor care.[20] Rather, such an inadvertent public is available to sanction poor performance only at the behest of elites or demagogues, if then. Thus, the most modest concession to realism in representing the interactions of citizens with judicial journalism results in freeing judges and journalists from the very prescriptions and proscriptions (that is, the statements of mission) that define the Inside-Out Perspective.

From Information Flow to Drama and Spectacle

As a result, assuming an "inadvertent public" would compel Outside-Inners to reconceive the flow of information from legal and media elites to masses—a second shift from the Inside-Out Perspective. If most judicial opinions and journalistic reports do not reach most citizens, it seems reasonable to expect that for most legal news there is only a trickle of information to an attentive minority in elite media. Instead, the Outside-Inner might expect that citizens who use mass media confront a flow that is less information than entertainment. Let us see why this budding Outside-In Perspective forces us to this conclusion.

To overcome the indifference of most citizens to legal news, both mass media and decision makers must reassure or threaten the inadvertent public with dramatic spectacles.[21] Bombast is much more "newsworthy" than tight, technical reasoning and takes up less space and time, so we might expect judges and especially litigants, advocates, and their sympathizers[22] to politicize legal issues and escalate conflict beyond the confines of adjudication. Interpersonal conflicts, adversarial maneuvers, shocking outcomes, and community outrage are far easier to report than accurate descriptions of more normal legal work, and journalists have little stake in covering what they understand almost as poorly as their readers and viewers. Thus, the presumption of an inadvertent public would lead Outside-Inners to expect drama and spectacle at least to compete with and probably to overwhelm information in court coverage. Let us see where that insight might lead.

From Objective Accuracy to Inexpensive Hype

Whenever they strive to maintain drama and spectacle, reporters will focus on intriguing story lines rather than less newsworthy, less popularized, and hence more revealing details. Mass media tend to prefer stories that may be covered easily, cheaply, and in a manner that generates attention and sales.[23] Thus, the third contrast between the Inside-Out Perspective and an Outside-In Perspective concerns views of the mission of the media. Accurate, objective coverage makes a lofty mission statement and must characterize much coverage lest the attentive public give up on a news outlet. Nonetheless, Outside-Inners expect low-cost, exaggerated coverage (that is, "hype") to meet the abilities of citizens and reporters and the demands of the marketplace. At the very least, then, an Outside-In Perspective directs attention to many significant lapses from the objective, laudable coverage that the Inside-Out Perspective presumes.

From Craft and Candor to Cunning and Cant

Lawyers and judges sometimes furnish the raw material for dramatic spectacles of adjudication. All but the most dogged Pollyannas expect lawyers to play to the grandstand, especially after decisions. However, judges on even the highest courts may succumb to such temptations as well. In an era dominated by propaganda, public relations, and mass media, judges would not be human if they did not at least occasionally avail themselves of imagery for strategic ends.[24] Well-crafted and fearlessly honest judicial accounts do not pander to the inattentive public and spectacle-mongering media, so the information trickle we discussed earlier limits the influence of the judicial decision maker. If judges believe that they have something to say to any but the narrowest audiences, they must indulge in some strategic rhetoric to be heard. Thus, an Outside-In Perspective might lead us to expect judges to "get in the game" far more often than the Inside-Out Perspective would.

From Idealistic Prescription to Critical Description

Such harsh portraits of citizens, media, and politicians are so outside the mainstream of politics in the United States that we must label the outsiders' stance as predominately descriptive. That is, the Outside-In Perspective urges attention to how citizens, reporters, and courts often interact, not to how they *ought* to interact. This alternative perspective overcomes the complacency of traditional assumptions by presuming that critical accounts of citizens, journalists, and lawyers contain some truth. Those who take an Outside-In Perspective may concede that media, courts, and citizens ought to behave as the Inside-Out Perspective assumes. Indeed, Outside-Inners may even concede that participants often behave as the Inside-Out Perspective demands. The key difference between the views is that Outside-Inners focus on deviations from the Inside-Out Perspective as very important for evaluating coverage of courts.

Two Examples of Outside-In Perspectives

Perhaps because swimming outside the mainstream requires more caution, Outside-Inners tend to be more explicit about which aspects of the conventional, Inside-Out Perspective they reject. However, please do not expect Outside-Inners to articulate full-blown alternatives. Partial critiques of the Inside-Out Perspective—by lawyers suspicious of journalists' motives and competence but confident of the virtue of bench and bar, for example—do not even try to refute each Inside-Out assumption. It is far more manageable for critics to assume, at least for the sake of argument, all of the standard understanding except the assumption they want to attack.

Professors David Paletz and Robert Entman

Two scholars have provided an explicit and fairly complete alternative to the Inside-Out Perspective. Professors David Paletz and Robert Entman have argued that the Supreme Court of the United States appears to need and use mass media less than any other national institution but, in fact, plays mass media politics quite deftly.[25] I will generalize their argument to all courts to reveal one external view of judicial journalism.

Paletz and Entman argue that courts employ a twofold strategy to control their images. First, they take advantage of every symbol and ritual to emphasize the majesty of the law and the formality of the judicial process. While dramatizing their transcendence of politics and the mundane center stage, courts simultaneously minimize public access to the backstage operations of the judicial system.

> What reporters see inside the courtroom — all they see — is designed more to elevate than to display the judicial process. The ornate setting, the ritual, the ceremony, the way the justices preside in their robes and high-backed chairs, physically and metaphorically raised up, occasionally deigning to pose and press questions while the lawyers plead their cases below; all sanctify the authority of the Court and its members.
>
> Meanwhile, the crucial decisions are reached in private,

out of sight and earshot of reporters. For, of all the institutions of American government, the Supreme Court is the least permeable to the press. As Congress is relatively open to the mass media, as its members court publicity, the justices shun it. How decisions are reached; the kinds of informal contact among the justices; the appeals and persuasion; the sometimes pragmatic compromises, negotiation and bargaining; all are kept confidential. . . .

Access denied is reinforced by information controlled. Supreme Court justices—all judges—preside, commune alone or deliberate with one another, and reach their decisions. They speak to the mass media—when they speak at all—through official spokespersons, not in person. The representative, in turn, is mainly a conduit for transmitting the decision and servicing reporters; he or she neither expounds on [sic] the decision nor describes the process by which it was reached.

. . . Yet the media themselves contribute to deferential coverage, most importantly by their adherence to the myth of the judicial exception. Most reporters seem to think that the Supreme Court is above and beyond politics, unsullied—in contrast to the executive and legislative branches. . . .

Journalists who cover the judicial system accept and respect the majesty of the law as it issues from the Supreme and lower federal courts—and most state courts too. They sense, if they do not fully comprehend, the vulnerability of the courts' legitimacy. To dissect the courts, expose the fallibility and frailties of judges, could undermine the legal system by encouraging disrespect for court decisions by the public officials who should execute, and the public who should obey them. [26]

In this excerpt I detect multiple, mutually supporting departures from the Inside-Out Perspective. First, Paletz and Entman notice that the justices (and remember, I am generalizing their argument for all courts) need not practice their craft with the candor that insiders implicitly expect. Rather, they assume that judges and justices, like other political officers in modern politics, fashion rhetoric that will satisfy an audience and preserve the delicate legitimacy of courts. The judges may be relatively straightforward and clear, as the Inside-Out Perspective assumes, but they may also be cunning, as any sophisticated observer of politics would expect.

Second, Paletz and Entman note the complicity of reporters in conveying, if not co-producing, the majesty and eminence of the courts. Rather than embracing the Inside-Out assumption that reporters strive for accuracy and objectivity, Paletz and Entman insist that reporters strive to maintain the myths and imagery of their subjects.

Having posited different missions for the courts and the media, they take the next Outside-In step: they presume that most of the audience is not very adept at seeing through the production of legal majesty by courts and media. Although Paletz and Entman do not explicitly note that most of the audience is quite inadvertent and perhaps indifferent, they must assume that most of the judges' audience is neither astute nor attentive, else they would see through the mediated courts. However, Paletz and Entman explicitly characterize the flow of information as primarily "drama and spectacle" and not a two-step that informs the audience.

This unabashedly descriptive and analytic look at court journalism contrasts starkly with most scholarship on the subject. Most studies of judicial journalism are informed, implicitly or explicitly, by the Inside-Out Perspective far more than by alternatives.

Justice Antonin Scalia

By no means is Paletz's and Entman's Outside-In Perspective the most extreme alternative. Consider the views of Justice Antonin Scalia.[27] In a 1990 speech, Justice Scalia differentiated between legally astute audiences, whom the justices may inform, and lay audiences, whom the justices cannot reach. The primary audience for courts must consist of the Bench and Bar, in Scalia's view, for no other public can fathom the justices' language and reasoning. Judicial results and reasons flow from the courts to the elite, jural public.

To Justice Scalia, the flow from legal elites to attentive and mass publics is, apparently, at best a matter of indifference and at worst an obstruction of justice. Specialized media (such as law reviews and reports of decisions) transmit judges' reasons to lawyers and judges because mass media are ill-equipped to do so. Mass media may induce acquiescence or reinforce judicial authority, but they have only a minor role in relaying reasons. Instead, mass media report results and consequences of decisions and avoid the arcane reasoning of judges that neither reporters nor readers can comprehend. Justice Scalia believes that the intricacies of judicial reasoning are essential information for evaluating the work of the courts. "You cannot reasonably expect to get all that information from a newspaper account, at least not a newspaper that wants to remain in business. That's why the *University of Chicago Law Review* is not sold in 7-11 [sic] stores."[28] Table I.2 displays my best formulation of Justice Scalia's "model" of legal reporting.

Table I.2   Tentative Formulation of Justice Scalia's Perspective

	Scalia Model
Primary Audience	Legally astute
Information Flow	From courts to Bench and Bar
Media Mission	Elite media inform Bench and Bar; media entertain masses
Judges' Job	Formulate reasons for Bench and Bar
Valuative Criteria	Hyperformal

Justice Scalia is not alone in his concern about mass media and courts (especially appellate courts). Tarr and Porter summarized the experiences of the Ohio State Supreme Court with news coverage in a similar manner:

> . . . [T]he media, with the exception of a handful of newspapers and reporters, are not equipped to handle courts. And courts, in turn, with fewer exceptions, are even less prepared to handle the press. *Ordinarily this failure of communication is of no great consequence.* However, when for whatever reason a court becomes news, run-of-the-mill misunderstandings may result in rancor on both sides. Further, as this chapter illustrates, the public, heretofore mostly ignorant about judicial functions and processes, may be made aware of the third branch only through sensationalist accounts of possible skulduggery in high places. The result is that the press, not having taken the time or not having cared about educating readers about courts, presents an erroneous and distorted view of the third branch and its purposes. . . . More sophisticated and in-depth coverage—once reporters had put the court on their beats—would have provided the Ohio electorate with more information upon which to base their decisions. [29] (Emphasis added)

The Multiplicity of Perspectives Available and Useful

Obviously, inside and outside perspectives inform different researchers and different projects to various degrees, so we should expect neither coverage nor research about coverage to match either perspective or any alternative in every particular. Realistic readers and viewers expect neither perfection nor perfidy from media, courts, lawyers, and scholars. Knowledgeable observers anticipate that some citizens are attentive to some cases and controversies but apathetic about and/or ignorant of other legal matters. Critical citizens will not settle for the glib, safe assumption that "the truth is somewhere in between." Realistic, knowledgeable, and critical students of court coverage will insist on using multiple perspectives to see judicial journalism from many angles.

For example, Paletz and Entman, the authors whom I cited to exemplify an Outside-In Perspective, introduced their work with a remarkably balanced view:

> This book is personal, interpretive, openly speculative; but it is not ideological. We critically analyze the media to be sure. We are not apologists. But we show how the media simultaneously disrupt and defend the status quo, how they can both assist the radicals and marshal the forces of reaction. Most important, we reveal how they inadvertently promote confusion, discontent, discord. In other words, we try to portray the effects of the media on American politics in all their complexity and contradiction. [30]

Paletz and Entman are too astute to assert that their Outside-In Perspective, by itself, explains everything. Instead, they insist that media politics is subject to complex contradictions and can be understood well only by taking countervailing influences into account.

I shall follow their example. I introduced only two perspectives to remind you that there are many ways in which to understand even the simplest social processes and events. Court coverage is not a simple social process or cultural artifact, so it can and should be seen from a variety of perspectives. However, even the two perspectives already defined will yield insights and implications.

Implications of Internal and External Perspectives

The two perspectives outlined generate at least four expectations for judges and reporters, even if we ignore audiences and the flow of information. Journalists who try to optimize the newsworthiness (which I shall call "news-worth") and timeliness of coverage may strive for accuracy (as the Inside-Out Perspective predicts) even as they strive for expediency (as an Outside-In Perspective might predict). Judges who try to convey reasonably sincere accounts of decisions may produce the Judicial Candor that insiders expect, but, to defend the legitimacy of their decisions, judges must also provide a rhetorical account shaped to the expectations of presumed audiences. Call this Judicial Suasion. Thus, the Inside-Out and Outside-In Perspectives furnish the four expectations in table I.3.

The four possibilities in table I.3 are not equally likely. The ideals of journalism and jurisprudence demand that formality prevail routinely and, more to the point, seem to prevail almost always. Most cases conform to the needs of both mass media and the legal system because both enterprises are designed around ordinary reporting of ordinary adjudication. Thus, we should expect coverage of the courts to approximate the combined expectations of insiders much, perhaps even most, of the time.

Table I.3 **Four Possibilities That Follow from Inside and Outside Perspectives**

	Inside-Out Media strive for accuracy	Outside-In Media strive for expediency
Inside-Out *Judicial* *Candor*	Idealism: Precise media carefully relay candid judicial decisions to audiences	Distortion: Judges are candid but mass media cut corners
Outside-In *Judicial* *Suasion*	Mystification: Mass media carefully relay judges' cunning deceits at audiences' expense	Pragmatism: Media and Judges both pursue institutional interests

However, this routine formality should not distract us from the ever-present possibilities of distortion, mystification, and pragmatism. Truly ordinary, truly formal cases are the ones least likely to be covered, because they are not news by the most conventional journalistic definitions of the term. More newsworthy cases are likely to tax mass media, the legal system, or both. When complex or prolix decisions defy journalists' and editors' best efforts to cram coverage into an ever-shrinking "news hole," distortions are inevitable. When media uncritically convey to their audiences indefensible judicial decisions, they abet judges in mystifying the citizenry. Finally, if Gerald is correct in claiming that "[m]uch of what the media and the judges communicate about themselves is refracted through the lens of self-interest,"[31] judicial journalism will often be pragmatic.

Conclusion

The implications are that even the two perspectives will yield intriguing possibilities, especially once we factor in audiences and the flow of information. From the possibilities in table I.3, I have determined that the elementary tensions between two opposed perspectives are sufficient to allow us to "triangulate" chronic and occasional features of court coverage. Thus, in the remainder of this book, I shall describe the coverage of courts and then assess the coverage with the aid of these two main perspectives. As alternative views, such as those of Justice Scalia, seem apposite, I shall remind you of them. You will formulate your own views as you review each chapter.

To understand coverage of the courts completely, one must master both the normal and the everpresent threats to the norms. When you are adept at seeing both the ordinary and the extraordinary in adjudication, journalism, and scholarship, then you will be a sophisticated student of coverage of the courts.

CHAPTER 1

Construction of Judicial and Journalistic Authority

Even if the Inside-Out and the Outside-In Perspectives defined in the previous chapter improve our vision by enabling us to see court coverage stereoscopically, how can I maintain that those opposing perspectives are complementary rather than contradictory? These two main perspectives seem to be combatants, not companions.

To understand the two perspectives as complements, you must understand how courts and news media legitimize their decisions and accounts. This chapter explains how courts and news media, separately and interactively, re-create and maintain *authority*. With authority, courts are entitled to be obeyed and mass media to be believed. Absent authority, judges and reporters alike lose some of their privileges and must compete with stronger political and social interpreters. Thus, we must presume that reporters and editors and judges and justices hustle to defend their respective authorities.

To defend their authorities, judges and reporters direct their audiences to *standards* by which audiences may satisfy themselves that decisions and accounts are legitimate. Legal practitioners invoke formal standards and journalists brandish professional canons, both of which consist largely of ideals that must be compromised greatly when novelties or other difficulties loom. Those compromises threaten the legitimacy of decision makers, so decision makers must stress the impossible ideals and minimize their deviations from those ideals as much and as often as they can.

Enter our two main perspectives. The Inside-Out Perspective presumes that courts, news media, and citizens play roles very similar to the ideals prescribed for each. Our Outside-In Perspective—remember, it is only one of many possible alternatives—presumes that judges, reporters, and consumers deviate from those prescribed ideals significantly and habitually. My survey of courts and news media reveals ample support for both views, setting up assessments of each view in subsequent chapters. We shall discover that courts and media usually approximate the Inside-Out ideals but often justify our Outside-In suspicions as well. That is why I have counseled you toward "both/and" thinking and away from "either/or" thinking.

Creating and Managing Authority Through Standards

Courts and news media, like most decision makers, depend on authority—the ability to command or expect deference, credence, or compliance. Without authority, decision makers cannot expect to be heeded. Since as children we learn simultaneously who authorities are and what authority is, we may mistake authority for a possession of those in positions of public trust. Authority, however, is more a matter of performance than position. Judges, editors, and reporters who shape and then meet the expectations of their audiences achieve credibility and deference. Those who fail to shape or to meet those expectations must rely on raw power denuded of authority.[1] Since courts and mass media have little raw power, such reliance will often be misplaced.

Tradition, Charisma, and Standards

Students of society usually identify three sorts of legitimate authority: tradition, charisma, and what I shall call "standards."[2] Traditional authority legitimizes decisions by their correspondence to habits and expectations long established and widely approved. Charismatic authority legitimizes decisions by their resemblance to deeds and dogmas promulgated by one or more exemplary individuals believed to be inspired by insight above and beyond ordinary people. "Standards," in contrast, legitimize decisions by stipulating ideals, aspirations, and criteria that the decisions meet. Any institution, actor, or system of decision making must rely on all three sources to legitimize its authority, but standards are most important for courts and news media.

Tradition and charisma provide a foundation for judicial and journalistic authority by supplying customary routines and approved examples to which the decision maker may conform safely because the routines and examples predate decisions and thus seem largely beyond the decision maker. Tradition and charisma may be said to be "suprahuman" or transcendent authority because they are so well established that authority emanates from immemorial practices, time-tested processes, and widespread consent. Long-standing, transcendent authority will often prove unresponsive or maladapted to novel demands and specific decisions, however, because traditions must endure to be authoritative and charismatic exemplars die. The institutions that concern us here—courts and news media—require less transcendent but more malleable authority if they are to adapt and prosper.

Standards furnish the less transcendent but more malleable authority that courts and the press require. Standards are less transcendent because humans create and reformulate them deliberately and obviously, sometimes ad hoc and often haphazardly. Audiences, once aware that authority comes not from long ago or far above, may feel free to judge decisions for themselves using the very standards that decision makers adduce. Still, standards promote adaptation and rationalization to a far greater extent than traditional or charismatic authority. Standards dictate certain steps to be followed or certain thresholds to be met before decisions can be authoritative. If decision makers follow the steps, they often "discover" authority that warrants extraordinary, if usually gradual, changes and that adapts to unforeseen, complex circumstances.

The relative malleability, flexibility, and responsiveness of jural and journalistic standards also leave judges and reporters considerable discretion. Like traditional and charismatic authority, standards usually conserve norms, discourage deviations, and moderate change by forcing agents to legitimize their actions by reference to legal or professional standards. However, law and journalism teem with ways to adapt settled standards to new social, political, and economic situations. Since judges and reporters may disagree intensely about the nature of the situations and the standards applicable, decision makers have considerable "leeway" for judgment calls and audiences have ample room to doubt that judgments comport with standards.

If the superior malleability of standards enables judges and reporters to persuade audiences that discretion has been exercised legitimately, the inferior transcendence of standards compels judges and reporters to persuade audiences that decisions amount to more than unbridled discretion. Judges, reporters, and other decision makers must justify decisions by citing as their standards ideals and criteria that are widely accepted. Traditional and charismatic legitimation may be closely guarded mysteries largely beyond ordinary comprehension, but standards must be more accessible to persuade critics and attentive citizens. In sum, standards authorize discretion but force decision makers to defend their exercise of that discretion in public accounts that overcome the deficit of transcendence.

Practical Idealism

In practice, judges and reporters must compromise ideals to reach decisions, just as each of us must do in everyday life. Parents, baby sitters, and teachers use malleable standards to justify the judgment calls, discretion, and flexibility that complex situations necessitate, so most of us long ago mastered the distinction between "principled" and "practical" decision making. Like those authorities from our childhood, the authorities of our adulthood justify their decisions by referring to some standards. As children we rejected justifications that ranged too far from accepted standards. As adults, too, we are prone to reject justifications that compromise ideals and principles too much by challenging would-be authority: "You're just making that up as you go along!"

Forced by their audiences to justify their decisions with reference to established standards, judges and reporters confront a bruising choice: the more ideal the standards they invoke, the less often they will be able to measure up to such standards in practice. Those who pursue excellence in judging or news reporting want to meet the most demanding standards, the better to persuade audiences that suprahuman transcendence is being realized. The ideals and aspirations that official standards incorporate can be so demanding that they deprive decision makers of much of the flexibility and malleability that they need and all of the discretion they want. Consequently, decision makers compromise principles in practice. They approximate ideals to claim some transcendence but deviate from ideals to preserve discretion, to accommodate other values, and to tailor decisions to the exigencies of specific cases. A common strategy by which judges and reporters avoid being bruised by choices is to persuade audiences that ideals and principles impel judges and reporters to decide as they have. The more persuasive these claims to transcendent authority, the more discretion and room for compromises judges and reporters secure.

When decision makers cannot persuade audiences that they measure up to ideals or other absolute standards, they may preserve some room for discretion and compromise by demonstrating that their decisions at least avoid the opposites of the absolutes. If reporters cannot show that they have been totally objective—and we shall see that usually they cannot—they must at least show that they have not been subjective. If judges cannot prove that they have been perfectly impartial, they must eliminate the most obvious signs of partiality if they are to protect themselves against attacks.

Decision makers may establish virtue by denying vice because most ideals are twofold: they exemplify both motives and conduct that good people emulate and motives and conduct that good people abhor. To distinguish saints from sinners, for example, religions must simultaneously identify good and evil, prescribed and proscribed, sacred and profane. The Ten Commandments of Judeo-Christian scriptures rely on negations of the most common vices far more than affirmations of the desirable virtues, presumably because measuring up to ideals ("Thou shalt be honest") is less practical and often impossible while avoiding the opposites of ideals ("Thou shalt not steal") is far less equivocal.

Because jural and journalistic standards are just as twofold as religious authority, reporters and judges too will find it practicable far more often to demonstrate that they have avoided the feared opposites of ideals than they will find it to show that they have achieved ideals. The judge on the bench and the reporter in the back of the courtroom may be unable even to imagine a perfectly just decision or an ideally accurate story in some cases, but both will be able to imagine thoroughly unjust decisions and fatally inaccurate stories. Thus, news media and courts may profit from showing that exercises of discretion resemble positive ideals far more than their negatives. We shall see throughout this chapter various examples of how the courts and the press affirm by negating.

Standards, Practical Idealism, and Perspectives

Once we understand that standards call for legitimizing persuasion and that such persuasion affirms virtues by negating vices, we expect both mainstream perspectives that focus on ideals that decision makers purport to be fulfilling and alternative views that emphasize how rhetoric disguises deviations from ideals. The Inside-Out Perspective, for instance, focuses our attention on the legitimacy of most judicial and journalistic decisions, the persuasiveness of most justifications, and thus the transcendent authority that judicial or journalistic ideals usually furnish. Alternative perspectives may acknowledge the transcendence that standards provide in routine matters, but they must direct attention to flexibility, malleability, discretion, and distortions in the use and abuse of standards and ideals. Since transcendence and discretion commingle, both the mainstream view and alternative views will never lack examples. Both inside and outside perspectives will usually apply to journalistic and judicial decision making.

Now that we understand the roles of transcendence and discretion and the interdependence of virtues and vices in the abstract, we must examine how courts and news media achieve transcendence without forsaking discretion in practice. We shall first see how the standards that orient judges deny opposites of formal ideals more persuasively than they affirm the formal ideals. This will reveal how, in practice, judges often alloy the Candor and Craft assumed by the Inside-Out Perspective with the Strategic Imagery highlighted by the Outside-In Perspective. After that, we shall see how the professional canons by which journalists swear deny opposites more persuasively than they establish press ideals and how reporters routinely trade Objective Accuracy for Inexpensive Hype. Having glimpsed such practical idealism in courtrooms and in newsrooms, we shall be equipped to look at judges' and journalists' interactions both from the inside and from the outside.

Managing Judicial Authority by Formal Standards

The most powerful allure of modern law is its formality. Formal standards specify precise procedures that courts must follow, rules that they must apply, and logical forms that decisions must take. Legal authorities *both* struggle to meet the most imposing formal standards they can create *and* labor to create the most imposing formal standards they can meet. The more imposing the formal standards, the more impossible they are to meet, so judges approximate jural ideals by distancing themselves from jural vices when appeals to ideals alone will not persuade. Let us review the most common devices by which jurists persuade their audiences and themselves that they realize formality by vanquishing informality.

In any stable legal order, ordinary adjudication will convey formality in most cases. However, less routine and more newsworthy litigation will tend to raise problems that force judges into practical idealism, the mix of transcendence and discretion that I discussed earlier. In such visible cases, courts must dramatize formality so that news media can convey judicial performances to viewers and readers. The most common devices for dramatizing formality deny informal vices far more persuasively than they affirm formal virtues.

If I succeed in convincing you that judicial formality, in the non-routine cases that mass media most likely want to cover, combines transcendent judicial craft and cunning judicial suasion, you will see why both the Inside-Out Perspective and our Outside-In Perspective pertain to visible, newsworthy adjudication. Employers of the mainstream view will find that courts approximate formal, jural ideals just as the mission of courts (Candor and Craft in table I.1) in the Inside-Out Perspective states, while those who wield our critical alternative will direct attention to the court's use of "strategic imagery." To be formal, judges and courts must be crafty, both in the sense of being skilled in applying formal principles to challenging cases and in the sense of justifying or hiding their discretion in clever ways. To understand completely how judges and courts maintain formal authority, we must understand their craft both from the inside and from without.

The Basic Social Logic of Courts

Professor Martin Shapiro has defined the universal logic underlying all courts by asserting a positive ideal and immediately noting the necessity of denying the opposite of that ideal:

> . . . Cutting quite across cultural lines, it appears that whenever two persons come into a conflict that they cannot themselves solve, one solution appealing to common sense is to call upon a third for assistance in achieving a resolution. So universal across both time and space is this simple social invention of triads that we can discover almost no society that fails to employ it. And from its overwhelming appeal to common sense stems the basic political legitimacy of courts everywhere. In short, the triad for purposes of conflict resolution is the basic social logic of courts, a logic so compelling that courts have become a universal political phenomenon.
>
> . . . At the moment the two disputants find their third, the social logic of the court device is preeminent. A moment later, when the third decides in favor of one of the two disputants, a shift occurs from the triad to a structure that is perceived by the loser as two against one. To the loser there is no social logic in two against one. There is only the brute fact of being outnumbered.[3]

In these two passages, Shapiro has shown us that the most elemental judicial authority follows from the *triad*, a three-way relationship among two disputants and a third party to whom they consent. This "basic social logic of courts" succeeds if losing litigants and, far more important in modern legal systems, their potential allies perceive a legitimate triad. The basic logic of courts fails when a sufficient proportion of the attentive audience sees the relationship as an illegitimate *diad* (two against one). Diads characterize warfare ("us versus them"), contests ("Whose side are you on?"), and especially politics ("The ayes have it!"). Diads are, in short, what the disputants had before they recruited a third party. Because judicial standards specify triadic virtues and diadic vices simultaneously, astute citizens learn the virtues of the triad as negations of diads. The universal definition of judicial proceedings implies both the presence of triadic virtues and the absence of diadic vices, so judges and courts must demonstrate to audiences through the media that this basic ideal has been realized and its opposite eliminated.

Courts realize their basic, social logic more by denying diadic vices than by proving triadic virtues, because denying that a decision was "two against one" will often be more persuasive than showing that a triad genuinely appeared. To see why this is so, we need only consider the most common formal devices by which judicial authority is maintained.

Independent Judges

The basic, social logic requires third parties to establish their independence of litigants lest the authoritative triad be seen as an illegitimate diad. Disputants locked in disagreements must consent to a third party if a diad is to be reshaped into a triad. Since courts so often proceed without the explicit consent of one or more parties, they preserve the logic of the triad by asserting "judicial independence," freedom from political, social, economic, or other informal influences. Like most ideals in most standards, judicial independence is *both* necessary in theory *and* impossible in practice.

So obvious is the desirability of judicial independence that we are startled to realize that not a single criminal trial even approximates this socially necessary representation! When the state prosecutes a party, the third party is an employee of the very state prosecuting the accused. Even outside the criminal courts, lawyers "shop" for judges likely to be sympathetic to the lawyers' cases and arguments. The independence of judges is a myth that judges always strive to maintain, observers usually strive to believe, and adversaries often strive to undermine.

Because judicial independence cannot be realized, it cannot be demonstrated in any compelling way. Instead, audiences and practitioners alike usually satisfy themselves that the judge appears to share no substantial, pertinent stake with either side. That is, judges can deny dependence but cannot prove independence, so they substitute plausible denials of sympathy to either litigant for preposterous demonstrations of indifference. Litigants are free to challenge judges for conflict of interest or probable prejudice. Most judges most of the time can persuasively deny prejudice or partiality but stand ready to disqualify themselves if litigants show even an appearance of judicial favoritism.

Most judges cannot establish their utter independence of all parties, especially if the advocates are familiar to the judges. Thus, judicial independence more often issues from performances that deny diadic sympathy than those that demonstrate triadic indifference. Judges then justify their discretion by establishing that, *in a particular case*, they have followed appropriate steps to eliminate or mitigate any major prejudice. Those performances satisfy because almost all members of the audience want to believe in the formality of their courts and the independence of their judges.

Impartial Juries

A second device for projecting and preserving triadic form is to assert that jurors and juries are impartial. In practice, this ideal often proves unattainable for many reasons, the most obvious of which is that lawyers choose jurors for sympathies to one side rather than true independence. Indeed, jury consultants advise lawyers how to stack juries in their favor.[4] Many citizens and lawyers rationalize this apparent contradiction of the triad by asserting that an adversarial process of juror selection keeps the most partial potential jurors off the jury, in which case impartiality is achieved more by eliminating the most biased jurors (that is, by negating partiality) than by guaranteeing the most impartial triers of fact (that is, affirming jurors' indifference). In sum, jury selection too negates diadic evils more than displays triadic goods because the logic of the triad demands disinterest and independence that seldom can be realized and thus must be dramatized. "Candid craft" by itself does not suffice; it must be supplemented by strategic defenses of the practical compromises necessary to preserve the jury system. Audiences suspend belief because they want to believe in the jury system, but compromises of ideals are ubiquitous.

The Myth of Preexisting Rules

Consider a third device for preserving the triad—use of preexisting rules by which judges are bound and to which litigants have consented to be judged. Triadic adjudication reproduces and then meets formal standards by reshaping disputes to suit rules and norms. Modern courts assiduously cite formal rules and procedures to justify their decisions so that losers and their sympathizers must admit that they lost according to norms to which all citizens, including the losers, are bound.

If dramatizing the triad meant demonstrating that the decisive norms actually antedated the decision, even routine adjudication would fail its own standards. Rules are often far from settled and lawyers exploit ambiguities in the rules as the most likely or only route to victory.[5] When rules contradict one another, judges use discretion to "discover" which rules should prevail and which should yield. When novel cases expose gaps in the law, judges and advocates must extend or reshape rules to patch up the law. Did the patch predate the hole? Even if legal norms were unequivocal and unavoidable, judges and juries would still possess sufficient discretion in "finding" facts to affect the outcomes of cases. Thus, we are left to wonder how the triadic requirement of preexisting rules usually elicits credence from even modestly informed laypersons, not to mention practitioners.

Once again the answer is that adjudicators need only deny the diadic vice to induce most observers, who want to believe in the judicial system, to perceive triadic virtue. No candid judge can show or even pretend that existing rules actually compelled his or her decision in any nontrivial case. Rather, judges show that rules, properly interpreted, warrant their creative, necessary discretion. If legal authority permits a judicial determination, the judge can deny personal responsibility for judgment calls and can direct the disgruntled to the legislature or other avenues of reform. Robert Cover used a wonderful pun to describe this tactic: "The judicial can't."[6] If judges can argue persuasively that rules compel a decision, then, no matter how absurd or unjust the decisions seem, judges can claim that they would love to do what they acknowledge is right, but they "can't." Of course, such statements underestimate the discretion available to judges and hence are cant—that is, meaningless or ambiguous phrases used by those inside one group to fool those outside that group. In sum, legal reasoning "positively" demonstrates that decisions were compelled far less often than it shows, "negatively," that the decision need not evince prejudice or preference for either litigant. Legal rituals manufacture preexisting rules that deny diadic influences as much as or more than they affirm the triad.

Credibility and Triads

If you suspect that I have merely emphasized aberrations from professed ideals, please consider Shapiro's findings. The formal standards by which lawyers and laypersons alike usually define courts are realized in practice without substantial compromises virtually nowhere on the globe throughout history.[7] So alluring are formality and the logic of courts, however, that Shapiro had to analyze them carefully to show readers that the devices only approximate formal standards, usually by denying diads more than by actualizing triads. Because most members of their audiences want to believe that legal ideals are realized and will settle for demonstrations that the feared opposites of formal ideals have not played a part in adjudication, jural decision makers come to regard denials of diadic vices as tantamount to attainment of triadic virtues. Thus can the affirmations and denials by which legal authorities "realize" (that is, make to seem actual) formal standards before lay audiences make believers of lawyers and judges as well. The amplitude of discretion and frequency of deviation may be hidden very well behind crafty candor so that judges and lawyers can believe in and reassert formal ideals and aspirations.

Biases in Legal Constructions of Authority

We have seen that hard cases compromise, however slightly, legal ideals presumed by the Inside-Out Perspective. As a result, judges must engage in some of the "strategic imagery" that our Outside-In Perspective stipulates as the mission of the courts. Now we shall briefly review how courts and the legal system compromise legal ideals across the board. Structural, systematic biases that judges, lawyers, and reporters too often ignore directly challenge the Craft and Candor expected of judges by those who take the Inside-Out Perspective. These systematic, structural biases imbue our Outside-In Perspective's phrase, Strategic Imagery, with a far more sinister meaning. They suggest that the ideals and aspirations that animate jural standards are often façades behind which the gross inequities of the law, the blatant injustices of courts, and patent insensitivities of judges all huddle. These biases do not merely compromise judicial ideals and standards; they utterly contradict the ideals.

Social Biases

Sociologist Donald Black has documented forces that routinely shape decisions and outcomes in courts. Differences in wealth, degree of integration into society, education and other "culture," membership in approved organizations, and moral rectitude shape the application of laws in and out of courts. Black has argued that the law reproduces the preferences and prejudices that govern "normal" (that is, nonjudicial or diadic) politics.[8] The poor, the marginal, the unconventional, the unorganized, and the deviant should not count too much on the alleged impersonality of laws or impartiality of courts, Black has warned, because social biases will creep in, subtly but decisively.

Social biases must creep in subtly because they flatly contradict the triad and formal standards examined above. Since judges will tend to be wealthier, more integrated, better educated, more cultured, more involved in "better" organizations, and more "morally upright" than almost all defendants and public defenders in criminal trials, the logic of the triad is imperiled. Many civil cases will similarly compel judges to decide between relatively privileged litigants, whom the judges resemble, and litigants from other strata. Truly "representative" juries will bring into deliberations social information that undermines juror impartiality. More, social biases will shape jurors' perceptions of testimony and assessments of credibility.[9]

These everpresent threats from social biases must not reach the public lest the triad and formal standards lose credibility. As a consequence, the social biases of the law are hidden "backstage" as audiences are regaled "frontstage" with reassuring ideals, aspirations, standards, and rituals of formality. Only rude outsiders (such as your author) in special media (such as this book) will note how social biases contradict the majesty of the law.

Organizational Biases

In defense of jurisprudential ideals, we might note that, while rules and decisions do not always vindicate formality, they routinely do or at least appear to. A sociological (that is, "outside") review of routines common in legal organizations undermines this defense, however. In a classic essay,[10] sociologist Abraham Blumberg dissected routines in ordinary criminal courts and found that the social structure of courts defined the role of defense lawyers in a manner far different from what legal ideals and widespread beliefs would predict. Courts imposed bureaucratic demands and organizational goals on defense attorneys, often in ways that compromised attorneys' zealous advocacy of clients.

Blumberg showed that public defenders and other attorneys who repeatedly practiced before the same judges and with the same prosecutors tended to become part of a team that induced clients to plead guilty and otherwise expedited the process. At worst, such routines made advocates agents of the system and subverters of their clients!

Blumberg entitled his essay "The Practice of Law as a Confidence Game" to make the point that legal ideals instill in too many clients a confidence that is misplaced. When lawyers and judges do not live up to the ideals of their profession, litigants' and citizens' confidence in legal procedures may work against their interests. Blumberg did not argue that lawyers and judges abandoned formality and autonomy. Rather, he noted how enduring relations among judges, prosecutors, and defense attorneys in the criminal justice system created incentives to sacrifice adversariness, on which the criminal trial is predicated, for cooperation. Defense attorneys may not deliberately barter this client or that case for better rapport with judges and prosecutors with whom they will work again and again. However, the organization of litigation and practice of negotiations is likely, over a long haul, to induce all participants to "play ball." [11]

Formality, Audiences, and Acquiescence

In routine cases, affirmations and denials should and will persuade most audiences. Settled law and routine techniques warrant the vast majority of decisions, making "extralegal inputs" almost as redundant as they are unwelcome to most observers. More, the proceedings, we have now seen, are designed to "realize" formal ideals by denying informal vices. Law school and experience train judges and lawyers to exclude all that conflicts with the autonomy on which not just courts but the whole legal profession hangs. Legal reasoning, jural rhetoric, and other formal imagery are thus crafted to secure the acceptance or at least acquiescence of lay and legal audiences.

These audiences include a minority who see formality as a set of rationalizations for a thoroughly social and political diadic process, and a majority who reassert formal standards as reasonable approximations of virtue that legal practitioners should redouble their efforts to achieve. The minority will tend to be much more attentive than the majority, so judicial suasion aims to assuage potential critics lest judicial performances be panned. Judicial rhetoric must maintain or increase the credulity of the majority if the triad is to work. Judges are aided in dramatizing standards by the fact that the majority are not very attentive and not very astute but eager to believe in adjudication and legal symbols.

The most important subset of the attentive publics will consist of legal practitioners. Morale and vigor within the legal system depend on the success of lawyers and judges in persuading their peers and, thus, themselves that adjudication truly transcends mere politics. For such suasion to succeed, judicial justifications and ideals must routinely resemble each other.

In sum, formality is produced, maintained, and reformed by standards that orient most observers of the legal system. Insiders, such as lawyers and judges, will realize that the system sometimes fails of its ideals and its imagery, but even major reforms must be defined and defended in terms that deny or disguise the role of rules and decisions opposed to formal procedures. Because formality is approximated far more easily by negating recognized vices than by measuring up to rigorous virtues, and because a legal order conditions its performers and audiences to dramatize the negation of vices as the attainment of virtues, the routine forms, processes, and reasoning of courts will reinvent and reinforce formality.

Rhetorical Constructions of Formality

This survey of the devices by which formal standards are re-created and maintained revealed some distinctively judicial symbols, myths, and rituals that maintain *both* the transcendence *and* the malleability that set standards apart from traditional and charismatic authority. Formality entails ideals. The more demanding the ideals, the more transcendent and authoritative the law and the courts will be. Realizing those ideals in even ordinary cases, we have acknowledged, is impossible, so adjudicators must settle for demonstrations that their practices are far closer to the demands of ideals than to the temptations of their opposites. In practice, then, legal standards are both transcendent and malleable because those who routinely invoke those standards dramatize the ideals in the context of real decisions.

I have *not* shown that formality, autonomy, and authority are illusions created to dupe the gullible. Rather, I have tried to show the degree to which the legal system uses standards to create as much authority as human frailty and complexity will abide and much more idealism and formality than otherwise would be possible. Ideals must be and in fact are arguably approximated at virtually every point of almost every case, lest formal standards lose their transcendence for outraged citizens, politicians, losing litigants, judges, and lawyers alike. Without widespread acceptance or acquiescence, the legal order would be a transparent employment of force that could hold the allegiance of neither insider nor outsider. Because formal standards are understood, valued, and employed, adjudication that fails of high standards will promptly be designated as aberrant malfeasance to be remedied by additional doses of formality.

We now begin to see why the Inside-Out Perspective might dominate thinking about judicial journalism. The mainstream view assumes the self-image and daily output of the legal profession. More, the mainstream view focuses on the symbols, myths, and rituals of the law as simple reality and not as strategic imagery. This dominant perspective conditions reporters to treat formal denials of vices as tantamount to achievement of lofty legal standards. As judges and lawyers spotlight that rarity, the formal trial, audiences—lawyers and reporters included—want to believe in the formal ideals and in the legitimacy of adjudication. Because the devices discussed above make it easy to believe and hard to doubt the formality of the judicial "frontstage," the press and other observers tend to focus on what the judges spotlight.

If the Inside-Out view tends to dominate coverage, however, the routine uses of strategic imagery to reinforce formal ideals should alert us to the relevance of outside, alternative perspectives. Only the most astute consumers of court coverage are likely to see formal rhetoric as rationalization, so systematic biases and pragmatic compromises in judicial decisions will be well hidden in routine cases. Less routine adjudication may force judges and courts to more visible compromises of formal ideals and thus may make more obvious the mix of strategic imagery in judicial craft. We have seen how Inside-Out and Outside-In Perspectives may both find evidence in ordinary judicial decision making. We shall see by chapter's end that we should expect one or the other to dominate in certain kinds of cases.

Maintaining Journalistic Authority by Professional Canons

The creation and maintenance of journalistic authority proceeds, we shall see, in much the same manner as for judicial authority. Canons—norms and guidelines—of professional journalism correspond to ideals that cannot be realized except through plausible denials of their opposites. As a result, publics tend to suspend disbelief, to accept or at least to acquiesce in decisions, and thus to supply the belief or nonopposition that constitutes journalistic authority. Readers and viewers want to believe and can be induced to put their faith in the ideals, aspirations, and standards that the press produces to justify its preeminence. We shall see that these ideals and standards must be compromised in practice, perhaps even more seriously than formal standards. As a result, Objective Accuracy in table I.1 turns out to be far more problematic than naive consumers of news realize.

Naive readers and viewers may mistake professional canons and justifications for accomplishments rather than aspirations. Our closer, more critical examination of canons and justifications will suggest that the Inside-Out Perspective overstates the accuracy and objectivity that news media manage. Our subsequent survey of systematic biases in the construction of news will disclose that one justification for the quantity and quality of coverage—"news-worth"—shelters a multitude of influences that make news resemble the Inexpensive Hype posited by our Outside-In Perspective. Once we realize the prevalence of "hard fluff," "info-tainment," and cost-effective coverage in television and even in newspapers, we shall see that alternative views of mass media are prerequisites to overcoming the naivete that journalistic standards and ideals encourage.

Credibility

The central canon of journalism, its minimal prerequisite for authority, is credibility. While judicial authority and other kinds of official or political authority entitle officers and decision makers to be obeyed, journalistic authority is more a matter of belief. An "authoritative" journal, like an authority you might cite for an argument you make, is entitled to be believed or at least to be taken seriously. A newspaper or news hour cannot expect obedience because even its editorialists do not issue orders. Rather, media offer descriptions, impressions, and interpretations that will not sell if potential clients or customers regard them as preposterous or incredible.

This ideal of credibility may be rendered as three, progressively less demanding standards[12]: *accuracy, objectivity*, and *fairness*. Each standard is laudable. Each is unattainable. Practical routines and everyday compromises of journalism compel reporters and editors to "realize" the ideal of credibility by means of standards that define and deny the opposites of those ideals. Press credibility, like judicial formality, is thus as much a denial of barriers to belief as it is a fulfillment of ideals. We shall see, then, that the Inside-Out Perspective's Objective Accuracy, in practice, amounts to coverage that cannot be shown to be too inaccurate or too subjective. Let us see why.

Credibility might be thought, at a minimum, to require *accuracy*.[13] However, accuracy in any truly rigorous sense is too much to ask of routine journalism. If critics assail the accuracy of accounts of the assassination of President John F. Kennedy thirty-five years after the event, it is unlikely that reporters on deadline can do much more than avoid disastrous inaccuracy in reporting any slightly complex matter. If the story concerns powerful officials, journalists must worry about suppressed information, disinformation, and misinformation. More, competing news values such as concision, interest, and intelligibility require reporters to leaven accuracy with selectivity and judgment, even in simple, everyday reporting.[14] Certainly, credibility will be enhanced to the degree that noticeable *inaccuracies* are minimized, but then the standard of accuracy becomes the standard of "not inaccurate."

If we relax the canon of credibility to demand *objectivity*, results are much the same. It is indisputably a canon of modern journalism that reporters must keep their views (and those of their superiors and owners) out of news copy. If this objectivity demands merely the absence of flagrant subjectivity, most news organs can meet that standard most of the time. However, if any positive showing of objectivity is required, the situation is hopeless. Human subjectivity makes social situations interpretable and intelligible. The story of any act or event assembles details of the actors, the context, and motives.[15] Historians cannot be objective when they decide which actors to highlight, which settings to define, or which motives to emphasize hundreds of years after the actors and settings have passed away. How much less objective must reporters be as they dash for deadlines? Truly objective reporting, like absolutely accurate reporting, would dash other news values. That's why reporting is not truly objective and cannot be.

The canon of credibility is impossible to realize even if it is diluted to demand merely *fairness*.[16] Maintaining a perfect balance among subjects or treating everybody alike is neither accurate nor objective, so the standard of fairness represents a considerable concession to the realities of journalistic practice. That concession is in vain. Treating everybody alike deprives a storyteller of heroes and villains, of normal and abnormal, of the explicable and the inexplicable. Truly balanced reporting would be news from nobody's point of view[17]: no actor's view, no rooting interest, no audience's concern would orient a story. Deprived of conventional coordinates, readers would become disoriented.

If accuracy, objectivity, and even fairness guide practice only from afar, they still legitimize journalism and sanction violations. The canon of credibility, however defined, legitimizes and sanctions in much the same manner as formality legitimizes courts. That is, the canon defines illegitimate and thus unprofessional conduct and threatens wrongdoers. Coverage that is more inaccurate, subjective, and imbalanced than normal is criticized and impossible ideals are reasserted as if they could be and usually are realized. Labeling journalistic failings as aberrations not only sanctions violators, but, far more important, reiterates ideals as norms in which readers and viewers may put their faith. Defenders of the press both assert credibility, the minimal prerequisite for journalistic authority, and measure up to that minimum by deploying accuracy, objectivity, and fairness as standards.

The Mirror Metaphor

A common professional rendering of "Objective Accuracy" (table I.1) in practice is "the mirror metaphor," which Edward Jay Epstein defined and analyzed:

> . . . If television news is assumed to be analogous to a mirror, in reflecting willy-nilly all that appears before it, questions concerning the selection and production of news become palpably irrelevant. . . . Conceiving of television news in mimetic terms necessarily requires a certain blindness toward the role of the organization and organizational routines in the shaping of news reports and pictures; . . .
>
> The mirror analogy also suggests immediacy; happenings are reflected instantaneously, as they occur, as in a mirror. The image of immediate reporting is constantly reinforced by the way in which those in television news depict the process to the public. . . .
>
> The notion of a "mirror of society" implies that whatever happens of significance will be reflected on television news. . . .
>
> The mirror analogy further tends to neglect the component of "will," or decisions made in advance to cover or not to cover certain types of events. A mirror makes no decisions, it simply reflects what occurs in front of it; television coverage can, however, be controlled by predecisions or "policy."[18]

Is this mirror metaphor merely a flimsy, hypocritical defense of inaccurate, subjective, and unfair journalism that should not be believed? I do not think so. Rather, the mirror metaphor marshals the aspirations of the media as a defense against the common charge that media create what they are reporting. As we have seen and social scientists have shown repeatedly and persuasively, media *do* create the news.[19] No candid representative of the media denies that. However, representatives of news media (and not just television news) offer the mirror metaphor as a professional upgrade of the playground reply, "The truth hurts!" They mean by the mirror metaphor that *if* reporters have obeyed the canons of good journalism, the resulting image has enough truth in it that the truth and not the media's storytelling annoys or injures.[20]

If I am correct about this, the mirror metaphor is—in professional usage and in context—neither a claim about the truth of media reports nor a collective, delusional defense. The mirror metaphor is a professional aspiration as well as an alibi. It promises that reporters who match proper journalistic techniques to fearless pluck will create stories in which truth will so outweigh the reporter's artifice that readers, editors, and publishers will defend and laud the reporter. The mirror metaphor will mislead the unwary, as Dr. Epstein showed, but misdirection of the unwary is a major function of standards.[21]

Journalistic Exemplars

The canons of journalism do not depend, of course, on the mirror metaphor alone. In journalism schools and in newsrooms and on the job, reporters learn various practical techniques that make "good journalism" attainable and "bad journalism" less likely. "How to" books exhort and entice fledgling reporters with ways in which veterans have made their reporting more precise, more authentic, and more eclectic. These are *practical* counterparts of the unattainable ideals we examined: accuracy, objectivity, and fairness.

More, exemplary reportage and reporters teach their public and their profession how accurate, objective, fair, and truthful journalism can be. Expert police reporters can instruct other reporters how to escape "press release" journalism to bring readers and viewers truths about law enforcement, crime, and social control even as they incline audiences to expect more than ordinary sensationalism.[22] Prominent reporters, especially those for elite newspapers and networks, not only teach their lesser known colleagues by example but also introduce readers and viewers to what reporting should be but so seldom is. Anthony Lewis, as Supreme Court reporter for the *New York Times*, wrote *Gideon's Trumpet* and showed a wide audience majestic struggles that defined constitutional law.[23] Investigative journalists Bob Woodward and Scott Armstrong showed a less majestic side of the Supreme Court in *The Brethren*, but out of the petty bickering the justices stepped as flawed human beings who nonetheless spent most of their time struggling to make sense of the Constitution and the law.[24] Such reporting is not without critics but sets high standards for credibility and authority nevertheless. Such work and the daily reporting of correspondents for national newspapers, television networks, National Public Radio, and other elite outlets show that journalism's search for truth, credibility, and intelligibility is not in vain. Such successes may even excuse many shortcomings elsewhere.

My point, of course, is not merely that the ideals of modern journalism are compromised in practice. That is true of all professions and especially true of academic professionals. The stories and beliefs that constitute professional socialization call trainees and tyros to be the best that they can be, so naturally ideals demand more excellence than we can expect. The myths of professional journalism, like the formal myths of the law, identify the most common pitfalls and urge practitioners to avoid them. Avoiding the most common sins is, in practice, tantamount to virtue because such avoidance can be dramatized when virtue cannot. In such a manner do canons of journalism create journalistic authority rather than merely recognize it.

"Source-ery"

Canons of accuracy, objectivity, and fairness teach reporters to dread and deny biases and to strive mightily to eliminate evidence of partisanship or prejudice from their reports. Professional ideals sustain problematic distinctions between reports of facts, which are indispensable to good journalism, and opinions, which good journalists are supposed to leave to editorials. Ideals and standards weave symbols of neutrality and impartiality into routine reporting. I want to note just one such set of practices by which journalists recreate and preserve their authority much as college students do—citing sources.

Reporters face a dilemma alluded to earlier: opinions, interpretations, and evaluations are seldom objective but usually essential to intelligible stories. The claimed, suspected, and ulterior motives behind any action, for example, are necessary to any complete account of politics, including judicial politics. However, suspected or ulterior motives contradict claimed motives and undermine justifications and authority. Reporters may supplement or complement actors' public accounts without compromising neutrality by attributing speculation about private motives to other actors. The resulting account is hardly objective or neutral, but the reporter cannot be attacked for relating to readers' reactions to public claims. As Sally Field noted in the film *Absence of Malice*, well-sourced news can be accurate without being true.[25] Sources plausibly deny professionally proscribed inaccuracy, nonobjectivity, and unfairness.

Citing sources for non-neutral material in news reports reinforces faith in objective journalism without forcing reporters to practice it. This "source-ery" is perhaps the most crucial means of suiting political coverage to canons of professional neutrality. Whether journalists seek sources similar to themselves in outlook or "shop" for experts who will say what the journalists want to write, *or both*, "source-ery" transforms sources' subjective views into apparently accurate, objective, and fair coverage.[26] After all, quotations can be and usually are accurate, objective facts recorded by multiple reporters and thus within the realm of fair use. That interpretations contained in the quotations can be wildly inaccurate, patently self-serving, and grossly unfair is unfortunate, but, as we learned in *Snow White*, we must not blame the mirror for reflecting reality!

Source-ery transforms the subjective into the apparently objective in at least two other ways. When journalists repeatedly use the same sources, those sources become well known for expertise irrespective of their qualifications, acumen, or accuracy. Even chronically misguided, wrong, or mendacious sources acquire favorable reputations through repetition.[27] When that happens, the sources' reputations make their subjective views seem more objective or expert. In addition, the selection of certain sources entails exclusion of other sources. Views that the media seldom disseminate seem strange and thus more subjective. Views that are heard daily are comfortable and thus seem more objective.[28]

Veteran correspondent David Broder has warned of too much source-ery:

> . . . Nonetheless, the close working relationships between journalists and public officials have led to what I call clique journalism. In recent years our reporting of government and national politics has narrowed to the coverage of the insiders, by the insiders, and for the insiders. I dwell on the dangers of

such coverage because I think it corrupts our character. It diverts us from our main function of serving the broad public and it alienates us from that public, whose support is ultimately the only safeguard of the professional freedom we require to do our jobs.[29]

Please note that Broder immediately marshaled a canon as remedy for the damage that "clique journalists" do to the authority of the news. Broder summoned the belief that the press serve and depend upon their public and, in a single sentence, juxtaposed that myth with the canon of "journalistic independence." I read Broder's argument as a recipe for overcoming the pitfalls of source-ery: journalists must tighten their relationship with their readership and relax their relations with their subjects. Having observed a practice more proximate to journalistic vice than to journalistic virtue, Broder implicitly advised his journalistic readers to put some distance between themselves and their sources.

The Beat

The image of reporters poised to record any events in their domains reinforces the myth that newspapers gather all the news accurately and objectively. Not content to be told what the "line of the day" or governmentally approved story might be, reporters, so the myth goes, are out exhuming leads, examining developments, and extrapolating events. Beats are routine methods for organizing news gathering because they are potent symbols of media vigilance and credibility. Ironically, however, the beat tends to deny vices it guarantees. Let us see how.

Beat is a journalist's term for a domain for which one or more reporters are responsible. This domain may be topical (e.g., the police beat), territorial (e.g., the county seat or state capital), or both (e.g., the Supreme Court beat). Beats have been the modal method of organizing newspapers for coverage in this century,[30] symbols of expertise and effort.[31]

As an ideal, this beat system encourages expert, vigilant, independent reporters to sift through happenings in a specified domain and to tell readers about the most significant. In practice, the beat system constricts the range of events to which beat reporters routinely expose themselves.[32] Deadlines, editors' expectations, efficiency, and other daily demands induce beat reporters to prefer events that are organized and usual (because such events are easily interpreted and reported—journalistic standards of efficiency and intelligibility), official and formal (because the storyline is built in so that reporters need not struggle to "find the story"), and well bounded (to minimize the time and costs of investigation). Moreover, newspapers do not send reporters out to beats to wait around and then to report if anything significant should happen. Rather, expenses and expectations compel beat reporters to insure a constant flow of stories.

Beat reporters, the very symbols of independent, journalistic expertise, thus become part of the reality to be reported. Institutions such as courts will take advantage of beat reporters' preferences for the routine, the usual, and the easily described by staging events to match expectations. The more successfully the institution handles reporters, the more pleasing the institution's coverage will likely be. Savvy operatives take advantage of "source-ery." They make themselves available for comment and will tailor their comments to the needs and desires of beat reporters and other news "gatherers." The more efficient and routinized the beat, the more difficulty less organized, less accessible, and more challenging interests will have finding and impressing the beat reporter. Beat reporters thus tend to get co-opted into the very system(s) they report.[33] The watchdog becomes a lapdog.

This co-optation is likely to be especially acute for reporters on judicial beats. Most legal beats are not desired and hence fall to inexperienced, inexpert reporters. Such laypersons and generalists are even more dependent on sources than more experienced and knowledgeable journalists. Legal insiders will be able to spin tales; legal outsiders will have too little access to insure that their sides of stories about cases get heard. Legal beats, far from increasing accuracy or objectivity, tend to increase the ability of insiders to get their cunning imagery amplified by credulous reporters.

Biases in Journalistic Constructions of Authority

This whirlwind survey of the creation and management of journalistic authority has emphasized how ideals are reinforced and amplified both in coverage and in many accounts of journalism. Every assertion of formal or professional virtue is designed, at least in part, to remedy some common professional vice, real or perceived. The creation and management of authority marry general, abstract, and majestic standards of formality and professionalism to specific, concrete, and mundane denials of common errors and sins.

This "marriage" suggests how the Inside-Out Perspective developed and why it dominates conventional observation and analysis. Consumers and observers of judicial journalism naturally apply conventional standards for journalistic authority. Those standards, we have seen, match affirmations of ideals and denials of the most common deviations from those ideals. Informed and persuaded by the yoked affirmations and denials, consumers and observers of judicial journalism are most attentive to journalistic practices designed to defy the very perils that journalists use to define their craft. The Inside-Out Perspective, in sum, directs its devotees to the "frontstage" of journalism and the standards for authoritative action dictate that journalists will put "up front" the vices to be ritually rejected!

Other vices, less easily rejected, show why Outside-In Perspectives are also justified. These vices less often grace texts intended for journalistic practitioners, so they are vices that the usual canons and reports do not deny. Because reporters do not routinely define their craft by reference to these biases, these biases provide outside information and ulterior motives from which more skeptical perspectives about journalism may be constructed to complement naive idealism.

Content or Angle Biases

Routine journalism exhibits tendencies that compromise the authority of news, tendencies that neither "the mirror metaphor" nor canons for professional reporting acknowledge. I have derived four such tendencies from the work of W. Lance Bennett[34]: *dramatization, personalization, normalization*, and *morselization*. Each tendency makes stories more newsworthy (recall that newsworthy events are those more suitable for dissemination as news) and intelligible by amplifying selected aspects of actions and contexts and de-emphasizing other, often far more significant, aspects. These systematic biases in story angles and content that journalism texts too seldom acknowledge transform "news-worth" from a common excuse for selective coverage into a critical exposé of subjective interpretation.

Modern mass media tend to *dramatize* events by defining as newsworthy aspects of events that grab attention. While dramatics may augment readership and ratings, the media's penchant for drama supplants routine but banal coverage that may have far more import for readers' and viewers' lives. Long-term regularities may affect our lives far more than almost all aberrations, but the immediate, the imminent, and the protean are far more dramatic and thus far more newsworthy, if by news-worth we mean *not* what audiences ought to learn but what audiences will buy. The pursuit of drama supplants gradual trends, directing the searchlight of the news more often to symptoms and events than to causes and processes, more to antics than to arguments.[35] More, news dramas encourage readers and viewers to adopt the passivity of spectators.

Media intensify dramatic impact when they *personalize* events and actions. Personalization reduces complex geopolitical conflicts to struggles between individuals. Saddam Hussein squared off against Norman Schwarzkopf and John Kennedy took on Nikita Khrushchev because media find international rhetoric wrestling easier to cover than complex processes. Disagreements over principles and policies tend to be portrayed as interpersonal difficulties or spats, as the demands and resources of storytellers dictate. Personalized news accounts implicitly displace institutional, structural, and historical explanations by eliminating forests in favor or closeups of trees, especially celebrated trees. The personal perspective or story angle is designed to elicit predictable, often visceral reactions, not to elevate or excite thought.

When mass media habitually use the same angles or formulas to dramatize or personalize events, they *normalize* the news.[36] Normalization is "the tendency to filter new information through traditional values, beliefs, and images of society and to deliver the filtered information through the reassuring pronouncements of authorities charged with returning things to normal."[37] Normalization developed contemporaneously with dramatization and personalization as the nineteenth century "reporter as independent interpreter of events" gave way to the twentieth century "reporter as objective observer."[38] "Instead of aiding his audience to come to terms with old realities in new ways, the journalist now tends to help his audience to come to terms with new realities in old ways."[39] News contextualized and interpreted to match conventional views is familiar and thus seems more objective than news that calls into question "what everyone knows." Normalization, then, represents an unacknowledged cost of the credibility and objectivity that media proclaim because normalized news reasserts conventional views, such as the Inside-Out Perspective.

Dramatization, personalization, and normalization compact happenings into morsels that seldom challenge readers or viewers. "[W]e receive our news extensively predigested, coded, and packaged in conventional parcels."[40] When media *morselize* coverage, they prefer news that readily and easily fits into their formats (such as the three angles we have discussed), their constraints (time in the case of broadcast news, space in the case of print media), and their markets (readers and viewers with short attention spans). Morselizing media tend to prefer the simple or simplifiable to the complicated, the discrete to the continuous, the localized to the global, the snapshot to the montage. News reporters are so constrained by their "news hole" (the space left over in a newspaper after the advertisements are situated) or their ninety seconds (the average time for a story on network news) that they must cut out much of what would have made the story interesting and informative in order to squeeze the story past their editors.

Dramatization, personalization, normalization, and morselization are tendencies that are understandable and in some cases praiseworthy. Each aids readers and viewers in understanding at least the surface of daily events. Still, each tendency represents a routine choice that compromises objectivity and accuracy in predictable ways. Dramatized coverage systematically favors the unusual over the usual. Personalized coverage chronically prefers individual to institutional causes. Normalized news typically suits information to expectations rather than schooling expectations with challenging information. Morselization routinely renders the world as a pile of building blocks, not a weave of interdependent strands.

These biases also guarantee a low common denominator of intelligibility. Intelligibility is important. However, when intelligibility is created by suiting the news to the expediences of journalists, the prejudices of readers and viewers, and the objectives of officials, "that's the way it is" becomes "that's the way we want it to be" or "that's the only way we can tell it."

As a consequence, biases that journalists vehemently deny all too often creep back into journalism unseen. Biases audiences are likely to perceive or suspect must be denied. Formats, however, tend to be transparent to most members of most audiences. Dramatization and personalization distort some happenings and cause other happenings that exist solely to be reported. That is not accuracy. Normalization imposes conventional views on reporting. That is hardly objectivity. All four angle biases prefer certain actors, causes, interests, and interpretations and ignore or scant others. That is not fairness.

Commercial Biases

The four content or angle biases reveal as well an implicit economy of gathering and disseminating news. Each bias follows in part from the demands of and on mass media as businesses. Each bias increases circulation or ratings through the same techniques that, for example, soap operas employ. Dramatized news titillates and fascinates; personalized news concentrates empathy and anger around heroes and villains; normalized news suits plots to audiences' hopes and desires; and morselized news delivers new installments in episodes that one may follow even if one has missed the show for weeks. Each bias, then, seems well designed to increase viewers' and readers' emotional stakes in stories, irrespective of any showing that stories truly affect viewers' and readers' lives. The content biases, then, are in part marketing ploys, hype that induces consumers to view advertisements.

In addition, each content bias may cut costs. Discovery of a dramatic angle saves reporters time and energy and allows editors and others to enhance the "production values" through good pictures or lurid reactions. Normalized coverage reduces research expenses by directing reporters to the usual sources and authorities for context or "spin" and makes news almost self-formatting. Personalized coverage minimizes investigative costs by narrowing the subjects of coverage to a few, usually very public persons (or personas). Morselized content excuses superficial but cheap reporting to keep content simple and accessible.

Beyond the four kinds of content bias discussed above, observers have easily discerned commercial tendencies that shape the news and shatter the mirror metaphor. Modern mass journalism is mostly corporate journalism, so most print and electronic media must please financial managers and stockholders more than readers.[41] This bias imperils reports that threaten the interests or images of advertisers and owners, close affiliates or subsidiaries of the owning corporations, or corporate culture or capitalism in general. Commercial biases do not prevent all unwelcome business news from emerging, as a glance at electronic or print media discloses. Rather, commercial biases subtly and sometimes surreptitiously sanitize image-threatening events into ideal-reaffirming news. Corporate owners and marketing magnates do not control the news, but they definitely manage it when they see a need to.[42] It cannot surprise us, moreover, that financial muscles usually need not be flexed because print and electronic media personnel will anticipate their superiors' preferences and will deliver "safe" coverage without having to be told to.[43] Commercial biases can induce newspapers and broadcasters, for example, to prefer news secured cheaply to important news that costs more to gather and report.[44]

Far subtler and perhaps even more pervasive are biases worked by the markets for mass media.[45] Robert Entman's analysis of the "marketplace of ideas" disclosed that economic and political competition among media actually constricted the flow of news and views that democracy demands of citizens—a form of normalization writ large. Economic competition among media narrows the range of news in the marketplace, which impoverishes political competition among ideas. On the demand side, media must not too far outstrip public tastes and abilities, because on the supply side, shareholders and owners demand low costs and high profits.[46] Little wonder that media insiders and outsiders alike cite commercial biases as the most serious threats to any free marketplace of ideas.

This is another, more ominous meaning of "news-worth": events and people are newsworthy if it profits news media and especially the owners and shareholders of news media to cover them. Ordinary usages of "newsworthy" point to what citizens have a right to know, need to know, or want to know. Commercial usage of "newsworthy," however, contradicts the very ideals and standards journalists cite to defend their profession.

Political Biases

Content biases and commercial biases are the most serious, chronic, and demonstrable tendencies in mass media, but less important, and more occasional and deniable biases tend to garner more attention in mass and specialized media. The very prominence of charges of partisan and ideological biases in mass media news leads me to downplay them here. More than other tendencies I have discussed, political biases are detected and stressed on newscasts and talk shows, in news columns and commentary. Powerful factions in politics are so vigilant for partisan and ideological slant in mass media that they can find it where it does not exist![47] Given these raucous critics in the front row of the audience, networks and newspapers would be reckless indeed to let their biases escape very often. Since representatives of the two major parties and of the ideological wings of those parties can get access to and bring pressure on mass media so easily, most news media will control such biases through the devices for tending credibility discussed earlier. In contrast, content biases and commercial biases need not be (and cannot be) closeted so assiduously because only a few academic outsiders will bother attentive citizens with charges of such biases.[48]

Jural Tendencies

Of course, the biases of the most direct interest in this book are those concerning courts and the legal system. Content biases, commercial biases, and political biases suggest ways in which judicial journalism should be expected to contradict professional ideals. While specific jural tendencies will be discussed in subsequent chapters, we may anticipate some findings that follow from the tendencies we have discussed.

The general implications of content or angle biases should be clear. Mass media's tendencies to dramatize news should lead us to expect coverage to prefer conflict—say, clashes between lawyers in trials and between judges in appellate cases—to cooperation. Personalization implies that coverage of cases with very sympathetic or very unsympathetic participants and victims will exceed even coverage of far-reaching cases whose "winners and losers" cannot be named and interviewed. Naturally, any complications or novelties in court must be easy to normalize or they are much less likely to draw attention. Even dramatic, personalized, and normalizable cases must be compacted to fit the usually limited "news hole," so cases that may be described alluringly, simply, and concisely—the morselizable cases—stand a much better chance than those that require more time, space, and resources.

We certainly should expect mass media to focus far more on decisions and their immediate results than on the process, evidence, and logic that justify decisions. In general, we should expect most cases to yield little that is newsworthy unless titillating or lurid details provide the drama for which mass media are looking. However, verdicts, sentencing, and deviations from routine may provide some spot news, but major coverage will require dramatic vignettes that personalize the process into gripping stories. However little coverage decisions get, expect reasoning and legal logic to get still less unless disputes over legal principles and rules can be dramatized, personalized, normalized, and morselized.

Commercial biases also yield general predictions. Certainly, mass media will tend to give most favorable coverage to extensions of First Amendment liberties that result in easing the burden or enhancing the profits of the press.[49] Beyond such self-serving coverage, we may also expect that verdicts and decisions that help or harm the corporate owners of the media will be evaluated with the interests and views of corporate headquarters in mind. Commercial tendencies may incline media to tabloid formats that cost little to produce but generate readers, so judicial difficulties or shortcomings may be exaggerated to sell the news. This may incline some mass media to accentuate the negative and eliminate the positive.

The Journalistic Construction of Authority

The authority of professional journalism follows, it now seems, from practices that insinuate the existence of ideals mostly by denying in a routine and plausible manner their opposites. These practices maintain journalistic authority as journalists create news, meet deadlines, and generate publishable copy. Attentive audiences propagandized in advertisements and talk shows may come to believe that the canons of professional journalism usually insure authoritative, credible coverage. If those attentive viewers and readers usually believe, then the coverage is credible and the content of the coverage becomes part of the common perspective on events and personalities. That is, coverage assimilates news to the shared, authoritative, credible "reality" being constructed by major actors and mass media. Since contemporary journalism is shaped by the vices to be avoided as much as by the ideals to be approximated, most coverage will live up to the standards of journalism. A cacophony of criticisms of media inaccuracy, subjectivity, and bias will usually be met by prefabricated defenses, because standard journalism is designed to deny such vices. Indeed, we have seen that the ritualistic denial and derogation of such vices often defines journalistic practices.

Because widespread recognition of content and commercial biases in the news would imperil the credibility of news media, publicized canons deny routinely suspected (and easily deniable) biases and assert that media are reasonably accurate, practically objective, and usually fair. Content and commercial biases pose systematic problems with objectivity and accuracy that defenders of media acknowledge and answer only in specialized media, if at all. Instead, mass media, socialization, and journalism texts regale viewers and readers with canons and concomitant denials of threats to credibility and intelligibility that mask the far more serious issues.

These conclusions have clear implications for the Media Mission entries in table I.1 of the Introduction. We have seen that journalistic standards and practices produce the Objective Accuracy that the Inside-Out Perspective must posit, albeit more by denying subjectivity and inaccuracy than by measuring up to usual definitions of the terms. We have also seen that mass media have profound incentives to pursue the Inexpensive Hype that my Outside-In Perspective presumed. Routine angle biases incline media to settle for hype. Commercial factors encourage inexpensive coverage. While I have slighted many interesting features of the journalistic construction of authority in my survey above, I trust that you now understand why both Inside-Outers and Outside-Inners have some justification for their views.

An interesting, ironic implication of the foregoing is that reporting is likely to be more objective and more accurate the less newsworthy the event or person to be reported is. If a story has actual or potential "news-worth" because it can attract readers and viewers, we must expect content and angle biases to sacrifice accuracy and objectivity for more marketable hype. The more that a story has "news-worth" because it coincides with the interests of the corporations that create the news, the more pressure that commercial biases are likely to exert. The good news is that stories that are newsworthy only because involved and astute citizens want to know about them will likely draw the accurate, objective coverage that the mainstream view assumes. The bad news is that stories that have more mass or corporate appeal are likely to leave little room or time for truly worthy stories.[50]

Table 1.1   **Supposed Intersections of Inside and Outside Perspectives**

	When cases are least "newsworthy"	When cases are most "newsworthy"
When cases are legally most routine	**Mainstream Standards:** The Inside-Out Perspective better explains both judges and reporters than an Outside-In Perspective.	**Media Distortion:** The Inside-Out Perspective better explains judges, but an Outside-In Perspective better explains reporters.
When cases are legally most challenging	**Jural Mystification:** An Outside-In Perspective better explains judges, but the Inside-Out Perspective better explains reporters.	**Dual Pragmatism:** An Outside-In Perspective best explains both judges and reporters.

How Jural and Journalistic Re-Creations of Authority Intersect

For clarity, we have examined jural and journalistic authority separately. The perspectives that orient this study, however, purport to explain not only how courts and news media behave but also how they interact. We now consider how judges and journalists manage their authority in the presence of the other.

Looking at the interactions that issue coverage of courts leads to a fascinating theoretical insight that will help us synthesize research findings throughout the rest of this volume. Suppose that the Inside-Out Perspective applies best to cases that are legally routine and not newsworthy, but that alternative perspectives apply better when cases are *either* less routine legally *or* more newsworthy. Suppose further that when cases are *both* legally uncommon *and* newsworthy, the Outside-In Perspective defined in table I.1 applies best. I have fashioned table 1.1 from table I.3 to display these suppositions.

We saw already that every judicial case and journalistic story must approximate formal and professional standards to some degree. If expectations of the Inside-Out Perspective are largely met by almost all courts and almost all news media, we should also expect that court coverage—the intersection of courts and news media—would closely resemble the Inside-Out Perspective most of the time. Thus, the core of my supposition is that the mainstream view *usually* describes court coverage fairly accurately. The common prescription serves as an apt description *very often but not always*.

Formulating this norm, however, immediately directs our attention to exceptions. Many of those exceptions, I suspect, are *not* accidental or random. Rather, I suspect (and I hope to induce you to suspect) that deviations from the Inside-Out "rule" result from conditions that challenge or undermine authority, conditions that I have tried to highlight throughout the previous parts of this chapter.

I have argued that formal standards dictate results in most court cases—that is, ordinary litigation—but must be compromised in less routine cases and may be compromised severely in extraordinary cases. I have also argued that news-worth often challenges or contradicts journalistic standards. That is, the more that an event or personality arrests or potentially arrests the attention of media consumers, the more that media will be tempted to enhance profits and cut costs by imposing one or more angle biases on the resulting stories. As we now consider adjudication and journalism together, we may supplement these two challenges—extraordinary cases and newsworthy stories—with a third challenge: overlap. Legally extraordinary cases will often (but not always!) be stories that journalists find extremely newsworthy. When the judicial and journalistic challenges coincide, I shall argue that we should expect court coverage to resemble the Inside-Out Perspective least and our Outside-In Perspective most.

Like Hercule Poirot, I have gathered all my suspects together and proposed a solution to the mystery. As in *Murder on the Orient Express*, all the suspects have played a part. Now I must define the parts my suspects have played and will play, suspect by suspect.

The Inside-Out Perspective Accounts for Routine, Nonnewsworthy Cases

The Inside-Out Perspective accounts for most coverage and most of our awareness of courts. It should. The Inside-Out Perspective represents the coherent model of how ideals for adjudication, journalism, and democracy conform. Tradition, charisma, and standards teach us ideals and expectations that define courts, the press, and democracy and that furnish "baselines" for performers and performances and for those who judge them. The Inside-Out Perspective, we have seen, combines standards. These mainstream standards tutor observers on what ought to happen (that is, they are prescriptive standards) and thereby induce observers to assume that what ought to happen ordinarily does happen (descriptive standards). Thus does a normative model *for* court coverage consistently become an empirical model *of* court coverage. The Inside-Out Perspective predominates because, most of the time, it prescribes the roles of courts, media, and citizenry, so each group aims to conform to the descriptions of the Inside-Out Perspective. If performances must routinely resemble normative expectations, the Inside-Out Perspective's connections between what ought to be and what is incline or impel officials to adhere to expectations and ideals.

Those expectations and ideals demand more than humans can usually deliver, so performances will often merely approximate prescriptive standards. That is, what decision makers cannot be or do, they must *seem* to be or do. Their representations simulate and reinforce the ideals and expectations as barriers to arbitrary or abusive decisions. If such representations often compromise ideals, nonetheless the ideals shape the real.

Let us review the Inside-Out Perspective to see how it choreographs the performances of news media, courts, and citizenry.

The press must encourage attention to and belief in its fearless vigilance and unstinting accuracy because objectivity and accuracy (Media Mission in table I.1) prescribe this watchdog role for news media. Via that watchdog press, courts must show an attentive public the prescribed denials of jural vice and approximations of jural virtue that define the judicial role. Judicial dramatizations of craft and candor (Court Mission in table I.1) must persuade media, citizens, and proponents of the Inside-Out Perspective. Of course, such journalistic and judicial image-making and ideal-approximating do little good unless most of the audience attends to the stage. Thus, the Inside-Out Perspective not only presumes and prescribes that attentive citizens outnumber inattentive ones as well as skeptical sophisticates (Extensively Attentive audience in table I.1), but presumes as well that the sole or most important Information Flow is from courts through media to attentive citizens. Thus, the prescriptions and descriptions of the Inside-Out Perspective dovetail judicial, journalistic, and citizens' roles.

Legally Routine Cases

The Inside-Out Perspective coheres better when cases are legally routine than when cases challenge prescriptions and proscriptions for judging. I define "routine" lawsuits and judicial decisions as those that elicit or are likely to elicit a great degree of agreement from disinterested legal experts. When legal rules are clear and only a few facts are disputed, or when only one or two issues of interpretation cloud the rules, adjudication may be said to be mundane, modal, ordinary, jurisprudentially insignificant, or—telling adjectives!—*standard* or *normal*. Whatever the "news-worth" of such cases, they have little "law-worth." Less routine cases will pose legal questions the answers to which many legal experts will be less able to predict. In jurally extraordinary cases, the law is "up for grabs" and most lawyers and judges will be unable to predict from preexisting rules what courts and judges will do. Unpredictable cases yield decisions that make law. These are truly "law-worthy" cases.

Routine cases, by definition, do not challenge judges. As a result, judges can approximate the most rigorously formal standards quite well. Let us not even tarry with the most routine criminal or civil cases, which are decided before trial in plea bargains or out-of-court settlements, except to note that some such cases are so routine and legally so unchallenging that they would waste the court's time. In most, and perhaps nearly all, cases that come to trial, substantial jural issues are few and not forbidding for the competent jurist. The fewer and the easier the legal issues, the more rigorous the formality that the court will dramatize.

When easy cases allow courts to strut their formality, the "Candor and Craft" posited by the Inside-Out Perspective should be forthcoming in abundance, and the court should need little of the Strategic Imagery charged by our Outside-In Perspective. Routine cases cannot challenge the craft of any competent jurist, and if every disinterested lawyer would reach the foregone conclusions, why shouldn't the judge be perfectly candid? In short, in such cases, the most strategic argument is to direct all parties to settled law.

When ordinary adjudication issues candor and craft, reporters will often provide accurate, objective coverage automatically, just as the Inside-Out Perspective assumes. Reporters will not need to worry much about balancing reports to make them seem objective, for the wholly or largely preordained decision will excite little opposition and the widespread agreement of Bench and Bar will be objective facts to be reported. The dearth of legally substantial issues or wrenching factual questions in routine litigation will leave the competent reporter little about which to be inaccurate. Indeed, reporters will probably find the most difficult part of covering routine cases to be persuading their editors to print the stories. With such minimal "law-worth," most judicial matters are not newsworthy and will not be reported. If reported, routine cases will likely be clustered in a box headed "Day in Court" next to birth and death notices.

There is no reason to suppose that even attentive citizens learn about most routine cases, but whatever they learn likely will reaffirm the Inside-Out Perspective. Courts and press will so easily fulfill their missions that authority will be reinforced. Audiences attentive enough to learn of routine cases will find the fulfillment of missions and the reinforcement of authority satisfying and reassuring.

Legally Less Routine Cases

When less routine cases pose trickier issues, the Inside-Out Perspective may be challenged by alternatives that propose less judicial candor and craft and more strategic imagery. Jurists may be tasked more and thus may approximate formal standards less. Judges will still be able to deny the vices opposite to prescribed jural virtues, but they will find that they have to engage in trickier and riskier arguments to support their rulings. Even as approximations of standards get rougher, judges may usually depend on their audience's willing suspension of disbelief, *provided that* the judges do not supply losing litigants or sympathizers with evidence that judges have abandoned solid, formal methods. To avoid arming potential detractors, judges must be far more strategic and rhetorical.

The legal cliche "Hard cases make bad law"[51] suggests the difficulties that extraordinary cases pose for judges and courts. There are few or no compelling routes from established law to decision(s), so the judge cannot employ judicial cant about being bound to follow the law. The judge's range of discretion is as patent as the "right" answer is latent. Losers and their sympathizers will decry the decision as "two against one," denounce the judge for making formal standards much too malleable, and declaim before any who will listen that, with far less manipulation and far more authority, the law would have supported them.

Nonroutine cases may confound reporters, especially reporters new to the court beat. The more remarkable the case, the more journalistic accuracy and objectivity will depend on the expert sources and other assistance that reporters secure. Astute legal reporters can unravel even convoluted justifications for puzzling decisions with little help, but such reporters are rare outside specialized media; most are assigned to the U. S. Supreme Court, and research shows that even they are often mystified.[52] For all these reasons, it is not clear how accurate or objective reporters can be when jural challenges incline judges and lawyers to strategic imagery.

What is clear is that nonroutine cases turn enterprising, accurate, and objective reporters into menaces to formality. The more that a hard case induces lawyers and jurists to manipulate formal standards, the more unseemly discretion they must deny if they are to secure any transcendence and authority for the decision. The more discretion involved in adjudication, the more questions an accurate, objective report must raise. Worse, the most obvious, accessible, and inexpensive sources for information to balance stories about close calls will be lawyers who represent or sympathize with the losing litigants.

Issues and decisions that perplex or divide legal scholars and stymie legal reporters will probably not make much sense to audiences, but many attentive citizens will gather from accurate, objective coverage that formal standards have not been fulfilled. Just as coverage of routine decisions will tend to amplify formal reassurances and insure acquiescence, so too coverage of extraordinary decisions will tend to trumpet discretion and dissension that may not reassure those who sympathize with the winning side and cannot soothe "losers." Even citizens rooting for the winning litigants may react negatively to insufficiently formal justifications, if for no other reason than the insecurity of the immediate victory.

So we see that nonroutine cases, by forcing judges to engage in riskier imagery, may undermine the Inside-Out Perspective. It is bad enough that cases with great law-worth may alert the media watchdog. Even worse, a barking watchdog may rouse a quiescent populace to legal threats, real or imagined.

To avoid such unpleasant situations, judges and lawyers have every incentive to be less candid and more cunning in justifying decisions. If reporters follow their professional canons regarding nonroutine cases, practitioners must insure that balanced reports include the spin that practitioners prefer. This result might be styled "jural mystification." Jural mystification can take many forms, but the most common is to simulate formal-legal decision making. Cover called this tactic, used by judges in antebellum slavery cases, "retreat into formalism."[53] The judges knew that they had no uncontroverted authority for any decisions but, to avoid criticism, they endeavored to depict their reasoning as utterly determined by inescapable rules. Critics might say they were mistaken about the rules, but at least no one would accuse them of the vice of writing their own political views into law.

Jural mystification is what we may expect if journalists on judicial beats adhere to their professional canons and provide objective, accurate coverage for judges who must mask their discretion and manipulation of authority. This is, as we shall see in the next chapter, Richard Davis's critique of coverage of the U. S. Supreme Court. Davis argues that Supreme Court justices take advantage of their mostly nonroutine docket to secure media coverage for their strategic imagery. Without professional assistance and with looming deadlines, reporters must rely inordinately on the justices for stories. Supreme Court coverage tends toward "press-release journalism," Davis argues, because in the short time between the announcement of decisions and decisions' "expiration dates," reporters cannot write careful, analytical, critical stories. Instead, they settle for accurate quotations and well-balanced statements from interest groups and other quipsters at the ready. The result is mystification, Davis claims, because reporters are forced to dance to the justices' tune.

If, following Davis, we decided that judicial outputs and not media outputs were *the* problem, then we might comfortably adopt the premises of the Inside-Out Perspective except for its Court Mission. In other words, the media largely accomplish their mission and convey to an extensive attentive public the strategic imagery of the courts (the Court Mission assumed under my Outside-In Perspective). Any judicial mystification hypothesis presumes a nontrivial attentive public lest there be no masses to mystify. More, such a view requires the two-step flow from courts to media to the public, or no mystification could take place. If the media do not convey judicial mystifications fairly faithfully, then the judges have less control over their media and hence over their messages.[54]

Table 1.1 reminds us that mystification is a possibility, but I have not highlighted it as a major alternative perspective for two reasons. First, I do not believe that mystification will be as common as dual pragmatism (the lower right cell of table 1.1), even at the U. S. Supreme Court. The Supreme Court devotes its time and resources to few run-of-the-mill cases, so I expect, and research has discovered, abundant use of imagery and discretion at the Court. However, for reasons that I shall detail presently, I expect the Court to make the most news and get the most coverage in cases that have the angles that media prefer. Cases that have news-worth (for examples, attractive angles or absorbing content) will tend to draw far more coverage than cases with less appeal. The angle biases or content biases will reshape stories in ways that compete with and crowd out the justices' attempted mystifications. The reporters, having internalized their organizations' preferences, are hardly helpless thralls of dazzling legal intellects. Rather, the state of coverage of the U. S. Supreme Court is as much a product of the proclivities of the press as it is the cleverness of the justices.

A second reason to suspect that jural mystification is relatively rare is, ironically, implicit in Professor Davis's own argument. Where but in the Supreme Court of the United States would we expect decisions that have great law-worth but little news-worth to get covered? Davis's thesis, which he limits to the Supreme Court, presumes that cases that lack conventional prerequisites for major coverage get coverage as accurate and objective as overworked reporters can manage in a short time. Once we consider other courts in subsequent chapters, we shall rediscover the obvious: only Supreme Court cases get more than mere mentions if they lack other attributes of news-worth. Thus, jural mystification is probably limited to the Supreme Court because no other court and no other judges get covered enough to mystify even the most attentive reader and viewer.

Newsworthy Cases

I noted earlier that most cases are so mundane that they lack both law-worth (that is, substantive impact on rules or laws) and news-worth (that is, suitability for coverage). The majority of cases and the vast majority of trials will pass with at most minimal press notice. Routine cases may get some perfunctory coverage if they involve celebrities or human interest. To get more than brief notices, cases must exhibit news-worth beyond the norm.

News-worth is largely a matter of reporters' and editors' perceptions about whether "there's a story there." Even cases that deviate from the routine and have great law-worth may fail of news-worth, because news-worth depends on the suitability of familiar media formats and angles. To be worthy of the news, cases must be adapted or adaptable to the requirements of the news medium and the tastes of that medium's public.

Novelty provides incentives for mass media to cover cases, so cases that are legally different from the norm have some news-worth. Still, accurate, objective coverage even of jurisprudentially weighty topics cannot compete with news tailored for media and audiences, so court coverage will tend to be covered far more if it presents angles that correspond to the content biases of modern mass media. In sum, newsworthy cases will increase the news media's incentives to engage in the inexpensive, hyped coverage that our Outside-In Perspective assumes.

Justice Antonin Scalia, we saw in the introduction, has warned that judicial outputs may be distorted by news outlets into hype. Justice Scalia claimed to assume that appellate decisions surpass the understanding of all but the legally trained members of the public. Specialized media might accurately convey legal reasoning from courts to lawyers and judges, but mass media cannot, in Justice Scalia's view, even pretend to grasp what the judges are doing and so must mangle judicial news in transmission.

To advance his thesis, Justice Scalia idealized judging:

In most areas of human endeavor, no matter how technical or abstruse the process may be, the product can be fairly evaluated by the layman: the bridge does or does not sustain the loads for which it was designed; the weather forecast is or is not usually accurate; the medical treatment does or does not improve the patient's condition. I maintain that judging, or at least judging in a democratic society, is different. There, it is frequently the case that the operation is a success, even though the patient dies. For in judging, process is a value unto itself and not—except in a very remote sense—merely a means to achieving a desireable [sic] end. The result is validated by the process, not the process by the result.[55]

Justice Scalia in effect married the ideal Court Mission posited by the Inside-Out Perspective to a commercial Media Mission outlined by my Outside-In Perspective. The justice goes the mainstream view one better by asserting that the courts exude "craft and candor" that is so formal and rigorous that it is quite beyond the comprehension of all but the legally astute. He then intensifies the Outside-In critique of news media by arguing that those media are well suited to convey melodrama and spectacle but utterly inept at accuracy, objectivity, and subtlety. Justice Scalia's "marriage" of perspectives issues a dichotomy— specialized, elite media (such as law journals) emulate the Inside-Out Perspective's Media Mission while generalist media entertain and distract the masses with nonsense.

Justice Scalia suggests an uneasy relationship between judges and reporters. Even trial courts will involve procedures that generalist reporters could neither fathom nor convey even if they had the airtime or news hole for such reporting. Appellate issues will prove even more inaccessible for reporters, editors, readers, and viewers. This alternative perspective depicts courts and media as mutually uncomprehending forces consistently forced to collide and to misunderstand. Ironically, Denniston and Gerald, whose remarks I used in the Introduction to exemplify the Inside-Out Perspective, characterized the relations between courts and reporters in the same terms but were convinced that the conflicts and misunderstandings could be overcome by effort on both sides. Justice Scalia professes to be more defeatist.

While Justice Scalia's view is presented for your consideration, I do not recommend it for a few reasons. In the first place, Justice Scalia enjoys playing the provocateur, so his remarks may have been intended to tweak his audience. If so, we should probably not put too much work into investigating a half-serious sally. Second, Justice Scalia has suggested several times in his opinions that judges and justices who disagree with him have failed to be forthcoming, to reason carefully, to take the logical path. Since the justice has thus admitted that much judicial image making is quite strategic, it is hard to take him seriously if he means to suggest that even law school deans could make sense of some of the output of the U. S. Supreme Court. Most important, I have used Justice Scalia's views to illustrate the theoretical possibility of Inside-Out judging combined with Outside-In reporting. In doing so, I may have overgeneralized his thesis. In a serious mood, Justice Scalia might not want to argue that ordinary cases exceed the ken of reporters. He certainly would not claim that most of the adjudication at the Court is so routine that formal, ideal reasoning alone will generate decisions. Still, keep this possibility in the back of your mind to force yourself to refute it in each chapter—if you can!

The Outside-In Perspective Accounts for Newsworthy, Uncommon Cases

The pride of place that I withheld from Justice Scalia's Media Distortion thesis and Davis's Jural Mystification thesis I have given to our Outside-In Perspective. I suspect that this perspective most likely explains court coverage in newsworthy cases that are not legally routine. Because I have already suggested why newsworthy cases will elicit expedient, hyped coverage and why nonroutine cases will feature more discretionary adjudication, I shall here rehearse why our Outside-In Perspective most coheres when cases are both newsworthy and law-worthy.

Our Outside-In Perspective is quite pragmatic. It coheres best in situations in which important ends demand compromises of ideals. Newsworthy cases that are out of the ordinary create such situations, for they force judges and reporters to pursue authority in ways that contradict mainstream expectations.

When cases are both law-worthy and newsworthy, judges must please more observers than usual. Clarity, candor, and craft are useful in all cases because judges have an audience of legally astute critics with whom to contend. The more attention a case garners from lay audiences, the more judges must disarm critics with arguments and imagery. While the strategic imagery expected by our Outside-In Perspective will be present in many cases, the increased visibility of newsworthy, nonroutine cases exacerbates the need for convincing rhetoric and, I suspect, inclines judges to leaven their formality with strategy, discretion, and manipulation.

News media must always meet Inside-Out standards for accuracy and objectivity, even if only by denying inaccuracy and subjectivity. As cases become more law-worthy, respectability to attentive, educated consumers of news requires news media to mention the decisions. What mass media must mention, they will have incentives to mention in the most marketable fashion. Thus, novelty alone predicts coverage, coverage implies media formats, and media formats imply angle or content biases. Even without much inherent news-worth, landmarks legal, political, and social would derive news-worth from the media's felt obligation to cover. That tendency, by the way, is why I discounted Davis's thesis and the lower left cell of table 1.1: law-worth tends to foster news-worth!

Whether law-worth or news-worth creates coverage matters little, for coverage brings with it inexpensive hype. Beyond minimal prerequisites for "facticity," balance, and intelligibility, news media must make money or lose less than competitors. To compete, media must cut costs and increase revenues. Our Outside-In Perspective presumes that this competitive pressure leads to inexpensive hype.

Inexpensive hype is also needed to capture audiences. An extensive attentive public for court news is a pleasant assumption and one necessary for the Inside-Out Perspective. If the attentive audience for court news is to grow to even a noticeable minority, the usually inattentive public must be persuaded to tune in. I have assumed in constructing our Outside-In Perspective that even judicial landmarks with drama, personalization, and other juicy angles and content will almost always escape popular notice. I note here the irony that the attentive public may be expected to increase beyond a small fraction of the populace only under conditions that make the rest of the Inside-Out Perspective far less likely than normal.

In sum, only when cases are legally momentous and suitable for media hype does an employer of our Outside-In Perspective expect much attention at all to befall court coverage. That is why our Outside-In Perspective posits "Drama and Spectacle" as the primary flow of information from courts, through media, to audiences. The "Mediated Two-Step" assumed by the mainstream view too often implies that portions of judicial outputs reach mass audiences. This implication the Outside-In Perspective contradicts. Instead, what is most likely to reach readers and viewers is whatever is cost effective, format friendly, and market savvy for media to hype. It is reasonable to assume that whatever the media leak to viewers and readers will be, for example, far more morselized and normalized than educational.

If coverage of newsworthy, out-of-the-ordinary cases tends to satisfy our Outside-In Perspective more than coverage of other cases, then the outside view is a useful complement to the mainstream view, even if the mainstream view still explains more about the coverage of this subset of cases. If such cases lead to media reports that resemble the alternative view or views more than the mainstream view, then the complementary alternatives seem indispensable. If the most covered and most absorbed stories about the most path-breaking cases seem to vindicate the outside view and to vitiate the inside view, then we must master *both* the inside *and* the outside if we are to fathom court coverage.

Conclusion

These possibilities are hardly the only ways in which we can see judicial journalism. Rather, the highlighted perspectives and the alternatives orient our review of the literature on judicial journalism with coordinates based on our attempts to think systematically about possible intersections and interactions between courts and news media. Now we must turn to empirical studies to see what support we can discover for the mainstream view and for alternative views.

It would be quite coincidental if the four kinds of courts—criminal, civil, lower appellate, and Supreme Court—discussed in this book each matched a different one of the four suppositions in table 1.1. Still, it should not surprise us much if reports of most criminal and civil trials tend to confirm the upper-left supposition, the Inside-Out Perspective. Most criminal and civil cases are neither newsworthy enough to justify much coverage, let alone hyped coverage, nor jurally unusual enough to push judges beyond ordinary formality. Many more appeals, however, are legally more challenging and significant, which should call for judicial imagery. Ordinary cases at the United States Supreme Court will be at least somewhat newsworthy, which may encourage hyped coverage. At the very least, then, appeals courts would seem much more likely to resemble the assumptions of our Outside-In Perspective.

I hope that this chapter has made it clear why it would also be unlikely that coverage of all four kinds of courts would best be understood by one and only one of the suppositions. If I was correct in the Introduction, however, the Inside-Out Perspective commands such allegiance that, in effect, the upper-left cell of table 1.1 provides and confines the conventional understanding of court coverage. The Introduction and Chapter 1 aim to alert you, the reader, to other possibilities so that your perceptions and cognitions will not be so confined.

I hope I have convinced you that the two main perspectives that will orient the rest of this book are indeed complementary. Even in the most routine, least newsworthy case, some of the presumptions of our Outside-In Perspective will round out our understanding, although the Inside-Out Perspective will usually suffice under those conditions. More newsworthy and extraordinary cases will feature Outside-In media and courts, but judges and reporters can fulfill the outside view only behind Inside-Out cover stories. Thus, the two perspectives complement each other case by case. They complement each other in general as well, as table 1.1 makes clear.

Now, let us turn to cases, courts, and coverage.

CHAPTER 2

The Supreme Court
of the United States:
Very Public
But Very Private

> The Supreme Court is a paradox for journalists, at once one of
> the most open and one of the least accessible of the major insti-
> tutions of government. Its openness derives from the public
> availability of nearly all documents filed with the Court; from
> public oral argument sessions; and the fact that it decides cases
> by written opinions in which the justices explain their reasoning.
>   At the same time, the actual process of deciding cases is
> not open to public view. Only the final product emerges from
> behind the closed doors of the conference room and the judges'
> chambers. . . . Justices are typically not available for interviews
> and, for the most part, shun personal publicity.[1]

Observers have scrutinized coverage of the Supreme Court of
the United States more than that of any other court. Despite differing
perspectives on Court coverage, these observers tend to agree that the
Supreme Court is very public but also very private. The High Court is
both open *and* secretive, *both* conspicuous *and* imperceptible, *both*
welcoming *and* forbidding. Linda Greenhouse, Supreme Court beat
reporter for the *New York Times*, pronounces this dual nature a "paradox for journalists."

Recent scholarship suggests that, far from a paradox, the Court
is a paragon of image politics.[2] When the Court chooses to "go public,"
the justices supply evidence for judicial virtues; when the Court "goes
private," its justices craft decisions and opinions by arts *both* political
and judicial. On display, the Court considers formal, written appeals
and entertains lawyerly oral arguments. The justices then retreat
behind purple curtains where they ponder and pontificate, niggle and
negotiate, write and wrestle. Their less decorous backstage allows the

justices to direct attention to a very proper frontstage where a deliberate, dignified Court again displays itself to reveal its decisions, opinions, and orders.

In this alternative interpretation, then, the public and private faces of the U. S. Supreme Court show us that the justices adeptly practice public relations in a manner *both* similar to *and* different from other modern institutions. Like other institutions, the Court tries to live up to ideals and, when unable to match those ideals, to seem to be what it cannot in fact be. Like other politicians, the justices try to control their images and their audiences' reactions by averring virtues and avoiding vices. Similar as the *ends* of the Court's public relations may be to the goals of other institutions and groups, the justices employ very different *means*. The justices profess to be bound by legal rules, beyond or above politics. Having imparted legal "spin" to their activities through official opinions, the justices must then remain silent lest they seem political. As a result, the most effective public-relations routine for the Court may be to shine judicial virtues and to shun injudicious vices but otherwise to skirt notice.

Because they look for conventional tools of public relations, reporters and observers who are otherwise astute often miss or misstate the justices' talent for matching their decisions to ideals and expectations. To me, the stunning paradox is that analysts who pity the justices and the Court for being so inept at controlling their image often document the very means by which the justices and the Court control their image! Let me try to heap this paradox atop Linda Greenhouse's.

Perhaps the archetypical reporter of the Supreme Court, Anthony Lewis, pronounced the Supreme Court to be as oblivious to public relations as a national political institution could be,[3] but he incorporated the justices' "spin control" into his book on the Court.[4] A pioneer in the study of Supreme Court coverage, Chester A. Newland, stated that "(n)o positive program of public relations exists in the sense of promotion or publicity of decisions, justices, or the Court as an institution," in the middle of an article that documented how the Court shaped its coverage.[5] Lawyer and reporter Fred Graham noted the absence of news management even as he showed how the justices kept reporters away from whatever they did not want reporters to see or report.[6]

The reporter, the political scientist, and the lawyer-turned-reporter overlooked the special public relations practiced by the Court even as they documented it. For most Washington politicos, getting ink (that is, notice in the written press) and air (broadcast notice) is an important means to their ends and, for some, an end in itself. The politicians in robes at the Court expose themselves more judiciously. At many points in the Supreme Court's process, the justices regard no news as good news and, unlike most politicians, seek anonymity. At other points, the justices regard controlled news as good news, just as other politicians do.[7] Restricting press and public to tightly controlled, official audiences with the Court, the justices largely ensure coverage that matches their professional ideals and image.[8]

To understand coverage of the U. S. Supreme Court, it follows, we must see that coverage both from conventional and from unconventional points of view. I try to present evidence for both views in this chapter. First, I explain coverage of the High Court by standard journalistic practices. This overview provides us some generalizations that characterize research to date and anticipate what research may find tomorrow. In addition, this survey of research shows how the Court manages to be so public yet so private. After this overview, I advance some specific hypotheses for your consideration. Extensive as studies of Supreme Court coverage are, few scholars in this area have systematized findings. This chapter will offer ways to make sense of what we have found to date by advancing hypotheses that studies have suggested and that the perspectives just identified might explain.

Standard Practices and Court Coverage

. . . For many journalists, the Court is a boring assignment. The decisions of the Court are highly complicated. The Court is the institution least willing to cater to journalists' needs, making their assignments even more burdensome. The exceptions are the stories encompassing policies that can be explained easily and possess a moral element and a high degree of passion on both sides. These types of Court stories more readily fit media values of news. Reporters may cover the Court in accordance with news values.[9]

The Supreme Court of the United States is, in general and on occasion, the most powerful judicial institution on the planet. When the Court exercises great power, it becomes very public. Some decisions achieve such notoriety through mass media that readers and viewers avoid reports only through conscious efforts. If we focus on stupendous decisions, we may overestimate how much of the work of the Court is routinely covered and underestimate how often the Court is routinely overlooked.

The Supreme Court becomes very public when its actions seem newsworthy. Two tendencies of mass media introduced in chapter 1— commercial biases and angle biases—inform judgments of news-worth for coverage of the Court, as they shape the news-worth of other institutions and actors. As a consequence, I may advance an unsurprising generalization: *The Supreme Court of the United States, its justices, and its work are most public when they match commercial biases and angle biases and least public when they flout commercial and/or angle biases.*

Commercial Biases and Coverage of the Supreme Court

Commercial biases, I hope you recall from chapter 1, concern mass media as businesses. Stockholders and executives demand that their employees project news to broad audiences at modest cost for immodest profit. As a result, editors and reporters strive to cover news according to the standards of journalism but within the demands of owners and proprietors for profit, cost containment, and marketing.[10]

Commercial biases apply to coverage of the Supreme Court in the same manner as other coverage, so we may presume that Supreme Court decisions that arrest attention and cost little to cover will be far more public than decisions that concern few consumers or consume journalists' resources.[11] This is simply a matter of supply-side media-logic.[12] Reporters and editors tend to attribute news-worth to events at the Court that they may cover professionally but profitably. Reporters and editors are professionals, so they will cover the Court with as much accuracy, objectivity, and comprehensiveness as profits and proprietors permit. The expense of securing information will direct reporters to less costly information, and thus news media will feature far more of the information the Court provides for free than that for which news outlets must pay.

Truly comprehensive and comprehensible coverage of the Supreme Court is rare because it is so costly: reporters must specialize in legal or Supreme Court matters; reporters require time to prepare for and to ponder arguments and announcements associated with cases; editors must understand enough about the Court or trust their reporters enough to critique and reform initial copy; then editors must scare up time or space enough for reporters to explain what the Court has done.[13] Even so brief a list of prerequisites for good coverage of the Court demonstrates how costly such coverage would be and shows us why few publishers and editors will be in a position to afford such extravagance. Concerns for circulation or ratings will prod news producers to provide less luxurious stories that entice news consumers.[14] As Justice Scalia has reminded us, "You cannot reasonably expect to get all that information from a newspaper account, at least not a newspaper that wants to remain in business. That's why the University of Chicago *Law Review* is not sold in 7-11 [sic] stores."[15]

Angle Biases and Coverage of the Supreme Court

Commercial considerations are often reinforced by angle biases defined in chapter 1, so we must see how mass media market news with standard story-telling devices that seize consumers' attention and hold it at manageable cost. Recall that W. Lance Bennett argued that journalists morselize, dramatize, normalize, and personalize reported events in ways that shape news to newspapers' needs even when inaccurate, unbalanced, and subjective reports result.[16] Other observers have suggested slightly different biases. Richard Davis includes "timeliness, proximity, and unusualness" among the news values that shape mass media coverage of the Court,[17] while Tim O'Brien has argued that networks have not one bias but several: in favor of those being interviewed at the moment, in favor of middle-American perspectives and values, in favor of bad news.[18] I shall indicate how I believe O'Brien's and Davis's formulations of angle biases might be included in Bennett's. You must understand how each angle bias—however formulated—applies to reports of the United States Supreme Court.

Morselization and Coverage of the Court

Bennett defined *morselization* as the tendency of mass media to reduce events and activities to "bite-sized" stories with little of the context and process that might lead to deeper understanding.[19] Morselizing reporters pare away complicating details and ignore ongoing aspects in favor of immediately completed action. Thus, Bennett's morselizing media prefer the timely and the proximate (Davis's formulation) and are biased in favor of those who compete hardest for media attention at any moment (reporter O'Brien's formulation). If reporters are assigned to a courthouse beat, for example, the very organization of their work will direct their attention away from the legal system as a whole and toward immediate, particular occurrences around the court-house.[20] This might explain the news media's habit of considering Supreme Court decisions as definitive resolutions of disputes or authoritative answers to questions rather than as responses in an enduring debate or as stages of a marathon.[21] At the least, morselization encourages journalists to look past trends, issues, and tendencies and to observe the Court in terms of self-contained cases.

Dramatization and Coverage of the Court

A second angle bias, *dramatization,* directs reporters and editors to the most arresting features of adjudication. Davis stresses reporters' yen for the unusual; O'Brien says reporters seek out threatening stories; both of these formulations specify aspects of dramatizing coverage, in my view.

As with other angle biases, dramatization is understandable and even laudable. After all, consumers of news often seek conflict, sensation, titillation, so it can scarcely surprise or disappoint us that verbal fisticuffs among justices or donnybrooks between the Court and powerful adversaries draw far more coverage than disquisitions on the intricacies of phrases from legal Latin. Coverage will emphasize surprising decisions over compelling justifications and conflictual more than unanimous decisions.[22] As a result, journalists will usually report the Court's results more often and more completely than the Court's reasons. Since most Supreme Court actions feature little drama that popular press may convey to their audiences and since other institutions will tailor their actions to secure coverage,[23] dramatization also accounts for prevalent noncoverage of the Court.

Morselization, Dramatization, Reporters, and "Spin Doctors"

Morselization and dramatization often reinforce one the other. Reporters routinely reduce decisions and opinions to *results*—the Court's specific determination of which side or sides win on which issues—and, less often, *holdings*—principles shaped to fit the specific case but to answer the more general, legal questions that the case raises. Reporters can then dramatize results and some holdings as *landmarks*. Landmarks are guiding precedents, holdings that define the law for some time to come. The more final, the more definitive that reports make the Court's decisions and opinions seem, the more striking their impact on consumers of news. When morselizing coverage sharpens decisions into very dramatic points, qualifications and nuances that the justices struggled to include must yield to journalistic imperatives for angles.[24]

In turn, reactions to reports may exacerbate dramatization or exaggerate morselization or both. Winning litigants and their sympathizers are likely to generalize the holding into an enduring landmark, even to the point of obscuring conditions and cautions with which justices qualify their opinions, opinions that the winners have yet to read. As winners inflate their victory into a landmark, losers may minimize their loss with inferences from reports of opinions of justices, contentions of lawyers, or facts of cases. Losers, that is, tend to accumulate context (de-morselize) to make decisions less discrete and to assemble details (de-dramatize) to make decisions less stark. However, if most media most of the time do not convey such context or details, losers will often have too little appreciation of the subtleties of decisions to deflate those decisions. All the worse for losers, journalists must morselize and dramatize reactions if they are to report them at all. Hence, losers' attempts to counteract morselization and dramatization *may* tend to lead journalists to reimpose angles on reports of reactions.

Normalization and Coverage of the Court

Journalists tend to morselize and dramatize even attempts to resist morselization and dramatization because they make their reports acceptable by fitting recent occurrences into familiar formats. This tendency to interpret "news" in terms of "olds" Bennett labeled *normalization*. O'Brien suggested that reporters tended to use the values of "Middle America" to orient their reports about the Court. Bennett might allow that as a subset of normalizing coverage. Clearly, we should expect the actions of the Supreme Court, like those of other news makers, to be interpreted to conform to jural norms as much as we have already seen that Court news will conform to journalistic norms. The Court cuts journalists' costs by displays of the most judicious, official, formal features of normal adjudication. The Court then imposes the strictest secrecy to deny journalists most information inconsistent with those jural norms tended and trumpeted by the justices. Costs and deadlines will often incline reporters to defer to the normalized output that justices provide. If they choose to challenge the justices, reporters undermine their own balance and objectivity unless they contradict the justices with reactions from litigants, experts, and sympathizers. These reactions will tend to refer to norms, the better to reiterate and to reinforce them. Indeed, even if reactions are so injudicious and political that they demand coverage, the very deviance of the reactions will tend to reaffirm norms. Normalization and commercial biases, then, explain the habitual deference and even indolence of many who report the Court. These biases are reinforced by work habits: " 'I've been in the business since 1948,' said Lyle Denniston, who covers the U. S. Supreme Court for the *Baltimore Sun* and is the author of the book *The Reporter and the Law*, 'and I know of no beat where reporters are lazier and do less to penetrate the process they're supposed to cover than legal reporting.' "[25]

The tendency of mass media to normalize news both follows from and conditions further their morselizing and dramatizing of the U. S. Supreme Court. Norms help readers and viewers interpret complicated legal events, so ordinary understandings and expectations assist morselization. On the other hand, as reporters write stories to fit the demands of editors and readers, they tend to omit from stories details that defy their editors', their readers', and their own presuppositions. Thus, morselization and normalization reinforce each other. As well, normalization often furthers dramatization and vice versa. Major conflicts supply drama but normalization frames conflicts in predictable, comprehensible formats and characters.

Personalization and Coverage of the Court

Personalization, Bennett's final angle bias, sometimes operates peculiarly in Court coverage. Chapter 1 showed that personalization is the tendency to construct stories around individuals rather than institutions. Certainly, coverage of the Supreme Court focuses on the Court more than the justices:

> The inaccessibility of the justices restricts the press from highlighting people-oriented aspects in Court stories. Stories of the Court are highly oriented toward discussion of public policy. In nearly two-thirds of the Court stories, most or all of the content consisted of policy discussion. Even CBS News' content overwhelmingly stressed policy discussion, though to a lesser extent than the print media. . . .[26]

Because personalizing the decision makers would be costly and would defeat morselization and dramatization, if not normalization, journalists often use litigants or third parties to personalize cases. At *CBS News*, for example, Fred Graham pioneered "personification" in coverage of the Supreme Court. CBS hired Fred Graham to improve its coverage of the High Court. Graham covered cases by going "on location" to show the individuals involved. This morselized, personalized technique made cases much more comprehensible, relevant, and real to ordinary viewers. This is an example of what Davis would call "proximate coverage." However, as other telecasters and many print journalists began to emulate Graham,[27] style began to subvert substance. Not only did certain dramatic plots—such as powerless versus powerful, traditional versus progressive, pluralistic versus absolutist—recur but they became formulaic. That is, coverage was not only morselized and dramatized but normalized as well.

A Generalization about Coverage

I hope that this review of commercial biases and angle biases makes sense of my generalizations about Supreme Court coverage. I might have generalized, following the lead of others, that mass media tend to cover the High Court when its activities have more "news-worth,"[28] but that generalization seems to me true by definition. Instead, I have defined *news-worth* by commercial and angle biases to enable us to begin from the more interesting, if unsurprising, proposition stated earlier: The Supreme Court of the United States, its justices, and its work are most public when they match commercial biases and angle biases and least public when they flout commercial and/or angle biases.

From this proposition, let us derive two implications. First and most obvious: *the actions and personnel of the U. S. Supreme Court will tend to be covered when those actions and those people conform to one or more of the biases.* When they fit none of the biases, they will tend not to be covered in mass media, although specialized legal media and other targeted media may find them newsworthy. Second and maybe less obvious: *when mass media cover the justices or their acts, they will tend to emphasize aspects that match the biases and will tend to de-emphasize or ignore aspects that do not.*

A Very Public Court— Result-Oriented Coverage

Only rarely do people know exactly what the Court has held, less often do they know why it has held as it has. And almost never do they appreciate the consequences of particular Court decisions.[29]

Any impressions of Supreme Court coverage that you brought to this chapter were probably influenced by recollection of this blaring headline or that interrupting bulletin. The Supreme Court is covered infrequently by most mass media, but when it is covered, it is covered prominently.[30] Your recollections may direct you toward unrepresentative coverage and away from the usually more modest news-worth of most activities of the Court. Only the largest and best endowed national and regional newspapers can note many of the thousands of decisions that the Supreme Court makes each year.[31] It is important at the outset, then, that I remind you that, for most readers and most viewers, the Court usually operates with minimal surveillance.[32] As we look at the public face of the Court and the justices, we must never forget that their faces usually are not public.

"The few systematic studies of news media portrayal of the Supreme Court have concluded that news coverage is infrequent and sketchy."[33] Sketchy coverage tends to be result oriented. Lawyers refer to the tendency of lay observers, including many journalists, to emphasize the winning and losing sides over the process of decision making and the quality of argumentation as result orientation. Lawyers sneer at result orientation because it falls far short of lawyers' professional ideal, reason orientation or process orientation. While this distinction is often overstated, results and reasons may be distinguishable enough to characterize reports about the High Court.

We may begin our survey of research, then, from a view held by justices, lawyers, and laypersons alike: *The results that the Court generates tend to be publicized far more and far more often than justifications for the results or other information about the process by which the justices reached their results.* If we compare this view with the general proposition that I stated above, we may infer that results are usually more newsworthy than reasons and hence are covered both more and more often.

Spot Coverage

Spot coverage barely improves on noncoverage, but spot coverage is the most the justices may hope for in many instances and too much to expect in many others. Even a national newspaper with an ample "news hole" can justify extensive coverage of Court-related happenings only when they are most newsworthy. Smaller newspapers and broadcasters may choose not to lavish space or air on modestly newsworthy stories and may scale back their coverage. In 1989, for example, only 11 percent of the Court's 144 full-scale decisions were covered by ABC, NBC, and CBS and only 24 percent drew coverage from at least one.[34] Many of those reports were capsules.

Since all journalists focus their reporting to enhance readers' and viewers' understanding and enjoyment, concision itself is a virtue and is *not* the problem with spot coverage. The *New York Times* lavished 9,200 words (roughly the equivalent of a forty-page, double-spaced paper!) on *Miranda v. Arizona* (1966), the Supreme Court landmark that resulted in the Miranda warnings that we hear and see everywhere in popular culture. However, the *Times*'s verbal investment represented less than a quarter of the words that the justices used in their opinions.[35]

Instead, problems of spot coverage are evident in this example from *ABC News*:

> [T]he Court has ruled that the state government in Ohio was wrong when it tried to bar the Ku Klux Klan from erecting a cross in a . . . park, near the state capital at Christmastime. "If other private groups can display religious symbols," the Court ruled, "such as a Menorah, the Klan can put up a cross."[36]

This brief item devoted three-fifths of its fifty-six words to a first sentence that expressed the specific result in *Capitol Square v. Pinette*, a Supreme Court decision announced on June 29, 1995. The twenty-two words in the second sentence suggest a lay version of the holding so simple that anyone may understand it.

You should have little difficulty seeing why justices and lawyers deride such news capsules. Other than the outcome of the case, pure spot coverage provides news consumers almost nothing. The capsule succinctly relayed the Court's specific decision—Ku Klux Klan wins and the Capitol Square Review and Advisory Board loses—with but a hint of the Court's reasoning. The second sentence suggests the peril of covering reasons in one sentence: viewers might read that sentence as a comparison of the Ku Klux Klan to Christian and Jewish groups. Little wonder that Justice Scalia, author of the opinion, excoriates Court coverage!

Results, Holdings, and Rigors of Reporting

> [I]t is the daily or periodic task of legal reporting to tell who won or lost. Of course, it is also part of the task to describe how the process went, and—if at all possible—how the ultimate result was reached.[37]

This quotation and the discussion that preceded it suggest that at least two aspects of cases will be highlighted if mass media cover cases at all. The most public aspects of the Court's work are specific *results* of decisions—which parties win and which lose. Less prominent but nonetheless common if a case is covered, holdings answer the legal questions that cases pose. Often, mass-mediated holdings will be so simplified and morselized that even attentive and retentive citizens will not discern the principles that the Court has articulated. This was the case when *ABC News* reduced *Capitol Square v. Pinette* to two sentences. When mass media simplify holdings and reasons, coverage of the Court may convey little more than who won and who lost.

Observers have generalized that, when the Supreme Court is covered, most mass media stories go beyond results and holdings rarely and barely.[38] This finding is implicit in the result-oriented generalization already stated: *Results usually and holdings often will be present if a case is reported but will be all that is present in news capsules.* It is nonetheless useful to remember that such bare bones coverage is more the norm than the extensive treatment that larger newspapers give a few landmarks per year. To the extent that results and holdings are disseminated widely with little else, the public Court is defined by winners, losers, and holdings.

Reporting Winners and Losers

The Court's results will be covered if the Court is covered at all because the stark conclusions of cases—who won, who lost—are essential for any story about any decision. However, please do not forget commercial biases and angle biases. Winners and losers coverage—especially when results contradict the intuitions and sympathies of ordinary folk—provides news that is inexpensive to gather, unchallenging to relay, premorselized by the Court in the final paragraphs of the majority opinion (and often elsewhere), and normalized by the forms that Court and news reports alike repeat. If reporters can reconstruct winning or losing litigants as familiar characters or stereotypes, winners and losers coverage may instantly dramatize coverage as well! Since coverage of winners and losers is relatively cheap and easily normalized and morselized, we expect it to be common.

Reporting winners and losers is also one way to manage the flow of news. Demands for speed and brevity exacerbate tensions between courts and all their coverers, but reporters usually can convey quickly and briefly who won and who lost. The pulses of Supreme Court decision making can overwhelm news media if reporters try to convey much more than who won and who lost. In sum, results match many requirements both of narrative and of newsworth.

Holdings, Deadlines, and Wire Services

One great virtue of holdings (and winners and losers) is that they may be reported within deadlines.[39] Indeed, results and holdings may be all that some reporters can cover on deadlines. Consider, for example, wire-service reporters, on whom many newspapers and some broadcasters across the nation depend for reports of the Supreme Court. Associated Press reporters

> must quickly identify a case, determine the decision, wade quickly through thousands of legalistic words of the majority and dissenting views, refer to the background which they have assembled and get the story moving by telephone dictation—all in a matter of a few minutes.[40]

Deadlines demand speed and concision[41]; winners, losers, and holdings may be identified quickly and recorded briefly. Elliot Slotnick has reported that Richard Carelli, a reporter for the Associated Press, reviewed the complex opinions of the justices in *Regents of the University of California v. Bakke* (1978) for three minutes before filing a "bullet lead" that contained—that could contain—merely the results and a hint of the holdings. Carelli often must create about two dozen or more Supreme Court stories in a single day.[42]

Concision pleases managing editors[43] because spot coverage morselizes and normalizes news into small news-holes and packed broadcasts. Indeed, wire service stories may enable newspeople to cover more decisions, albeit less extensively. David Ericson found in his study of newspaper coverage of the Court that the *Ann Arbor News*, which relied on wire services extensively, reported something about 87 of the 145 written decisions handed down by the Court in its 1974 Term (60 percent), while the *Detroit News* covered but 44 decisions (30 percent). The much smaller paper in Ann Arbor used wire-service stories with minimal revision. The much larger Detroit daily either went with more extensive coverage or skipped decisions altogether.[44]

Even for reporters with more time than wire-service reporters, cases are often complex, language confused and confusing, and arguments convoluted, but the bottom line is usually clear. Given short filing limits, multiple opinions turning on nuances, justices' indifference to explaining themselves to the uninitiated, and the news media's taste for emphasizing some cases and de-emphasizing others, we should be more surprised that reporters relay more than results and holdings than that they pass along only such reports.

If justices will not write for the usual journalistic audience, holdings may be the only legal reasoning that many reporters understand well enough to pass along! While many decision makers on many beats strive to suit their announcements to the patterns of coverage, the Supreme Court will often release multiple landmarks and a dozen or more decisions in a day, especially at the end of a term. John MacKenzie lamented his having to cover the 580 pages of Supreme Court output released on June 12, 1967.[45] Tim O'Brien of *ABC News* has made it clear that this is still a problem.[46]

To prepare for onslaughts of decisions, reporters who specialize in the Supreme Court may compose parts of their stories about cases in advance of announcements of decisions.[47] While this means that some of the legal arguments in briefs or oral arguments may contextualize holdings, it also implies that holdings will be the centerpiece of the report of the case. Holdings are not only more dramatic and comprehensible than predigested material but also more immediate. Reporters and editors will prefer the immediate reports, such as holdings and reactions uninformed beyond who won and who lost, to more dated material.

Dominance of Results and Holdings—An Example

If we conceive of Supreme Court coverage as ranging from non-coverage to true spot coverage to news briefs to full-blown stories about the Court, only at the lengthy end of this continuum would we expect reports to include much about the reasoning of the justices, precedents and legal language, and other formal aspects of cases. Reporters and editors with little space in broadcasts or on broadsheets need to grab consumers' attention. Results seize the eye and hold the ear to a far greater extent than reasons or anything else.[48]

If we return to *Capitol Square v. Pinette*, the Supreme Court decision covered in the capsule earlier, we may see that results and holdings dominate coverage longer than capsules as well. Just as ABC had, *USA Today* treated *Capitol Square* as an appendage of coverage of *Rosenberger v. University of Virginia:*

> A companion ruling Thursday said Ohio restricted the free speech rights of the Ku Klux Klan by refusing to allow it to erect

a cross in a public park near the state Capitol, even though other groups are allowed to erect signs and to demonstrate in the area.[49]

Those forty-eight words expended, reporter Tony Mauro speculated about political consequences that could follow from the result and the holding. Mauro's article adds eventual consequences to immediate holdings of both *Capitol Square* and *Rosenberger*, but results crowd out the justices' reasons in his story. Results, albeit extrapolated to other political arenas, predominate.

Of course, *USA Today* exemplifies coverage between newspapers of record and television news. Broadcast news and small newspapers can fit very little Supreme Court news into their reports, so results, holdings, and perhaps a little more incontestable information may use up the time or space available. *USA Today* may aptly represent modal coverage!

Table 2.1 **Composition of Linda Greenhouse's Report of**
Capitol Square v. Pinette

Paragraphs	Summary of Content	Number of Words
1	*Lead: Decision of Court*	**50**
2-4	Paraphrases/quotes majority opinion	159
5	*States reaction of Lubavitch Jews*	**33**
5	*Assesses implications for other cases*	**18**
5	*Reports Court action in related case*	**35**
6	*Identifies option available to states*	**34**
7-9	Paraphrases/quotes two dissents	116
10	Paraphrases/quotes concurring opinion	69
11	Characterizes divisions within majority	97
12	Notes unmentioned precedent	84
	All paragraphs in story:	695
	Result-oriented paragraphs:	**170**

More extensive coverage by national newspapers with ample news holes reveals just how far beyond results and holdings specialized reporters who are granted time and space can venture. Let's analyze Linda Greenhouse's article on the same landmark for the *New York Times*.[50] After leading with fifty words stating the result and the holding of the Court—which was about what *ABC News* did but about all that it did—Ms. Greenhouse paraphrased and quoted from Justice

Antonin Scalia's majority opinion. She then reported that Lubavitch Jews had declared the Klan's victory to be their own victory (reactions to winners and losers) and assessed implications of *Capitol Square* for other litigation (reactions to legal holdings). Greenhouse then reported that the Court had vacated a lower court ruling on a similar case. She then assessed consequences of *Capitol Square* for local governments. After that bit of result-oriented reporting, Ms. Greenhouse directed her attention to such reason-oriented aspects of the case as dissenting and concurring opinions, a split among the majority justices on state endorsement of religion, and the apparent demise of *Lemon v. Kurtzman* (1971) as the leading precedent in this field.

Ms. Greenhouse has added not merely words but legal and political contextualization. She has shown us that holdings and results need not exhaust coverage even of a relatively minor case. Indeed, I have juxtaposed her article to coverage on ABC and in *USA Today* to make the point that the result-oriented coverage of the latter two news outlets likely induced readers to regard *Capitol Square* as a sideshow to *Rosenberger* while Ms. Greenhouse educated her readers about perhaps unsuspected implications in the Klan case itself. Ms. Greenhouse captured results of the decision. She relayed the holding, the winners and losers and their reactions, and consequences political and legal, immediate and longer range, all in about 170 words. I have italicized in table 2.1 summaries of paragraphs that seemed to me result-oriented and I have used boldface for the number of words that those paragraphs consumed. Notice that my rough and ready estimate is that Greenhouse devoted about a quarter of her copy to results. In contrast, her paraphrases of and quotations from the majority opinion, concurring opinion, and dissenting opinions added up to at least 344 words, or nearly half her article.

While Greenhouse's coverage of this case shows us what other reporters might do if their editors granted them the space, such indulgence is exceptional. Most media outlets select the less expensive practice: they mention the work of the Supreme Court not at all. When Supreme Court decisions do not conform and cannot be made to conform to angle biases or time and space constraints, we should anticipate that the Court will issue little news. When one or more angles make Supreme Court news marketable, we may expect editors to find room for reporters' angles. Results and holdings adorned by only minimal details will occasionally provide a little drama in a morsel and thus may surface, albeit barely, in the news media. After no coverage at all, then, coverage of who won and who lost is the least expensive coverage and should be expected when decisions present reporters and editors with too few angles to exploit. Coverage that conveys even popularized versions of the Court's reasoning will be even less frequent unless the Court's holdings present commercial possibilities or attractive angles.

Beyond Winners, Losers, and Holdings

Court stories almost always began with words to the effect: "The Supreme Court, in a major ruling today . . ." or "The Supreme Court held today. . . ." The story then proceeded to identify the key issues of the case, to quote from the majority and dissenting opinions, to discuss the potential impact of the decisions, to place the decision in the context of previous opinions, and to include reaction by interested persons and legal scholars and practitioners. The decision was the focal point of the story.[51]

To go beyond merest mentions of results and holdings, the press must decide which details embellish stories without sacrificing angles and marketability. Enhancing details must be readily available or the costs of improvements will likely prohibit enhancements. Additions must not compromise angles (especially morselization) without great gains in other angles. Moreover, any embellishments and enhancements must be accomplished quickly and accurately.

Choices characteristic of various media will differ, of course.[52] "Newspapers of record" may enhance their coverage of decisions with summaries of the justices' opinions and of prominent reactions, as Linda Greenhouse's report of *Capitol Square v. Pinette* did. Other newspapers will lean on wire services for sparer copy that features little more than holdings and a pithy quotation from the majority opinion. Television may be expected to cover fewer decisions but to plunge beyond holdings into some analysis, personalized attention to litigants, or rather free associations.[53] While I know of no extensive research on this matter, I believe that I can make persuasive inferences from documented patterns of behavior by Supreme Court reporters. These inferences will help us to create hypotheses about reporting beyond results and holdings.

Votes

As a first, trivial example, consider the voting alignments of the justices. Please recall that such alignments occupied about one-seventh of Linda Greenhouse's article about *Capitol Square v. Pinette* (see table 2.1). Supreme Court reporter Dana Bullen tried in his newspaper stories to state the vote (for example, unanimous, or five to four) near the beginning, where the most important information was to be found.[54] Court provided summaries, called "syllabi," detail the lineup of justices, so the vote may be extracted for free. Ordinary readers and viewers will understand the vote immediately. Reporters may verify the vote quickly. Hence, we may expect Supreme Court stories to relay the Court's lineup as a routine embellishment of the decision.

Source-ery and Document-Centered Coverage

Probably just as obvious, result orientation, beyond emphasis on winners, losers, holdings, and votes, leads to document-centered coverage. Since the Court disseminates its holdings and reasoning and provides little other free information, journalists will be inclined to go with what they can quickly glean from official documents surrounding the decision and with reactions they can gather from readily available sources responding to that decision. Professor Davis has deftly connected styles of coverage to the sorts of sources that mass media use to endow their reports with credibility:

> One sign of the dominance of decisions in Court stories was the type of source employed. Documents—in this case, the opinions of the justices or written summaries—were mentioned or implied in a source in nearly every story. They far exceeded use of any other source-reporter observation, on-record interviews, backgrounders, etc.—for Court stories. By comparison, documents were mentioned or implied as sources in only one-fourth of Congress stories and less than one-fifth of stories on the presidency.[55]

We may also hypothesize that prior to announcements of decisions, accessible aspects of the Court's work will seldom surface except in elite newspapers.[56] Court specialists are expected to master lower court opinions, briefs, and oral arguments to be able to contextualize decisions when they are announced.[57] Thus, coverage that goes beyond results may add contentions of the litigants or of "friends of the Court" who have advanced arguments prior to the decision. Such official, legal contextualization is distinctly limited in all but the most elite news organs by producers' and consumers' knowledge and interest and by the usual angle biases. Details with drama and immediacy may enhance the marketability of the story. Details that merely add to the accuracy of the story and the comprehensibility of the decision, the Court, or the legal system in general usually will be squeezed out of copy by competing stories with greater commercial appeal.[58]

Syllabi and Headnotes—Court-Controlled Information

Even if most media had more room for legal details, their reports would abound with the Court's version of the law rather than independent, analytic, or even mildly critical coverage. The Court releases with its opinions syllabi that expedite coverage of legal factors in decisions. The Court does not, strictly speaking, control its coverage. Through syllabi, however, the Court makes it far easier for reporters to relay very formal, very official accounts that keep the Court above politics. Spot coverage and other stories that emphasize results need incorporate little from syllabi. However, stories that go beyond results may use the Court's syllabi extensively.

Each syllabus is a concise summary of the legal issues posed in the case, the Court's resolutions of those issues, the lineup of votes of the justices on issues, and the reasoning of justices who agree with the decision of the Court's majority. Reporters who rely on syllabi get a formal, apolitical view of decisions that may induce them to supplement holdings and results with reasoning that reinforces the image of the Court that justices prefer. Syllabi, then, provide reporters with an official, hyperformal "spin" on decisions in an offer many reporters will be unable to refuse. Please note well that the justices *do not* write the syllabi, but, since Chief Justice Warren Burger's tenure, they have authorized an employee, the Reporter of Decisions, to do so.

Headnotes are even more concise statements issued by case-reporting services. These services derive from the majority opinion (but not any concurring or dissenting opinion) the "rules" that the Court has "found." The Reporter of Decisions prepares these pithy statements of the main principles that justify decisions.[59] These notes restate the legal authority underlying the decision in a manner that makes issues appear so technical and esoteric that only the boldest layperson would dare to challenge the justices' reasoning. In headnotes as in syllabi, then, majority opinions are reduced to their most judicious and legalistic elements.

Do headnotes and syllabi shape coverage? Given deadlines, demands, and commercial considerations, how could reporters forego such cheap assistance, even if it is pure, judicial spin? Even reporters wary of the Court's "help" may be so accustomed to or comfortable with formal legal accessories that they acquiesce in "prespun" Supreme Court news.

Consider, for example, what Supreme Court reporters sought when the late Chief Justice Warren E. Burger asked them for suggestions for improving coverage and conditions. Reporters suggested improved access to official documents: simultaneous release of opinions, distribution of opinions in advance with lockup to prevent leaks, advance notification by docket number, release of headnotes with opinions, joint release of related decisions, and clearer definition of disagreements among concurrers, majority, and dissenters. In response, Burger agreed to release headnotes, to even out releases across the week, and to reschedule some oral arguments. Reporters expressed their gratitude for these improvements.[60]

Everette E. Dennis has suggested why such minimal, manipulative assistance satisfied the reporters:

> The reporters' attitude toward the information policies of the Court reflected a tone of resignation. Most reporters assumed the Court was unyielding in its basic stance toward disseminating information on its deliberations and rationale for decisions. Accepting this, they focused their concerns upon procedural problems which, if resolved, would result in some short-term gains. This acceptance sadly suggests a potential co-optation of some reporters.[61]

I disagree with Dennis only in that I do not see reporters' co-optation as potential. This example seems to me to demonstrate the extent to which Supreme Court reporters were coopted long ago into coproducing the public image of the Supreme Court.[62]

Paraphrasing Perilous Opinions

As Justice Scalia has observed, even considerable assistance to journalists may not be enough to make legal issues clear and understandable. Editorial responses to *Harris v. McRae*[63] (1980) reveal the difficulties that editorialists, an unusually well informed and thoughtful lay audience, had with even the simplest opinion. Let us see what we can learn from this example.

Most justices considered *Harris v. McRae* to be indistinguishable from the Court's earlier decision in *Maher v. Roe* (1977).[64] In *Harris v. McRae*, the U. S. Supreme Court upheld the Hyde Amendment, by which Congress had limited Medicaid funds for abortions and held that states were not required to replace Medicaid funds denied. In the earlier case, the same Court had held that Connecticut could withhold state Medicaid funds from poor women seeking abortions. A reader who but glanced at the syllabus for *Harris* should have gathered the connection between *Harris* and its precedent:

> 2. The funding restrictions of the Hyde Amendment do not impinge on the "liberty" protected by the Due Process Clause of the Fifth Amendment held in Roe v. Wade, 410 U.S. 113, 168, to include the freedom of a woman to decide whether to terminate a pregnancy. . . .
>
> (a) The Hyde Amendment places no governmental obstacle in the path of a woman who chooses to terminate her pregnancy, but rather, by means of unequal subsidization of abortion and other medical services, encourages alternative activity deemed in the public interest. Cf. Maher v. Roe, 432 U.S. 464, p. 315.[65]

I have highlighted one of two references to *Maher v. Roe* in the syllabus to *Harris v. McRae* to show that one need not read the opinion in *Harris* to grasp its relationship to *Maher*.[66]

Editorialists could read in the *New York Times* that the Court had previously held that state legislatures need not fund abortion through their appropriations. However, even the *New York Times* account failed to mention *Maher v. Roe* by name.[67] Editorialists who relied on *Preview*—a guide to Supreme Court decisions that lawyers prepare for nonlawyers—got no account of *Maher*. Worse, the officially provided syllabus does not summarize reasoning of dissents and concurrences, so justices who reconsidered *Maher* in their separate opinions did not get through to many editorialists.[68] One critic concluded that editorial responses to *Harris v. McRae* revealed striking ignorance or indifference to *Maher v. Roe*, a precedent that could greatly have enriched commentary. The critic found expressions of shock at *Harris v. Roe* misplaced given the *Maher* precedent.[69]

This example shows why opinions—the official, formal accounts that the Supreme Court supplies to reporters—are free but tricky. From this and from the few studies of the matter with which I am familiar, I formulate a tentative hypothesis: *Supreme Court reports will rely on quotations from opinions far less than on paraphrases of opinions and will seldom relay material from opinions*. The safest and cheapest course, and the one that reporters will most often follow, I have hypothesized, is not to address the reasoning of the justices at all. If reporters and editors wish to risk characterization of opinions, they are more likely to find syllabi, wire-service reports, and summaries by lawyers more useful because they reveal more than opinions more quickly.[70]

Opinions may add little to holdings in most news media and may even create or exacerbate confusion. Distilling pages and pages of the justices' prose to meaningful, accurate, morselized representations that readers may comprehend is daunting. Interpreting opinions or reading between their lines is even more treacherous, according to John MacKenzie, who covered the Supreme Court for the *Washington Post*. MacKenzie noted that to the extent that opinions are written to mask rather than reveal difficulties, accurate reporting of murky reasoning will tend to create murky stories.[71] At the very least, he claimed, opinions will often defy reporters' understanding and thus will propel reporters toward newsworthy trivia rather than "lawworthy" details.[72]

Still, we must expect news stories, if they go beyond holdings, to summarize written opinions by the justices.[73] If the report goes much beyond the skeletal summary in the syllabus, the justices' reasons get telescoped because justices and reporters write for different audiences and seem to live in different worlds. The author of an opinion devotes three pages to get just right a point that a reporter will render in three sentences if at all.[74] Television reporters will usually distill opinions still further:

> [T]elevision news reporters must provide the network with a story that describes the event in simple terms and within the organization's prescribed time limitations. In their reporting of the Court, the reporters' explanations of the decision are limited by these imperatives and pressures. Consequently, reporters revert to their own analysis of the decision rather than allow the decision to speak for itself. Reporters do paraphrase the justices' opinions. However, television news reporters rarely allow the justices' words to be directly conveyed.[75]

Newspaper reporters use more quotations from the justices than television reporters do, but even print reporters include precious little from majority and dissenting opinions.[76] Indeed, some reporters treat judicial opinions as they treat other justifications from political officials—as self-serving, controlled communications from manipulators who cannot be trusted.[77]

Journalistic routines, tailored to economic constraints and news-worth, explain the dearth of attributed quotations in broadcasts as in print. Lawyers and judges prefer complex, complete arguments, while news media crave brevity and simplicity. If the justices do not reduce reasons to sound bites, journalists will reduce those reasons for the justices.[78]

If, however, justices create sound bites, their phrasings may be disseminated. That is, we should qualify our hypothesis because journalists may quote from opinions if opinions cater to the angle biases of mass media. Morsels from opinions, for example, will be more likely to be printed or aired if they match journalists' demands for dramatic or personalized commentary. A justice's pithy attack on a colleague may be big news. A dissenter's parade of horribles that follow from the majority's opinion may be quoted rather than summarized if the dissenting opinion is flamboyantly alarmist.[79]

Political But Not Legal Context

What, then, is the substance of Court stories if not passages from the decisions themselves? Reporters use the alloted [sic] time or space to briefly describe and then attempt to explain and analyze the Court decision. Emphasis is placed not so much on the decision itself as on the potential implications of the decisions, the reactions of principals involved in the case or others in the legal profession, and, less frequently, the motivations of the justices. As a result, the quotations of the justices' opinions may well be overshadowed by the quoted reactions to the decision by others.[80]

Comprehensibility must matter to journalists, so reports of results, holdings, spot news, and all other journalism tend to eliminate what readers and viewers are less likely to understand in favor of stories that readers and viewers know and care about. Readers and viewers fathom far more about politics than they do about law. News consumers usually worry about policy more than doctrine, about results more than reasons, and about values more than rules.

For these reasons, I may reasonably hypothesize that reporters tend to preserve and present far more of the political context of cases than they do the legal context. I do not intend this generalization as an attack on Supreme Court specialists. Cynical political scientist though I am, I believe that reporters delight in enlightening their audiences but the economics of the news business and the angles favored by editors sharply circumscribe their ability to do so. Commercial biases and angle biases dictate that reporters and editors make Supreme Court stories consumer friendly. More, demands for speed and accuracy drive reporters and editors away from perhaps enriching but certainly challenging material.

Perils of Legal Context

To convey the formal significance and legal context of decisions to readers and viewers, reporters and editors would have to understand the jurisprudential logic underlying decisions. They would also have to document their understanding with ample citations to judicial and legal authorities. If professors at prestigious law schools take months and even years to unravel the reasoning of the justices, it is hardly fair to expect journalists to make sense of the justices in minutes or hours. Some justices' decisions and opinions simply do not make sense. In such instances, journalists would face a daunting decision: distort the justices' arguments so that readers might grasp what the justices were trying to accomplish, or restate opinions accurately but analytically to expose illogic. Either decision imperils reporters, editors, and news media.

Perhaps the most noted Supreme Court decision of this century, *Brown v. Board of Education of Topeka* (1954), exemplifies these perils. Chief Justice Earl Warren wanted the Supreme Court's unanimous but momentous decision to be understood by ordinary citizens, so he wrote a short, simple opinion which many newspapers reprinted in full. Cutting out media interpretation did not necessarily make the Court's opinion clear or cogent, however. Chief Justice Warren and the other justices offered a notoriously weak footnote ("Footnote Eleven") to document their claim that social scientists had amply documented the harms of states' segregating their public schools by race. The Court the same day found that public schools segregated by race were unconstitutional in the District of Columbia, a politically necessary but constitutionally suspect conclusion.[81] No objective, balanced presentation of the Court's opinions could have made the school desegregation cases legal rather than political documents. Indeed, the best that sympathetic editors and reporters could do was to omit mention or interpretation of the Court's reasoning.

To generalize from this example, we might expect that a safe, cheap choice is to skimp on legal detail in favor of political conflict.[82] The public Court, it follows, will often be defined by reactions from lawyers and laypersons.

Leeways of Political Context

Reporters for mass news media enjoy and employ considerable discretion in selecting cases to cover and in framing stories. Consider an example mentioned by Richard Davis.[83] The U. S. Supreme Court decided a minor blood-alcohol case from South Dakota. The reporter for *CBS News* stated the result and immediately launched into a discussion of questions surrounding common use of breathalyzers. A Court decision was pretext for the more newsworthy and accessible topic of breathalyzers.

The justices frequently pursue a legally warranted tactic that virtually elicits politicized coverage. Since the Supreme Court is not authorized to decide cases that are not yet before it, the justices are not supposed to anticipate conflicts or issue prospective decisions or opinions. As a result, justices often strive to deny that an announced decision predicts what the Court will do in future cases. This tactic is politically expedient in that it saves the justices from having to speculate about cases that may never arise, but it strikes many or most lawyers and judges as the legally and constitutionally proper posture to take.

However, this judicious stratagem often encourages journalistic license. Deprived of the sources that legitimize interpretive coverage of other institutions, reporters covering the High Court become interpretive authorities themselves, at least for the minority of Americans who attend to Court coverage. Some journalists will understate the import of decisions and issue cautious interpretations.[84] Others will hype decisions to enlarge their audience and augment the significance of their stories.[85]

Of course, even well crafted decisions and accurate coverage may result in politicized transmission, as when those who publicize an opinion politicize it as well. For example, consider the school prayer decisions of the Warren Court. Justice Tom Clark objected to coverage of *Engel v. Vitale* (1962), claiming deadlines had led to inaccurate stories that elicited baseless, vituperative criticisms from readers. Wire-service reporters, among others, protested that their reports were not inaccurate. Remarkably, scholars found that both Justice Clark and the reporters were correct![86] Initial wire-service stories were professional and objective, but they were also terse. This concision, the scholars concluded, permitted misinterpretations by readers, some of whom denounced the Court for kicking God out of schools or taking "In God We Trust" off coins. The Court had rendered no decisions about coins or currency and no school's roll listed any divinities, but the limits of the Court's decisions were lost in editing the copy to fit the news hole. In addition, headlines exaggerated to sell papers facilitated misinterpretations.[87] Hyped headlines and spare stories provoked overwrought responses that then reverberated over the wires and made the news.[88]

Reaction-Oriented Coverage

> First-day reaction about a decision is almost always based only
> on wire-service reports and these, owing partly to time and
> space problems, have always been skimpy at best and at times
> misleading or downright inaccurate. For that matter, most sub-
> sequent reaction is also based on press reports.[89]

As politicization—that is, the emphasis of political over
jurisprudential context—of *Brown v. Board of Education* and *Engel
v. Vitale* has illustrated, reactions to decisions correspond to media
angles and commercial biases much better than judicial reasons ever
could. It can hardly surprise us, then, that the public Supreme Court is
created by lay reactions to decisions more than by informed considerations of opinions. Because reasons and judicial opinions are over-
matched by reactions and lay opinion, even landmarks that were not
covered in an acutely result-oriented manner may, in mere hours and
days, come to be dominated by reaction-oriented coverage.[90] Lawyer
Lionel S. Sobel suggested that reaction-oriented coverage tended to
supplant what the Court said with propaganda from overwrought
opponents of decisions and doctrines, especially when the press supplied the public with little countervailing information about decisions
and opinions.[91]

One consequence of such reaction orientation is that reporters
relay inaccurate, demagogic, or manipulative views of cases. While
reporters may alibi away such coverage by insisting that quotations
and paraphrases accurately convey actual responses to the Court, such
source-ery leaves the Court open to ill-informed criticism and citizens
open to propaganda. After the Court's decision of *R. A. V. v. City of St.
Paul* (1992)—a cross-burning case—was announced, for example,
many local newspapers quoted and paraphrased angry activists and
posturing politicians and thereby introduced inaccurate, impertinent,
and insolent reactions into early reports of the decision and opinion.[92]

A second consequence of reaction-oriented coverage is that justices may monitor the reception of decisions among attentive, active
citizens.[93] The more result oriented and politicized the portrait of the
Court's opinions, the less useful lay reactions may be, for members of
the public may be reacting to decisions that the justices never made
and doctrines the justices never would have endorsed. On the other
hand, justices may be able to defend subsequent decisions more persuasively if they know what misconceptions rampaged through the
polity after previous decisions.

Rights, Social Issues, and Judicial Activism

Beyond the basics above (winners and losers, holdings, votes, paraphrases, and reactions), we should expect coverage of social issues to be far more detailed than coverage of other sorts of litigation. Scholars have noticed that cases that concern individual rights, for example, are reported more often and more extensively than many other sorts of cases. Social issues suggest that the hypotheses presented earlier must be qualified to a degree.

A recent study confirmed the tendency of news media to cover cases concerning the rights of persons accused of crime and, especially, freedom of the press more than other cases on the Supreme Court's docket.[94] This study reinforced earlier findings about the press's alacrity at covering freedom of the press even more than freedom of speech.[95]

Angle biases make it clear why we should expect news media to cover cases that concern human rights. Such cases usually involve individual Davids fighting governmental Goliaths (did you spot personalization and dramatization biases?), expansions of democracy and equality that match expectations engendered by popular culture and traditions (normalization), and basic choices among common values and absolutes (morselization).

Typical televised reports of Supreme Court cases suggest how angle biases generally coalesce in cases concerning individual rights. I related how Fred Graham pioneered personalized coverage by broadcasting the stories of people involved in cases. Other television reporters and some print reporters have followed Graham's example.[96] Given the individualistic values that many Americans continue to cherish, such coverage seems bound to encourage talk of rights at the expense of community and tradition.[97]

As a result, cases that concern individual rights are covered in reports about the Supreme Court beyond what their contribution to the caseload of the Supreme Court would predict.[98] Television reporters may insist that such reporting tracks audiences' interests and values,[99] but that explanation merely reiterates angle biases and concedes the rights orientation of Court coverage.

Scholars have also noticed that social issues, such as abortion, sexual harassment, and discrimination bristle with the drama and melodrama that attract coverage.[100] Many such cases, of course, involve individual rights, but I stress them separately to reinforce the point that relevance to partisan and ideological conflict and high stakes for important groups will encourage journalistic attention whether individual rights are prominently at stake or not.

Still another qualification of our hypotheses about coverage might follow from journalistic preferences for judicial activism. Judicial activism has many meanings, but in this context let us agree that, when justices choose to go beyond narrowly circumscribed and stringently legalistic bounds, they court charges of activism. Economist and commentator Thomas Sowell recently named a fascinating proposition "the Greenhouse effect"[101] after Linda Greenhouse of the *New York Times*. Sowell proposed that reporters and commentators lavish praise on activist justices. Professor David Barnum has found that the press had abetted the activism of the Warren Court.[102] Veteran Court reporter John MacKenzie believed that activism made more news and secured more exposure for the Court.[103]

I know of no systematic studies that confirm these contentions, but angle biases would certainly support their plausibility. After all, sweeping change is far more dramatizable than painstakingly gradualistic decision making. Grand political deeds will be far easier to personalize for viewers and readers than petite legal documents. Great judicial leaps forward may strike the only occasionally mindful citizen as business as usual for the High Court, in which case abnormal leaps are easier to normalize than ordinary decisions!

I suspect that any relative overreporting of activist decisions probably cuts both ways, contrary to Sowell's presumption. That is, decisions portrayed by mass media as portentous judicial departures may terrify and enrage opposition far more than they rally support. After all, if I see a decision as self-evidently correct constitutionally and morally, I give little credit to the Court for discerning the obvious. In contrast, when the Court embraces obvious (to me) evils out of a proclaimed fidelity to judicial restraint, I am all the more likely to castigate the justices for preferring legal niceties and procedural technicalities. Thus, even if Sowell is correct about more than a few reporters and editors, the consequences of activism-orientation may be quite the opposite of those that Sowell intuited. Only careful research will tell us how many Greenhouse effects we may identify and to what consequences they may lead.

Conclusion

Each tendency noted above has been explained in terms of commercial and angle biases. These biases imply that decisions that conform to biases are more likely to be covered than those that do not or cannot be made to conform. I have hypothesized that any coverage of the Supreme Court will tend to stress aspects that conform or can be made to conform to biases and will tend to eliminate or devalue all other aspects.

Remember that my explanation of relatively reported aspects of the Supreme Court is only one way of making sense of the findings to date. I believe that these generalizations suit the evidence. However, exceptions abound, and other biases may affect coverage, so I have suggested qualifications for the suitable generalizations.

The Very Private Court

For many people, the Supreme Court appears to function behind a shroud of formality and secrecy. This shroud of secrecy surrounding the Court and its activities is reinforced by the infrequent nature of newspaper and television stories about it.[104]

Many aspects of the Supreme Court will ordinarily escape consumers of all but the most specialized media, such as legal records, law journals, and other lawyerly publications.[105] Specialists on the Supreme Court who write for newspapers of record may introduce readers to some of these features in the most newsworthy cases, but even such beat reporters will seldom secure much space—here, too, the final frontier—for coverage of trends in cases both in the middle and long ranges, denials of *certiorari*,[106] and oral arguments.

You should be able to anticipate the obscure and obscured aspects of the Court's business. Simply invert the scale used to explain the public Court. The less news-worth an action or decision has—that is, the less it comports or can be made to comport with commercial or angle biases—the less likely it is that it will secure mention in media. If an action or decision does get covered, its least newsworthy aspects are likely to be unmentioned or barely mentioned.

If you invert the scale of coverage to anticipate when the Court will be private, I hope you remember that noncoverage is very common. Most of what happens at the Supreme Court is, for all but media of record, not newsworthy at all. For example, when Richard Davis undertook to study Supreme Court coverage on *CBS News* and in the *Los Angeles Times* and *Syracuse Post-Standard*, he found his study impaired by the infrequency of Supreme Court coverage.[107]

Throughout this chapter, then, keep in mind that even the Supreme Court of the United States is covered rarely as well as barely!

Noncoverage makes the private face of the Court easy to explain. Deprived of inside information, helpful sources, and the usual angles, editors and reporters are unlikely to find in most of the Court's activities anything that looks like news. Indeed, given the steady diet of managed news from the justices through which reporters must wade, the justices may get their just deserts when their work is not covered at all.

My present concern is not noncoverage, however, but slight coverage. These are the aspects of the Court, its justices, and its actions that seldom surface even when the Court gets covered. To be sure, the Court is a very private institution because its ordinary practices insure such privacy. However, my point here is that when the Court is public enough to draw mention in the press it is nonetheless usually quite private.

Trends and Interpretations

Newspaper articles that are meant to be interpretations of events fill 8 percent of the Washington news hole, but constitute 11 percent of the stories about foreign policy, 11 percent of government operations stories, and 9 percent of economics/ finance stories. This compares, for example, with 3 percent for law.[108]

Thus did a prominent observer of news media, Stephen Hess, document the extent to which stories about law lacked the interpretive and analytical qualities of other sorts of stories. Although the Court may draw more coverage than the average for law, we have rehearsed reasons to expect little interpretation, analysis, or even contextualization of Supreme Court reports. First, commercial pressures will usually not justify the space and research necessary to analyze or interpret in any depth. Second, few viewers or readers expect or demand such coverage, so coverage of trends would not match customary mass media marketing. Third, specialized media provide more and better coverage than all but a handful of Supreme Court reporters could produce even if their news outlet considered such journalism economically feasible. Fourth, the justices can confound prognosticators and pundits. Supreme Court reporter Dana Bullen, for example, claimed that he tended to understate consequences of decisions lest justices veer off in subsequent cases.[109] Finally, interpretation and analysis of cases and trends seldom will match any angle biases, for such scholarly journalism is neither timely nor lively to most readers and most viewers.

Some mass media, especially newspapers, *do* highlight very recent trends and *do* hazard interpretations and predictions of the Court's tendencies. However, only mass media that cover the Court most assiduously are likely to feature such contextualizing coverage more than once or twice per year, at the conclusion and commencement of the Supreme Court's year. In June or July, after the justices have announced the end of the term that began the first Monday in the previous October, the glut of published decisions and opinions provides reporters and commentators an opportunity to recap the monumental events of the previous months. Again in October, at the start of the new term, some media will synopsize recent decisions and anticipate the next term's docket.[110] These considerations suggest a generalization: Only at the beginning and near the end of the Supreme Court's term will most media discern or interpret trends in the Court's actions.

Seth Goldslager has discovered an interesting "disconnect" in coverage of trends: managing editors claimed to welcome both reports on legal trends and more interpretive copy, but reporters did not perceive such wishes.[111] Whatever the explanation, most reporters devote minimal attention to trends.[112] Goldslager's disconnect suggests why we should anticipate little discussion of trends most of the time.

Noncoverage of Supreme Court trends can deprive news watchers of perspectives that might inform and enlighten them. Historical perspective can fit this week's decision into a sequence with discernible direction. Appreciation of historical direction may provide the attentive citizen a base from which to extrapolate the Court's tendencies. Such perspectives are especially useful for fending off overreactions to predictable rulings, such as reactions to the abortion-funding and school-prayer decisions. Attention to trends might also enable more citizens to appreciate the emphases and predilections of justices, individually and collegially.

If the media seldom cover justices as individuals with personal agendas or the Court as an institution with collective goals, media reinforce institutional perspectives on the Court. If so, "the Court today said" is less shorthand than media-assisted judicial imagery. Uncritical reporting of holdings and opinions, for example, may distract citizens from the political roles that justices routinely play.[113] By uncritically relaying the justices' institutional imagery, mass media both depersonalize and personalize news about the Court. Institutionalized coverage depersonalizes the justices if they seldom emerge as individuals. Unlike presidents and prominent members of Congress, justices are often granted a distance or transcendence that enhances authority and majesty.[114] However, the usual angle bias of personalized coverage is not abandoned entirely. Personal milestones on the Court and other biographic information unrelated to policy-making or ideology are readily available, cheap to publish, and unthreatening to institutional image.[115]

Among the trends that most mass media will not cover are what Stephen Wasby has labeled "impact" and "aftermath."[116] We observed above that immediate, often thoughtless reactions from various publics and officials and counter measures undertaken by groups and governmental officials will tend to be covered when they suit commercial biases and angle biases. Less immediate responses, we must hypothesize, will match commercial biases and angle biases almost as seldom as other, more legal trends. The direct and indirect consequences of specific judicial decisions—"impact"—and the complex of developments subsequent to decisions, opinions, and judicial policies—"aftermath"—should be expected to be among the trends that most mass media will interpret seldom.

Control of the Docket:
"The Road Not Taken"

The Supreme Court controls its own docket. Because its justices choose which cases they will hear and which they will not hear, the Court has immense discretion. The justices decline to hear many times more petitions than they hear. That is why Justice Brandeis maintained that the most important thing that the Court did was "not doing."

Despite such importance, denials of hearings are covered rarely. In raw numbers, denials each year are many but denials covered by media are few. As a percentage of all instances of "not doing," of course, stories about the justices' deciding not to decide appear quite exceptional. Capsules about denials are more frequent, especially from Supreme Court beat reporters and in cases with local salience for newspeople's clientele. However, even such exceptional coverage— easily explicable by news biases—likely will suffer because denials of cases are so difficult to interpret.[117] Commercial and angle biases will undercut the likelihood of much coverage of nondecisions.

Often such noncoverage of nondecisions is just as well, for, in dramatizing nondecisions, mass media often get the denials that they do cover wrong! This sin is most grievous with regard to decisions not to hear cases.[118] When the justices decline to hear a case, we may conclude only that fewer than four justices voted to hear it. The Court issues no definitive decisions on the merits of the case, so mass media err when they report denials as if they were decisions.

However, we ourselves must take care not to overstate or to oversimplify. While it is technically and formalistically the case that the justices insist that a refusal to hear a case may not be construed as any indication of the justices' views of the merits of the case, it is empirically and realistically the case that denials of *certiorari* do indicate substantive views.[119] As a political science professor, I may sniff that all of my students know that a denial of *certiorari* ends the case without an authoritative declaration of views. However, as a political science professional, I must concede that extensive research indicates that many denials do represent justices' views.[120] If you and I are going to criticize journalists when they take legalistic distinctions at face value, we cannot demand that they take formalism at face value when the Court denies a writ of *certiorari*.

Thus, reports that treat denials of *certiorari* as equivalents to decisions on the issues may misinform readers and viewers. Formal dogma would lead us to conclude that such reports are always in error. Practical consequences, in contrast, will justify some reports, as when spot news of a denial of *certiorari* assesses the denial as a setback for one side or a particularized victory for another side. Ignoring formalistic distinctions will infuriate legal cognoscenti, but cognoscenti are too few for the press to notice.

Oral Arguments

Because oral arguments would seem inexpensive to cover and unthreatening to the image of the Court, we might expect mass media to cover them extensively. Further reflection suggests that oral arguments seldom meet the requirements of mass media. Viewed from a commercial perspective, oral arguments are readily observed by reporters but difficult to contextualize and to summarize for lay audiences. The market for oral arguments thus must be narrow. We reach much the same conclusion from Bennett's four news biases. While this oral argument or that may feature dramatic conflicts or iconoclastic moments, any dramatic or personalized morsels will be extremely difficult to contextualize concisely but precisely.

Such generalizations regarding content in mass media are reinforced by the little time that even Supreme Court beat reporters devote to oral arguments. Dennis estimated that specialists devoted only about 5 percent of their time to observing oral arguments.[121] Famed Supreme Court reporter Anthony Lewis purported to read all petitions and then to consult lawyers and the solicitor general's office and staff before he attended oral arguments.[122] Such work appears to be extraordinary.[123]

In addition, oral arguments are seasonal. The justices hear arguments on Mondays, Tuesdays, and Wednesdays for two weeks each month from the start of term in October through April. For the months May through September, then, reporters have no oral arguments to report.

While I know of no study of how often oral arguments are reported, I shall hazard a generalization: *Newspapers of record will cover oral arguments far more extensively than other major newspapers and small papers will seldom cover oral arguments.*

I intend this generalization to convey the truth that newspapers do cover oral arguments, especially in cases that feature some titillating political hook or journalistic angle. Newspapers of record—nationally oriented newspapers that pride themselves on their compendious coverage—will keep their readers abreast of newsworthy arguments. Table 2.2 shows just how much coverage such national papers give oral arguments. It also shows how little coverage some less national but nonetheless important newspapers gave oral arguments. Table 2.2 provides rough but revealing confirmation of the tentative generalization in italic above.

Table 2.2   Coverage of Oral Arguments, Calendar Year 1994

Newspapers	Total Stories about the Court	Total Stories about Oral Arguments
Paul M. Barrett, *Wall Street Journal*	75	2
Joan Biskupic, *Washington Post*	122	18
Linda Greenhouse, *New York Times*	100	14
Tony Mauro, *USA Today*	90	15
David G. Savage, *Los Angeles Times*	38	7
Houston Chronicle	48	3
Christian Science Monitor	29	2
San Francisco Chronicle	44	1
Denver Post	32	1
Times-Picayune (New Orleans)	11	0

In table 2.2, Supreme Court specialists from five such newspapers of record are compared with coverage in five newspapers that cover national politics less thoroughly. The five specialists are listed by name alphabetically. The five contrasting newspapers are listed in declining order of coverage of oral arguments. I used *FirstSearch Newspaper Abstracts* to locate all stories concerning the United States Supreme Court from January 1, 1994, through December 31, 1994. Any mention of or reference to oral arguments in the abstracts for the articles counted as coverage of oral arguments. This method overlooks mere mentions of oral arguments, which might not be mentioned in the abstracts, to concentrate on articles in which oral arguments were a major focus. If that selection seems imprudent to you, you can probably use *FirstSearch* in a library near you. Check my work! I bet you find coverage to be sparse.

The Secret Court

> The Court begins as a mystery, and the reporter or editor who fails to appreciate the fact that certain things about the Supreme Court will remain unknowable and unprintable simply does not understand the situation.[124]

The Court sometimes is hidden from public scrutiny and other times it hides. While the economics of news gathering and angles that shape a news product may disincline the press to cover less accessible aspects of the Court's work, the justices make some aspects of their work inaccessible. We have seen which aspects of the Court's work are more newsworthy and which aspects less newsworthy. Now we turn to the aspects of the Court's work that seldom see the daylight of media attention.

One reason that the justices make these aspects of their work inaccessible is to cultivate their authority. Judicial authority depends, we saw in chapter 1, on judges' transcending disputes. The more remote the justices from interests involved in cases and the more independent the Court of improper influence from other branches, the more judicious the justices and the Court are likely to seem.[125] Justices protect their remoteness to perpetuate their authority.[126] Little wonder that justices seldom emerge as individual decision makers in stories about the Court.

Justices' Interactions

Covering the Supreme Court was like being assigned to report on the Pope. Both the justices and the Pope issue infallible statements, draw their authority from a mystical higher source, conceal their humanity in flowing robes, and—because they seek to present a saintly face to the world—are inherently boring. They also both have life tenure, which implies a license to thumb their noses at the news media. . . . The justices were so withdrawn that covering the Court for any news medium was in a journalistic class by itself.[127]

If seemly, legal aspects of Supreme Court litigation, which are easy to cover and to document, draw little coverage, we should expect even less coverage of seamier, political aspects of cases that the justices want to obscure. To keep up their "papal" image, the justices must keep much of their work and many of their decisions shrouded. Welcome to the "Secret" Supreme Court, an institution protected by secretive justices and conforming journalists alike.

Scholars often have noted the lengths to which Supreme Court justices go to protect their privacy and the secrecy of their deliberations.[128] Reporters have agreed: "There was an understanding in my dealings with them that all conversations were off the record, and confidential Court business was usually not discussed."[129] Davis has noted that, for other officials, discussions with reporters are presumed on the record, while for justices, discussions are assumed to be "on background"—that is, for reporters' edification but never to be printed or aired—or "off the record"—available for dissemination but without attribution—unless otherwise stipulated in advance.[130] Indeed, the justices' passion for anonymity led many observers to regard them as indifferent to imagery.

Exceptions to this pursuit of anonymity actually reinforce the secrecy of the Court. Davis has noted:

> . . . The justices were rarely direct objects of news media attention. The stories were almost never about the people on the Court. Court stories stressed the institutions with the justices as parts of the whole, but not covered as individuals. Those very few stories in the sample about justices as individuals consisted primarily of features on nominees for the bench moving through the confirmation process, specifically John Paul Stevens, Clement Haynsworth, and one justice who resigned, Potter Stewart.[131]

Dennis noted that personalized coverage might also include personal appearances, anniversaries on the Court, or birthdays.[132] These safe subjects direct reporters and audiences alike away from other aspects of the Court that might contradict the Court's image even as they direct reporters to other aspects that provide reporters with the newsworth that they crave.[133]

Davis has identified the source and some consequences of High Court secrecy:

> The justices' relative invisibility to the press, separate from the institution, is a Court-determined phenomenon. Justices have chosen to avoid the public spotlight. Though a few of the justices have made tentative steps toward the press, the norm of aloofness has not yet been significantly altered. . . .
>
> The inaccessibility of the justices restricts the press from highlighting people-oriented aspects in Court stories. Stories of the Court are highly oriented toward discussion of public policy. In nearly two-thirds of the Court stories, most or all of the content consisted of policy discussion. Even CBS News' content overwhelmingly stressed policy discussion, though to a lesser extent than the print media.[134]

The justices, we may surmise, enjoy their privacy precisely because it compels the press to disseminate official outputs and innocuous personal information. If reporters penetrate secrecy, the Court redoubles security.[135] Lower-court judges occasionally explain their decisions beyond formal outputs, but not the justices of the United States Supreme Court.[136] The justices and their Court, to put the matter bluntly, usually need nothing and usually want nothing from reporters.[137] They may occasionally bestow a "backgrounder" on a reporter but seldom cultivate personal relationships with reporters, the sorts of relationships that yield coverage of other officials.[138] Having scaled a pinnacle of their profession, the justices have long since acquired an interest in the system and the Court. It cannot surprise us, therefore, that their norms discourage self-interested behaviors that might imperil their institution.[139] While a few justices have been close to at least some reporters,[140] most justices have engaged reporters at the justices' peril.[141] The safer course has proved to be to let opinions stand alone as the authoritative output and to avoid public division.[142]

In sum, the Secret Court flaunts its judicious authority and hides disconfirming information, all without overt public relations that would contradict judicial imagery. The Court, for example, must respond to public opinion in ways that do not appear to respond to public opinion, lest it vitiate its vaunted judicial independence. The justices maintain their image by stressing their disdain for image making.[143] The best way to maintain such an image is through secrecy. Secrecy keeps disconfirming information from appearing.

Reporters' Interactions with the Secret Court

If the "Secret" Court serves the interests of the justices and preserves the image of the Court, a secretive Court may serve reporters as well. Above we saw that the Court, when on display, furnishes mass media with authoritative documents that are normalized, morselized, and inexpensive to distill and to disseminate (commercial biases). The justices-in-public normalize decisions and opinions by crafting jural justifications suited to attentive audiences. Reporters, then, are literally handed by unimpeachable sources documents that portray decision making as exactly what it is supposed to be. Only in the rush at the end of terms do the justices pile such decisions and opinions on reporters. Even then such outputs are easy to morselize because they are handled by judges and handed to reporters as discrete cases. Throughout the term, the Court uses its Public Information Office to deluge the press with official reports that must be summarized on deadline. The justices keep their secrets so that they will not contradict their image and their messages, but in so doing the justices also spare reporters a lot of work.

The justices keep reporters quite busy with official documents.[144] Opinions and decisions created—at least in part—to be covered in an ordinary fashion do not call for additional scrutiny. In addition, what cannot readily be covered usually need not be covered. Routine reportage and normal noncoverage habituate viewers and readers to the judicial party line. Indeed, we might suspect that the accessibility of official documents and unavailability of alternative perspectives confines most lay and much legal understanding of and debate about cases. In any event, most users of mass media are so habituated to normalized and morselized coverage that we must imagine that they expect the Public Court and do not notice the Secret Court. Reporters, then, may find it in their interest to give their readers and viewers what they have become used to reading and viewing.

Even if the justices were not adept at producing and performing in the Public Court and even if reporters were not experienced at summarizing the staging of the Public Court concisely, and even if attentive citizens were not accustomed to formal motifs, each set of actors would find it costly to change roles and behaviors. The justices would be accused of overtly political decision making, reporters would be liable to charges of editorializing, and readers and viewers would find stories suspect. Viewed as a shared ritual, then, Supreme Court decision making demands a degree of deference and fidelity from reporters.

Paletz and Entman have theorized that reporters have a stake in the Public Court and thus acquire a stake in vouchsafing the Secret Court:

> Journalists who cover the judicial system accept and respect the majesty of the law as it issues from the Supreme and lower federal courts—and most state courts too. They sense, if they do not fully comprehend, the vulnerability of the courts' legitimacy. To dissect the courts, expose the fallibility and frailties of judges, could undermine the legal system by encouraging disrespect for court decisions by the public officials who should execute, and the public who should obey them.[145]

If this critical theory sounds too far fetched, consider the following passage from a recent essay by ABC Supreme Court reporter Tim O'Brien:

> If the American people could see the Supreme Court from my vantage point, I believe they would be as impressed—and proud—as I am. . . . I have learned that our legal system is genuinely committed to [due process, fair trial, free speech, and equal protection] and I am inspired by it. . . . I believe the best kept secret of the judiciary is how well they work.[146]

We should expect little critical distance from O'Brien.

Observers have made it clear that O'Brien is hardly the only beat reporter seduced into cheerleading or deference.[147] Perhaps the most influential reporter of the Supreme Court, Ms. Linda Greenhouse of the *New York Times*, has indicated that she opposes leaks and reporting leaks because such breaks in secrecy undermine the mission of the Court.[148] Lyle Denniston has suggested that reporters justify the aloofness of the Court.[149] It is difficult to imagine such attitudes from any reporter not invested in the Public Court.

In addition, reporters who share with justices the rhythms of workload and the rush at the end of the term may lose sight of ordinary journalistic norms and ideals.[150] Davis has speculated that the routines of the public Court allure reporters and numb them, thereby inducing norms of noninvestigative reporting. The Court may exacerbate uncritical reporting by the justices' indifference to conventional public relations. Deprived of a reasonable chance at scoops, reporters settle into the dissemination of opinions.[151] Denniston has even opined that the Supreme Court beat may have some of the laziest reporters because of the numbing routine and seductive legal viewpoint.[152]

In contrast to the indolent and the mesmerized, industrious reporters who come to understand and respect legal norms are especially susceptible to accepting the Public Court and ignoring the Secret Court. For example, at least some reporters who undertake specialized legal training to do their job better must be expected to come to share the formalistic frame of the Public Court and to want to share the rigors of the legal turn of mind with their viewers and readers.[153]

The Secret Court, then, is a joint production of justices controlling their images and reporters giving those justices the coverage that the justices seek. Davis has argued that the justices choreograph reporters by making it inexpensive to cover the Public Court and next to impossible to document the Secret Court.[154] The aloofness of the justices and the Court's indifference to public relations, in Davis's view, are public relations coups. The Court, wrongly pitied for its ineptitude at public relations, in fact largely guarantees coverage that will direct audiences to the Public Court and away from its actual workings. Although Davis and I differ in how much responsibility we assign to the press for their own subduction, we agree that the Secret Court follows from strategic staging. David Grey, who repeated the superficial judgment that the Court tended to ignore modern public relations, later saw the matter more clearly:

> By not *trying* to manipulate public opinion, the Court paradoxically *is* manipulating public opinion. The Court controls the flow of news by releasing only what it wants to say and by often leaving vague what it does not want to say. There is no direct answer from the public. No press conferences or defenses are needed. The Court simply speaks and the country and parts of the world listen. Thus, while it can be argued that the Court shows great restraint and wisdom by being silent, it also can be observed that this silence may serve best the Court's self-interest. Not only may the Court feel it does not need or should not have public relations, it may also not want public relations.[155]

Qualifying Our Hypotheses

Generalizations are always risky. My generalizations cry for some qualification. Since most of the research from which I have derived generalizations and hypotheses concerned print media and much of that concerned newspapers, I want to balance this discussion with some attention to newsmagazines, television, and books. Media that offer only occasional coverage of the Court—such as newsmagazines and books—cover fewer cases but generally cover the cases more deeply than all but a few newspapers. Television covers fewer cases and covers them more superficially than most newspapers, but may digress into broader coverage.

Newsmagazines

Newsmagazines—such as *Time, U. S. News and World Report*, and *Newsweek*—differ greatly from daily papers. Weekly magazines have smaller news holes, so we should expect them to cover fewer cases than dailies. On the other hand, weeklies should be able to investigate the Court and its activities far more deeply than all but a few dailies. The studies of newsmagazine coverage with which I am familiar suggest that newsmagazines offer less coverage but better coverage.

Quantity of Coverage

Newsmagazines call for no reconsideration of our conclusion above that Court coverage is occasional. Indeed, newsmagazines cover the Court less often than even small newspapers. Both Michael E. Solimine and J. Douglas Tarpley have reported that the three major news magazines mentioned only about 15 percent of the decisions with full opinions that the Court issued each year.[156] Dorothy A. Bowles and Rebekah V. Bromley scaled Solimine's and Tarpley's estimates down to less than 10 percent.[157] Compare that figure with the percentages reported by David Ericson for three newspapers in the Court's October 1974 Term. According to Ericson, the *New York Times* reported on 77 percent of 145 written opinions in that year, the *Ann Arbor News* on 60 percent, and the *Detroit News* on 30 percent.[158]

Solimine found an average of 22.4 decisions with full opinions reported for each of three terms 1975-1978. He noted as well that references to pending cases and cases in which the Court refused review raised the average to 32.3, but the increase of 9.9 cases on average is an infinitesimal fraction of the cases pending and refused in each term.

Tarpley noted that two-thirds of all mentions were published in April, May, June, or July for the three subsequent terms (1978-1981) that he surveyed. Bowles and Bromley found less coverage in eight Supreme Court terms, 1981-1989 and agreed that stories tended to accumulate at the end of terms.

Quality of Coverage

The three studies cited allow us to generalize that newsmagazines tend to provide coverage in more depth than almost all other mass media. Newsmagazine stories usually include much more than winners, losers, and holdings, in part because capsule coverage and spot news are rarer in newsmagazines than on television and in newspapers. Moreover, newsmagazines, as we might expect, better cover legal and political trends, both because stories are longer and because deadlines are relaxed.

Bowles and Bromley have most completely analyzed the quality of newsmagazines' content. Their findings contradict some of my generalizations and thus should be kept in mind. Beyond the barest rendering of the holding, the 221 newsmagazine stories coded mentioned or discussed in impressive proportions the vote of the justices (91.4 percent), the reasoning of the majority (88.7 percent), the facts of each case or the path it took to the Court (87.3 percent), the name(s) of parties (86.0 percent), the impact of the decision (82.4 percent), reactions to the decision (78.3 percent), applicable rules, statutes, or precedents (67.0 percent), and dissenting opinions (58.4 percent).

In sum, coverage of the Supreme Court in newsmagazines, while quite occasional, is thorough when it appears.

Television

We should expect television to exacerbate some of the tendencies about which I generalized earlier. We expect commercial biases to prey upon television reporters, editors, and executives to a greater degree than for respective decision makers at newspapers. Consider the chief difference between televised and printed news. Readers may skip items of little interest to them in a newspaper, so each added item of coverage may increase the interest of some readers without alienating others who turn to other items of limited appeal. Television, in contrast, faces the problem that viewers must be induced to wait through every item. Viewers may turn off the set or channel-surf away.[159]

For televised news, angle biases are usually more acute than for newspapers. Television favors interviewees who are not camera shy, "mainstream" values, and the negative, for examples, beyond even the predilections of newspapers.[160] Expect more emphasis on "infotainment" and dramatization because televised pictures tend to become the whole story and spectacle overwhelms analysis.[161] Expect more personalization from television as reporters follow Fred Graham's pioneering personification of Supreme Court cases.[162] Tim O'Brien claimed that television demanded so much titillation and drama that a reporter might get more substance into thirty-five seconds on radio than twice as long on TV.[163]

Deadlines, brevity, and high-speed editing afflict all Court reporting but particularly plague television coverage of the Court. Television news thrives on immediacy. No blaring headline can match an interrupting news flash. To maximize their advantage over print media, television reporters may go to great lengths. Tim O'Brien recounts networks efforts to be first to announce the outcome of *Regents of the University of California v. Bakke* (1978). All networks wanted to be first on the *Bakke* decision. ABC had a camera and correspondent waiting in front of the high court each day from April 1 until June 28 and a courier in track shoes ready to sprint outside with the decision. When the highly complex decision came down, a reporter read from the Court's syllabus the contorted lineup of justices: Justice Powell joined four justices on the first major issue but he agreed with the remaining four justices on the second big issue.[164] Despite these formidable obstacles, NBC went on the air with the decision ninety seconds after its release.[165]

Preposterous demands for speed yield habitual emphases and omissions. Paletz and Entman have noted that wire service reporters tended to emphasize litigants' identities, disputed issues, snippets of legal history, and decisions, but seldom outcomes or impacts. They noted that major newspapers tended to go beyond wire services to balance specific decisions and ramifications. Television, they found in contrast, tended to cover results, to skimp on details, and to concentrate on political reactions, social outcomes, and personalized impacts.[166]

Thus, while television has covered the High Court more in recent years,[167] it does not follow that citizens know more, except about landmarks covered at great length in newspapers and on networks.[168] The effects of the practices of television news are especially important if most viewers receive all their news from television, as they repeatedly report.[169] Russell Neuman and his coauthors have argued that broadcast news is so common that it can introduce ordinary observers to subjects. That is the good news. The bad news is that "telenews" seems more realistic and dramatic but is actually less capable of considering matters thoroughly and is prone to oversimplify or reduce news due to its acute constraints.[170] Superficial, facile reports on television may incline some viewers to become readers some of the time, but at the price of distortive and often nonexistent coverage.[171]

Books

Our survey of mass media and the Supreme Court would be incomplete without a brief mention of books, a mass medium that fosters more reflection due to different commercial concerns and less regard for the angle biases that plague television and newspapers. I shall not consider textbooks or scholarly works to which ordinary citizens have little access. Instead, I shall mention *The Brethren* by Bob Woodward and Scott Armstrong (Simon and Schuster, 1980), a journalistic treatment of the Burger Court that took readers inside conferences and decision making. *The Brethren* exemplifies journalism that provides extended albeit occasional coverage.

While academics have wrested from the secretive justices truths and anecdotes about the Court,[172] most of their research concerns historical esoterica and biographical minutia. Much of this material greatly enriches the understanding of scholars and students; little of it reaches ordinary citizens. *The Brethren* should be noted, then, less because it revealed politicking about which scholars already knew and more because it publicized judicial politicking for a broader audience.

Even a casual glance at *The Brethren* discloses that the bulk of the book concerns the Secret Court. The aspects of the judicial process least likely to be covered by most journalism—conferences and voting, negotiation and writing, intra-Court conflict and cooperation among justices and clerks—are center stage. Decisions and opinions are present but hardly the center of attention. This book stunned reviewers and laypeople precisely because it presented the information that workaday journalism so often cannot.

As an alternative to daily coverage, then, books such as *The Brethren* might seem ideal. However, the evidence and inference that constitute this exposé will seldom be available and usually only at high cost. In addition, even best-selling exposés will reach few citizens. Such books remind us how much information we know little about through no fault of mass media. What we may be less likely to appreciate is how challenging many lay citizens will find such investigative reporting to be. Even as we enjoy and profit from *The Brethren*, we should see that such literature cannot substitute for mass media tailored to commercial biases and angle biases.

Putting Supreme Court Coverage in Perspective

We may summarize the foregoing chapter by noting that the very public Supreme Court tends to resemble the Inside-Out Perspective while Outside-In Perspectives tend to explain the very private Supreme Court. If *both* the Public *and* the Secret Court interest you, then *both* the Inside-Out Perspective *and* Outside-In Perspectives will be indicated.

From the Inside-Out Perspective

The Public Court conforms to prescriptions of the Inside-Out Perspective. That cannot surprise us. The professional ideals and norms that created this conventional view inform justices and journalists, if not readers and viewers. Justices shape formal, official outputs to showcase judicial virtues and mold the process of decision to obscure less formal, overtly political inputs. Reporters may convey the public, seemly side of the high court inexpensively in stories virtually preformulated by the justices. The less the decision process mirrors ideals, the less access reporters may expect and exploit. As a result, the press conveys the Public Court objectively and handily but conveys the Secret Court only awkwardly and haltingly. The prescriptions of the Inside-Out Perspective, it seems, nearly create the two-step flow of formal documents *from* decision makers *through* decision reporters *to* decision receivers. We expect this most visible of courts to conform to mainstream expectations. Usually, it does.

Davis's Outside-In Perspective

Richard Davis argues that the justices, schooled by reactions and sanctions, have developed methods of managing their press to preserve the image of transcendent impartiality and to maintain aloofness. The justices carefully choreograph the Public Court to suit mainstream images of adjudication. They also circumspectly conceal the Secret

Court to avoid contradicting conventional beliefs. The judicial craft and candor that the mainstream view prescribes are too often products of strategic imagery in Davis's view.

Justice Scalia's Outside-In Perspective

You might suspect that graduates of law schools would attach more blame to reporters than to the justices. We have seen that Justice Scalia takes this position. However, some experts on journalism with no apparent stake in legal training fault journalists as well. These critics often take a position that echoes the view of Supreme Court reporter James E. Clayton more than a quarter century ago:

> All too frequently, the press lays the blame for this lack of communication between the Court and the public totally on the Justices. Some of the blame is rightfully theirs. But the press is hardly in a position to complain when it has done so little to make communication possible between its reporters and the Court.[173]

Justice Scalia and other critics cite journalists' penchant for cheap, ill-informed, sensational, and superficial coverage as *the* culprit.

The Outside-In Perspective of Paletz and Entman

Paletz and Entman allow *both* Davis *and* Justice Scalia to be correct. Let us review their account of the public and private Court.

Paletz and Entman agree that the Supreme Court *seems* above politics, an elite institution that relies on other elites to implement its decisions and reaches them through specialized media. However, implementation demands perceived legitimacy, which means justices must tend their image. Hence, justices and Court are far less independent than they let on. Perhaps aware of the flimsiness of their authority, justices tend it in myriad ways—prudent self-restraint in decision making, reticence, sops to powerful elected officials, and delayed implementation.

Paletz and Entman examined the Supreme Court and concluded:

> But the justices, like politicians, know that the reality of their behavior is often less important than its image. Enter the media.

> There are two main strategies: accentuate the majesty of the
> Court, and minimize access to its inner workings.[174]

The two main strategies that Paletz and Entman discerned in the
Court correspond neatly to the views, respectively, of Scalia and Davis.
Scalia noted that the Court surpassed the understanding of reporters.
He thereby accentuated the transcendence if not the majesty of the
Court. Davis emphasized the means by which justices restricted the
press's access to the business of the usually secret Court.

As a result of the twin strategies, Paletz and Entman inferred,
reporters overreported what little the Court let them see and underreported what the Court kept from them. The majesty of furnishings and
setting and snippets of learned discourse were readily available to
reader and viewers; the actual manner in which justices deliberated,
negotiated, and decided cases seldom reached even inquisitive consumers of mass media. By denying access, the justices controlled their
images and that of the Court. By acceding to the justices' strategies,
reporters abetted this supreme image control.

Paletz and Entman seem to offer too extreme a perspective
until we observe that many observers and even Supreme Court
reporters confirm the very symbiosis that the political scientists have
espied. Graham, Supreme Court reporter for CBS as well as a lawyer,
has told us straight out that the late Chief Justice Warren Burger
wanted reporters to convey uncritically whatever the Court had to say
and to avoid digging up anything else.[175] Davis, while faulting justices
for controlling reporters and reports, admitted that Ms. Greenhouse,
perhaps the Supreme Court reporter from whom more network leaders and academics get their Supreme Court news than any other, is so
concerned for the image of the Court that she opposes leaks. O'Brien
has gushed about the admiration with which he swells when he covers
the Supreme Court. These reporters do not sound very independent!

A Tentative, Inconclusive Conclusion

If all four perspectives on the Supreme Court seem to suit at
least some cases, which perspective or perspectives ought we to
apply? I suggest you answer this question with two other, rhetorical
questions. Why not keep all perspectives at the ready to account for
specific instances of coverage? Why not have four possibilities that
keep us open to seeing more and remaining critical of what we read?

If that conclusion is too tentative and inconclusive, however, let me suggest that you use the four perspectives and perhaps even others to revise or recycle an earlier hypothesis. Let us revise table I.3 and recycle table 1.1 to organize predictions from four of the sources reviewed in this chapter. While I know of no data with which we might assess the relative preponderance of the sort of coverage predicted by reporter Greenhouse, Justice Scalia, and professors Davis, Paletz, and Entman, we may anticipate the conditions under which each perspective might apply best.

Table 1.1 suggested when "Mainstream Standards," "Media Distortion," "Judicial Mystification," and "Dual Pragmatism" might each be expected. I have recycled the dimensions of news-worth and law-worth as the columns and rows, respectively, of table 2.3. Table I.3 displayed the intersections of "Media Mission" and "Court Mission" under the Inside-Out Perspective and my Outside-In Perspective. I have revised the dichotomies of journalistic accuracy versus expediency and of judicial candor versus suasion from table I.3 to yield the perspectives taken by four prominent observers of Court coverage. If this genealogy of table 2.3 confuses you thoroughly, please review tables I.3 and 1.1 to spot family resemblances in their progeny, table 2.3.

Table 2.3 provides a basis for critical anticipation. Even at the level of our highest court, most cases are not particularly newsworthy and not overwhelmingly significant legally. Hence, you should expect that Greenhouse's view of unproblematic, routine decision making and coverage will obtain much of the time. However, when cases are newsworthy, expect coverage to increase and, with the increase in coverage, expect commercial and angle biases to shape the Court's press. Legally important cases may receive good coverage in specialized media, but mass media will tend toward superficial, expedient coverage, so expect law-worthy but unnewsworthy cases to draw so little reporting that laypeople are mystified. When cases raise the most notice socially, politically, and legally, beware of deviations from ideals on the part of justices and reporters alike.

Table 2.3 Intersections of Inside-Out and Outside-In Perspectives at the Supreme Court

	When cases are *least* newsworthy	When cases are *most* newsworthy
When cases are legally most routine	**Linda Greenhouse**[a] Mainstream Standards: Judicial Candor matches Journalistic Accuracy in coverage of the Public Court. The Inside-Out Perspective best explains both justices and reporters.	**Justice Antonin Scalia**[b] Media Distortion: Judicial Craft loses out to Media Expediency, thereby distorting the Public Court. The Inside-Out Perspective better explains justices but an Outside-In Perspective better explains reporters.
When cases are legally most challenging	**Richard Davis**[c] Jural Mystification: Journalistic Craft cannot ordinarily overcome Judicial Cunning that shields the Secret Court. An Outside-In Perspective better explains justices, but the Inside-Out Perspective better explains reporters.	**Paletz and Entman**[d] Dual Pragmatism: Judicial Cunning colludes with Media Expediency to disguise the Secret Court. An Outside-In Perspective best explains both judges and reporters.

a.   See her entry "Press Coverage" in Kermit L. Hall, Jr., ed., *The Oxford Companion to the Supreme Court of the United States* (New York: Oxford University Press, 1992), pp. 666–67.

b.   Refer to M. L. Stein, "Scalia Discusses the Press," *Editor and Publisher,* 123 (Sept. 8, 1990):16.

c.   See *Decisions and Images: The Supreme Court and the Press* (Englewood Cliffs, NJ: Prentice-Hall, 1993).

d.   Consult *Media Power Politics* (New York: Free Press, 1981).

CHAPTER 3

Modest Coverage
of Appellate Courts

When journalist Max Freedman called the Supreme Court of the United States the "worst reported and worst judged institution in the American system of government,"[1] he might have said "least" rather than "worst." He might have improved his accuracy still more by redirecting his comments to the subjects of this chapter. Appellate courts other than the Supreme Court may be the least reported and least judged institutions in the American system of government.[2] This chapter examines why appellate courts get far less coverage than *both* trial courts (covered in chapters 4 and 5) *and* the U. S. Supreme Court (covered in chapter 2).

This chapter concerns noncoverage rather than coverage of appeals courts because, aside from a very few decisions, appellate courts are *not* covered. This modest coverage of appellate courts belies the importance of appeals and thus challenges *both* the Inside-Out Perspective *and* the Outside-In Perspectives considered so far.

If we presume the Inside-Out Perspective, we may explain noncoverage by saying that most appellate decisions in courts other than the U. S. Supreme Court lack news-worth. The perspective incorporates assumptions that media accurately cover candid courts for vigilant citizens. We saw in the introduction that Inside-Outers expect media to serve as watchdogs who inform attentive citizens when legal officials or institutions compromise or flout values, norms, and conventions.[3] An Inside-Outer might explain appellate noncoverage by the need for a good watchdog to alert its owner to threats but not to rile the neighbors about nothing. Taking the metaphor of the watchdog quite seriously, then, the user of the Inside-Out Perspective might even salute noncoverage as necessary and virtuous because the press cannot cover everything and, if they did, the significant would be lost amid the trivial.

Without elaboration, however, that explanation immediately proves less than satisfying. News-worth tends to be defined as the likelihood of coverage, so lack of coverage —by definition—implies a lack of news-worth. It is true that appellate courts tend not to be covered much because most of what they do is unlikely to be perceived as news, but that hardly tells us why. Thus, the challenge for Inside-Outers is to show that news-worth describes the highly trained sense of astute media watchdogs, lest skeptics suspect that news-worth is just a way to let sleeping dogs lie.

The more we explore and elaborate news-worth, the more we find that coverage of appellate courts seems to resemble the habitual news biases discussed in foregoing chapters. While some coverage and some noncoverage will be fully justified by the mainstream, Inside-Out view, much noncoverage seems expedient and efficient but hardly accurate or thorough. We shall find ample evidence that dramatization, morselization, personalization, and normalization, combined with the commercial predilections of modern mass media, define news-worth in appellate courts other than the U. S. Supreme Court. Angle biases and commercial biases, in short and in sum, explain why the media watchdog so often doesn't hunt.

Yet I shall not be able to find, amid the biases, much evidence for any of the three Outside-In Perspectives that I have introduced so far. Contrary to the primary Outside-In Perspective (defined in the Introduction in table I.1), coverage of most appellate cases other than those of the U. S. Supreme Court is not inexpensive hype. It is inexpensive, but that is because it usually is nonexistent. Appeals courts do disseminate strategic imagery, but the strategic images are legally crafted because about the only audience at all attentive to most appeals courts consists of lawyers and judges. There is very little drama and spectacle communicated by these national and state appeals courts, so the primary Outside-In Perspective does not describe ordinary noncoverage.

The "external" view I have attributed to Justice Scalia (table I.2) fares a little better, for popular media seem to give the irrepressible Scalia the sort of noncoverage he would prefer for the U. S. Supreme Court. However, Scalia complained of the press's distortions and oversimplifications. This empirical claim cannot be sustained with regard to almost all appeals courts. Judges and lawyers pronounce most appellate coverage, we shall see, to be competent, balanced, and accurate. Juridical elites are disappointed in the *quantity* of coverage more than in its *quality*.

Nor can I recommend the "external" view I have imputed to Richard Davis (see table 2.3), although his view of coverage of the

U. S. Supreme Court does apply in at least one respect to other appellate bodies. Like the justices of the U. S. Supreme Court, other appellate judges carefully regulate their communications with reporters and the mass public. However, I am aware of no evidence that lower appeals judges use cunning rhetoric to control their images. Instead, sketchy studies done to date suggest that appeals judges usually make few or no concessions to reporters or other laypeople. Indeed, appeals judges seem generally indifferent to coverage.

Before I suggest an answer to the puzzle of appellate noncoverage, let me review what little scholars have discovered about appeals courts other than the high court.

Appellate Courts— Distinct and Important

Major differences between appeals courts and trial courts make appeals courts relatively and absolutely important to citizens and media who would monitor the legal system or adjudication, but those differences also make appeals courts much harder for mass media to cover. As a result, we might begin with sharply contrasting expectations of coverage of appeals. The distinctive importance of appellate adjudication—that is, its relative law-worth—might incline us to expect that the media cover appeals more thoroughly than trials. In contrast, distinctive difficulties of understanding and explaining appellate adjudication might incline us to expect media to cover courts more selectively than trials. So which is it? Is appellate coverage generally more thorough or more selective? Both!

In this regard, as in so many others in this book, I urge you to prefer "both/and" to "either/or." *Both* of the contrasting expectations seem justified in the sketchy literature that I shall review with you. Appeals are relatively and intrinsically important, so mass media tend to cover a greater *proportion* of appeals, even excluding coverage of the United States Supreme Court, than the *proportion* of trials they cover. However, due to the challenges of reporting appellate adjudication, journalists tend to restrict themselves to cases that suit citizens' and reporters' training and habits. Inevitably, far more trials than appeals will suit reporters and readers and viewers. To fathom coverage of appeals courts, then, we must understand *both* the challenges *and* the importance of appeals.

Appeals Are Distinctive—
And Distinctively Challenging

Appellate courts review cases already decided in some other court or courts. The evidence, testimony, motions, rulings, and arguments that constitute a criminal or civil trial are preserved in a trial record. Appeals courts consider whether that record shows that the trial court applied laws and procedures correctly. Some appellate courts at the apex of the hierarchy in some states and the United States Supreme Court may also hear appeals from other appellate courts. In such cases, the higher court determines whether its subordinate correctly interpreted and applied the law.

Focusing exclusively on meanings and applications of legal rules, appeals judges dispense with features of adjudication familiar from television and films. Appellate courts rarely gather or admit new evidence, almost never hear witnesses, and never feature juries. They seldom concern themselves with factual questions such as the truth of a verdict or veracity of a key witness. It is only a slight exaggeration to say that the facts of cases are frozen in trial courts so that only questions of law matter for appeals. The major issues of trials—guilt or innocence, liability, balancing of equities—are usually far easier to comprehend than the often recondite, always challenging issues that bedevil appeals courts. The eyes of even astute laypersons will usually glaze over as appeals detour from ordinary questions of culpability and reasonability into conundrums of jurisprudence.

Because facts are frozen and only legal questions are at issue, appeals resemble debates between lawyers into which the judges may regularly intervene to question, argue, or prod. Advocates submit briefs, written summaries of the best arguments for each party's preferred outcome(s). Appeals judges may read these written arguments before oral arguments and may even decide the case on the basis of the briefs. Appeals judges may avail themselves of oral arguments, during which lawyers are at the judges' disposal and the judges may pose hypotheticals, interrupt polished presentations, and even argue among themselves. Appellate arguments in general resemble grueling examinations in which the best students in class are pitted against each other before probing professors. The "professors" then assess the arguments and issue a decision about which parties should prevail on which issues. In sum, if trials resemble mundane debates in which advocates often tailor arguments to twelve ordinary citizens, appeals proceed as specialized, abstruse debates that only lawyers and judges may follow. Sometimes even they lose their way.

Trials and appeals are alike in at least one respect: far more cases fail to make it to formal proceedings than succeed. Yet even this similarity may make appeals harder for the unschooled to comprehend. Every informed citizen knows that far more cases are plea bargained or settled out of court than adjudicated. Many well read citizens may not realize how few cases merit and receive appeal. Even those citizens aware of the many barriers to appeal may not understand why a court dispensed with an appeal, while most can grasp the calculations that lead to pleas and other bargains. The U. S. Supreme Court and supreme courts in states with intermediate appellate courts— appeals courts above the trial level but beneath the ultimate state court—may refuse to hear appeals and need not say why. Even if the reasons for ending the process short of a hearing are stated, the average newspaper reader may not comprehend them. Thus, formal trials and appellate arguments are both rare, but consumers of mass media are likely to understand why trials end and unlikely to understand why appeals are dismissed.

The rare, full, formal proceedings issue distinctive justifications that match the distinct audiences of trial and appeals courts. Trial courts depend mostly on ritual to assert that justice has been done, while appeals courts rely far more on reasoning. Ordinary trials end in verdicts that are clear to all. Appellate hearings end in decisions and opinions that must be stated clearly and defended persuasively if the appeals court is to guide other courts, judges, and lawyers. Appellate judges defend their decisions in opinions that are usually scholarly and often lengthy but almost always beyond the ken of the average viewer or reader.

Appellate decisions and opinions are predominantly collegial products of at least three and sometimes nine or more judges or justices. When an appellate judge issues an opinion that states his or her reasons for deciding as he or she did, such an opinion may approximate the coherence and consistent focus of an individual speaking her or his mind. However, most appellate opinions are joint ventures explaining decisions made, in effect, by committee. Usually, the author of the joint opinion does not even have the division of labor that comes with coauthorship. Rather, the author is expected to craft a justification for the collegial decision and must write and rewrite to please the other judges enough that they will endorse the collegial opinion. Constructing a paper to suit coauthors is tricky. Collegial opinions are more like writing a paper for a panel of readers whose objections must be met before the paper is acceptable. The distinctively collegial process of deciding and justifying appeals makes appellate results far harder to summarize or understand.

Finally, appellate decisions usually have more extensive consequences than verdicts or results of trials. Because appellate decisions are made from some height in the judicial hierarchy, the issues resolved often have very general ramifications for many courts under the appeals court. Trial courts usually resolve the instant case alone. The higher in the judicial system an appeal goes, the more courts the decision of that appeal will usually affect. Every competent jurist is expected to ponder and heed the authoritative declaration of her or his superiors, but no jurist reads fast enough to skim the results of most trials. Hence, appellate results, because they are far more portentous than trial results for everyone except the parties to the trial, must be stated subtly, precisely, and reflectively. Subtle, precise, and reflective prose is hardly a habit for most television viewers and newspaper readers.

In sum, basic features of appellate decisions challenge readers, viewers, and reporters far more than the essentials of trials do. Such challenges explain, if they do not justify, noncoverage of appeals. Now we shall see that the importance of appeals demands that coverage overcome at least some of the obstacles to coverage. If the obstacles to understanding that we have reviewed above incline us to expect less coverage of appeals, the ramifications of appeals for citizens and officials must incline us to expect more coverage.

Appeals Are Absolutely and Relatively Important

To convince you that appeals matter, I point out three functions that appeals courts serve. Appellate courts routinely *make law, guarantee justice*, and *secure order*, so appellate adjudication is crucial in any legal system. Having seen already the distinctive difficulties that might explain a paucity of appellate coverage, you will now see the distinctive importance that demands extensive appellate coverage.

Both the relative importance and dearth of appellate decisions explain why appellate opinions are available in most law libraries while most trial records are not. Appellate litigation is important, we have seen, because appeals make and remake the law. Appellate rulings and opinions create precedents, authorize dispositions of legal questions in recurring situations, and circumscribe or control lower courts. Over time and many cases, appellate adjudicators and appellate litigants weave precedents into doctrines that reinforce or reinvent existing law. Settled or resettled doctrines are called *black letter law* because they state in boldface the general policies that judges have made and remade and that legislatures have accepted or modified. In a common law system, appellate courts are a major source of law. Appellate judges create precedents and rules, monitor applications of law in specific cases, and reconcile discordant rulings into statements of new rules or restatements of old rules. This law-making function of appellate courts is absolutely important both to media that purport to monitor institutions and to citizens who purport to attend to self-government.

Appellate courts also verify that justice has been done by reviewing how trial courts have applied law when a dissatisfied party to the trial requests such a review. That justice be done and be seen to be done is perhaps the most crucial goal of any judicial system, so assessing whether laws have been properly applied and procedures assiduously followed is absolutely important. A miscarriage of justice in a specific case is hardly trivial, but general injustice would seem the far greater concern for most citizens. In sum, the verdicts of trials tend to have consequences that are far more limited than appellate decisions and opinions. Absolutely and relatively, then, appellate courts are crucial guarantors of justice.

Absolutely and relatively as important as making law and guaranteeing justice is securing order, the third appellate function I showcase here. Appellate courts insure order by resolving ambiguities and filling gaps in the system of rules so that the law tends to be internally consistent and uniformly applied throughout the jurisdiction of the appellate court. Laws are not truly uniform and general if verdicts and judgments depend on which judge or which court happens to apply the laws. The consent of the governed to courts depends in part on the existence and use of settled rules. If gaps or overlaps in the legal system permit similar cases to be resolved disparately, the perceived fairness and actual coherence of the legal system must suffer. While a particular trial may slightly test faith in the rule of law, appellate disorder frontally assaults that faith.

Thus, we find that appeals, individually and collectively, tend to matter more for the maintenance of justice and order in the legal system than trials, if for no other reason than that most appeals have more extensive consequences for subsequent trials and appeals than most trials have. The relative and absolute importance of appeals would incline the conscientious citizen and the watchdog press that the Inside-Out Perspective presumes to attend to appeals far more assiduously than the distinctive challenges of understanding appeals led us to expect.[4] The distinctive difficulties of understanding appellate adjudication and the distinctive importance of appeals, considered together, suggest that mass media must trade off some comprehensiveness in pursuit of comprehension. That is, the more time, effort, and space that media devote to reports of appeals, the less time, effort, and space they can direct to explaining the issues and decisions involved in any appeal.

As we shall now learn, however, mass media tend instead to sacrifice *both* comprehensiveness *and* comprehension to other values. To see how the press neglects *both* quantity *and* quality in appellate coverage, let us survey the research.

Noncoverage of Appellate Courts

Most judicial journalism concerns trials or the rulings of the Supreme Court of the United States. Between profane, titillating trials and the sacred, imposing Court, state appellate courts and United States courts of appeals receive very little coverage from mass media. Indeed, so minimal is the coverage that scholarship about appellate coverage is almost nonexistent.[5] However, from the few studies extant, I extract four generalizations. These four generalizations support my contention that the press covers appeals courts—other than the United States Supreme Court, which I discussed in chapter 2—not only seldom but superficially, too.

Generalization One:
Routine Noncoverage

Routinely, appellate courts other than the United States Supreme Court are not covered. Subsequent generalizations show how poorly appellate courts are covered when they are covered. The most important fact you should know about coverage of appeals courts, however, is that, for most readers, viewers, and auditors, it is minimal.

Consider the views of one justice of the Ohio Supreme Court:

> The media coverage reflects a lack of knowledge about how the court functions and what its purposes are. This lack of knowledge is consistent, generally, with that of the general public. The real business of the Supreme Court of Ohio is not of any interest to the media and so *is barely reported.*[6]

Chief Justice Thomas M. Kavanaugh of the Michigan Supreme Court stressed the same shortcomings, then offered an explanation for the sparse coverage:

> [T]oday it is a rare news operation—electronic or newsprint—that assigns a reporter full-time to the courts. Sports, yes; courts, no. Yet, management expects its reporter to dash into a hall of justice in between covering a fire or city hall, and in fifteen minutes find out all there is to know about a trial that has been in session all day or more. You say, that's what general reporters are supposed to be capable of doing. I suggest this is unfair to the reporter. I suggest, also, that the net result can be unfair to your viewers, to the persons whose lives and livelihoods are involved in the judicial process, and to the courts.[7]

Justices of the Washington Supreme Court tended to voice similar complaints and suggestions.[8] They believed that reporters were ill-trained and overworked and that, as a result, the court received coverage inferior to that of other state agencies.

Scholars reiterate the scarcity of appellate coverage. When Professor Jack C. Doppelt surveyed judges in Chicago to get their views of judicial journalism, he chose not to interview appellate judges—state appeals judges and judges from the United States Court of Appeals for the Seventh Circuit might have been available—"because of the relatively limited media coverage at the appellate level."[9] In their study of state supreme courts, G. Alan Tarr and Mary Cornelia Aldis Porter implied the same judgment: "In our study of the Ohio Supreme Court, we have focused on a number of idiosyncratic factors that would have little bearing in a study of other state high courts — media coverage of the court, for example, . . ."[10]

F. Dennis Hale found so little coverage of the California Supreme Court that he had to redesign his study. Regarding 139 decisions in 1972, Hale found that ten California newspapers featured 277 reports. More than half of the California Supreme Court's decisions in 1972 went unreported in *all ten newspapers*. Hale calculated that 19 percent of the decisions were reported in three or fewer newspapers, 18 percent were reported in four to six newspapers, and a mere 8 percent were reported in seven or more papers. *Only six decisions (4 percent) were reported by all ten newspapers!*[11] Hale's sample included large, respected newspapers. The *Los Angeles Times*, for example, reported 29 percent of the decisions of California's highest court; the *San Francisco Chronicle* reported 33 percent of all cases;

and the *San Diego Union* reported 21 percent.[12] On average, the ten papers reported but 20 percent of the court's decisions that year. In an earlier study of the Washington State Supreme Court, Hale found that the Associated Press covered 90 percent of the court's decisions while the United Press International covered merely 37 percent. Six Washington dailies ran wire service stories of 3 percent to 37 percent of 30 decisions from the court, with 13 percent the mean.[13] Such wire coverage is crucial: Robert E. Drechsel found, for example, that one law reporter he observed had such a huge beat that he relied on the Associated Press to cover the state supreme court.[14]

Reporters agree that even state supreme courts in large states with major newspapers are famous for their anonymity.[15] Hugh J. Morgan, former Associated Press wire-service reporter who covered supreme courts in Louisiana, Mississippi, and Michigan, has said courts received and deserved only nominal coverage, not close scrutiny.[16] Another reporter explained the lack of coverage just as Chief Justice Kavanaugh did:

> State supreme courts and appellate courts are a vast no-man's land as far as the press is concerned. There are reasons and excuses, of course. In most states, no newspaper, and not even the press associations, can afford to have a trained reporter keeping constant watch on the higher courts. The result is that when developments in those courts are covered at all, they are covered by innocents in the law. At no time is there good analytical coverage of the courts' accomplishments during a given session or of any trend of opinions in the courts.[17]

My first generalization about coverage of appellate decisions is the *noncoverage generalization*—expect most decisions of appellate courts, the U. S. Supreme Court excepted, to go unreported in almost all newspapers. Do not expect the press to report most appeals poorly; expect the press to cover most appeals *not at all*.

Generalization Two:
Some Outcomes Are Newsworthy

For the minority of cases covered, coverage consists of who won and who lost and little else. This is the *results-coverage generalization*—expect reports of appellate decisions to state the winning and losing parties but not reasons, reactions, or other contextual aspects. Most mass media stress "who-just-did-what-to-whom rather than the more substantive issues of what-is-going-on-and-why."[18] Often wire-service stories supply only a brief paragraph for each decision, if that.[19] Newspaper rewrites of those wire-service stories may cluster together unrelated decisions.

In a systematic study of routine coverage of a state supreme court, Hale found that the Washington Supreme Court seldom achieved news-worth in the eyes even of reporters who routinely covered the court. Reporters usually covered cases only when the state supreme court filed decisions and opinions. They seldom paid attention to preliminary phases in the appeals. The Associated Press tended to summarize each decision in its own paragraph as the court handed down decisions. The United Press International saw even summaries of holdings as excessive: " 'I see no reason for complete coverage of the court's output. . . . We're concerned with cases of substantial public importance. Many routine appeals get no news coverage at all and don't deserve any. . . . ' "[20]

Beyond specific news about winners and losers, Hale found little attention to appellate decisions. The reporters he interviewed did not even want the court to supply aids to understand the legal reasoning and significance of decisions because they believed that nonetheless they would have to mine opinions for newsworthy angles and elements that *summaries of legal significance would only obscure*.[21] These reporters also approved of the court's practice of releasing decisions on a single day each week because that routine ensured predictability and, perhaps, restricted reports to only the most noteworthy cases.

Generalization Three:
Appeals Have Mostly Derivative Significance

Appeals tend to derive their rare news-worth from some source external to the appeals court. This is the *derivative coverage generalization*. Hale's study of the Washington Supreme Court in 1968 showed that clashes between officials, a First Amendment case, and a major change in the common law made the front pages while other decisions did not.[22] Hale's later study of the California Supreme Court yielded similar findings: contests between prominent officials and cases involving famous litigants drew the only widespread coverage.[23] These studies warrant tentative specification of usual sources of derivative importance. Please recall that these speculations and hence this third generalization follow from a few, preliminary studies. Appellate courts other than the U S. Supreme Court will need much greater scholarly attention before any reliable propositions will be available to us.

Significance Derived from Trials

Cases well publicized in the past are much more likely to be covered on appeal. Hale's wire-service correspondents who covered the Washington Supreme Court told him that the news-worth of cases tracked trial coverage. Reporters actually criticized coverage of appeals that did not elicit extensive coverage as trials![24]

Significance Derived from Future Adjudication

Cases that may proceed to the United States Supreme Court will draw coverage that they otherwise would not get. The mere possibility that Guam's law against abortions might lead to an appeal in which the Supreme Court would overrule *Roe v. Wade* induced some coverage by national papers, for example. One would be hard put to find the *Washington Post* reporting on another Guamanian case on federal appeal in Hawaii.[25]

Significance Derived from Local Relevances

Coverage of appeals derives mostly from local salience—that is, the relevance or interest of the case to readers or viewers toward whom a local medium aims. Hale's wire reporters claimed that most of their clients picked up reports about the state supreme court only if cases had some local relevance.[26] Local interest thus directly shaped the quantity and quality of coverage. Since Hale also discovered that the California reports tended to emphasize immediate consequences of decisions if they mentioned consequences at all, we might hypothesize that when decisions' immediate consequences have local salience or obvious implications for politics or business, decisions had much more news-worth.

Significance Derived from Conflict

Finally, conflict within a court and especially political conflicts that erupt from the court will generate coverage. In their study of state supreme courts, Tarr and Porter examined extensive coverage of the Ohio Supreme Court but barely mentioned the press in discussing state supreme courts in New Jersey and Alabama.[27] The coverage of Ohio's supreme court that Tarr and Porter called "idiosyncratic" followed from partisan judicial politics. We might generalize this lesson to state that when appellate judges enter the arena of mundane politics, they may become far more newsworthy because far less law-worthy. Coverage in such cases derives more from political drama rather than from legal importance.

Generalization Four:
Most Aspects of Appeals Have Little News-Worth

This generalization is largely the flip side of the previous three generalizations. Because most appeals have at most derivative news-worth, they will not be covered based on any inherent news-worth. Even decisions that derive some salience from a local angle or an electoral connection will tend not to be covered during preliminary stages or subsequent developments. That is, derivative significance tends not merely to be rare but also to be circumscribed. Aside from such derivative significance, appeals have negligible news-worth, so only the immediate outcome and direct effects on the people or groups from which the case draws its news-worth will be reported. That is, even derivative coverage (generalization three) will justify only results-coverage (generalization two). Consequently, most reports of appeals will leave most aspects of the appellate process unreported (generalization one).

Certain aspects of appeals tend to be remarkable by their absence: public arguments heard before the appeal is decided; deliberations and negotiations by appeals judges; reasons and justifications in appellate opinions; and the immediate and eventual consequences of appellate decisions. Each aspect reminds us of the importance of commercial biases.

Briefs and Oral Arguments Are Usually Overlooked

Reporters might discern important legal aspects of the appeals if they looked over written arguments in briefs and oral presentations of arguments to the justices. Usually, however, reporters overlook them:

Few cases were covered by the wire services when initially argued before the court, the stage often referred to as hearings or oral arguments. Reporters disagreed on quoting judges' comments from oral arguments. About half felt that the briefs, not the oral arguments, contained the meat of the case. Others felt that the judges, acting as devil's advocates, did an excellent job of spotlighting the law.[28]

Since Hale found that reporters encountered most cases immediately after they were decided and while deadlines loomed, the reporters' estimates of the value of written briefs versus oral arguments were perhaps sincere but certainly academic. Without coverage of briefs and oral arguments, only reporters with extraordinary memories and spectacular files could elaborate the contexts and legal issues that decisions often leave implicit. Perhaps the most telling aspect of the debate just quoted is the pervasive practicality of the reporters. They implicitly, perhaps automatically, disregard the best coverage—attention to both briefs and oral arguments that would both enrich appreciation of eventual decisions and yield stories about the appellate process—in favor of expedient coverage that would satisfy press clients. This is one indication of how expediency and efficiency tend to compromise coverage so that news-worth becomes a commercial calculation rather than a journalistic judgment based on what the public ought to know about. In this instance, news-worth seems to follow directly from a commercial bias.

Deliberations Are Almost Always Secret

Appellate coverage, even at the level of the Supreme Court, will very seldom mention or describe deliberations of any courts or judges. While trial courts, to a large extent, impress their publics with the majesty, order, and justice of adjudication by publicizing their process, they do not put judges or jurors on display during deliberations. In a similar manner, appellate courts keep their decision making quite private. As a result, reporters almost never have access to sources who can confirm suspicions about appellate decision making, deliberations, and interactions. Since accounts of deliberations are so rare, reporters need not fear being scooped by competitors. This absence of competition will also free the press from any impulse to investigate or to analyze deliberations, however, so the black box within which appeals judge decide and negotiate will almost always remain dark.

I note noncoverage of deliberations so that you will see that media usually cannot penetrate judicial deliberations and thus reporters will usually depend on judges' formal justifications. However, I also hope to direct your attention to a less obvious point. If reporters ordinarily covered oral arguments and if media regularly ran reports on preliminaries in appeals, readers and viewers might have more access to and understanding of judicial decision making. At the very least, a diligent reader might supplement the formal motives proclaimed in opinions with ulterior motives evident from briefs or oral arguments. If reporters routinely reviewed briefs, for example, they would learn the range of options among which appeals judges might choose. The logic trumpeted in an opinion is seldom the only argument available and knowing what arguments the judges neglected to consider or ignored without explicit reason can be crucial to understanding appeals. Even more obvious is the utility of covering oral arguments. If judges publicly question attorneys in ways that betray values or preferences, readers—especially those expected to vote for appeals judges in the near future—might profit from such knowledge.

In sum, the absence of reports about private decision making is not that remarkable, but the dearth of inferences about the process is debilitating and disserves readers and viewers. The expense and bother of such comprehensive and comprehensible coverage would, perhaps, be too much for any but the largest news organs to bear. However, to put the matter in such a way makes my point: expediences and expenses define news-worth far more persuasively than any premonitions about what audiences demand or might want. If we assume that the press exists to make money, noncoverage is inevitable. If we assume that news media are supposed to increase public awareness, noncoverage is indefensible. However, I see noncoverage as *both* inevitable *and* indefensible.

Appellate Opinions Are Not Often Reported

Deliberations yield opinions that make appellate judges' justifications for decisions public. They are available to all reporters. They too usually go unreported. While an occasional florid phrase or devastating dissent may make the wire, such exceptions truly prove a rule: they are news because they are rare and conflictual, not because they bode well or ill for the public weal or the law. Aside from titillating tidbits from opinions, the official accounts of appellate courts do not reach the lay population. Even when appellate judges clash in opinions, the conflict may not be enough to make news. James S. Granelli, legal affairs reporter for the *Los Angeles Times*, is not sure if readers care about personal bickering among judges on collegial courts.[29]

Spotty coverage of appellate opinions is, like noncoverage of deliberations, to be expected or excoriated depending on the perspective one adopts. Viewed from an accountant's bottom line, opinions are unlikely to appeal to most consumers and are very likely to exceed the comprehension of reporters, editors, and their clientele. As a business decision, then, modest coverage of opinions makes sense and cents. Viewed from democracy's bottom line, however, minimal coverage of appellate opinions eliminates the bulk of the citizenry from the courts' audiences and renders voters too ill-informed to cast a meaningful vote for state appeals judges and too ignorant to know what national appellate judges are up to. As a result, attentive citizens are more susceptible to caprice or mistake in judicial elections and are more vulnerable to activists' propaganda in the selection and promotion of national judges. If "all the news that's fit to print" were practical aspiration rather than advertising slogan, reporters and editors might strive for critical or at least competent recounting of opinions. By keeping lay readers in the dark, news media save themselves the costs of educational, edifying coverage. When public officials trade personal profit for their public responsibilities, journalists rightly condemn them for bribery. When journalists swap inexpensive hype for objective accuracy, however, that is just standard business practice.

Decisions' Consequences Are Seldom Explored

Nor do reports tend to assess legal or political implications without conflict or novelty or some other angle. Appeals courts' reactions to lower or higher courts will draw comment only if they are intemperate or inordinate (again, the Supreme Court of the United States excepted). The routine tasks of appeals courts that I highlighted above—*to make law, to guarantee justice*, and *to secure order*—have profound legal, political, social, and cultural import. These implications will tend to elude consumers of mass media, if the sparse scholarly evidence to date is reliable.

Coverage Neither Comprehensive Nor Comprehensible

We see, then, that coverage of appeals courts is sporadic and shallow. Faced with a choice between quantity (covering most appeals superficially) and quality (covering a few appeals insightfully), most papers appear to have compromised by covering a few appeals superficially. I said earlier that "the challenge for Inside-Outers is to show that news-worth describes the highly trained sense of astute media watchdogs, lest skeptics suspect that news-worth is just a way to let sleeping dogs lie." Our survey of appellate noncoverage—a survey limited by the paucity of studies—shows that challenge to be daunting. How can we explain or justify coverage that is minimal when it is not altogether absent? I have shown throughout this section of the chapter that commercial biases that inform both journalism and our Outside-In Perspective seem to explain noncoverage. Now we shall explore other reasons for shallow, sporadic coverage.

Why Appellate Adjudication Is Not Newsworthy

We can understand readily why state appeals courts and U. S. courts of appeals are generally less newsworthy than lurid trials and momentous Supreme Court litigation. However, the news values that best explain the news-worth of titillating trials and landmark Supreme Court cases resemble angle biases introduced in chapter 1 far more than they match any watchdog metaphor. A mutt that sees little and barks less may be a valued pet, but it is not much of a watchdog.

Challenging Cases Are Less Accessible, Hence Less Covered

I shall quickly reprise three contrasts between trial and appellate courts that explain why appeals make the news far less than their relative and absolute importance might lead us to expect. The three contrasts—the relative complexity of appellate issues and decisions, the relatively sophisticated audiences for which appellate judges write, and the collegial decision making characteristic of appeals but not trial courts—do not exhaust the challenges of appellate reporting. Rather, I review them now because they seem to me the most compelling reasons for appellate noncoverage.

Appeals may attain less news-worth because, first, general and specific intricacies of appeals will impair coverage. Appellate adjudication is relatively esoteric and perhaps even absolutely recondite. Few nonlawyers could or would fathom the issues and the arguments even with reviews and summaries that most media will not or cannot provide. Perhaps a simple contrast captures this difference between trial and appeal. In trial courts, witnesses must understand the questions and, often, jurors must understand the issues. On appeal, neither questions nor issues need be understandable to ordinary citizens, and answers to the questions and resolutions of the issues will usually elude all but the most sophisticated.

Second, trial and appellate courts target different audiences. Trials are supposed to instruct the community on the rules of conduct and the costs of disregarding those rules. Appellate adjudication, in contrast, aims to systematize the law and reinforce judicial authority and hierarchy. The targets of appellate decisions are predominantly the Bench and the Bar. When asked about their audiences, appeals judges mention other judges and other lawyers, legislators and executive, and even future generations. Only a minority, however, see themselves writing for ordinary citizens.[30] Appeals judges focus on issues they regard as crucial for the polity but they do not accept the role of popularizing or even publicizing their efforts to secure justice and order under the rule of law.

Appellate decision making is, third, often complicated by multiple voices involved in decisions. Oral arguments among two or more lawyers and three or more jurists are far more difficult even to describe than colloquies between a single judge and, usually, two advocates. A singular trier of fact will usually yield tidy verdicts, and even juries will usually speak *officially* with only one voice. Appellate triers of law, in contrast, may speak in as many tongues as there are triers.[31] Thus, appeals can issue conflicting judicial opinions and clashing legal logic that even law professors cannot comprehend. Under such circumstances, the press may distort understanding far less by reporting nothing from justifications than by selecting the arguments most easily rendered in lay terms.

In sum, an obvious and common explanation for the quantity and quality of coverage of appeals is the absolute and relative difficulty of conveying issues, reasons, context, and ramifications to a predominantly lay audience.

The three challenges reviewed here would explain the mediocre *quality* of appellate coverage, but they do not explain the modest *quantity* of such coverage. Indeed, if newspapers provided mere lists of cases with one sentence per case—that is, minimal *quality*—the papers would cover more than the small fraction of appeals that researchers have found.

Angle Biases

Angle biases explain the modest *quantity* of appeals stories. Because media may dramatize, personalize, morselize, and normalize civil suits and criminal cases far more easily than most appeals, and because media have far more trials from which to choose, media will find more stories in trials than in appeals.

In subsequent chapters we shall see that civil and criminal trials tend to draw attention more for their potential for human interest or entertainment than for their substance. Trials with titillating conflicts, remarkable litigants or advocates, or intriguing episodes or vignettes tend to appear in print and on the air. They are, to use that murky term again, newsworthy. At least in metropolitan areas, editors have many trials from which to choose the most interesting, so it should not surprise us that they tend to emphasize trials that make the best stories.

Appeals, in contrast, seldom attain news-worth. Appeals usually are not dramatic and, on the rare occasions when they are, appellate conflict will not lend itself to dramatized coverage. Appeals do feature characters, virtues, and vices suitable for personalized coverage but fewer of them than the far more numerous trials going on at any moment. We have seen that appeals often defy lay understanding, which makes them far harder to morselize for daily consumption. Nor can the media readily normalize appeals as they can trials, for the latter will approximate everyday notions of justice to a far greater degree than technical, abstract appeals can.

Finality and Focus Induce More Coverage

We have seen that challenges of covering appeals explain too little to account for the scarcity of appellate reportage. However, once we consider the U. S. Supreme Court, the challenges may explain too much! Relative to state appellate courts and U. S. courts of appeals, the Supreme Court decides fewer cases, confronts cases of at least equal complexity, writes for at least as sophisticated a readership, and is usually subject to more opinions and clashing voices. The three challenges reviewed above and the other challenges detailed earlier cannot tell us why the Supreme Court of the United States is covered far more than any other appellate court, especially if we are to use those challenges to explain why trial courts are more accessible to reporters, viewers, and readers.

Offsetting the Challenges of Covering the Supreme Court

If we try to offset the equal or greater challenges of covering the Court by citing special advantages that reporters might have, we do not get very far. The Supreme Court decides for the country as a whole, so it might be believed to have more general importance. Perhaps the greater importance spurs reporters and editors to overcome the challenges? This explanation is undermined, however, by the scope of state supreme courts and U. S. courts of appeals. For media that serve the jurisdiction of such appellate entities, decisions are very important. Most appeals courts are just as final as the United States Supreme Court because their superiors review far fewer cases than they let stand.

We might offset the challenges of covering the Court by citing specialists on the Supreme Court or federal law beats. The knowledgeable, experienced reporters on these beats dictate some coverage, because what they produce is cost-effectively reproduced and disseminated and because the news organizations that pay their salaries must have something to show for the expense. However, this explanation tells us that news organizations meet the challenges of appellate coverage by assigning reporters with legal training and acumen to cover appellate courts. That explanation implicitly admits that newspapers do not cover other appellate courts because they do not value such coverage enough to send specialists. The more surmountable the challenges at the Supreme Court, the more surmountable those challenges in state capitals or in national appellate venues as well. The dozen or so reporters assigned roughly full time to the Supreme Court must be there because news organizations believe that the Court has newsworth. What makes the Supreme Court so much more newsworthy than other appeals courts?

Angle Biases Accentuate Finality and Focus?

Angle biases may make the high court much more newsworthy than other appeals courts. Relative to other appeals courts, the Supreme Court enjoys advantages in perceived *finality* and *focus*. I have noted that most cases stop well short of the U. S. Supreme Court, so the finality of the high court characterizes appeals courts and, for that matter, trials. However, because the losers of every trial and most appeals might want to take their case to the Supreme Court, and because celebrated cases often seem preordained to make the Court's docket, the Supreme Court exudes finality that eludes other courts. The Court is also focused for coverage: nine justices in a single courtroom rather than many cases in many places with many different judges and clashing rules. Let us see how finality and focus translate to the dramatized, personalized, normalized, and morselized coverage that media favor.

The finality and focus of the United States Supreme Court encourage drama. As the final round of any contest arrests attention far more than preliminary rounds, so does litigation before the High Court. That finality intensifies the media's spotlight as out of a welter of state or federal rulings, the Court imposes its views on all other courts. Singular focus and judicial finality make major Supreme Court cases the main event, while other appeals may seem more like warmups.

Finality and focus not only encourage dramatized coverage, they also tend to personalize cases. Finality and focus make public figures of Supreme Court litigants far more often than in almost any other court. Educated citizens are far more likely to remember Linda Brown or her father, Oliver Brown, than any of the other schoolchildren or parents involved in the fight to desegregate public schools, because the Browns gave their name to the Supreme Court decision *Brown v. Board of Education* (1954). Finality without focus may not make litigants famous, as the pregnant woman in *Roe v. Wade* (Norma McCorvey) could attest. Focus without finality may short-circuit fame as well. Marco DeFunis made roughly the same arguments against affirmative action as Allan Bakke made, but DeFunis's case was left undecided by the Supreme Court while Bakke's was decided at the Court.

It is ironic that the finality that many citizens attribute to the Court reinforces the normalization of what are actually quite rare events. The less that viewers and readers know about the judicial system, the more they may suppose that the United States Supreme Court polices the judiciary, state as well as local. If so, such ordinary consumers of mass media will take Supreme Court decisions to be the normal consummation of a legal dispute. The frequency with which print and broadcast media focus on such cases reinforces this impression. Since the justices will restrict the Court to cases that they find most crucial and since many such cases have concerned and will concern constitutional rights or other issues of national significance, extensive coverage of the Supreme Court will incline routine viewers and readers to expect judicial resolutions of political or publicized issues at the Court. Coverage thus tends to normalize not only judicial extensions and proliferation of constitutional rights but also the widespread belief that the Supreme Court is where all the action eventually takes place. Because finality and focus reinforce normalization and vice versa, expect extensive coverage of the U. S. Supreme Court and skimpy coverage elsewhere.

If the perceived finality of the Court encourages coverage, and if that coverage in turn encourages the belief that monitoring the Court is tantamount to monitoring the legal system, then the relatively intense focus of the media on the Supreme Court virtually dictates morselized coverage. In covering the Supreme Court, quantity and quality of coverage may truly trade off. The more cases that the media report as decisions defined by justices' opinions, the more cases the media may cover. The more space that media devote to details, arguments, nuances, context, and implications, the fewer cases the media may cover. We saw earlier that media coverage of other appellate courts tended toward minimal quantity and modest quality. The finality and focus of Supreme Court reporting allows for a better mix of quantity and quality but only if that coverage is morselized to fit into the small news hole available in most newspapers and the even smaller "air hole" available in broadcast news.

Focus and finality at the Supreme Court—actual or attributed—will also encourage groups, lawyers, and officials to accentuate Supreme Court cases far, far more than they stress lower-court appeals. Participants and practitioners adapt to the angle that media prefer. That is how one gets publicity, support, and funds for one's side. Mass media tend to cover those who play the media's angles far more than those who do not. In this way, focus and finality, in concert with angle biases, create more news at the Supreme Court than at any other appellate court, more than at all other appellate courts combined.

Spare That Watchdog!

If angle biases seem to explain the greater news-worth of both trials and the Supreme Court, both the Inside-Out Perspective and the watchdog metaphor are imperiled. The Inside-Out Perspective presumes that reporters closely monitor judges and courts to keep them honest, but angle biases indicate that courts and judges satisfy reporters by supplying newsworthy—that is, cost effective and preformatted—tidbits that eliminate most scrutiny. In other words, the watchdog seems to be fed the news routinely. The watchdog metaphor may be retained only if we modify or qualify it. One usual means of saving the watchdog metaphor is to claim that the watchdog media serve the whims of their masters: the citizenry.

I have argued that the work of appellate courts is important and that law-worth (that is, the social, political, and legal significance of cases and decisions) should insure news-worth if objective accuracy is actually a mission of mass media. However, the import of courts and cases at various levels is hardly a simple or incontestable conclusion. While some appellate judges have expressed regret at the *quantity* of coverage, most claim that the *quality* of their coverage is acceptable, and many judges agree that most of what they do is *not* very important to anyone except the Bench and Bar.[32] Even scholars and highbrow journalists, not slaves to mass audiences and deadlines, tend to study and to write about trials and especially the Supreme Court far more than other courts. Whatever their protests about importance, academic critics must acknowledge that their own estimates of importance seem curiously like those of the mass media. Thus, proponents of the watchdog metaphor might exclaim to critics, "Doctors, heal thyselves first!"

Even if scholars professed interest in appellate decisions equal to the importance that I have asserted and then presumed earlier, I should be hard pressed to demonstrate that readers and viewers share my estimate of importance. Media watchdogs, we must assume, have been trained to alert their client-masters to matters that concern the client-masters. When Hale found, for example, that local salience tended to determine whether newspapers used wire stories, this finding merely demonstrated that state supreme court rulings most interest local editors because they most interest local readers. While I may be correct to claim that appellate rulings are relatively and absolutely more important than trial results *in general and in the abstract*, specific and concrete stories interest ordinary people and authors alike more when those stories concern people and places close to home. Importance is relative and editors and reporters must tailor coverage to their clients, not their critics.

I may have gone too far in showing that angle biases best explain skimpy, superficial coverage of appellate courts, for I have thereby shown that mass media supply their clients what their clients have become accustomed to, what their clients tend to purchase, and what media professionals have learned to create. For example, an exciting new study of political communication suggests that television news—shorter, more superficial, and even more subject to angle biases than many newspapers—tends to inform and involve viewers with only modest interest in complex, abstract, or recondite issues. Once viewers are involved in an issue, they are more likely to seek out newspapers and other media that make more demands and deliver more dividends.[33] If Neuman, Just, and Crigler are correct, dramatized, personalized, morselized, and normalized coverage of courts may interest and involve far more viewers and readers than less superficial and hence less intelligible reporting. To steal from Justice Scalia again, that is why your local 7-Eleven stocks newspapers and *TV Guide* but not the *University of Chicago Law Review*.[34]

Thus, the Inside-Out Perspective might suggest we take a different view of the quality of appellate reporting. To get the quantity of coverage in perspective as well, take a second look at the numbers of stories of trials and appeals. The press reports *more* appeals than trials once we take into account the sheer numbers of cases involved at each level. In raw numbers, of course, we find much more coverage of trials. However, there are so many more trials than appeals that far more appeals are covered than trials *as a percentage of all court coverage*, and the average appeal is far more likely to receive some notice from the press than the average trial.

More, Hale himself has provided evidence that important appellate cases elicit better coverage. He identified ten important Washington state cases and found that wire services and dailies tended to report them more often and more extensively. Defenders of the watchdog metaphor would note that a discriminating press rations coverage to public demand and public interest. Newspapers and television identify the most newsworthy appeals and skip most appeals because their space and air can be put to better use. To mix metaphors—a good watchdog doesn't cry wolf unless a wolf is there.

In sum, the watchdog metaphor survives the findings above once we remember to place new information in perspective. Mass media monitor appellate courts other than the U. S. Supreme Court selectively—and "selectively" serves here as a euphemism for "haphazardly" or "minimally." Such selective, haphazard, minimal coverage is as expedient, inexpensive, and hyped as our Outside-In Perspective expects. However, when we look at skimpy and superficial reportage from the Inside-Out Perspective, we can see that the limitations of audiences' attention, media's expertise, and judges' explanations may dictate modest coverage. Although this "any more coverage would be wasted" defense of the media watchdog undermines idealistic claims of the Inside-Out Perspective that media pursue accuracy and courts practice candor before the watchful public, more practical understandings of the interactions of judges, reporters, and citizens survive—barely.

A Symbiotic Hypothesis

Our "both/and" guideline demands that we accommodate the predilections and interests of judges, audiences, and journalists in a representation that satisfies *both* the Inside-Out Perspective *and* our Outside-In Perspective. Rich as we have found the very few studies of appellate journalism, their paucity counsels us to be quite tentative in formulating any representation. Allow me to advance a tentative but tantalizing possibility: a representation I call the *Symbiotic Hypothesis*, in keeping with hypotheses common in studies of other kinds of political journalism.[35]

Recall from high school biology that symbiosis is a mutually beneficial relationship between two or more organisms. The Symbiotic Hypothesis here introduced suggests that spotty, superficial coverage of appellate courts allows judges, reporters, and citizens to exchange benefits that otherwise might not be forthcoming. Let us examine these hypothesized exchanges.

Noncoverage gives appeals judges insulation and anonymity, both of which enable judges to pursue their professional goals. Insulation and anonymity insure some autonomy, so that judges may devote themselves to formal duties without scrutiny, lobbying, or meddling. Judges who have political agendas may pursue those agendas as well because non-coverage protects them from discovery unless their violations of judicial roles are too flagrant. For judges who seek to be appointed to other positions, anonymity and insulation minimize the "paper trail" that can obstruct their candidacies. For judges who face reelection, a name barely recognized that calls up no scandals or controversies may be the greatest asset. Thus, for U. S. and state appellate judges alike, no news is usually good news.

Judges seek little publicity, their courts maintain only skeletal public information services, and most of them do not talk to reporters about cases and legal issues. Hale found that most judges disparaged the quantity of their coverage but not its quality. From this finding, I suspect that many appeals judges want more of their decisions to be covered but want them covered superficially. Superficial coverage of appeals amounts to "press-release journalism,"[36] in which public officials feed reporters words and images that the officials want the reporters to amplify and relay to their readers and viewers. When reporters relay (1) the bare facts of a case, (2) the holding of the appeals court, (3) a few words quoted from formal opinions, (4) minimal assessments of the direct, legal impact of the decision, and (5) *not much else*, the reporters assist the judges by directing readers and viewers to the formal, jural aspects of cases and thus distracting readers from more political interpretations of the judges' actions. Commentary will almost always come from disgruntled parties or sympathizers—"losers" whose overheated rhetoric will do little to undermine the judges' claim that the law requires the result reached and whose calls for redress move the issue out of the autonomous judicial system and back into the wider polity.

What do media get in return for press-release journalism? First, minimal coverage reduces costs. Reporters may be assigned beats wider than specific courts because appellate coverage consists largely of encapsulating formal opinions. Since appeals judges hand reporters the greater part of stories, writing the stories takes less time and the stories occupy less space or air. While judges would prefer to see more of their cases reported, media are able to monitor courts and maintain acceptable surveillance by covering a few cases that can be hyped through angle biases. Such modest coverage gives judges control of their images while it gives audiences news values that they want or expect. More important, modest coverage allows media to cover cheaply the rare appeals that achieve news-worth and to save precious space and air time for more newsworthy and hence profitable coverage.

Thus do courts and media provide readers with reassurance, accessible and acceptable surveillance, and entertainment masquerading as information. Noncoverage assures widespread acquiescence because what almost all citizens do not know cannot arouse them. Judicial opinions, written to justify and to legitimize appellate decisions, dramatize formality and legality, especially when they are conveyed uncritically by journalists. Except when powerful groups or interests can break through the apparent formality and absence of information, readers and viewers get either reassuring reports or none at all. If readers and viewers believe the watchdog metaphor, they also get from their media reassurance that they are easily and readily fulfilling their duties as citizens to monitor courts. Reassurance and surveillance come easily and readily when news is made entertaining. News crafted by mass media to suit entertainment values will tend to skimp on appeals, for appeals will have less potential for entertainment than selected trials and Supreme Court landmarks.

Of course, entertainment potential is not an inherent or invariant quality of appellate decision making or of any political process. While appeals probably must be dauntingly technical and rigorous, appellate coverage could be augmented and enhanced if courts, media, and citizenry had incentives to do so. However, the hypothesized symbiosis persists because there are so few incentives to exit satisfactory relationships. Television news viewers habituated to arresting pictures, unchallenging angles, and recurrent fantasy themes have dozens of alternatives and soon will have hundreds of alternatives with which appellate news can never compete. As mass media grow ever more attentive to profits, edifying and upgrading the audience are foolhardy strategies, at least in the short-run calculations imposed by stockholders and accountants. Appeals judges who enjoy their autonomy and solitude are unlikely to want to exchange it for the hurly-burly of political institutions that cater to the press. If courts and media could make appellate news more accessible, it is difficult to imagine why they would.

Even if courts and media wanted to make appeals more accessible, it is not clear how they could. That is, the symbiosis that I am hypothesizing may follow far less from strategy than from structure. In many ways, the appellate process is structured to eliminate newsworth. To maintain judicial independence and jural rigor, judges are trained and admonished to blind themselves to drama and personality. Appellate opinions are supposed to resonate with Bench and Bar, not with Brokaw. A few trials and some Supreme Court cases achieve news-worth despite procedural limitations, but we have seen that appeals lack the lurid actions, suspenseful testimony, theatrical advocacy, and community concern of trials as well as the focus and finality of the High Court. Both strategy and structure, then, seem to incline appeals courts and news media to minimal coverage that suits the interests and structures of both sets of institutions.

Finally, the few brushes of appeals judges and courts with public scrutiny remind them of disincentives to make the news. When news is limited to the formal outputs of courts, judges have maximal image control. Once intracourt squabbles or extracourt pressures subject appellate judges to the rigors of media politics, judges find how little image control they can manage. Chief Justice Frank Celebrezze (defeated for reelection after a politicization of the Ohio Supreme Court), Chief Justice Rose Bird (defeated for reelection after a politicization of the California Supreme Court), Judge Robert Bork (denied confirmation to the U. S. Supreme Court after a politicization of his record), and Justice Clarence Thomas each can testify to the consequences of forsaking the security of judicial robes and rhetoric for the scrutiny of citizens and legislators. Ill-equipped for mass-mediated combat, appeals judges are well advised to stick to the arenas they command.

From our Outside-In Perspective, the hypothesized symbiosis represents judicial and journalistic collusion. Judges control their images and legitimize their rule with the complicity of cost conscious, indolent journalists. Courts mystify the population by strategic employment of myths, rituals, and symbols not only because media fail to contradict jural imagery, but also because media amplify and disseminate courts' mystifications. Little wonder, then, that appellate judges lament the paucity more than the superficiality of appellate coverage! Superficial coverage furthers mystification far more than critical or investigative coverage could. If, following our Outside-In Perspective, we assume that the mission of judges and courts is strategic imagery, uncritical reporting that mainly summarizes judicial opinions is all that judges could want. The judges would love more such doting coverage. However, the mission of journalists, according to the "outside" view, is inexpensive hype. Since trials and High Court cases will supply more hype and may be covered about as cheaply, reporters and editors may be very selective about covering other courts.

If Outside-Inners complain that the three-way symbiosis obstructs change, awareness, arousal, and demystification, Inside-Outers may respond that such obstructions undergird any stable judiciary and legal order. The hypothesized symbiosis guarantees that courts and media will regularly fulfill audiences' expectations and the missions specified by the Inside-Out Perspective. First, the insulation and isolation of appeals judges will incline them to write and rule for Bench and Bar. However much strategic imagery appellate judges wield, we should expect them to wield more when laypersons and political potentates are paying attention and less when only lawyers will know. Second, the occasional coverage adds so little to appellate outputs that it usually cannot help but be objective and accurate. Thus, the hypothesized symbiosis suits the "inside-out" media mission. Finally, the sparse, superficial coverage is designed to seize readers' and viewers' attention, so the symbiosis augments the attentive public of appeals courts beyond what it would otherwise be, albeit not to the degree that extreme versions of the Inside-Out Perspective might assume.

In sum, we have good reason to represent the interplay of courts, media, and publics as a symbiosis. That symbiosis can be understood and evaluated from each perspective. However, so sparse is information on coverage of appeals courts other than the Supreme Court that extensive research will need to reinforce the generalizations in this chapter before the symbiotic hypothesis may be advanced with any confidence. For now, the symbiotic hypothesis is the best way to make sense of the minimal knowledge we have.

Exemplary Coverage of Appellate Courts— An *En Banc* Controversy

Conflict in U. S. courts of appeals in the 1980s exemplifies how mass media neglect newsworthy stories by coverage that is inadequate or absent. However comfortable non-coverage may be for appeals judges and other officials, non-coverage costs citizens knowledge from which they might profit. A judicial controversy that went almost unnoticed outside academia will illustrate both the extent and the costs of noncoverage.

During the Reagan presidency, critics of the judiciary claimed that Reagan's appointees were abusing procedure to accomplish political goals. Clearly, political manipulation of appeals is news, even if the charges prove groundless. Moreover, members of the second most powerful court in the land, the Court of Appeals for the District of Columbia, publicly excoriated each other for misbehaving. Thus, not only was the story news, it was ready-made for publication. Yet, this judicial flap barely drew notice. Let's take a look at this example of ordinary noncoverage of appellate news.

The conflict concerned *en banc* rehearings of cases already decided by three-judge panels of circuit courts of appeals. To manage their caseload better, U. S. courts of appeals randomly assign panels of three judges from the court to decide cases. Only in cases of "exceptional importance"[37] may a majority of the judges on a circuit court of appeals vote to rehear the case *en banc*—that is, with all of the judges sitting in on the case. When an *en banc* rehearing is voted, the original decision is deleted and the appeal is reargued.

In 1987, the Court of Appeals for the District of Columbia erupted after a conservative majority on the court had voted for eleven *en banc* rehearings in the first half of the year, three times the usual rate of rehearings. Judge Laurence H. Silberman, a Reagan appointee, voted with five judges appointed by Democrats to stop *en banc* rehearings of three cases in July. Those judges outvoted five Reagan appointees who wanted to rehear the cases. Clashing judges then issued their opinions.[38]

Judge Edwards, in an opinion joined by the other Democrat-appointees, suggested that "dissenters would like to rehear Bartlett *en banc* so that they might create some 'sweeping and revolutionary' new law in the area of constitutional adjudication. This would be a gross abuse of the *en banc* process."[39] Judge Edwards also attacked the "self-serving and result-oriented" reasoning of the dissenters and their specious characterization and flagrant mischaracterization of precedent. Judge Edwards continued, "Underlying the dissenters' calls for rehearings *en banc* . . . is the implicit view that every time a majority of the judges disagree with a panel decision, they should get rid of it by rehearing the case *en banc*."[40] He then concluded with an ominous prediction:

> Collegiality cannot exist if every dissenting judge feels obliged to lobby his or her colleagues to rehear the case *en banc* in order to vindicate that judge's position. Politicking will replace the thoughtful dialogue that should characterize a court where

every judge respects the integrity of his or her colleagues. Furthermore, such a process would impugn the integrity of panel judges, who are both intelligent enough to know the law and conscientious enough to abide by their oath to uphold it.[41]

The few press reports of this squabble did not miss the thinly veiled charge that the conservative judges appointed by Reagan were playing politics with the *en banc* process.

This charge the dissenters denied in an extensive and scholarly opinion that nonetheless managed to suggest that the decisions reinstated were so wrong and so ominous that *en banc* rehearings were necessary. While the dissenters did suggest that one of the decisions was "sweeping and revolutionary . . . quite aside from its gratuitous dicta concerning congressional power over the Supreme Court's jurisdiction," their tone was very judicious (the better, the Carter appointees might note, to deny any political motivation). However, Judge Kenneth Starr (later to become a special prosecutor for Whitewater) suggested that the decision not to rehear the cases *en banc* was dangerous:

> . . . [I]t is destabilizing and unseemly for courts, which should be solid rock in a world filled with rolling stones, to lurch suddenly from one course to another. . . . [I]t is, in my judgment, unwise to tear asunder in one mighty blow that which was duly considered and decided upon after careful reflection by the full court. It is quite unlikely that a "mistake," which obviously could infect the exercise of judgment as to one case, would suddenly spread with prairie-fire speed to consume three cases of significance.[42]

If ever the output of a U. S. court of appeals had news-worth, this public, political brawl was the one. "Liberal" judges who had run the D. C. court of appeals for years now confronted an ascendent "conservative" majority bent on redressing rulings of which they disapproved. More, the ideological clash occurred in public, in opinions to which any journalist had ready access. Some declarations were intemperate and transparent, stripped of legal jargon.

This news competed with little else that sleepy August, except perhaps the nomination of Judge Robert H. Bork, of the very same court of appeals, to the Supreme Court. Judge Bork was one of the Reagan appointees who had voted to rehear the cases *en banc*. Judge Bork and President Reagan had called for judges to abjure politics and stick to the law. Now liberal judges accused Judge Bork and his ideological soulmates of precisely the judicial politicking that Judge Bork and President Reagan had denounced.

Despite its obvious news-worth, I found but three references to this extraordinary event in U. S. newspapers:[43] one each in the *Washington Post*, the *Wall Street Journal*, and the *New York Times*. The day after the opinions were filed, the *Post* devoted part of its front page and 1,012 words to the controversy:

> A long-simmering split in the U.S. Court of Appeals here erupted into a public squabble yesterday, with liberal members of the court accusing their conservative colleagues of deciding cases by majority rule instead of rule of law.
>
> The conservatives countered that the liberals don't know an important case when they see one.[44]

The following Monday, in its first edition since the news broke, the *Wall Street Journal* noted the controversy and explained its nation-wide ramifications.

> Sharp ideological differences flared publicly in one of the nation's most important courts, the U. S. Court of Appeals for the District of Columbia. . . .
>
> The actions represent an unusual public display of politics in judicial decision making. They also demonstrate the increasing polarization occurring in the country's federal appeals courts, . . .[45]

The author then suggested that squabbling over *en banc* rehearings and other decisions was hardly limited to the D. C. court, a news flash otherwise available only to those who read the *Wall Street Journal*, law journals, or law books.[46]

The *New York Times* mentioned the incident two weeks later as part of a story about another D. C. court of appeals case. Judge Abner J. Mikva, a Carter appointee, issued a dissent that accused his two "conservative" colleagues on an affirmative action case of ravaging and distorting the law. Judge Kenneth W. Starr, writing for himself and his fellow Republican appointee, characterized Judge Mikva's dissent as feverish. To contextualize this incident, the reporter recalled the earlier incident:

> The decision dramatizes the deep split between the six Reagan appointees and the five Democratic-appointed judges

on the appeals court, which was long dominated by liberals until Mr. Reagan tipped the balance. The long-simmering feud had previously erupted in an extraordinary series of opinions by the full eleven-member court on July 31.[47]

I found, however, that this "extraordinary series of opinions" had not achieved notice in the *New York Times* before this date, nor did this self-proclaimed "newspaper of record" note that similar divisions were occurring in other U. S. appeals courts.

Nor did my searches disclose reports of the opinions in any other newspapers. Despite the public charges of partisan or ideological judging, despite the role of Supreme Court nominee Judge Bork in the *en banc* flaps, and despite the ready availability of the story to any subscriber to the *Post* or *Times* news services and any reader of the *Wall Street Journal* or the *Washington Post*, this clearly newsworthy story became a nonstory through noncoverage. Discussions in legal media, books, and law reviews persisted because this story was clearly significant, not just for the D. C. court of appeals, but for a federal judiciary increasingly dominated by nominees of President Reagan and, thus, for all citizens.[48]

However, a similar search led me to dozens of notices of *Steffan v. Aspin* (1993), a decision by three Carter appointees on the D. C. circuit court of appeals that ruled unconstitutional the ban on homosexuals in the military. Although the policy considered by the court was now so obsolete that the Clinton administration would choose not even to appeal to salvage that policy, the story derived news-worth from the administration's fight over gays in the military and from Mr. Steffan's personal and dramatic struggle against an indifferent or hostile military bureaucracy. As a result, *Steffan* made better theater and was covered while the *en banc* controversy, with its national implications, was not covered.

I do not contrast *Steffan* with the *en banc* skirmish merely to show that "derivative news-worth" elicits coverage for intrinsically less law-worthy cases while more important news goes largely unnoticed. In addition, I use *Steffan* to underscore the superficiality of coverage when it comes. *Steffan* was decided by the only three liberal judges left on the D. C. court of appeals. It was decided eight years to the date after the same court had upheld the Navy's right to discharge a homosexual.[49] The three judges who awarded Steffan a victory had dissented from the earlier decision. More, conservatives complained that three important civil liberties cases in the last thirteen months had been decided by these three remaining liberals without any of the eight judges appointed by Presidents Reagan or Bush participating.[50] In short, the ideological polarization of the Court of Appeals for the District of Columbia Circuit—commonly reckoned the second most important court in the nation—continues to be a story that is barely covered.

The *Steffan* case deserved to be covered and was, but with its derivative features center stage and its political and legal importance unremarked or barely mentioned. The *en banc* controversy likewise demanded coverage if the watchdog were to do its job. Only three newspapers mentioned it. *Steffan* and the *en banc* cases exemplify superficial coverage and noncoverage respectively.

Theoretical Scorecard

Now we must attempt to explain noncoverage of appeals other than those in the U. S. Supreme Court. I have argued that commercial biases and angle biases make sense of noncoverage. The predominance of such noncoverage would seem to render the Inside-Out Perspective less pertinent to almost all appeals than we should prefer. However, I have also claimed that these two sets of biases do little to support the three Outside-In Perspectives examined so far. Where does that leave us?

What the Inside-Out Perspective Accounts For

I have salvaged the Inside-Out Perspective in this chapter only by amending it severely. The four generalizations extracted from the literature contradict "objective accuracy," the media's mission posited by the Inside-Out Perspective in table I.1 in the Introduction. Instead, media exhibit *selective acuity*. When appeals conform or can be conformed to angle biases or commercial biases, cases may be covered superficially and efficiently due to the media's eye for dramatic, personalized, normalized, and morselized details and for profit. However, many politically, socially, and legally important details will escape the media. If we try to excuse this selective acuity by the suggestion that only angle-biased coverage will attract mass scrutiny, then we must modify the Inside-Out characterization of the audience as "extensively attentive" because coverage is tailored to uninformed, unsophisticated tastes. More, we must adjust the mission of the appellate judge—craft and candor—because judicial outputs are targeted at Bench and Bar and not at the mass public. If appeals judges profit from noncoverage, as our symbiotic hypothesis suggests, then the craft and candor posited by the Inside-Out Perspective and the strategic imagery posited by our Outside-In Perspective are usually indistinguishable.

Why save the Inside-Out view at all? I propose to keep the mainstream perspective at the ready because those rare cases that are covered will be covered about as accurately and objectively as reasonable observers of mass media can expect. While noncoverage overwhelms coverage, I know of no study that suggests that coverage is inadequate, inaccurate, or otherwise substandard. Indeed, I have reiterated the finding that most legally astute observers, albeit in a small sample, found the quality of reports of appeals to be acceptable. The minimal quantity of coverage, when it comes, apparently is quality coverage.

What the Outside-In Perspective Accounts For

Our Outside-In Perspective anticipates symbiotic relations among courts, the press, and audiences but, as I observed at the start of this chapter, it explains too little. Appellate coverage little resembles the inexpensive hype expected by our Outside-In Perspective. Angle biases may foster some hype, but most coverage is acceptable to at least some jural audiences. Noncoverage saves money and conserves profits, but virtually any student of mass media expects coverage to be circumscribed by costs and space. I have already remarked that appellate opinions often elude most reporters because well crafted, candid opinions aimed at the legally astute will amount to strategic imagery. That is, such appellate opinions force reporters to choose between noncoverage and coverage in judges' preferred terms. Either way, judges can insulate themselves from citizens in cocoons of jural argot. This does, of course, minimize the portion of the audience capable of understanding opinions, which makes the audience for appellate courts mostly inadvertent, as the Outside-In Perspective predicts. The exceptions that we discovered in the literature—when politics in appeals courts results in public flaps that derive news-worth from elections and politicians—may spur appellate courts to avoid candor about judicial politics lest the symbiosis of noncoverage temporarily break down, but that contradicts the Inside-Out Perspective more than it supports the Outside-In Perspective.

I hasten to add the lesson I draw from the *en banc* controversy: breakdowns must be chronic and vivid to overcome the media's usual indifference, so even flawed imagery will almost always secure the noncoverage to which appeals judges have become accustomed. This example provides little support for either the Scalia model of journalistic distortion or the Davis model of judicial mystification. While I do believe that noncoverage deprives citizens of knowledge, I cannot declare that to be distortion. And how may I infer mystification when judges send out so few messages to any public other than legal elites?

Table 3.1   Table 1.1 with Noncoverage Included

	When cases have no news-worth	When cases are less newsworthy		When cases are most newsworthy
When cases are legally most routine	**S Y M B I**	*Mainstream Standards:* The Inside-Out Perspective better explains both judges and reporters than our Outside-In Perspective.		*Media Distortion:* The Inside-Out Perspective better explains judges, but our Outside-In Perspective better explains reporters.
When cases are legally most challenging	**O S I S**	*Jural Mystification:* Our Outside-In Perspective better explains judges, but the Inside-Out Perspective better explains reporters.		*Dual Pragmatism:* Our Outside-In Perspective best explains both judges and reporters.

Still Another Perspective?

We must remember how inchoate the literature on appeals courts remains. So sketchy and dated are the findings on which I have depended that all four of the intersections that I discussed in chapter 1 remain possibilities. Indeed, my review of studies persuades me of a fifth possibility. The Symbiotic Hypothesis partakes of some contentions of Outside-In perspectives but focuses on noncoverage rather than on coverage. As indicated in table 3.1, we may revise table 1.1 to account for symbiotic noncoverage.

When cases are at least somewhat newsworthy, we anticipate the same tendencies as we hypothesized in table 1.1. As in table 1.1, legally uncomplicated cases with at least minimal news-worth (that is, angles or commercial value) may be covered and, if covered, will be covered so concisely that "Mainstream Standards" for accuracy, balance, and objectivity will largely be met. As legally unimposing cases become more and more newsworthy (for example, their angles increase in number or variety or both), they secure more coverage but the very notoriety of the case encourages sensationalism or other forms of media distortion introduced earlier. If, instead, minimally newsworthy cases pose questions or puzzles that task the legally astute, in table 1.1 we hypothesized that conditions were right for "Jural Mystification": any coverage would be relatively brief and would tend to relay what authorities, especially judges and justices in the majority, had decided. Our final expectation in table 1.1 was that the cases that demanded coverage for *both* their law-worth *and* their news-worth would tend to be sensationalized by reporters and "sanitized" by judges. In sum, we hypothesized that the most reported cases would likely be subject to the missions attributed to judges and press by Outside-In Perspectives, a condition that I labeled "Dual Pragmatism" earlier.

After that brief review of table 1.1, it should be apparent that table 3.1 merely adds a possibility. Suppose that cases have very little or no news-worth. That is, they seem to match neither commercial nor content biases. In that case, the symbiotic non-coverage that I have discussed may be expected to prevail, whatever the law-worth of the event, decision, or case. For routine appeals and ordinary decisions, such noncoverage matters little. I have noted more than once that a watchdog that barks at every motion is worse than useless. However, when an argument or a writ is fraught with legal or social consequence but is neglected or ignored because the press cannot find angles, profit, or space for the report, the symbiosis disguises the discretion of courts and media alike. We have hypothesized above what payoffs such a symbiosis might have for news makers and decision makers. I only want to add that this symbiosis seems to me especially pertinent when judges must stand for reelection. Under such conditions, we shall see in chapter 6, the anonymity that noncoverage affords the judges may be very valuable indeed.

However, I suggest caution in wielding this new hypothetical possibility. Judges, we have seen, are reportedly fairly satisfied with the *quality* of their coverage but disappointed in its *quantity*. That dichotomous datum, should it hold up in additional studies, issues at least two implications. A defender of the Inside-Out viewpoint might note this datum as evidence that judges are *not* implicated in any symbiotic relation with the press. The judges want more coverage even though the Symbiotic Hypothesis that I have crafted above posits their professional interest in less coverage. An Outside-Inner might rebut this first implication with a second: of course judges tend to like the *quality* of their coverage; four of the five expectations in table 3.1 redound to the benefit of the judges; little wonder that they would like more such advantageous and unthreatening coverage when the majority of their activities draw no coverage at all.

As always, I urge you to take a "both/and" stance. Symbioses probably work better the less aware that each symbiont is of its benefits to the other. The symbiosis that I have created to explain the skimpy research on appeals courts other than the U. S. Supreme Court need not be conscious. Perhaps relations would break down if symbiont reporters and judges saw their relations as I have represented them. Nonetheless, what research we have suggests that noncoverage overwhelms coverage to the benefit of media and courts alike.

The only certain conclusion we reach at the end of this chapter is that the media watchdog is at best a peculiar pet with regard to appeals. We have seen that the dog's vigilance is so spotty that we can save the Inside-Out Perspective only by compromising its tenets until it almost converges with our Outside-In Perspective. Indeed, the idealistic possibilities of earlier chapters survive this chapter only as a façade behind which the other possibilities hide. Outside-In Perspectives seem better suited to findings but the pragmatism and symbiosis they predict leave us with a media watchdog that responds to rewards from courts to give the kind of scrutiny that they welcome. A watchdog who works for those whom we want to monitor is worse than useless because such a pooch lulls us into false security. The alternative perspectives of Davis and Justice Scalia demean the watchdog as well. Justice Scalia believes that the watchdog is so easily befuddled that we should put the dog to tasks suited to canine discrimination—watching politicians, for instance. Davis sees the watchdog as a judicial lapdog whom cunning judges can feed and whom citizens therefore ought not to trust.

CHAPTER 4

Covering
Criminal Justice

In this chapter I shall argue that coverage of criminal courts tends to conform to expectations derived from *both* the Inside-Out Perspective *and* our Outside-In Perspective and, thus, tends to confound expectations derived from either perspective alone. We shall consider the possibility *both* that courts and reporters tend to measure up to mainstream standards *and* that two ironies of court coverage compel us to combine expectations from the Inside-Out Perspective and our Outside-In Perspective to explain how media report criminal adjudication. I shall claim that these two ironies reinforce the advisability of the "both/and" approach that I urge throughout this book.

Irony One: *most coverage of criminal courts fulfills mainstream standards but the cases most covered fulfill mainstream expectations least.* Most criminal justice cases are not covered at all. Of the few covered, almost all are relegated to news briefs and spot news that meet mainstream standards and achieve the accuracy and objectivity expected of media by the Inside-Out Perspective. However, the very few cases covered extensively will often detour judges and reporters from standardized coverage toward the expedient hype that the Outside-In Perspective predicts. It follows from this first irony that criminal court coverage confounds expectations drawn from one or another perspective because different perspectives best explain different styles of coverage.

Irony Two: *routine reporting tends to emphasize "Crime-Control" values, while extraordinary reporting is much more likely to feature "Due Process."* We might expect reports of routine criminal adjudication to abound with the values and principles distinctive of judges and lawyers: concern for procedural regularities, attention to rules of law, debates about legal ethics, and so on. If we look at coverage of criminal courts, however, we find that routine reports often play down such values and often play up competing values, such as security from wrongdoers, just deserts, and punishment. Sensationalized stories will tend to secure space sufficient to explore procedural issues, questions, and resolutions. This may imply that coverage according to mainstream standards tends to give procedural values short shrift while less frequent media distortions tend to feature due process more prominently. That is the second irony.

Your job is to pay close attention to see if I can make these two ironies clear. If I can and do, you must accede to the wisdom of seeing coverage of criminal justice from more than one point of view, for neither perspective alone permits you to fathom the ironies of criminal court coverage. However, remember that propositions and hypotheses adduced must be tentative. While we are blessed with solid studies of the reporting of criminal courts, our theoretical synthesis must anticipate further studies. Our reach in this chapter will exceed our grasp.

Symbiosis, Source-ery, and Routine Coverage

Journalists on law enforcement beats (crime reporters) and journalists on court beats (court reporters) cultivate relationships with regulars on beats in ways that exemplify both symbiosis and source-ery, discussed in chapter 1. Such relationships bombard reporters with views from insiders in law enforcement and legal institutions, encourage reporters to cover some aspects of the news more than others, and ease reporters' burdens when they report in ways that insiders prefer. Attentive readers will immediately deduce that symbioses and source-ery thereby insure both incentives for reporters to take the inside view and disincentives to seek information outside the usual rounds. Because symbiosis and source-ery tend to normalize most court and crime coverage to suit Inside-Out assumptions, Inside-Out assumptions (see table I.1 about judicial craft and candor and about journalistic accuracy and objectivity) will tend to shape journalistic routines. Let us examine each factor that molds court coverage to mainstream standards.

Symbiotic Relations Between Reporters and Sources

Crime reporters routinely rely on police officers, police officials, and the police bureaucracy as sources. Law enforcement officials routinely rely on reporters to amplify and to spread law enforcement messages.[1] Such reliance and routine reliability create symbiosis, the mutually beneficial relations among journalists and sources that I discussed in chapter 1 and applied to appeals courts in chapter 3. An observer recently described this symbiosis:

> [Newspapers and police] both need each other and both are partners (not necessarily equal) in the process of news construction and dissemination. The partnership may be that of the rider and the horse and which is which may depend on the issues involved, the presentation of these issues and the interpretation of news by the public. But the media need the police to furnish their programmes [sic] and publications with entertainment and information while the police need the media to gain and maintain support and seek the help of the public in their detection of crime or the presentation of their arduous duties. Many senior officers of the police believe that police image is everything and the media can be "a very good friend and a very bad enemy."[2]

For similar reasons, court officials and especially court clerks[3] must assist the press if they are to tend the image of their courts.[4] Court reporters must cultivate sources in the court bureaucracy to produce news predictably and efficiently.[5] From reciprocal needs and assistance symbioses grow. As veteran court reporter Lyle Denniston put the matter:

> A community cannot monitor its courts, judges, prosecutors, lawyers, and police if its information about the legal system is unreliable or inaccurate. The journalist and the legal professional, then, must work as partners not adversaries in the pursuit of this information. A legal reporter's information is no better than his sources, and there will be few good sources in the law for a reporter who is seen as a careless and uninformed adversary.[6]

Even astute court reporters will routinely require interpretations and confirmations, so they must rely on court insiders for assistance.[7] Indeed, court reporters become astute in part by learning the points of access, information, focus, and confirmation that are most likely to yield stories and details in a cost effective manner.[8] Court sources make manageable sprawling "justice beats," one of which included thirty-six state and local judges and their staffs; seventy-two attorneys in the county attorney's office and twenty in the city attorney's office; fifty public defenders; about twenty private criminal defense attorneys; fifteen private attorneys; court administration staff; the U. S. attorney's office (twelve prosecutors); four federal judges and their staffs; three federal magistrates; bankruptcy court; the FBI; the Drug Enforcement Administration; the Secret Service; clerks in federal law enforcement and judicial offices; bar associations; the Minnesota Supreme Court (although he generally relies on AP coverage of it); the state Lawyers Professional Responsibility Board; and the state Board on Judicial Standards.[9]

Source-ery among Court Reporters

Symbiotic exchanges between court reporters and court bureaucrats will tend to draw court reporters inside the court bureaucracy, usually insuring favorable coverage to courts. Lawyer-novelist Charles Sevilla overstated the matter but indicated a thoroughly outside view when he attacked

> the rule of indolence which prevailed with the reporters who covered the courts. Most of them were spoon-fed all of their news from the press releases or authorized "leaks" of information from the DAs or the cops. This they gobbled uncritically, digested, and regurgitated to their papers as news.[10]

Just as police sources manage their images in mass media by cultivating relationships with crime reporters, so too do court sources "feed" court reporters, and thus the news is largely what the reporters have "eaten."

Reliance on sources, we saw in chapter 1, often leads to source-ery, the journalistic practice of citing sources to validate or authenticate inherently subjective or partial reports. Sources make stories seem factual because quotations and paraphrases are presumed by many readers to be fairly accurate: Senator A may be wrong in expressing opinion B, but Senator A's expression of opinion B is a social fact. Source-ery transforms subjective, partial, and even outrageous views into reasonably accurate and apparently objective accounts of happenings. How accurate and objective accounts truly are depends on how eclectic and representative the sources are. The narrower the range of sources habitually cited, the fewer the perspectives routinely represented in the press.[11]

One court reporter phrased a consequence of source-ery pungently: ". . . after too long on the beat, a reporter either hates all his sources or becomes one of them, writing for them."[12] The longer the reporter endures the court beat, the more that cooperation must outweigh conflict. Inexperienced court reporters rely on court sources to learn the beat and to file copy of sufficient quality and quantity to stay employed, thereby incurring debts to sources and accruing reasons to rely on the kindness of sources. As they gain experience, reporters are likely to assimilate at least some of the views of insiders. If reporters do not incorporate such views, sources are likely to complain that reporters show bias, animosity, or poor news sense. That means that insiders' views create baselines against which reports are judged. We expect veteran court reporters, then, to share many of their sources' views of law and law enforcement. Since insiders' views do not exhaust the perspectives available, court reporters will tend to reinforce, amplify, and disseminate insiders' perspectives at the expense of alternative perspectives. That is court source-ery. That is also how source-ery and symbiosis may conform news about criminal courts to mainstream standards.

In at least one respect, court reporters are even more reliant on a narrow range of sources than most beat reporters. The law is more esoteric than most domains that mass media routinely cover, in part because legal processes and argumentation are seldom crafted for lay understanding. Court reporters must hurdle legal technicalities if they are to be credible to key sources[13]: "The journalist who is truly trained in the law . . . will be quite fully accepted, most of the time, by his sources on the beat. He may be a good deal more efficient in getting to the core of legal or judicial developments." Since court reporters rely on legal insiders far more than on parties to litigation,[14] insiders shape court reporting.

Journalistic Routines

Symbioses and source-ery remind us that routine relations among bureaucrats, media, and officials develop and adapt to suit the self-images and norms of each group. Routine relations not only "fit" professional and political imagery and norms; ordinary practices display or dramatize images and missions. As a result, daily court journalism is designed to meet mainstream standards. Let us examine briefly two examples of how mainstream standards for law and journalism shape court reporters' practices and values.

Bureaucratic Stages Preformulate Routine Coverage

Mark Fishman has shown that reporters and officials whom they cover tend to interpret the world in ways distinctive of their professions.[15] In my terms, professionals and specialists adopt habitual perspectives. Beat reporters, Fishman found, tend to validate or objectify their reports by fitting those reports within the perspectives characteristic of official, authoritative sources, a routine that I have related to symbiosis and source-ery. Fishman followed a reporter on the justice beat and showed how that reporter suited stories to the perspectives of law enforcement and judicial organizations and officials. Fishman's findings show how sources' perspectives shape court journalism.

Organizing court reporters' beats into "rounds" (that is, scheduled stops and sources regularly consulted by a beat reporter) insures that they will learn of key events, but they still must interpret events to create news stories. Fishman found that the justice reporter whom he followed had absorbed the "phases" of legal agencies and officials.[16] While any web of experience that resulted in a court proceeding would warrant perhaps dozens of stories and angles of view, court reporters tended to organize their stories in keeping with the sequence and duration of events dictated by law enforcement and judicial agencies. Accepting the agencies' official, formal, and routine division of legal stories into discrete but related stages (an aspect of what I have called morselization), beat reporters then extracted stories with sufficient news-worth to fill a news hole.

As a result, Fishman found, "journalists simply do not expose themselves regularly to unofficial interpretive schemes."[17] That generalization applied with particular force to Fishman's justice reporter:

> [T]he justice reporter steered clear of suspects, victims, and their families on his round. The only routine occasion in which the reporter was exposed to the suspect's version of events was during formal court hearings. But these were settings in which the suspect's version necessarily had been reformulated through an attorney to fit the legal-bureaucratic definition of events. In general, reporters in courtrooms will seek out lawyers, not their clients, as news sources.[18]

Court reporters rely extensively on official files and other legal documents that incorporate the same stages, formal perspectives, and words that lawyers and judges employ in the courtroom.[19] Reporters on the legal beat encounter events and actions in neatly preformulated phases and cases. This is a species of normalization of news. That busy reporters and harried editors do not reorder such preformulated stories cannot surprise us!

If Fishman is correct, we should not wonder if routine reporting tends to portray legal officials and agencies as fulfilling their missions. Since most events come to reporters preformulated to suit agencies' and officials' ideals, reporters will seldom be assisted or encouraged to see aspects of stories that contradict ideals. Official or agency deviations from ideals or norms might be newsworthy if perceived and reported, but preformulation of phases will tend to make deviations hard to see, harder to document (or source), and almost impossible to defend as accurate and unbiased.

Even this brief survey of Fishman's rich analysis inclines me to expect that the "Mainstream Standards" intersection of insiders' images of courts and news media (see the upper-left cell of table 1.1) describes most coverage of courts because courts—that is, judges, staff, and other sources—preformulate most events and outputs to which reporters have access. Courts create cases to match courts' formal mission. More, their creations then shape news coverage so that reporters may most easily, efficiently, and quickly cover court news by beginning from judicial and legal formulations. Coverage that contradicts or unmasks legal forms will be vulnerable to attack for inaccuracy and bias. All legal reporting must be at least somewhat imprecise and informal if readers are to fathom stories, so reporters will almost always be open to charges of inaccuracy. All reports inconsistent with official accounts will seem to take a party's or other outsider's side against officials, subjecting the press to official suspicions of bias. To match "Mainstream Standards" for accuracy and objectivity, then, reporters and editors will usually have to adhere to an official "line."

We must wonder, then, not that criminal court coverage approximates "Mainstream Standards" for courts and the press. We should be amazed only if any mass medium routinely departed from the safety and predictability of such normalized coverage. Journalistic routines build on agencies' routines to insure that coverage will be regarded by powerful sources and audiences as accurate, objective, credible, and intelligible.

Bureaucratic Values

If authorities tend to enshrine values chosen by bureaucratic routines, then reporters who treat those routines as objective facts tend to bolster those values. As a result, certain legal values influence court coverage more than other legal values. For this reason, I hypothesize that court coverage tends to reflect crime control values more than due process values. Let me define each set of values.

Crime control and due process values define an ambivalence that courts, police, reporters, and some attentive citizens share in the United States.[20] Because all parties share the ambivalence, they all value crime control and they all value due process. However, various parties and citizens are likely to disagree about priorities assigned to the sets of values when they conflict.

Table 4.1   **Crime-Control and Due Process Perspectives**

	Crime Control	Due Process
Primary Values	Efficiency Celerity Certainty	Formality Deliberation Appellate Review
Defendants' Status	Presumed guilty	Presumed innocent
Preferred Actors	Police and prosecutors	Defense attorneys and appeals judges
Metaphor	Assembly line	Obstacle course

Crime control values proceed from the importance of suppressing crime in an efficient, speedy, and certain manner. Efficiency dictates that police and prosecutors, given their funding, maximize rates of apprehension, conviction, and punishment. Speed justifies avoiding lengthy, formal proceedings in favor of expedited processing such as plea bargaining. Certainty demands that appeals and other delays of punishment be minimized. Crime control values proceed from the high probability that police and prosecutors would have abandoned a suspect if he[21] were not guilty. Herbert Packer labeled this the "presumption of guilt." Proponents of a relatively crime control perspective place more confidence in police and prosecutors than in defense attorneys and adjudication.[22] Their concept of criminal justice resembles an assembly line or conveyor that should be halted or slowed seldom and then only for the most compelling reasons.

Due process values, in contrast, emphasize the importance of affording the accused every opportunity to get off or impede the criminal justice conveyor belt. Those most sensitive to the propensity of police and prosecutors to err are likely to stress formality over efficiency and to insist on appellate review of convictions to preserve individual rights and security from crime control corner-cutting. While those who take relatively due process positions may agree that almost all persons charged are in fact guilty of criminal conduct, their skepticism of the process and concern for the accused moves them to insist that the presumption of innocence guide formal processes.

Since the crime control bureaucracy routinely interacts with mass media more than advocates of due process do, journalistic routines should be expected to bias reporters and reports toward crime control more than toward due process. Crime control values tend to shape the reporting and definition of stories because law enforcement sources impart that view[23] long before lawyers attempt to redefine the stories during formal procedures. In addition, crime control bureaucracies tend to control scheduling more than agents of due process.

Why might court reporters be more likely to absorb and to amplify crime control values than due process values? First, crime control is far easier to understand for reporters, their editors, and their audiences. Struggles between cops and robbers, good guys and bad guys, protectors and perpetrators are easy to write, to source, and to read or to view. Arcane rules and technicalities elude readers and viewers, many of whom have no idea what the rules are or what they mean. Crime control tends to be less expensive to cover than due process, so crime control tends to suit news media's commercial biases better as well. Routinely, law enforcement sources want to be covered, beat reporters are adept and experienced covering them, and there is a ready market for police coverage, as episodes of *Cops* demonstrate.[24] Crime coverage better suits audiences' tastes than the social significance of individual crimes, polls on most significant social problems, or crime statistics.[25]

Crime control caters to angle biases better than due process does. Normalization, morselization, and dramatization[26] in crime and criminal court coverage match news themes to audiences' beliefs and fantasies.[27] Vicious crimes and consequent trials dramatize stories, so violence is overreported while other crimes and trials are underreported.[28] Most crimes and almost all trials are self-contained, which may serve morselization better than many due process issues.[29] Stories about crime are easily normalized, with police and prosecutorial jargon making the themes and angles of stories familiar or predictable, if not interchangeable.[30]

Third, judges, staff, and attorneys are bound by legal ethics to avoid using publicity and news media to interfere with processes of law and justice.[31]

For all three reasons, we should expect crime control coverage to outweigh due process coverage. If so, accuracy and objectivity will, in practice, favor certain widespread values over other widespread values due to symbioses, source-ery, and journalistic routines. Norms for accurate, objective reporting accommodate jural, journalistic, and popular expectations so that court coverage ordinarily satisfies most observers.

Normalization

We have seen how court coverage accommodates the needs, norms, and values of courts and press alike, so we should expect routine court coverage to match insiders' perspectives on the missions of the courts and the press. Let us conclude by reviewing how symbiosis, source-ery, and journalistic routines may generate normalization.

Routine normalization follows directly from symbiotic relations between court reporters and courts. Each party to the relationship anticipates and meets ordinary, predictable needs of the other. Court personnel provide information to familiar reporters based on newsworth, knowledge of the sorts of stories that reporters habitually cover and newspapers usually print. Courts and their personnel have strong incentives to suit such free information to their institutional image, so symbiosis tends to normalize. In turn, reporters try to cooperate if sources cooperate but get aggressive if sources will not cooperate. When sources are fecund and habitual, reporters protect sources while conveying sources' information to readers and viewers.[32]

Normalization also results from source-ery, although court reporting introduces us to a different sort of source driven reporting from that discussed in chapter 1. Court reporters tend to rely on official records more than on court or court officials. Direct observation in courtrooms is too inefficient, so court-beat reporters gather most news and spend most of their day outside courtrooms.[33] While court reporters rely on interviews, informal discussions, and tips, court documents are the most important sources.[34] Drechsel's survey indicated that, on average, 49 percent of reporters' information came from documents, 28 percent from observation of proceedings, and 20 percent from interviewing.[35] Court reporters normalize court news, then, because they routinely treat official files, formal briefings, and officials speaking on the record as facts that require no further research.[36] Since canons of objectivity prohibit reporters from leavening official accounts with reporters' doubts, analyses, or inferences, it follows that news briefs, spot news, and wire-service stories will tend to track official documents. This will especially be so when the demands on reporters—deadlines, small news holes, multiple stories—deprive reporters of the time and resources necessary to supplement or supplant official accounts.

Criminal courts, it follows, may safely expect routines of court reporting to build on courts' self-images because court reporters usually depend on legal documents. Officials tend to disclaim any ambitions to spin[37] (that is, to interpret events in ways favorable to officials or their superiors) in part because official records spin stories the way officials prefer.

After immersion in formal documents and the automatic spin cycle, beat reporters may rely heavily on court clerks for tips and favors, which means that clerks have opportunity as well as motive to normalize news.[38] While reporters strive to maintain independence, they need assistance to do their jobs well but have little that courthouse staff need, want, or could use. As a result, reporters are not equipped to resist much of the normalization that court staff are employed to render.[39] Drechsel's reporter admitted that he dared not alienate courthouse sources,[40] from which Drechsel inferred that sources and reporters engage in implicit exchanges: sources gave tips, interpretations, and reactions in return for objective or flattering coverage of their courts.[41]

Judges and attorneys usually need not to respond to negative coverage if the local bar association or other colleagues stand ready to reinforce formality as image and reality.[42] When such sources speak to reporters, they expect competent and complimentary coverage that reinforces the formality and normality of proceedings.[43]

Routine Criminal Trial Coverage Meets Mainstream Standards

We have reviewed reasons to expect most court coverage to meet mainstream standards and to propagate sources' images of criminal proceedings. Now we review evidence to support that expectation. This supporting evidence confirms part of the first irony noted at the beginning of this chapter: most coverage of criminal courts fulfills mainstream standards. Having shown that such is the case, I shall examine the two ironies in later sections.

Routine Coverage Is Accurate, Objective, Episodic, and Selective

Courts strive to insure coverage that highlights the formal and judicial. Journalists tend to generate coverage that is as accurate—that is, authenticated by citation to official authorities—and as objective— that is, legitimated by location within routine bounds—as mainstream journalistic standards demand. Routine coverage tends to be acceptably accurate and objective in part because court coverage is very selective: the fewer the cases reported and the less reported for each case, the fewer the situations that threaten accuracy or objectivity as mainstream journalists define those ideals.

Drechsel discovered by following a reporter on a justice beat that the reporter covered startlingly little of court activities. For example, of sixty-nine cases available one day, this reporter filed spot news on none.[44] Doppelt confirmed the paucity of coverage: in May 1987, the *Chicago Tribune* and the *Chicago Sun-Times* averaged five court stories per day, counting all trial and appellate courts.[45] Thus, we must never forget that *the most routine coverage of criminal trials is no coverage at all.*

The few cases covered tend to elicit news briefs and spot news, in court news[46] as in crime news.[47] Drechsel estimated that most court reporters spend a majority of their time reporting spot news and that very few reporters lavish much time on features or other extended treatments of the work of courts.[48] In addition, coverage of legal processes is especially episodic because courts approach their work in discrete cases.[49]

Selective, episodic coverage is forced on reporters. First, we have seen that the justice beat may be immense.[50] Second, court reporters tend to be far less experienced than most of the officials and sources with whom they deal,[51] so many cannot supplement their sources to cover more cases. Third, daily deadlines circumscribe even veteran reporters' ability, inclination, and resources to provide broader, richer context for reports of cases.[52] Fourth, canons of objectivity and balance, exacerbated by routine source-ery and symbiosis, tend to deplete the details that court reporters may relay to readers. Fifth, editors in charge of a shrinking news hole will eliminate any unnecessary details or stories.[53]

We expect editors and reporters to select stories and details to report based on routines that cater to and were long ago shaped by sources, journalistic norms, and markets. Routine selections should satisfy mainstream standards. Features of court happenings that might compromise or contradict such standards are more likely to be omitted than aspects that at least appear to conform to norms for court coverage. While selected episodes of coverage are likely to be acceptably accurate and objective because doubtful details and subjective subtleties will be peeled off by editors and reporters, details and subtleties may provide the most insights—especially outside insights—into criminal justice in practice.

News Briefs

Because episodic coverage will tend to be quite concise, it is likely to be selective but accurate. Examine the following news briefs:

> Burglary: James Buchanan, 19, of 1856 Democrat Drive. Charged with second-degree burglary, pleaded guilty to amended charge of first-degree criminal trespassing. Charges of third-degree criminal mischief and two counts of fourth-degree assault dismissed. Placed on probation for two years.

> Robbery: Andrew Johnson, 37, of 1865 Republican Road. Charged with second-degree robbery, pleaded guilty to amended charge of theft by unlawful taking of under $100. Charges of second-degree criminal mischief and resisting arrest dismissed. Placed on probation for two years.

> Drunken Driving:
> Millard Fillmore, 50, 1850 Whig Way, fined $350, sentenced to 10 days. Second conviction.
> John Tyler, 27, 1841 Tippecanoe Trail, $500, 30 days. Third conviction.[54]

To be sure, such briefs select only the most official aspects of the case and relay almost nothing about the lives or views of those accused. Still, official acts are reduced to facts that make the report seem objective, precise, and legally complete. Information provided is so limited that occasions for inaccuracy or subjectivity are minimized.

Spot News

Journalistic reports that single events out of a continuing stream of actions are often called "spot news" by journalists and students of journalism. While many judicial events do stand alone or largely alone, most trials are continuous sequences of action that can be separated into moments only arbitrarily. We have seen how journalistic routines divide judicial continuities into phases that tend to draw spot coverage.

Although the literature on judicial spot news is spotty, we can formulate a reasonable hypothesis: *the more distant the judicial proceeding from the targeted audience of a reporter or medium, the fewer spots or events from each judicial proceeding we may expect media to feature and the briefer we should expect spot news to be.* For example, U. S. newspapers seldom lavish words on foreign judicial events:

> Cairo—An Egyptian military court yesterday charged a third group of suspected Muslim militants with plotting to overthrow the government and re-forming the outlawed group that assassinated President Anwar Sadat in 1981, defense lawyers said. The 33 suspects, who were put on trial in Alexandria, were also accused of forming a group to overthrow the constitution, illegal possession of weapons, and hiding fugitives. They could face the death penalty if convicted.[55]

Each of these three sentences in the *San Francisco Chronicle* is accurate and objective. The first two sentences report formal utterances that are "performative":[56] the reported actions ("charged" and "accused," respectively) are self-fulfilling expressions. When a court charges or accuses suspects, it transforms them into defendants, by definition. I presume that the court did in fact charge and accuse, so this spot is accurate and objective. The last sentence, I further presume, is based on Egyptian law and is therefore accurate and objective.

An inquiring, discerning reader might criticize this spot for paring away answers to who, what, where, when, and how questions that would contextualize the spot. If this is a third group of militants, *who* were the first two groups? *What* views or agenda do these militants advance besides those named in the article? *Where* were the militants in the twelve years between the assassination and the accusation? *When* and *how* will the trial proceed? Are the defendants as good as dead already?

The reader who asks such questions, however, misapprehends the economy of the news medium. Spot news allows the news medium to fit more stories into a small news hole. Mass media offer consumers a little about an array of topics. Consumers who require more information will turn from headline news or *USA Today* to media that provide more detailed reports. To dissect the Egyptian court coverage, then, is to misunderstand the point of concise spot news.

You should expect longer spot reports to provide more information. However, you should not expect reporters or media to risk much inaccuracy or subjectivity. Instead, journalistic routines (and underlying symbiosis and source-ery) aim to insure accuracy and objectivity and to preserve the economy of the news medium by eliminating controversial elements of context. Consider this report:

Portland, Ore., May 16 (AP)—The man who whacked figure skater Nancy Kerrigan on the knee and his getaway car driver were sent to prison today to serve 18-month terms.

Shane Stant, the hit man, and Derrick Smith, his driver, received no fines under their plea agreements with prosecutors. They were convicted of conspiring to assault Kerrigan.

But Shawn Eckardt, the sometime bodyguard for rival skater Tonya Harding, pleaded guilty to racketeering for helping to hatch the plot. Circuit Judge Philip Abraham set Eckardt's sentencing for July 11. His plea agreement also calls for an 18-month term.

Eckardt first contacted Smith about the plot. Smith then contacted Stant, who is his nephew.

Kerrigan was struck with a metal police baton Jan. 6 as she left practice at the national skating championships in Detroit. She was named to the United States Olympic team anyway, recovered from the injury and earned a silver medal in Lillehammer, Norway.

Harding, who went on to win the national championship and an automatic spot on the United States Olympic team, finished eighth in the Olympics. She is on three years' probation for conspiring to hinder prosecution.

Her ex-husband, Jeff Gillooly, pleaded guilty to racketeering and is scheduled for sentencing July 5. His plea agreement with prosecutors calls for a two-year term.[57]

This longer spot concisely summarized five months of developments for any reader who had forgotten the general story. We might well wonder whether any reader oblivious to anything in the last four paragraphs of the story would get that far, but perhaps the *New York Times* decided to run those paragraphs to refresh readers' memories.

Notice that this story relays simple facts and "performatives" as much as the Egyptian story. As readers, we presume the two men were sent to prison, performatively if not yet in actual fact. We have little difficulty believing that the men did plead guilty, were convicted, and were sentenced—all performative utterances. Because performative statements constitute many formal, legal actions, spot news that relies on performatives will almost always seem accurate, objective, and formal.

However, because it has been stripped to its accurate and objective facts, this report misses the story. This story omits from the "Saga of Nancy and Tonya" virtually every interesting aspect. The style of this spot, it seems to me, makes the story accurate and objective at great cost to context and thus to interest. Most readers want to know the implications of the pleas for the timing and degree of Tonya Harding's involvement in the plot to injure Nancy Kerrigan. Compare this story from the *St. Petersburg Times:*

> Shane Stant and Derrick Smith came to court in Portland, Ore., on Tuesday and pleaded guilty to conspiracy to commit assault on figure skater Nancy Kerrigan. Stant admitted hitting Kerrigan above the knee with a metal police baton as she practiced in Detroit Jan. 6, and Smith, his uncle, acknowledged driving the getaway car. A third defendant, Shawn Eckardt, pleaded guilty to racketeering. Stant, 22, and Smith, 29, were led away in handcuffs to start 14- to 18-month prison sentences. Eckardt, facing the same term, had his sentencing delayed until July 11.
>
> Stant, 22, and Smith, 29, admitted they conspired with Eckardt and with Harding's ex-husband, Jeff Gillooly, to assault Kerrigan. Gillooly has pleaded guilty to racketeering in an agreement that calls for a two-year prison term and a $100,000 fine.
>
> As he left, Eckardt reacted bitterly to the fact that Kerrigan's rival, Tonya Harding, did not go to jail for her role in the case. Harding pleaded guilty March 16 to conspiracy to hinder prosecution and received three years' probation.
>
> "I feel she wasn't honest with her attorney. Otherwise he wouldn't have made such a fool of himself in his representation

of her," Eckardt said. "I feel that if she's going to continue to act in the manner in which she has, she should become a better liar."[58]

This story is three words longer than the one in the *New York Times* but quotes Eckardt and thereby introduces some remaining issues. While most spot news on the matter was brief and thus stripped of details in favor of the incontestable facts and performatives,[59] quotations such as the one above were available but unused.

We could analyze even longer spot news to see how large a story must get before media risk inaccuracy and subjectivity to convey context. However, a sturdy generalization awaits more systematic research. For now, let me offer a suspicion and an inference. While a few criminal cases demand extensive coverage, routine criminal court coverage will be concise. Concision dictates not only selective, episodic court coverage but also the elision from selective, episodic copy of most or all contested, contestable, and contextual materials. Eliding controversial elements will minimize criticisms and insure a common denominator of accuracy and objectivity. When controversy goes, interest will often go, too.

I believe the following inference follows from the analysis of briefs and spots. *News briefs and spot news must morselize events to fit tiny news holes.* Recall from chapter 1 that morselization is an angle bias. When media strip stories of context and connections, they morselize events and persons. Reports may seem accurate and objective, but they achieve accuracy and objectivity by stripping away many of the most revealing aspects of stories and cases. Newspapers and broadcast media cover news in less episodic ways, to be certain. Dramatic, personal cases may encourage daily running stories that supply ample detail. Some media will run features on adjudication in general and institutional problems in particular. Still, most court stories are far more morselized than the stories reporters could tell with more space. As Denniston stated the matter:

There is a great deal that must be left out in legal reporting. That is perhaps the most rigorous aspect of this specialty. For any given story, news or feature that a courthouse reporter will write, he will or should know a great deal more in detail and breadth than he can expect to convey to his audience.

The facts are as important as the legal principles. The personalities or institutions involved are as important as the legal results. But, still, it is *the law* that one is dealing with, and it must be the core of any story originating on the legal beat.[60]

Plea Bargains But Not Plea Bargaining

To appreciate the costs of concision in court reporting, let us consider a most common event in criminal courts—plea bargains. Formal criminal charges result in guilty pleas more often than any other disposition by a ratio of about three to one.[61] Many but hardly all pleas result from plea bargains:

> Plea bargaining is the process by which the defendant in a criminal case relinquishes his right to go to trial in exchange for a reduction in charge and/or sentence. Most cases in most criminal courts in this country are plea bargained; notwithstanding the nomenclature, the "trial court" is really a "plea bargaining court."[62]

Plea bargains are one reason that criminal trials account for one-tenth or less of resolutions of criminal cases.

Most citizens do not realize how rare criminal trials are, in part because plea bargains seldom make much news. Fishman has noted that guilty pleas are likely to be reported while the process that generated the pleas is likely to go unremarked:

> Rarely do journalists report negotiated pleas as negotiated pleas, even though they will write feature stories, news analyses, and editorials about negotiated pleas in the abstract. It is mainly the guilty plea itself which is newsworthy because it represents a disposition of the case. That the plea was bargained over is a detail which, more often than not, is omitted in brief news reports focusing on how defendants plead.[63]

Fishman also observed that reports of guilty pleas usually are brief and that negotiations leading to pleas usually are not covered. Of course, we should not expect prosecutors, defense attorneys, and judges to haggle over pleas in public. Thus, we should not expect reporters to be privy to many aspects of negotiations. An unavoidable consequence of the relative privacy of plea bargains, however, is that the modal criminal justice process is underreported in routine court coverage unless a celebrity is involved.[64] Fishman provided an example of a story about a guilty plea:

> Martha Mungan pleaded guilty today to a charge stemming from a predawn shootout last December that left her wounded and her common-law husband dead from police bullets.
>
> Mrs. Mungan pleaded guilty to one count of threatening and interfering with police officers, and a second count was dismissed.
>
> Her sentencing was set for March 22 in the court of Superior Judge Lloyd Bennett.
>
> Police were called to Mrs. Mungan's home at 410-B Oceano Ave. last December by Rodney Charles Harvey, her common-law husband, during a family fight. In the ensuing gunfight, Mrs. Mungan was wounded and Harvey was killed when he retrieved the pistols and shot at police.[65]

Fishman seems to regard this story as reasonably accurate and objective. Review the story to see how accurate and objective you might take it to be. For example, why is it important to note twice that Ms. Mungan and Mr. Harvey were not formally married to one another?

This account excluded significant facts of both the shooting and the plea bargaining. Ms. Mungan had become intoxicated and was waving Mr. Harvey's guns at the police called to quell a disturbance on her front lawn. When she raised the guns toward the police, the police wounded her. Mr. Harvey, who had been trying to persuade her to drop the guns, then shot at the police. After he wounded an officer, the police killed him. An inquest exonerated the police.[66]

Details of perhaps most interest to ordinary citizens would concern the reduction of Ms. Mungan's charge from assaulting a police officer to interfering with a police officer. If the inquest had determined that police acted properly and if Ms. Mungan had set in motion the death and woundings, "interfering with an officer" seems an extravagant reduction in charge. Was the prosecutor trying to make the whole matter go away?

I cite this example at some length to exemplify Fishman's contention that readers and viewers get far less accurate, objective detail from plea bargaining than journalistic ideals might lead them to believe that they do. What little consumers get is likely to be accurate and objective. The greater portion that consumers do not get compromises ideals.

Inputs More Than Throughputs and Outputs

If a defendant does not plead guilty and opts for trial, journalists nonetheless tend to report formal charges and formal decisions more than the processes that link accusations to verdicts. Just as negotiations leading to pleas tend to be reported less often than the pleas do, so too the progress of trials tends to find print less often than their formal starts and finishes. We might explain this tendency by noting that the most objective features of criminal adjudication are the prosecution's and defense's official "inputs"—that is, actions that start a process in motion, the earliest court phases—and the court's official "outputs"—that is, actions that signal an official completion of the process, concluding court "phases." Between inputs and outputs, actions are adversarial, less official, and hence subject to contested interpretations. Reporters, we have seen, prefer the objective to the subjective, so inputs and outputs are far more likely to suit court journalism than anything in between.

We may appreciate the emphases inherent in routine court coverage by examining stories in newspapers. Table 4.2 summarizes newspaper coverage of courts.[67] Formal commencement and formal conclusion of court cases, in this simple sample of four days from 1993, drew more ink than formal procedures in between commencement and conclusion. Stories of indictments and arraignments drew more coverage than tales of plea bargaining, *voir dire* (juror selection), advocates' motions, statements and summations, judges' rulings, and judges' and juries' deliberations. Coverage of criminal cases resembles submarines: usually submerged, cases "surface" in the media when launched and show up less often at other times. It would seem that an inevitable result of this surfacing is routine emphasis on charging and pleading at the beginning, less emphasis on decisions at the end, and marked inattention to most of the ordinary process of trials. If differences between decisions and midtrial events seem from table 4.2 to be minimal, please remember that many trials present events across multiple days while announcements of decisions take far less time. Thus, events during trials have more opportunities, on average, to make the news but make the news less often.

Does television exhibit similar selections? I know of no research on the matter. However, everyday observation of television's tendencies inclines me to conclude—tentatively—that inputs and outputs are reported far more often. Cases surface in the news at their conclusions and perhaps at their inceptions but remain submerged most of the time.

Table 4.2   **Newspapers' Coverage of Selected Aspects of Criminal Process**

	Number of Articles	Percentage of Total	Average Length
Pretrial: Arrests, Indictments, Arraignments	240	40.7%	446 words
Trial: Jury-Selection, Testimony, Motions, Rulings, and Arguments	139	23.6%	473 words
Decision: Verdicts, Holdings, or Sentences	164	27.8%	417 words
Posttrial: Reactions	4	0.7%	1,277 words
Unfocused: Stage(s) Inexplicit	42	7.1%	648 words
Total: All Stages	589	100%	466 words

Angle biases, bureaucratic stages, and the limits to lay appreciation of criminal procedures would all account for submersion and surfacing. Arraignments and verdicts not only dramatize and personalize the confrontation between isolated defendant(s) and the omnipotent state, they also inspire morselized news briefs or spot news in most cases.[68] More, as Fishman observed, movement of cases into a new bureaucratic stage signals reporters that it may be time to file a story. Because most happenings during the trial are harder to relay to consumers of news than the beginning or the ending of the case, inputs and outputs surface in the press while most developments in between do not.

We must not overstate the findings from the rough-and-ready survey reported in table 4.2. Further studies will be necessary before we can generalize with any confidence. My "Submarining Hypothesis" might have to give way to an "Interest Wanes Hypothesis" if it turns out that beginnings dominate, and other phases of trials, including decisions, make news only occasionally. In addition, you must not forget that trials are exceptional and that guilty pleas and dismissals of charges usually complete formal proceedings.

Routine Coverage Stresses Crime Control

The tendency of court cases to surface in court reporting at the beginning and end of formal litigation shows that routine coverage stresses crime control aspects over due process aspects of cases. I hypothesized that crime control dominated due process in ordinary coverage. I have no studies to cite to demonstrate this tendency empirically. Instead, let me ponder my hypothesis as a plausible expectation that future studies might test.

Please recall why reporting from a crime control viewpoint should be expected to outweigh reporting from the viewpoint of due process. Crime control is easier to report than due process. Crime control stories better match angle biases, commercial pressures, and limits on reporters' time, energies, and resources. Crime control stories are preformulated—that is, officials tend to release information in formats that are already morselized and normalized for reporters—by a bureaucracy while due process stories are contested by the state, so reporters will tend to avoid the latter lest they seem to be taking sides. More, crime control bureaucracies tend to be far more organized and far better funded than the forces of due process. In addition, crime control bureaucracies are led by elected and appointed officials, while many advocates of due process are unofficial or even "out of the mainstream."[69] Crime-control bureaucracies also get the jump on reporters and defenders of due process because the former create cases and disseminate information long before the latter groups "get in the game."

Table 4.2 may be interpreted to support the tendency of coverage to understress due process questions, which disproportionately arise during the phases of trials that are *not* covered. When the press cover pleas far more than plea bargains, formal charges far more than formal proceedings, motions, and rulings, and decisions of juries far more than selection of juries, we must anticipate that the average media consumer has fewer and circumscribed opportunities for learning about due process. The aspects of the judicial system most important from a crime-control viewpoint—that is, the inputs and outputs—are far more likely to penetrate the consumer's awareness. For these reasons, we might expect the crime-control conveyor belt to dominate the due process obstacle course.

I also suspect that a primary concern of the crime-control perspective—factual guilt—implicitly and explicitly dominates a corresponding concern of the due process perspective—legal guilt. That is, court reporters may routinely devote far more attention to establishing whether the accused actually did what he or she is accused of doing (factual guilt) than they expend on assessing whether guilt or innocence were established according to the highest standards of criminal procedure (legal guilt). Factual guilt is of greater interest to many readers. Moreover, legal guilt is a difficult concept for many citizens to master.

If future studies find that crime-control perspectives do dominate due process perspectives, such findings would reinforce my contention that most criminal-court coverage meets Mainstream Standards: news media accurately and objectively relay crime control even as courts showcase due process with craft and candor. While outside observers might attribute the predominance of crime control in court coverage to expediency, inside defenders of the press may respond that crime control is the greater concern of most consumers of court coverage and hence, if coverage is said to be biased, it is biased in favor of the majority view of criminal justice. As I have throughout this book, I hold that *both* outsiders *and* insiders are correct. Crime control overwhelms due process *both* because it is cheaper and easier to relay *and* because it is truer to the values and views that characterize most readers and viewers.

Criminal Court Coverage as Usual

We may sum up ordinary coverage of criminal trial courts in some simple theses that deserve study. First, because almost all media, specialized and mass, have too little space or time for most criminal trials, the modal criminal court story is no story. Second, the next most common criminal court story is a news brief or spot news stripped of most content, context, and controversy to fit the news medium. Among criminal court stories published, the usual story is a note about inputs or outputs. Third, few stories will be long enough to include more than spot news about beginnings, endings, and legal performatives. Such occasional episodes will ordinarily be accurate and objective by prevailing standards. My conclusion then is that most criminal court coverage probably meets mainstream expectations.

However, our findings may also warrant a less simplistic, less cheery conclusion once we take a second look at the prevailing standards for accuracy and objectivity. We have seen how angle biases, commercial biases, journalistic routines, and bureaucratic stages coalesce to shape coverage. Criminal court happenings usually do not surface in the news. When they surface, the usual story presumes the authority and legitimacy of insider accounts and attends to the views of citizens, clients, and outsiders little if at all. If crime control informs reports far more than due process, due process and most aspects of criminal procedure will ordinarily be submerged in mass media.

If I am correct about what gets covered and what does not, what court news surfaces and what is submerged, and which values (crime control) tend to dominate which other values (due process), we must conclude that the accuracy and objectivity that the Inside-Out Perspective presupposes must be reconsidered. We must understand that the accuracy and objectivity incorporated in mainstream standards are conditioned by mainstream beliefs, attitudes, and preferences. What accuracy and objectivity do routine standards demand?

Accuracy in Routine Practice

Reporters may efficiently and effectively authenticate stories by citing authorities to whom audiences will give credence or at least deference. Reporters almost always get participants' names and performative utterances correct. Beyond that modest threshold of accuracy, however, reporters routinely depend on files and officials. We have acknowledged that quotations and paraphrases afford reports one form of accuracy: whatever the veracity of what was said, the source was cited accurately. Now we must acknowledge that official files and sources tend to make criminal court reports somewhat partial.

While reporters will shy away from sources who give them "bum dope," the inaccuracies to which inside sources are liable are products of official perspectives, not usually deliberate deceptions. Reporters, due to deadlines, sloth, expediency, or necessity, must rely on courthouse sources. Those sources take the official perspective of criminal cases. That official perspective, we have seen, stresses a formal view of the stages of the criminal trial and crime control. Thus, official sources compromise accuracy, albeit in ways that reporters and consumers are unlikely to detect.

Consider prosecutors, for example. Reporters cite prosecutors as the most helpful sources to clarify facts, to decipher formal technicalities, to proffer tips about stories, to interpret other sources' motives and actions, to confirm the accuracy of details, and to provide general background about the legal system.[70] Defense attorneys are slightly more likely to try to manipulate reporters or spin stories.[71] Since most criminal court coverage comes from files and sources rather than from courtroom observation,[72] it is little wonder both that prosecutors shape the news far more than defense attorneys and that prosecutors are far more contented with routine court coverage than defense attorneys.[73] Given symbiotic relations to prosecutors, reporters are unlikely to notice and unlikely to resist the prosecutors' perspective on the news. Enter, among other things, the crime control bias. Audiences partial to crime control over due process and accustomed to the prosecutor's view of criminal trials are likely to take that view to be accurate, objective, and real.

Proprosecution biases in ordinary news media are not objective, accurate or fair, Alan Dershowitz has recently shown.[74] Modern prosecutors try their cases in mass media as well as in courtrooms, with the result that defense attorneys who eschew media often fail to defend their clients competently. Dershowitz noted that prosecutors maintain public relations experts, accomplished spinners, and masterful leakers to win battles for public opinion, which in turn can win wars with juries. Dershowitz emphasized how much greater access to confidential information prosecutors have and how much of that confidential information prosecutors might leak to their advantage. He noted that defense attorneys have far less confidential information and do *not* want most of it released. More, Dershowitz observed that prosecutors' offices have ongoing relations with the press, while defense attorneys deal with reporters more episodically. This is especially the case for the majority of head prosecutors who face reelection and thus want to assist reporters and impress voters. As a final point, Dershowitz noted that prosecutors—directly or through police or other bureaucracies—have used leaks to intimidate or cajole witnesses by convicting the accused in public long before the protections of the criminal trial surround the defendant.

In sum, the advantages of prosecutors over defendants in coverage of criminal courts should be expected to extol crime control over due process and to extend the source-ery that, in routine practice, undermines accuracy and objectivity.

Objectivity in Usual Practice

Formal values and crime control values so suffuse criminal trials that, for insiders at least, they define events and decisions. When news reports mirror these legal and official preferences, no authoritative, credible critics are likely to obtain much of an audience. If news reports contradict those preferences, on the other hand, judges, lawyers, and courthouse staff are likely to regard the reports as subjective, unfair, and biased. From this I infer that "objectivity" in routine reporting about criminal courts is the quality of agreeing with the partial perspectives of court insiders.

This inference has lurked not very far beneath the surface of my remarks throughout this chapter. Court-media symbioses, source-ery in reportage of the criminal courts and other journalistic routines, and press adaptations to the phases of criminal adjudication all suggest that courts and criminal justice sources draw beat reporters inside. To report on criminal courts, reporters must fathom formal legal views. The formal legal view acquired is the common perspective on events and decisions. In effect, reality as construed by legal insiders bounds news reports. Accounts that contradict common legal assumptions will usually seem subjective—partisan, ideological, extreme, personal, or aberrant—or evidence of limited understanding of legal and judicial contexts and processes.

To consider the possibility that "objective" coverage of criminal courts is coverage that conforms to insiders' assumptions, hark back to our exploration of the "Judicial Construction of Authority" (chapter 1). There we rehearsed the evidence, arguments, and interpretations of two prominent debunkers of formal-legal presumptions. Donald Black[75] showed us that the jurisprudential perspective common to modern legal systems was in many respects wishful thinking. He showed that around the world legal and judicial systems discriminate against the poor and other minorities in many of the same ways that electoral or other political institutions do. Ample historical evidence supports Black in this respect.[76] The late Abraham S. Blumberg likened much of criminal justice to a "confidence game," a scam in which knowing insiders took advantage of the credulity of defendants.[77] The objects of defendants' credulity, please recall, were exactly the presumptions of the formal legal insiders that news media disseminate and amplify.

When I said that criminal court coverage is designed to meet mainstream standards for accuracy and objectivity, I conveyed both good and bad news. The good news is that news media usually meet

Inside-Out expectations. The bad news is that news media will often meet expectations by adhering to inside views that deny or denigrate other insights and perspectives.

Judicial Craft and Candor

I have not said much about the craft and candor that the Inside-Out Perspective expects of judges because, in almost all cases, craft and candor will come forth. Routine criminal adjudication requires little craft or candor from judges. We have seen how the prevalence of pleading and other alternatives to trial guarantees that. Reports of judges' performative utterances may usually be relied on, so even outside critics must presume that judges have repeated ritualized remarks and recited formal formulas as the law and the record required.

Still, the predominance of judicial craft and candor has important implications for our scrutiny of coverage of criminal courts, for it tells us that the lower row of table 1.1 will seldom apply to criminal cases. That is, almost all criminal cases are so mundane that they have few legal, social, or other ramifications. Such cases do not challenge the law or judges and so almost never tempt judges to dishonesty, artful dodges, or cunning arguments. As a result, our Outside-In Perspective seldom will contribute much to understanding routine criminal adjudication or adjudicators. To see judicial craft and candor from the outside requires another outside perspective, schooled by insights such as those of Black and Blumberg. I shall suggest such a perspective at the end of this chapter.

For now, readers need only see why a distinction important for the Inside-Out Perspective and our Outside-In Perspective lies between routine coverage and extraordinary coverage. Routine coverage, I have shown at length, is designed to meet mainstream standards and almost always does so. Extraordinary coverage, I shall now show, often compromises mainstream standards.

Recall the two ironies with which I started this chapter. Coverage extraordinary for its length and depth will diverge from the routine coverage we have already explored. It will do so first because cases must be sensational or sensationalized to secure sufficient space or time for length and depth. That is irony one. Stories that secure space and time will have room for procedures and details and so will emphasize due process more than routine cases do. That is irony two.

Unusual Criminal Trial Coverage

Doppelt and Drechsel have reported that legal officials tend to object most to inaccuracy[78] and sensationalism[79] in coverage of criminal trials. We have seen, however, that coverage seldom extends to most aspects of trials that challenge accuracy or fuel sensational coverage. Thus, we must rethink and perhaps reverse the usual criticism. Reporters usually do not sensationalize. Given the brevity of most reports, reporters could not sensationalize much even if they wanted to. However, when they cover cases with sensational features or matters that lend themselves to hyperbole, reporters might tend to fulfill mainstream expectations less (irony one) and discuss due process more (irony two) than they ordinarily do.

Reporters who stray from routine coverage will rely on less official or even disreputable sources, so they will be stripped of the protections of source-ery. Worse, reporters who investigate issues of due process may imperil police and prosecutors. When former symbionts become intense adversaries, routine symbioses disintegrate. This decline of source-ery and symbiosis will incline insiders, especially those legally trained, to trumpet inaccurate and subjective coverage as evidence of poor journalism. Let us see how extraordinary coverage may lead to inaccuracies, hype, and the ironies with which I began this chapter.

Table 4.3 **Word-Lengths for Criminal Court Stories**

	Number of Articles	
Fewer than 100 words	65	(10.9%)
100–200 words	97	(16.3%)
201–300 words	90	(15.1%)
301–400 words	53	(8.9%)
401–500 words	82	(13.8%)
501–600 words	57	(9.6%)
601–700 words	36	(6.1%)
701–800 words	32	(5.4%)
801–1,200 words	50	(8.4%)
More than 1,200 words	33	(5.5%)
Total articles	595	(100.0%)

Nonroutine Coverage and Dramatization

Table 4.3 reminds us that everyday court coverage, for the minority of cases reported, consists mostly of news briefs and short spot news.[80] A majority of the articles in the four-day, random sample of coverage ended before the four-hundredth word. That is little more than a page of double-spaced prose with a twelve-point font. Nearly two-thirds of these criminal justice articles did not reach the five-hundredth word. A student who filled three standard pages (8.5 by 11 inches) with twelve-point type would create as much copy as fully 86 percent of the articles in the sample!

The examples I have used in this chapter further illustrate the brevity of most stories about most criminal trials. The news briefs into which I substituted presidents' names, for a first example, measured 41, 39, 10, and 7 words in length. My example from the Egyptian military court consumed a mere 69 words, excluding the dateline. The two stories I reproduced concerning the men who pleaded guilty to assaulting Nancy Kerrigan measured about 210 words—I could have used stories that were a third as long. The example of a plea bargain that I took from Fishman occupied but 108 words.

Full-fledged coverage of criminal courts is rare. Perhaps we overestimate the comprehensiveness of coverage because such coverage, when it appears, tends to be dramatic. Newspapers from which data were gathered to create table 4.3 are larger than most, so table 4.3 at best roughly approximates coverage of criminal courts in major papers. Still, such data show us why coverage stories measure up to the accuracy and objectivity demanded by the Inside-Out Perspective: it is hard to stray in so few words!

Atypical stories tend to make the news while ordinary happenings do not. I do not presume to criticize mass media for stressing the unusual and the fascinating—that is their job! My point here is merely to call to mind what you already know. News about criminal courts tends to issue from dramatic cases, while run-of-the-mill cases issue less coverage. Now let us see why this lengthening dramatization tends to introduce due process into court coverage.

Our confidence in what we discover must be leavened by our reliance on a few cases. To my knowledge, more systematic, substantial research has yet to be done to establish the general characteristics of court coverage of extraordinary cases. Perhaps such research has been stymied by the relative infrequency of extensive coverage, by the lack of comparability among extensively covered cases, or other obstacles. The cases that follow, then, should be regarded as suggestive rather than definitive.

Dramatization and Normalization

To be covered extensively, cases must be newsworthy. To be newsworthy, cases must be inherently dramatic or dramatizable. Newsworthy, dramatic, or dramatizable cases must go to trial lest most of the coverage be performed by crime reporters. We have already seen that even notorious matters that result in pleas will seldom generate extensive coverage: Tonya Harding's plea largely ended media discussion of her case. Thus, newsworthy, dramatic cases must go to trial or coverage will be truncated.

Extensively covered trials may seem normal to lay observers who have been conditioned by television and movies to believe that criminal trials are the norm. We have learned (if we did not already realize) that such trials are quite occasional. We stumble, then, onto the conclusion that *extraordinary coverage makes the abnormal (full trials) seem to resemble what the poorly informed regard as normal.* Such distortions are *not* necessarily examples of inaccuracy or subjectivity that contradict mainstream standards. However, they do compromise mainstream standards in pursuit of dramatized normality.[81]

I use the term *dramatized normality* to convey two features of extensively covered criminal trials. First, extraordinary coverage of criminal cases so highlights dramatic morsels that even attentive citizens may be deceived by such coverage. Indeed, attentive citizens may be more likely to monitor court news and thereby become more susceptible to deceptive coverage than the majority. Some observers of extraordinary coverage may forget that dramatic narratives intensify and reconstitute prosecutions and dramatizations diverge from actuality. Second but related, as dramatic criminal trials supplant more common criminal cases, ordinary observers' notions of normal cases may converge upon normalized coverage. In sum, we may hypothesize that *news media dramatize abnormal cases until, over time, they have normalized dramatic cases.*[82]

Media-savvy citizens will know that mass media often exaggerate abnormalities until distortions become normal to the uncritical. Even relatively realistic television, for example, exploits courtrooms for ratings. The lawyers of *L. A. Law* spent much more of their time in court than most litigators do in real life. Less realistic television, such as daytime dramas, may distort lawyers' and judges' activities to an even greater degree. Even passive documentary coverage such as that available on *People's Court* will tend to imply that trials are where the legal action is to be found. Classic theatrical and cinematic dramas, of course, will overstate the importance of the adversarial, public stages of the law even more. For example, *Inherit the Wind* and *The Caine Mutiny Court-Martial* climax in cross-examinations. Witnesses break down, spectators confess, and lawyers seize cases in episodes of *Perry Mason* and its cinematic progeny (*Jagged Edge, Nuts, True Believer, Suspect,* and *Presumed Innocent* are examples).[83]

Dramatized Normality in Less Popular Mass Media

Newspapers and broadcasters, novelists, and screenwriters may excuse their dramatizations of normality and normalizations of drama by marketing and other commercial considerations. Academics and practitioners have fewer and less persuasive excuses. Nonetheless, too many academics characterize systems based on exceptional cases. Two examples from recently published books and articles should suffice.

An egregious example of dramatized normality is *With Justice for Some: Protecting Victims' Rights in Criminal Trials* by George P. Fletcher of Columbia Law School.[84] Fletcher has long argued for victims' rights. In *With Justice for Some,* however, Fletcher dwells on dramatic, atypical cases that involved Americans often disadvantaged by adjudication: women, racial and ethnic minorities, and gays. These include cases that well-read Americans would likely recognize. Mike Tyson's rape conviction, William Kennedy Smith's rape acquittal, and the acquittals and convictions of the police officers who beat Rodney King are probably most prominent, although Fletcher included an afterword on the O. J. Simpson case.

Fletcher would compromise the rights of defendants to advance the rights of victims. That is, he would drastically change the norms and procedures of the law on the basis of a few sensational cases. As a reviewer of the book noted:

> At a time when the O. J. Simpson trial has exacerbated many Americans' contempt for the criminal justice system, Fletcher provides academic cover for the view that notorious cases are representative and that defendants typically avoid justice because of procedural advantages.[85]

Whatever the merits of Fletcher's contentions, his focus on infamous outcomes and his inattention to far more common results reinforces the preference of other, less intellectual mass media for the sensational. Fletcher encourages his readers to see outrages as normal, a clever tactic for an advocate but bad journalism.

Alan M. Dershowitz likewise treats dramatic cases as representative examples of social trends in a recent book that collects his columns and essays from print media.[86] Professor Dershowitz excoriates the defenses of Lyle and Erik Menendez, Lorena Bobbitt, Tonya Harding, and other infamous defendants. He even anticipates and attacks a defense for Orenthal James Simpson before joining the "Dream Team."

Dershowitz fails to alert readers, in my reading, to the differences between the *cause celebre*, an extraordinary result that outrages or enraptures observers, and the ordinary prosecution, in which psychologists and other experts play far more unremarkable roles. Gerald F. Uelman, a fellow member of the Dream Team, saw even greater problems with Dershowitz's coverage:

> I was concerned by the public misunderstanding of what was really at stake in the *Menendez* case. No one was arguing the boys should be *excused*. The only issue was whether their crime was murder or manslaughter. On that issue, I thought evidence of prior abuse was highly appropriate and certainly did not warrant the jury-trashing and lawyer-bashing that Dershowitz and others were engaged in. . . . I concluded with a sarcastic personal dig at Alan for forsaking his roots as a criminal defense lawyer to become a media hype spinner.[87]

To be sure, practitioners and academics analyze more representative cases. Judge Harold J. Rothwax in *Guilty: The Collapse of Criminal Justice*[88] strives to characterize the criminal justice system accurately. Judge Rothwax discusses prominent cases but apprises readers of far less notorious instances of abuse as well. To cite a second example, *In Spite of Innocence: The Ordeal of 400 Americans Wrongly Convicted of Crimes Punishable by Death* makes a Herculean attempt to document shortcomings of U. S. criminal justice in capital cases.[89] I could cite many other examples. Thus, my point here is *not* that books and articles always sensationalize the atypical into the normal. Rather, my point is that even those who should know better may give in to sensational coverage. This is the problem of dramatized normality. The more mass media are tempted to sensationalize, the more likely it becomes that uncritical consumers of mass media will take media caricatures for normal trials. This is one reason for the first irony in this chapter—that extensively covered cases tend to resemble our Outside-In Perspective far more than the Inside-Out Perspective. Even when the reporters are experts, greater coverage tends to lead to inaccuracy, subjectivity, and cheap hype.

The second irony that I noted at the beginning of this chapter— that greater coverage leads to more attention to due process—seems evident in the dramatized and personalized prosecutions described by Dershowitz and Fletcher. While Dershowitz usually invokes norms of due process of law in *The Abuse Excuse* and Fletcher tends to stress crime control outcomes in *With Justice for Some*, both assess crime control and due process imperatives in the criminal justice system. Such assessments contribute to awareness among readers. Such awareness is not necessarily good. If readers become ever more aware of dramatized normality, they may become less familiar with criminal justice actualities. Dershowitz and Fletcher may not mean to raise the costs of due process or to amplify the drumbeat for crime control. Such outcomes are among the risks, however, when tabloid coverage invades legal and popular discourse about courts.

The People of the State of California v. Orenthal James Simpson

If you wondered where, in a book about mass media and courts, O. J. Simpson was going to show up, your long wait or cheerful respite is over. That Simpson's trial should be remarkable by its absence reflects the conditioning that news watchers underwent between June 1994 and October 1995. No matter how many times commentators warned us not to conclude anything about criminal justice from the Simpson prosecution, that case constitutes perhaps the bulk of what many of us "know" about criminal cases. If we adopt a "both/and" view of the Simpson trial, I believe that its very atypicality may furnish insights. That is, O. J. Simpson received a wholly atypical criminal trial the coverage of which tells us little about most coverage. Because it was so atypical, the O. J. Simpson trial magnified the shortcomings of the press and revealed the characteristics of sensationalized, albeit very unusual, coverage. In the dramatized normality of coverage of the very abnormal Simpson trial, we may see how extensive coverage veered away from expectations in the Inside-Out Perspective and fulfilled the descriptions in our Outside-In Perspective.

If you saw coverage of the Simpson trial, you should have little difficulty seeing how extensive coverage failed of mainstream standards. Source-ery and symbiosis interfered with the preliminary processes, leading a judge to cancel the grand jury because of undue publicity. Print and broadcast "tabloids" led the way by speculating and by paying witnesses. Participants, practitioners, and pundits spun each day's events in the court of public opinion, thereby undermining objectivity and accuracy in coverage and, perhaps, leading Judge Ito and the attorneys to adjust their behavior to coverage. The Simpson trial, then, suggests why I opined in the first irony that cases most covered fulfill mainstream expectations least.

In this regard, consider the views of Robert C. Lind:

> Although the performance of the press has become more objectionable over the years, the Simpson case has allowed for a culmination of all that is wrong with our modern media, reaching crescendo with its coverage of the Simpson murder trial. Any semblance of journalistic ethics and responsibility has been left in the hallowed halls of journalism schools. The media has violated court orders by broadcasting confidential conversations between Mr. Simpson and his attorney, interviewing attorneys in the hallway outside the courtroom and televising the identity of an alternate juror. In addition, the media has rushed to judgment by relying on single sources, used digitally distorted photographs on magazine covers, compromised witnesses by paying for interviews before they testified and hounded others.[90]

Thus, I presume that I need not dwell on the inaccuracy and subjectivity of coverage.[91]

The Simpson trial also reveals why I have hypothesized that extraordinary reporting is much more likely to feature due process. This second irony is driven home by the due process orientation of the trial. Both for viewers and readers who made up their minds long before the verdict and for those who reserved judgment until the jury came in, the factual guilt of O. J. Simpson was not at stake in day-to-day coverage. Rather, strategies and tactics, rights and responsibilities, and fairness and legality dominated coverage. While Simpson's trial was—I hope!—at the very limit of coverage, it did show that extensively covered cases permit emphasis on due process as well as crime control.

Beyond showing the validity of the two ironies at an extreme, coverage of the Simpson trial showed how the utterly abnormal may become normalized through dramatization. Perhaps the clearest illustration of normalization would be CNBC Network's *Rivera Live*, which served as the broadcast of record for the Simpson trials. Virtually every night, Geraldo Rivera hosted four or more guests to discuss the day's or week's developments. Guests and Rivera alike reminded viewers how uncommon the proceedings were, but most of the program contradicted that reminder.

First, the vast majority of the guests were legally trained (as was Rivera). While nonlawyers were occasionally interviewed and ordinary folk phoned in, judges and lawyers dominated the conversation.[92] Despite the uniqueness of the case and the peculiarity of a television program dedicated to a trial, a form of source-ery ruled the airwaves. Each development was interpreted from and fitted into legal frames of reference. It should not surprise us that lawyers' and judges' interpretations imposed legal norms and especially due process concerns on proceedings. The utterly unique trial became, I argue, normalized despite protestations about its abnormality. This jural normalization is treacherous because it is so superficial and misleading: "As coverage of the Simpson trial underscored, the new legal journalism has ghettoized legal coverage, providing an unprecedented amount but of a blindered, ingrown kind."[93]

Host Rivera strove for balance, but the balance itself reinforced biases on and of his show. That is, Rivera tended to offset prosecutors and former prosecutors with defense attorneys, judges with advocates, and Caucasians with African Americans. This balancing act was virtuous in that Rivera's show allowed viewers to see how racial the Simpson trial was from its very start. However, a host of alternative equilibria got represented less and less often: police officers versus knowledgeable critics; spousal-abuse experts who believed that Simpson fit the profile of a spouse killer versus those who did not; experts on forensics in general and on the Los Angeles laboratories in particular; and representatives of various communities interested in the trial. Too many repeat guests seemed to be chosen for glibness and entertainment value and for the conflict or hyperbole they generated. It seems to me that the frequent guests imported some norms and missed other norms that might have generated different perspectives. This is a second kind of normalization.

Nor was normalization by legal celebrities and by spokespeople for causes the only problem. More normalization followed from treating O. J. Simpson's trial as if it were another athletic contest:

> When I found time to watch the evening talk shows after a day in court, I often found it hard to believe these were intelligent adults speaking. The events were being reported like a football

game, with the same testimony being characterized as a touch-down for the defense or a twenty-yard loss, depending on the commentator.[94]

Much as reporters too often cover presidential campaigns as if they were horse races, network newscasts and cable talk shows alike labored to discern the net effects of each development in the case. This sportscasting normalization was, of course, subject to the usual pitfalls of predicting horseraces: "It treats the law as a game of strata-gems—a tendency exemplified by the televised coverage at the end of the Simpson trail [sic] especially, when virtually everyone in the pack of predictors . . . was proven wrong."[95]

Perhaps the most pernicious normalization effected by the Simpson trial was the triumph of inexpensive hype that our Outside-In Perspective posited as a mission of mass media. As the Simpson circus plunged onward and downward, many outlets indulged in tabloid cov-erage. Lawyer Lincoln Caplan characterized Simpson coverage as the new journalistic norm: "It is information delivered without knowledge, often escorted by opinion without explanation and soothsaying with-out heed of consequences."[96]

I suggest that this species of normalization may harm us most because it turns prominent criminal trials into events subject to ordi-nary rules of public relations. Normal public relations presumes that events exist to be reported as inexpensively and as advantageously as possible. O. J. Simpson's celebrity guaranteed extensive coverage. However, mass media, prosecutors, police, defendant, defense attor-neys, survivors, hangers-on, jurors, and witnesses all exploited such free media to promote themselves or their causes.

Although the Simpson trial has inspired quick fixes for free media and public relations, we cannot be confident that any of them will address problems of normalized, dramatized coverage of celebrity trials. In the civil case against Simpson, Judge Hiroshi Fujisaki banned cameras from the courtroom and sharply limited out-of-court utterances by participants.[97] Commentators reevaluated the advisability of televised trials.[98] Prosecutor Hank Goldberg hoped that "televising high-profile trials will never happen again."[99] Other critics suggested reforms of police procedures, lawyers' tactics, judges' permissiveness, and jurors' decision making based on this highly atypical case.

Erwin Chermerinsky, a frequent guest on *Rivera Live*, has reminded us how different the Simpson trial was but how influential it will be:

For years to come, people will view the justice system through the prism of the O. J. Simpson case, and it is a very distorting lens. . . . There is nothing typical about this case. But it has become so much a part of our shared culture that it's going to have profound effects.[100]

The Simpson trial will have profound effects in part because it is such an extreme example of ills to which the U. S. adversarial system is subject. However, it should have important implications for dramatized normality, of which it is a polar instance.

Battling Sound Bites—*New York v. Colin Ferguson*

The lessons of dramatized normality are unlikely to be taught or learned if observers of the Simpson murder trial attribute public relations and spinning to the Dream Team alone. Unlike Simpson's attorneys, most defense attorneys must overcome daunting obstacles to get due process more play in news media, even in cases already extensively publicized by police and prosecutors.[101] The following excerpt from the *New York Times* illustrates the uneven playing field on which criminal justice games are usually played:

Mineola, L.I., April 1—Several weeks after the lawyers William M. Kunstler and Ronald L. Kuby brought their high-profile approach to the defense of Colin Ferguson, who is accused of killing six people aboard a commuter train, the Nassau County District Attorney has requested a gag order for all lawyers involved in the case.

In a memorandum to the court, the District Attorney, Denis Dillon, said Mr. Kunstler and Mr. Kuby have "fueled the media's interest" in the case and "sought to influence public opinion by publicizing 'their side of the story.' "

According to court papers, Nassau County prosecutors are concerned that the defense lawyers may be presenting arguments or evidence that would be inadmissible in court, and that they have made it more difficult to find impartial jurors by holding news conferences, giving interviews, and discussing their strategy on television.

. . . [Paragraph four deleted]

But Mr. Kuby, who took over the case with Mr. Kunstler a few weeks ago, said he was astonished by the move. In a statement from his law office, he noted: "Nassau County Executive

Tom Gulotta calls Ferguson an 'animal,' the Nassau County police hold press conferences to publicize the evidence taken from Mr. Ferguson, he is almost lynched in Nassau County jail and we are accused of prejudicing the proceedings. Is this an April Fool's joke?"

... [Paragraphs seven through twelve deleted][102]

We need not concern ourselves with the specific merits of this procedural wrangle. What interests me here is how some state officials (that is, the county executive and the police) have tried Ferguson's case in the media while other state officials (the prosecution) are demanding that no lawyers engage in prejudicial activity. Is it any wonder that the defense attorneys felt that they were being prevented from doing what parts of the state's "team" had already done?

For our purposes it suffices to note that crime control concerns dominated initial coverage of this matter, long before due process issues were raised and far beyond the coverage such issues received. Only the unorthodox, sensational defense has revealed the ubiquitous domination of criminal justice by the state.

A Note on "Fair-Trial/Free-Press" Issues

It is almost an axiom that the press is most interested in those trials that are likely to be "notorious" in a community; those in which the crime is a serious or even a heinous one; or those in which one or more of the principal figures is prominent. . . . But those are the very cases that may cause judges, prosecutors, and defense lawyers to be concerned about "prejudicial publicity."[103]

Articles, chapters, and books on court coverage tend to concern clashes between defendants' rights to a fair trial and reporters' rights to inform their clientele. Because such cases are quite rare, studies of such cases supply precious little insight to students of everyday court coverage. Imagery of a watchdog press straining to inform the public about every nuance of trial strategy and every tidbit of personal history may serve the news media well or poorly. I suspect such imagery both glorifies and vilifies reporters. However, such cases are so atypical that they mislead us.

Still, to complete our survey of criminal court coverage, I describe in table 4.4 classic cases that have raised issues of fair trial versus free press. This table shows how truly rare such troublesome matters are and how localized many of the most egregious violations have been. It also reinforces the irony that the most publicized and sensationalized trials raise the most due process issues.

Table 4.4   Classic Fair-Trial/Free-Press Landmarks

Classic Supreme Court Cases	Classic Supreme Court Responses
Pennekamp v. Florida (1946)	Courts cannot cite newspaper editorialists for contempt just because they comment on ongoing cases.
Irvin v. Dowd (1961)	Publicity produced by prosecutors, law enforcement, and press compromised fairness of Irvin's trial.
Estes v. Texas (1965)	Live electronic coverage of pretrial actions denied Estes a fair trial.
Sheppard v. Maxwell (1966)	"Carnival atmosphere" fomented by media denied Sheppard a fair trial.
Nebraska Press Association v. Stuart (1976)	Judge's "gag order" to protect fairness of trial contradicted freedom of press.
Gannett Company v. De Pasquale (1979)	Accused enjoys right to public trial, but reporters do not, so judge may protect fairness of trial by barring press from pretrial hearing.
Richmond Newspapers v. Virginia (1980)	Constitution protects rights of press to cover criminal trials.
Chandler v. Florida (1981)	By itself, televising a trial does not make the trial unfair.

Theoretical Scorecard

What the Inside-Out Perspective Accounts For

Since the Inside-Out Perspective is defined by the same ideals that inform routine court coverage, it cannot surprise us that most reports from criminal courts conform to those ideals. Symbioses among the personnel of criminal courts and media generate, efficiently and predictably, what symbionts need or want. Sources—court personnel, judges, lawyers, and law enforcement officials—serve up tips, quotations, and stories that further the images and agendas of the institutions for which they work and by which they can be disciplined. Sources who contradict the preferred imagery of criminal courts will usually be outnumbered by sources in most strategic positions and of more long-term utility to the press. Disgruntled participants must avoid judicial censure so their protests are likely to be feeble and ignored. Judicial routines rely on source-ery and symbioses to produce reports that are documented and official, which in ordinary practice is tantamount to the accuracy and objectivity that form the mission of news media.

We have found that almost all coverage of criminal courts will meet Mainstream Standards and thus will greatly resemble the upper-left cell of table 1.1. News briefs and spot news will not merely adhere to judicial and journalistic mission statements but will in fact be produced by processes defined by those mission statements.

What Our Outside-In Perspective Accounts For

Nonetheless, our Outside-In Perspective complements the Inside-Out Perspective with regard to reporting criminal cases. First, we have found that almost all criminal cases will receive morselized and normalized treatments if they are covered at all. While news briefs and spot news suit the formality of courts and the commercial exigencies of the press, even attentive citizens gain little knowledge of the actualities of criminal justice unless they turn to specialized media. Second, we discovered that extensive coverage is reserved for sensational, dramatic cases. Dramatization and/or personalization may overcome morselization and normalization, but the very provision of details and context relaxes journalistic routines that generate official documentation for reports. In the more provocative language of our Outside-In Perspective, expedient hype will tend to overwhelm accurate, objective copy as cases become more visible in the press.

Third, we have found that extensively covered cases are more likely to raise questions about due process while ordinary reports tend to emphasize crime control perspectives. This finding implies that, while judicious, formal procedures subsumed under craft and candor are presumed by routine coverage, extraordinary reports will expose the strategic imagery necessary to construct criminal justice. Please recall that our Outside-In Perspective expects judges and lawyers to wrangle over procedures while striving to preserve the formal images and myths of adjudication. That is why our Outside-In Perspective presumes strategic imagery is necessary. Almost all criminal cases only minimally challenge adversarial ideals and institutions, whether because ideals are approximated or because organizational momentum overwhelms challenges (most likely, *both*). However, almost all cases are not covered or are covered modestly. The cases most likely to be covered will tend to proliferate due process issues and those issues will defy definitive answers. As a result, the craft and candor assumed by the Inside-Out Perspective must give way to strategic imagery.

Thus, most criminal court coverage fulfills mainstream standards but the most publicized and noticeable cases will draw coverage distorted by dramatization and due process. From our Outside-In Perspective, the accuracy and objectivity of routine coverage is severely circumscribed. That much reportage in criminal courts and instruction in the due process perspective depend on sensationalized coverage when such coverage is cost effective—that is, the two ironies around which I constructed this chapter—strikes me as telling evidence for the utility of the outside view.

What Neither Perspective Accounts For

As indicated earlier, it is possible to indulge hypotheses about Jural Mystification or Dual Pragmatism (see table 1.1) in the context of coverage of criminal courts, but only by going outside even our Outside-In Perspective. How might a thoroughgoing, sociological realist or cynic perceive the findings and gaps in this chapter? I believe that such an outsider might find the entire debate between Inside-Outers and Outside-Inners pointless because the two perspectives that I have defined are so conventional and safe. Let's take this walk on the wild side.

Table 4.5 **Adding the Outside-Out Perspective**

	Inside-Out Perspective	Outside-In Perspective	Outside-Out Perspective
Media Mission	Objective accuracy	Inexpensive hype	Crime Control coverage
Court Mission	Craft and candor	Strategic imagery	"Safe" due process
Audience	Extensively attentive	Mostly inadvertent	Attentive selectively
Information Flow	Mediated two-step	Drama and spectacle	Social dialectic
Stance	Primarily prescriptive	Primarily descriptive	Unabashedly critical

Suppose one begins far outside legal and journalistic circles and strenuously judges court journalism from outside those circles.[104] While Outside-Inners presuppose that commercial and angle biases (inexpensive hype) often overwhelm the objective, accurate coverage expected by the Inside-Out Perspective, Outside-Outers might expect ideological biases to matter more. One bias common to many reporters and readers, especially those unschooled in due process, would be a fierce preference for crime control. Threats to security would often prove to be draws too terrific for many mass media to pass up because crime seems ubiquitous and threatening both to those who produce the news and to those who consume it. By reporting serious crimes, personifying crime in villains, and dramatizing the processes by which lawbreakers are neutralized, mass media reassure their audiences. Since few defendants will have the wherewithal to stop or slow up to the crime control conveyor belt, media will usually supply both threats and reassurances. One on the outside and intent on staying out might posit a cycle of arousal and quiescence as permanent, common features of news about crime and about criminal courts.[105] This important Media Mission would neither be conceded nor explained by the views that I have defined.

What of the mission of courts? If the juggernaut of the state seldom loses to the accused, prosecutors may be generous in preserving the rights of the accused. Of course, the state may be most generous when it bestows rights that are seldom used or useless in practice. Rigorous guarantees of due process comfort law-abiding citizens and ennoble criminal courts. If, however, due process guarantees even threaten to release or to advantage many accused, then due process becomes costly and the public and the state may be aroused. The mission of the courts, in this view, is to lavish due process on the accused as long as such process is unlikely to free the accused, who is presumed guilty by most observers. If prosecutors and police may count on winning, they may tolerate citizens with rights and may convict the accused lawfully. If victory is imperiled, Outside-Outers should expect more desperation from the state: prosecutors steal every advantage even as they attack judges who deny them advantages for lenience; judges (especially those who must stand for election) pretend to believe perjury and pretend not to see police misconduct; and when constitutional rights become expensive, they become expendable.[106] Even if defense attorneys were not routinely tugged toward cooperation and cooptation, the state and its courts would often undertake the mission of subordinating citizens' rights to citizens' reassurance.

In their missions, the press and the courts would be assisted by the habitual inattention of almost all of the populace to the actual work of the criminal courts. Viewed Outside-Out, criminal justice and due process are achieved more through cinema, novels, and especially television than through other news media. If citizens select dramatic normality over actuality—keeping in mind that the latter is prohibitively expensive relative to the former—then mass media assist in the misdirection of citizens' scrutiny. Attentive to ubiquitous, soothing dramaturgy, most citizens miss even the misleading imagery that mass news media gush.

If citizens attend to pleasant depictions of criminal justice, the Outside-Out theorist might reason, they will be greatly disconcerted when they learn or believe that the guilty have gone free or when the innocent are incarcerated. For example, a large group of citizens who believe that a defendant is in fact guilty will likely care little that legal forms have been followed or that defense attorneys have won a fair fight (or at least an adversarial adjudication less unfair than normal). The Outside-Outer would predict backlash from such an agitated citizenry, particularly if prominent persons whip up citizens and backlash. While the Inside-Out Perspective and our Outside-In Perspective predict one-way flows from news makers to news consumers, an Outside-Out Perspective might anticipate that media and courts rile the observant and are riled in return by the obstreperous. While more conventional thinkers may presume that mass media and courts will not give in much or often to uninformed or hysterical criticisms, a more critical observer might expect pundits and politicians, if no other actors in the public sphere, to profit greatly from propaganda and frenzy.

I have outlined this third option because I want you to keep in mind what I have said from the start: the Inside-Out Perspective is the most common view but it is a highly selective view. Our Outside-In Perspective is more daring and thus more controversial than the Inside-Out Perspective that it counters, but it is hardly the most daring view. The Outside-Out Perspective that I have barely sketched above would enable us to reconceive court coverage in every chapter of this book. It is thus bold and perhaps even Promethean. However, that I can find this view has informed little of the scholarship that I have undertaken to summarize in this volume. This view does instruct a few students of crime,[107] so I have alerted you to its existence.

This Outside-Out Perspective accounts for the first irony that I posited at the start of this chapter. Of course, the Outside-Outer might say, mainstream standards apply best to cases that are covered least. The least dangerous cases may be covered objectively and accurately because readers and viewers interpret events in keeping with mainstream values and fears. More spectacular cases, in contrast, challenge modal views of crime and criminal justice. Such challenges must be exploited for their potential to arouse but then processed into reassurance. The more prominent the challenge to or the more obvious the departures from crime control or due process values, the more that both courts and the press must repair or manage their images.[108] When, as in *California v. Simpson*, shortcomings of both mass media and courts are too apparent, journalistic and judicial reforms and reformers will proliferate until some of the problems identified have been addressed.

Irony Two is no irony to one who takes the Outside-Out view. Only extraordinary reporting will cover due process under most circumstances because crime control is the major concern of authorities and citizens. When due process is covered, Outside-Outers expect more coverage that reassures viewers and readers that due process usually is forthcoming than coverage that exposes systematic shortcomings in the criminal justice system. In the most visible cases, such as *California v. Simpson*, an Outside-Out view readily accounts for commentary that argues that the process granted the defendant was not due. Pundits and reporters will blame jurors, judges, defense attorneys, and other obstacles to crime control for perversion of due process into a genuine obstacle to conviction and punishment. They may even blame reporters or prosecutors. The one proposition that most opinion leaders will not countenance is that due process, rightly understood, will on occasion result in freeing the guilty. Civics books may proclaim that it is better that one hundred guilty go free than that one innocent be incarcerated, but this is easier and better said than lived by.

CHAPTER 5

Covering Civil Litigation

While we know a good deal about coverage of the Supreme Court of the United States and something about coverage of criminal courts, we know very little about coverage of civil cases. Civil cases—those in which one party sues another party in pursuit, ordinarily, of redress—have tended to draw little attention from the press and even less from students of the press. Many media, mass and specialized, have paid more attention to civil litigation as a source of waste and outrages. While scholars have begun to unravel facile and fallacious criticisms of civil litigation,[1] mass-media coverage of civil litigation as a whole has been as fragmentary, melodramatic, and superficial as most news. Scholarship concerning coverage of civil courts has been rare as well.

Given the modest visibility of civil trials, civil cases, and even civil litigation in most mass media, we must focus on how we might learn more about trials, cases, and litigation outside criminal and appellate arenas. We begin with a few general observations and then move to a tentative hypothesis. Once we have a set of tentative expectations, we will briefly explore some exceptional litigation. While the exceptions challenge and qualify the expectations, the chapter concludes with contrasting perspectives on what the skimpy evidence uncovered to date shows and what we might discover that would affect our expectations, hypotheses, and theories.

Civil Law Is Private and "Privatized"

The most elementary expectation from which to begin to understand mass media coverage of civil litigation and cases is paradoxical: dockets of civil courts bulge while coverage of civil courts remains paltry. Let us learn once again from perhaps the most experienced judicial journalist in the country, Lyle Denniston:

Civil law is the growing side of the reporter's beat. The new and novel controversies that a complex society has produced have not been left routinely to be settled by other branches of government, but have rather gone to court. . . . For every newsworthy civil case, there will be perhaps scores that simply will make no news at all.[2]

Having seen that coverage of criminal courts was modest, you may be startled to learn that reporters are even more selective regarding civil courts. Yet Denniston notes that newsworthy civil cases are outnumbered by those that are not newsworthy by a factor of forty or more! Civil cases proliferate but make little news. How can this be?

Once we reflect on what we have learned about news coverage, the lower profile of civil cases seems understandable and even predictable. First, civil cases seem and often are much more private than criminal cases. Criminal cases pit the community against the accused (*The State v. Jones* or *The People v. Johnson and Brown*), so readers and viewers are in a sense parties to the case, and prosecutors, police, and jurors purport to represent communities to which viewers and readers belong. In contrast, many civil suits involve individuals or private parties whose problems concern ordinary people little if at all.[3]

Second, and as a consequence of the first reason, most civil suits are more humdrum than even ordinary crimes that offer little drama or titillation. Even daily occurrences such as purse snatchings or drunken disorderliness may offend communities and merit readers' and viewers' attention and concern. Bill collection, fender benders, and frauds may be fraught with momentous consequences for ordinary people, but those people may seldom see the ramifications even if such matters make the news.

Third, no matter how technical criminal trials get, their beginnings and endings usually grab ordinary folk. When a citizen is accused or exonerated, guilty or innocent, imprisoned or freed, vindicated or vanquished, viewers and readers sympathize with defendants, with victims and victims' friends and relatives, and sometimes even with attorneys and jurors. Civil litigation, in contrast, may defy laypersons' and even lawyers' understanding and thus elude their empathy. What are laypersons to make of contributory negligence, easements, rules against perpetuities, and other doctrines that are hard to explain in law school and nearly impossible to convey in interesting, concise prose in newspapers?[4] When lawyers and judges battle over technical matters and motions, even lawyers can be mystified by the results. Civil judgments often split differences, assigning blame and money proportionately to plaintiff and defendant. Both the jury's calculations and its results are far easier to fathom in criminal trials, in which the defendant is either guilty or not of each charge.

In sum, civil cases tend to be more private, more humdrum, and more technical than newsworthy criminal cases, so we should not be surprised that they are covered less often. We might even go further and suspect that since news media usually overlook or underemphasize civil courts, scholars who study news media tend to overlook or underemphasize coverage of civil courts as well. My researches support that suspicion, which is why I must so often speculate throughout this chapter. We have to create our intellectual starting points because scholarship about civil court coverage is even skimpier than the coverage.

Table 5.1   **Coverage of Civil Trials on Four Dates**

Newspaper	Civil Cases Reported	Civil Cases per Date	Criminal Cases Reported	Civil Cases per All Cases
Atlanta Journal and Constitution	24	8.0	30	43%
Arizona Republic	6	2.0	9	32%
Boston Globe	13	3.3	27	31%
Buffalo News	10	3.3	57	14%
Chicago Sun-Times	15	5.0	15	50%
Chicago Tribune	9	4.5	5	60%
Christian Science Monitor	0	0.0	1	0%
Cleveland Plain Dealer	22	5.5	38	32%
Dallas Morning News	29	7.3	19	56%
Houston Chronicle	19	6.3	27	37%
Los Angeles Times	38	9.5	58	36%
Louisville Courier-Journal	28	7.0	51	35%
Minneapolis Star and Tribune	14	3.5	16	36%
New Orleans Times Picayune	9	3.0	15	33%
Newsday	13	3.3	27	32%
New York Times	30	7.5	26	48%
Orlando Sentinel	16	4.0	25	36%
Phoenix Gazette	9	3.0	10	39%
Sacramento Bee	16	4.0	16	46%
San Diego Union Tribune	19	4.8	14	58%
San Francisco Chronicle	7	1.8	8	39%
Seattle Times	10	2.5	5	31%
St. Louis Post-Dispatch	15	3.8	21	38%
St. Petersburg Times	22	5.5	20	50%
USA Today	8	8.0	17	24%
Washington Post	22	5.5	16	52%
Washington Times	12	3.0	16	38%
Totals	435	4.5	589	39%

Skimpy Coverage of Civil Cases

To grasp the degree to which news media overlook civil trials, glance at table 5.1. To construct this table, I counted the number of civil and criminal cases featured in several newspapers.[5] Since the selected papers serve large markets and may choose from hundreds of cases, my selection may yield greater than average counts of civil litigation. However, both raw numbers of cases mentioned and percentages of court cases that are not criminal make it clear that civil law stories are not as common as criminal justice cases. Indeed, on the four random dates in 1993 on which table 5.1 was based, these large papers averaged less than five stories about civil trials. Doppelt reported similar findings for newspapers in the Chicago area.[6] Criminal trials, appeals, and juvenile cases make up about 61 percent of the cases covered in the twenty-seven newspapers in the sample.

The modesty of civil coverage need not reflect badly on the press. Reporters cannot be faulted for failing to cover trials that never happen, and parties in approximately 90 percent of civil cases do settle before a court decides or entertains an issue.[7] Just as news media tend to report only a small fraction of *criminal* cases that end before trial, news media tend to report few *civil* settlements. More important, civil suits that end before trial challenge news media more than pleas because many civil settlements are truly out of court. When prosecutors drop charges or defendants plead guilty, the official conclusion of the case takes place in a courtroom to which the press and public will usually have access. Criminal defendants may not plead guilty on the condition that no one will find out what happened. Civil litigants, in contrast, often settle cases with an explicit agreement that the terms of the settlement will not be revealed in or out of court by any parties or officials. Defendants may pay to avoid a finding of fault or to keep the public from discovering what fault had been or might have been found. If perhaps nine-tenths of the civil iceberg is unseen and practically invisible, civil litigation will elicit neither journalistic inquiry nor popular interest.

Biases Explain Skimpy Coverage

Three reasons that explain and perhaps justify the modesty of civil coverage relative to reportage of criminal cases have already been listed: civil cases tend to be or to seem private while criminal cases are inherently public; civil cases tend to be or to seem more humdrum while many criminal cases are arresting; and civil cases tend to be or to seem unintelligible while criminal cases usually feature clear findings of guilt or innocence. These three reasons reiterate common biases in media that we have already considered in previous chapters. Reports of civil cases will often be harder to dramatize, to personalize, to morselize, or to normalize than criminal cases and other news with which civil litigation must compete.

How Biases Reduce Civil Coverage

While it might be too facile to say that angle biases tend to contradict one another in civil cases, one angle may interfere with other angles in more civil cases than in criminal cases. Let us examine each of Bennett's angle biases in turn to see why this is the case.

We have already seen why criminal trials are easier to dramatize than civil trials:

> Criminal law is simply more "newsworthy" than civil law. More often, a criminal case will have in it the ingredients of human interest, public policy, and clearcut controversy that make news. At a more fundamental level, criminal law provides the most vivid test of the community's sense of justice and morality. Moreover, every criminal case can involve the basic guarantees of the Bill of Rights of the Constitution, at nearly every step.[8]

In this passage, Denniston deftly cites three ways in which civil cases are less dramatic or dramatizable than criminal cases. First, few civil trials can compete with visceral criminal matters for audience interest. Second, public policy—the social, economic, or political importance or relevance of matters—attaches more obviously to publicized or sensationalized criminal trials. Too often the importance and relevance of civil issues will seem more private and personal, especially to laypersons who do not fully grasp legal implications of cases. Third, clearcut controversy is virtually guaranteed in criminal trials. Civil cases are far less likely to furnish reporters with disagreements that constitute a controversy. Even if some controversy ensues, it is not as likely to pose clearcut choices, issues, or characters. Without much interest, policy implications, or understandable conflict, most civil cases are not very dramatic.

Civil cases that involve multiple parties, various jurisdictions, and complicated facts may be dramatic enough to justify coverage, but such drama may prove harder to morselize (Bennett's second angle bias). The criminal justice bottom line may justify a news brief even after almost all the facts have been pruned by reporter and editor, but pruning the complexities of the civil case may leave the reporter and editor no discernable or communicable bottom line. Hence, in civil cases, dramatization and morselization may conflict more often than cohere. The brief or report about civil courts that is simple and concise enough to fit into a news hole will likely be supplanted by another pithy story with drama intact.

Dramatic because consequential civil suits that nonetheless fit into news holes are not likely to suit personalization and normalization. Adding parties and major organizations to a case may make it more dramatic and hence more newsworthy if the resulting conflict reduces to an episode. However, class action suits or other ways of widening conflict to include more parties (and thus, I presume, more drama) will challenge personalization as well as morselization. We may also view the matter from a very different viewpoint. Sympathetic victims, vicious predators, villainous litigants, or other fitting subjects for personalized coverage can be discovered or created by reporters or press agents, but at some cost *both* to morselization, because character development takes space and words, *and* to dramatization, because personalized coverage often detracts from the institutional and community stakes that yield drama.

Some civil cases will feature drama because the persons involved in the case or the litigation arouse viewers' or readers' interest, but morselized coverage of such cases will often hinder normalization. Cases often offer clashing normalizations, for example. Is the plaintiff in a medical malpractice suit a victim seeking modest compensation from a quack, or is that plaintiff a chiseler extorting money from a blameless healer? Competing normalizations challenge journalists because virtually any judgments they make are likely to require extensive exploration (thereby impeding morselization) and complex characterizations (thereby complicating dramatization).

We have hardly surveyed the permutations of angle biases above, but our brief look should show that civil cases will often tax the best efforts of journalists to make the news. When we consider the four angle biases together, we see immediately that the four endanger the balance of news reports about civil litigation. When reporters dramatize, personalize, morselize, and normalize, they tend to create protagonists and antagonists, heroes and villains. Since few parties welcome the role of villain or foil, parties so positioned by reporters will challenge reports, reporters, and media. Every combination of angles will tend to the advantage of one side or the other, so every report will seem and may even be slanted. Of course, noncoverage is hardly neutral, but it is harder to complain about. We shall see that balance is particularly a problem amid civil trials. To report dramatic testimony on one day and to find little drama when the other side believes that it did well, for example, is likely to strike the side covered less as unfair. Comparable imbalances that disfavor criminal defendants matter less because most criminal defendants will not be in a position to complain much and many media customers would be indifferent to the complaint in any case.

I have stressed angle biases to explain the low profile of civil cases both absolutely and relative to criminal cases, but commercial biases enter as well. Each angle bias represents reporters', editors', and publishers' best judgments of long-run marketability and profit. Angle biases thus represent the habitual predictions of journalists of what readers and viewers will buy and what they will not. I have proposed no invariant rule, but I suggest that criminal cases are far more likely to yield copy that may be produced at lower cost in time, energy, personnel, and sources to greater interest among consumers. Thus, commercial biases, like angle biases, favor criminal coverage over civil.

Civil Practitioners Tend to Shun Publicity

Commercial biases and angle biases are not absolute bars to coverage. Rather, those biases and others reinforce journalistic habits. Journalists can break out of their routines *if* they have the will and opportunity. When journalists fear that biases or documents may unbalance their presentations, they chronically seek confirmations and denials from authoritative sources.

In civil litigation, however, many of the most authoritative sources are not talking to reporters. Judges and jurors, of course, must remain quiet. Lawyers, in addition, are not supposed to try their case in the press. Strictures on lawyers' comments apply to the civil realm as well as criminal cases and may apply with greater force when loose lips threaten to sink settlements. With much to lose and usually little to win by making themselves and their stories available to the press, civil litigants and lawyers may see even less incentive for cooperating with reporters than they do in criminal cases.[9] This reduces the symbiosis and source-ery on which the press so often depends.

The civil trial of Orenthal James Simpson may seem to exemplify the muting of what had been a raucous criminal case, but I urge you not to use that civil trial as an example. The criminal trial of O. J. Simpson and the subsequent wrongful death lawsuit are atypical and hence poor examples of anything. Perhaps Judge Hiroshi Fujisaki would have stifled parties to the civil suit in any case, but Judge Lance Ito's indulgence of attorneys, witnesses, and relatives of the slain probably contributed to Fujisaki's gag order. Without a video feed, coverage of the second trial was far less extensive and far less hysterical, but I draw no conclusion from that fact. Instead, the dearth of sources and possibilities for exchanges seem to me the more systematic factors.

Observers of court coverage document the absence of symbiosis and the dearth of source-ery. Jack Doppelt reported that 95 percent of the lawyers in civil practice whom he interviewed had had little or no contact with reporters.[10] Media critic David Shaw of the *Los Angeles Times* has noted that the 99 percent of lawyering that never makes it to court often goes underreported or unreported.[11] In criminal cases, even defense attorneys who routinely plead their clients out will appear in courtrooms and courthouses where reporters might try to recruit them as sources. Civil cases, however, expose attorneys to the press far less often, especially when those attorneys are deep in secret negotiations.

Scholars have found that reporters' relatively diminished interest in and work on civil cases also obviate press source exchanges. While two-thirds of the court reporters Drechsel studied spent a majority of their court reporting time on criminal cases, only one in eight devoted a majority of their court reporting time to civil cases. Given that the vast majority of Drechsel's reporters devoted *at most* a quarter of their time to court reporting (and spent most of their day on government reporting, general assignment, and other chores), even the one reporter in eight who reported spending the most court reporting time on civil cases should be expected to cover civil litigation for perhaps 15 percent of his or her day.[12] No wonder the press under-covers the volume of litigation and litigiousness.[13]

Even after the case has been concluded, the results are not truly final. Appeals or subsequent negotiations may be impeded or distorted by thoughtless remarks, so that even after the case is over, lawyers, judges, jurors, and litigants may choose not to cooperate.

In conclusion, we may generalize that journalistic routines tend to favor criminal coverage over civil coverage and noncoverage of civil litigation over coverage because fewer incentives induce cooperation between reporters and expert sources. Drechsel reported that such was clearly the case on the justice beat that he studied. His justice reporter explicitly preferred criminal to civil cases.[14] Indeed, that reporter's routine rounds insured far more exposure to criminal cases while exposure to potential civil law news was accidental. The reporter tended to pursue civil cases only if clerks or other courthouse personnel or observers gave him a tip.[15] We have seen why the reporter might despair of tips elsewhere.

Accuracy, Objectivity, and Sources Winnow Civil Coverage

We have now seen that biases characteristic of media and the professional ethics and practices of lawyers tend not only to reduce coverage directly but also to deprive reporters of symbiotic relations and routine sources. Journalists may cover civil cases with fewer assurances of accuracy and objectivity than the Inside-Out mission statement presumes. Deprived *both* of official parties who represent the community or another source of authority or expertise *and* of familiar proceedings that routinize interpretations, reporters of civil cases may struggle to achieve accuracy and objectivity.

In chapter 4, we saw that prosecutors and law enforcement, like other sources, rely on their presumptive expertise and their performative expressions. Presumptive expertise grows when the accounts and utterances of official sources, in courts and elsewhere, are treated as facts by journalists because officials are presumed by reporters and audiences to be in a position to know. What sources do or should know tends to trump other interpretations, so official utterances, promises, and opinions are presumed accurate and objective while other sources must compete for credibility and dissemination in mainstream media.[16] Presumptive expertise is assisted by performative expression. We saw in our exploration of criminal court coverage that official sources possess authority to express themselves in words that amount to official actions. When police pronounce arrests and read rights, when prosecutors file charges, and when judges pronounce sentences, their expressions constitute verbal actions. Official utterances do not merely recognize action; they *are* action.

Most parties to most civil suits lack the presumptive competence and the performative capacity of criminal justice officials and sources. We have no reason to assume that such unofficial sources are less competent, less trustworthy, or more self-interested than routine sources in criminal cases, but we may assume that journalists seldom accord them the same deference and authority that criminal justice sources enjoy. Private litigants are presumed self-interested unless they can allege that their case advances some public interest. Their civil-law opponents will obviously contest any such allegation of public interest, which vitiates immediately any objectivity and credibility that might have been attributed to either source. Accuracy yields to contradictory accounts that cannot both be true and objectivity yields to battling interpretations. Source-ery demands sources who can authenticate reports. Most civil cases feature few such sources and, hence, may result in stories that are eclectic and balanced, but the accuracy and objectivity of which may be contested.

Reduced Coverage and Patterns of Surfacing and Submerging

To sum up discussion to this point, we may say that difficulties in demonstrating accuracy and objectivity, shortages of official sources, conflicts among the usual angles, and limited marketability afflict civil cases more than criminal cases. If criminal cases are seldom covered for these and similar reasons, we should expect even less coverage of civil cases. Such features seem to account for why civil cases are so seldom visible.

Beyond such an explanation for reduced coverage, we may speculate that civil cases, like criminal cases, will surface in the media at their beginnings and at their conclusions, if they become visible at all. However, we also expect that, unlike criminal cases, civil cases usually will lack recurrent, built-in angles to orient reporters and audiences. If so, civil trials will usually be submerged more and more often than criminal trials.

Surfacing

We saw that the stages of criminal cases most likely to be reported were beginnings (indictments, arraignments, and opening statements) and conclusions (closing statements, verdicts, and sentencing). I called this "surfacing," likening criminal court reports to submarines that usually stay beneath the surface except at the beginning and end of a voyage.

We should expect civil cases to surface in the media when those cases offer reporters the same advantages as competing news (including competing court cases and criminal trials). When civil cases are filed, reporters may avail themselves of public events, official sources (such as courthouse clerks and public information officers), formal files and documents, and routine, performative utterances. Opening statements in public court likewise offer reporters a synopsis of what each side will try to prove. Both statements made when commencing a suit and statements made when introducing the suit to juries will likely stress substantial injustices in nontechnical language that jurors and viewers and readers can comprehend. When civil trials reach a public decision, the same sorts of accurate, objective, preformulated advantages *may* obtain. Before filings, between filings and opening statements, between openings and closing statements, and after verdicts, civil cases are, if anything, more daunting challenges to concision, accuracy, and objectivity than most political events.[17]

The foregoing considerations in mind, we may reasonably hypothesize that *the minimal coverage of civil cases will emphasize inputs (official, public filings of cases and dramatic, public opening statements) and outputs (official, public, and often dramatic decisions) over almost everything else.*

Table 5.2 shows general trends in coverage of civil cases, by arranging the number of stories according to the stages of the civil action.[18] I divide civil cases into Pretrial (every report before the plaintiffs formally open their cases with motions or statements), Trial (everything between Pretrial and Decision), Decision (every report after plaintiffs and defendants have rested their cases), and Posttrial (every report of a reaction after the trial).

As expected, newspapers tend to cover opening and closing stages of civil trials but much less in between. Indeed, table 5.2 shows us that in civil trials, pretrial and especially decisional phases surfaced and the trial phase submerged more than in criminal trials. For civil litigation, roughly two out of five articles concerned verdicts and damages. If the eighty-five articles in which no stages were mentioned explicitly are excluded, reports of decisions would account for almost half (47.6 percent) of all articles. This, we can see, contrasts with criminal coverage, in which the pretrial stage predominated even though the two kinds of litigation led to roughly equal numbers of stories about decisions.

In passing, please let me mention that civil litigation is covered at slightly greater length, on average, than criminal cases. This accords with my observations about the relative difficulties of covering civil cases, especially the relative challenge of morselizing such cases. Only among articles for which no stage of litigation could be coded did criminal justice stories average more words than civil justice stories.

Table 5.2 **Stages in Reports of Civil Cases**

	Civil Litigation	Criminal Litigation
Pretrial:		
Number	128 articles	240 articles
Percent	29.5%	40.7%
Mean Length	507 words	446 words
Greater Length	+13.7%	—
Trial:		
Number	54 articles	139 articles
Percent	12.4%	23.6%
Mean Length	568 words	473 words
Greater Length	+20.1%	—
Decision:		
Number	166 articles	164 articles
Percent	38.2%	27.8%
Mean Length	519 words	417 words
Greater Length	+24.5%	—
Posttrial:		
Number	1 article	4 articles
Percent	0.2%	0.7%
Mean Length	1720 words	1278 words
Greater Length	+34.6%	—
Unfocused:		
Number	85 articles	42 articles
Percent	19.6%	7.1%
Mean Length	581 words	648 words
Greater Length	—	+11.5%
Total:		
Articles	434 articles	589 articles
Percent	99.9%	99.9%
Mean Length	537 words	464 words
Greater Length	+15.7%	—

Expect Outrageous Inputs to Surface in News Media

If surfacing and submerging are to be expected in general, we may fine-tune our expectations a bit. *Expect civil inputs to be emphasized when the filing of a case itself is newsworthy.* If allegations or other issues submitted to litigation surprise, infuriate, or intrigue ordinary citizens, the mere submission of the case may make the news. The press will often cover such inputs as events rather than legal tactics. One such case was that of Paige Goodman.

With many Americans irate that trivial squabbles tie up their civil courts, news media might have anticipated that even the filing of the following suit would anger readers and viewers:

> One contender for valedictorian of the class of 1996 at Bayside High School in Queens was shy, studious, a soprano in the chorus; the other, the popular senior class president and captain of the tennis team. But their grade-point averages were practically identical, separated by just 0.05 points. And at different times, each girl was told that she, and she alone, would address more than 600 graduating seniors on June 25.
>
> Both students have already been accepted to Ivy League colleges, so the choice of valedictorian has strictly symbolic importance. But in what seems to be a case of academic competition run wild, the fight has pitted two Queens families against each other and left one girl a "wreck" and the other "devastated," according to family and friends. And, inevitably, it has ended up in court.
>
> The Board of Education had ruled that the two girls should be co-valedictorians, prompting the senior class president to sue to have the honor to herself. Yesterday, a State Appellate Court judge in Brooklyn upheld the school board's decision, but that ruling could change when a panel of judges hears the case next Wednesday, said Frank Sobrino, a spokesman for Chancellor Rudy Crew.[19]

Quoted here are the three opening paragraphs of the story carried by the *New York Times*. What do we see in those paragraphs? As I interpret this story, the journalists who produced it have explicitly chosen to play this as another episode of civil litigation run amok. The report almost asks readers to disdain this litigation and those who have clogged courts with an intramural spat. More, the report conveys weariness with petty cases. That, at least, is what I make of the clause "inevitably, it has ended up in court."

While I have cited this example to reinforce the point that newspapers' coverage routinely stakes out positions that are hardly objective in any strong sense, the more important moral of this story is that the reporter and the editor probably had to play the story in the way that they did if it was to make the *Times* at all. I read their angle as a device to normalize this dispute. That is, the report incorporates an interpretation that makes the story more intelligible by asserting that Goodman is engaged in litigiousness as usual.

By itself, a tiff between graduating seniors scarcely qualifies for our national newspaper of record. I concede that the story is morselized. Indeed, most of us would have trouble finding in this story much more than a news bite. It takes journalistic talent to swell a tidbit into a tale. I also concede that this trivial pursuit is personalized. The lead paragraph focuses on the personal angle. But where's the drama?

To me, the drama lies in symbolization. The journalists made this quarrel stand for a host of unimportant cases larding our civil courts. The report seems to me well crafted to irritate or enrage readers that this case was ever entertained by crowded courts and overworked judges. The item thereby performs remarkable alchemy: a spat so unimportant that the report concedes its triviality becomes a tale pregnant with import for our polity.

Such trivial filings may make the papers if they consume little of the news hole and offer readers a chance to laugh. Consider this morsel:

> Lansing, Mich.—A man is suing Michigan for $1 million because he says he caught cold in the drafty Capitol rotunda.
>
> Chris Morris filed the suit in the Court of Claims, saying he caught "a cold and hard cough" while visiting an African American art exhibit in February.
>
> Chris DeWitt, spokesman for state Attorney General Frank Kelley, said the whole thing seemed pretty funny.
>
> "But as ridiculous as this seems, we have to take it seriously. And keep in mind that one of our assistants will have to spend time on this lawsuit, so it does end up costing taxpayers money." A clerk at the Ingraham County Courthouse said the $90 fee for filing a suit was waived because Morris, according to court documents, is broke.
>
> Mark Behrens, an attorney and expert on lawsuit abuse, called the case "a paradigm for frivolous lawsuits." Said John Truscott, spokesman for Gov. John Engler: "The irony is we've heard for years the Capitol's full of hot air. I don't know where the cold air is coming from."[20]

While these 170 words provided droll filler and thus were, in that limited sense, newsworthy, the Gannett News Service that provided the story was able to tie the incident to the issue of frivolous lawsuits. This example of "kidding on the square" reminds us that reports of questionable lawsuits may persist in the minds of readers long after suits have been dismissed. Neither court nor judge may spend an hour on the matter and attorneys may dispose of this nuisance quickly, but that will be neither funny nor news.

To sum up, when the commencement of a case promises morselized, normalized, and personalized drama or when reporters and editors can make the mere filing of the case fit angle biases, expect inputs to be covered. Frivolous lawsuits without journalistic angles will prove harder to transform into news and thus should not be expected often. Ordinary lawsuits with predictable impact or high-profile forces (that is, celebrated litigants or renowned lawyers) may merit coverage in some news organs if there are angles. Normal inputs, however, will seldom make the news.

Expect Outrageous Outputs to Surface in News Media

Just as cases that will strike many viewers or readers as absurd may make news at their filing if they match the angle biases of mass media, results that will infuriate ordinary viewers or readers may make the news as well. Consider the following item that the *Washington Times* featured on its editorial page:

> When taxi driver Holden C. Hollum caught a mugger in the act, he knew what to do. He chased him down in his cab and pinned the thief against a wall. Well, the verdict on the case is in. A jury has awarded Ocie McClure, the confessed mugger, $24,595 because Mr. Hollum used excessive force in capturing him.[21]

The few readers of this editorial item, I imagine, went ballistic at a blatant miscarriage of justice. This capsule is adroitly crafted to provide just enough dramatization and personalization to make readers scream. However, pay attention to what the capsule *does not contain*: any legal or factual complexities that might make the result less perverse. To create such a "man bites dog" morsel, the editorialists normalized a unique or nearly unique outcome. It is difficult to read the item and not leap to the conclusion that something is very wrong in our courts.

Expect some outrageous outputs and obscene outcomes to make even national news outlets. If such items contain great possibilities for journalists to exploit angle biases, expect lengthy treatment that drives home injustice, perversity, corruption, and insanity (even if the reporters, editors, and producers have to create them). If, in contrast, civil courts dispense their ordinary outputs, expect the powerful, the white, the wealthy, and the celebrated to triumph with little notice.

In short, anticipate that the usual will go undercovered or uncovered while the bizarre and the aberrant will surface.

Submerging

The second part of our preliminary hypothesis incorporates the advantages in angle biases that, I have argued, criminal trials have over civil trials.[22] Criminal cases and civil cases dramatically present those who threaten society. Threats who are defendants in civil actions usually have in their deep pockets the wherewithal to strike back at news media, whereas defendants in criminal litigation tend to have less money and less clout (O. J. Simpson to the contrary notwithstanding). Few contract disputes or fights over copyright infractions will provide heroes and villains or other normalized, personalized angles, although some liability or pollution cases will. The bulk of business litigation cannot be dramatized, morselized, personalized, or normalized and so must be left for specialized media that cover business or law. Many private cases about real estate, employment, malpractice, or insurance may be fraught with far more danger to the press (from libel actions, for example) than angles of interest for most viewers and readers. While some recurrent themes, stereotypes, and characters encourage coverage of civil actions, most civil cases lack such news pegs. When the news pegs are lacking, expect little or no coverage.

Expect Throughputs to Be Covered Less

Between the official openings and the official closings of cases, civil procedures determine the course of trials. Television (such as *L.A. Law* and *People's Court*) and movies (*The Verdict* and *Class Action*) may have conditioned many citizens to believe that civil trials are riveting, but "Court TV" or a visit to our local courtrooms should extinguish that belief. Civil trials tend to be complex, technical, and confusing. To understand why we should expect throughputs to war with journalistic biases more than inputs and outputs, we need only apply the same media logic we have applied to civil coverage in general.

Inputs and outputs are largely prescribed and performative and thus more formal, more authoritative, and more predictable. To file a case with a civil court, to make an opening or closing statement, and to render a verdict are each routinized actions for which coverage could be just as routine. That is, a reporter who missed the actual event could cover it nonetheless by filling in details on a standard form. Throughputs are generally less circumscribed and hence more variable. Reporters must be present, attentive, and retentive to render ongoing examination and cross-examination. That increases the cost of coverage.

Civil liability may turn on legal subtleties that reporters cannot distill for viewers and readers as easily as reporters can define wronged parties and trespasses at the beginning of disputes or winners and losers at disputes' resolutions. Let us take care not to overstate this distinction: in civil actions, inputs may include suits and counter-suits, claims and counterclaims (the accused cannot officially counter prosecute, the defense of O. J. Simpson to the contrary notwithstanding) and outputs may defy description. Nonetheless, throughputs are often far less defined, distinct, discrete, or determinate than inputs and outputs.

Tending toward the ill-defined, indistinct, and indeterminate, civil throughputs are very hard to normalize, although dramatization, personalization, and morselization are hardly easy. Introduction of evidence and cross-examination can be very dramatic and very per-sonal, so reporters might have as little difficulty dramatizing or per-sonalizing such actions as they would with inputs. Most thoughputs are harder to separate from sequences of action and strategy than inputs and outputs, so journalists usually must morselize without rec-ognized, authoritative phases or rituals to guide their readers or view-ers. Normalization of civil procedures and proceedings, however, is probably most challenging. Every motion and ruling embodies lan-guage and learning that audiences for mass media have never mas-tered and seldom confronted. Viewers and readers will want to inter-pret events in terms of culpability (Who is guilty of what?) when judges, jurors, and lawyers are considering liability (Who owes what to whom?).

While commercial and angle biases may impede coverage of throughputs in civil cases even more than they hinder coverage of beginnings and endings, I have still another reason to expect through-puts to be under-covered. Ordinary judgments about news-worth can become treacherous if one or both parties charge reporters with unbal-anced coverage. This is less so at the beginning of a lawsuit, when defendants may dismiss the suit as frivolous and a collage of wild alle-gations and willful distortions. Nor are ordinary news judgments sus-pect when settlements or verdicts are reported, for journalists may publicize reactions or spin from many parties and observers. Amid a trial, however, parties are likely to think that judgments about news-worth reveal reporters' and editors' preferences or prejudices. The more that parties believe that they have at stake in a civil case, the more attentive to coverage of throughputs they are likely to be.

Objectivity Up in Smoke

I realize that my point about the balancing act inherent in covering throughputs in cases with high stakes for public images may be a little obscure or abstract, so let me illustrate this point with an example. Author Richard Kluger has recently supplied us an example of the stakes of covering throughputs.[23] Amid a lawsuit against three tobacco companies for causing a smoker's death, Kluger tells us, only one reporter was astute and attentive enough to sort through the various documents and testimony that plaintiff's attorneys, led by Marc Z. Edell, introduced. Morton Mintz covered the trial for the *Washington Post* and was afforded ample space in which to explore its complexities. This made him a special target of the publicist for the defendant companies, who provided texts and transcripts helpful to the tobacco companies and interpreted each day's events in the light best for his clients. When Mintz nonetheless covered the parade of internal documents and witnesses that made Edell's case seem meritorious and the defendants' conduct seem questionable, the publicist warned Mintz that the publicity agency planned to take the matter up with Mintz's superiors at the *Post*. After the trial, the publicist wrote a four-page letter to Mintz's boss alleging imbalances in Mintz's copy.

That the publicist for tobacco companies would assist the press in getting good coverage for the industry and would punish a reporter who covered the plaintiffs reiterates that commercial biases are occasionally reinforced by advertisers, publicists, and other commercial powers. What fascinates me about Kluger's account of the imbalance in Mintz's and the *Post*'s coverage of *Cipollone v. Liggett Group, Philip Morris, and Loews* is that Kluger admits the imbalance:

> The charge was correct, because in Mintz's view, the witnesses and documents that Edell was presenting were hard news, while the defense case consisted largely of familiar recitals by longtime recipients of tobacco money and a protracted examination of Rose Cipollone's medical history in order to plant doubt among the jury that smoking had caused her lung cancer.[24]

I see in Kluger's account the very sorts of angles that characterize news. That is, Kluger claims that Mintz covered the plaintiff's presentations more than the representations of the tobacco defendants because the plaintiff's exposition had greater news-worth. See if you can discern the angle biases before I assess them.

Mintz had covered startling revelations in internal letters and memoranda from the tobacco industry, I read Kluger to argue, because they were dramatic and morselizable, if not personalizable as well. The tobacco defendants, in contrast, were presenting expert witnesses who contested whether smoking caused any health problems. Kluger asserts that Mintz did not cover such testimony as much as the startling revelations because they were old news. Mintz may have chosen to cover the defendants' claims less because they depended on highly technical testimony of which ordinary readers could make little sense.

News-worth, Kluger has shown us, may create imbalances, real or concocted, in coverage. The *Post* stood behind Mintz; less experienced and less respected reporters working for less formidable news organizations might not enjoy such support. As a result, many reporters may dodge civil litigation to cover parties less likely to sue or strike back.

To sum up, we may reasonably predict less coverage of throughputs than of inputs and, especially, of outputs. Throughputs suit journalistic biases and routines less well and less often than the beginnings and endings of cases. In addition, reporting throughputs challenges the balance, actual or apparent, of media. As a rule, *throughputs will be "under-covered" both absolutely and relative to outputs and inputs.*

Exceptions to the Rule

Having created a reasonable hypothesis about civil coverage, I must now qualify that hypothesis. I have claimed that most civil cases are not newsworthy. However, large newspapers will daily feature one or more civil matters. To account for such covered civil actions, I have further hypothesized that outputs are most likely to manifest angles or news pegs characteristic of modern mass media and hence to elicit coverage. Inputs may be harder to morselize and are harder to assess in advance, but they are cheap to cover. We may expect fewer inputs to be covered than outputs, but we expect many commencements of litigation to make the news. I hypothesize further that civil throughputs, which usually accommodate angle biases and commercial incentives less, will not be covered often even in cases that merit coverage at preliminary or concluding stages.

Having related routine coverage and noncoverage to angle biases, I now test these tentative findings against anomalous cases. I have selected three sets of product-liability cases to reveal exceptions to the tentative rule. These exceptions will remind us that this chapter speculates about coverage because so little work on civil coverage has appeared.

Did Fuming Corvairs and Exploding Pintos Normalize Accelerating Audis?

We will examine very briefly liability litigation regarding the Audi 5000. I chose this set of cases because I believe I have a defensible suspicion from which to begin. I suspect that each episode of litigation normalizes such litigation, which in turn makes subsequent episodes more newsworthy because more intelligible. In the case of suits against automakers, each instance of corporate greed or substandard production, alleged or proved, makes subsequent instances more familiar.[25] Truck and automobile cases other than Chevrolet's Corvair and Ford's Pinto may have inclined viewers and readers to credit claims about the Audi 5000, but those two predecessors seemed to me to have been most widely known.

Ralph Nader attacked General Motors' Corvair and other American cars in a widely known if not as widely read book, *Unsafe at Any Speed*.[26] The Corvair and other inadequate automotive products provided stereotypes for a subsequent set of cases concerning Ford Motors' Pintos. In the case of Ford's Pinto, Mark Dowie revealed secret Ford documents in an article for *Mother Jones* that claimed that Ford's executives determined that it would cost them less to settle or to lose dozens of civil suits than to fix the gas tank in the Pinto.[27] Ford maintained that nothing or not much was wrong with Pintos but began to settle and to lose suits.

Coverage of the Corvair and Pinto cases in turn meant that, once the Audi 5000 came under suspicion, news organs might join the civil fray early and often, for they could be confident that readers and viewers would have a ready frame of reference. In sum, these cases suggest that the *usual indifference of mass media toward civil litigation can be overcome if stereotypes have so suffused the population that news media have news hooks to expand stories that they would normally morselize or ignore.* This is an important exception to the general rule that I have formulated.

Accelerating the Audi 5000 into the Courts

In *Galileo's Revenge: Junk Science in the Courtroom*, Peter W. Huber has argued that lawyers in pursuit of wealthy defendants and reporters in search of gullible consumers braked sales of the Audi 5000.[28] Mr. Huber's tale of pseudoscientific studies broadcast by uncritical media is fascinating. What interests us most about this story is how the Audi 5000 surfaced in mass media.

As Huber tells the story, a few owners of Audi 5000 automobiles had connected with each other and lawyers. The owners insisted that, despite their jamming on the brakes, their cars had surged out of control for no reason. They labeled the problem "sudden acceleration" and claimed that the Audi 5000 was liable to race forward or backward despite the best efforts of competent, responsible drivers to stop the vehicles. United by a label if not an explanation, outraged consumers and experienced automotive consumer advocates banded together. Lawsuits lurched toward Audi.

60 Minutes raced forward as well. In April 1986, the weekly televised newsmagazine aired stories of careening cars, including the devastating story of a minister's wife helpless to stop her Audi 5000 from propelling her six-year-old son through her garage and a partition. Her boy was dead because she could not stop the sudden acceleration of her car. Enter dramatization and personalization. Other drivers ended up on diving boards, inside homes, and down elevator shafts. All claimed to have been braking as hard as they could but to no avail. These mutually reinforcing anecdotes improved the credibility of the litigants, making them sources on whom CBS could rely. While claims against this model appeared elsewhere, *60 Minutes* beamed an arresting story to 30 million television sets in twenty minutes:

> Plaintiffs' lawyers could hardly have produced a better story on "60 Minutes" if they had written the script themselves. The newsmagazine happily tracked [auto-safety advocate Clarence] Ditlow's line, heightening the drama by mixing the diabolical with the inexplicable.[29]

Huber proceeds to show how little hard information backed up the mysterious allegations against the Audi 5000 and how suspect were the authorities and data on which reporters relied. Such shaky source-ery, we saw already, routinely characterizes mass mediated stories. Source-ery excused clumsiness:

> L'affaire Audi had now become viciously circular: the publicity attracted suits, the suits generated publicity, and the more people heard about sudden acceleration, the more they came to believe in it. As soon as you're *told* that your car is possessed by engineering demons, you're likely to understand in a flash just what it was that caused the stupid accident you were in last week. Last week you thought it might have been your own dumb fault, but now the matter is suddenly clearer.[30]

Huber may be correct about the circularity of this story. However, Huber may have overlooked that the starting points of circles often are hard to detect. The Audi 5000 careened into a segment of *60 Minutes* because reporters and editors were prepared to believe that automobiles' manufacturers were covering up when they claimed that "sudden acceleration" was not possible. I suspect that the Corvair and the Pinto and other wrangling over automobiles' safety inclined both producers and consumers to believe that the cars and not the drivers were at fault. I wonder if the sins of Chevrolet and Ford were visited upon Audi at least in part because the Corvair and the Pinto had normalized defective car stories? Whatever the merits of my suspicion that the Corvair and the Pinto normalized automobile-liability cases, Huber directs our attention to two aspects of the Audi saga. The amazing, accelerating Audi surfaced when some cases were being filed. This is consistent with our preliminary hypothesis that civil cases tend to surface, if at all, during inputs and outputs. However, Huber maintains that coverage of sudden acceleration led in turn to a new spate of complaints. This second point suggests an exception to the rule that civil cases are not covered except at their beginnings and their endings. If Huber is correct, many Audi cases emerged before formal litigation was underway. This qualifies my claim that pretrial negotiations and legal maneuvering tend to be submerged. In Huber's view, coverage begat litigation. Cases not previously contemplated began to take shape in lawyers' minds and offices because of coverage that Huber regards as precipitate. In this sense, *60 Minutes* made the news with which the Audi Corporation would live for years.

Results of cases were somewhat mixed: some plaintiffs won at trial but many lost. In 1988, the mother who drove into her six-year-old lost in a jury trial.[31] While newspapers covered the trials, often in capsule form, I doubt that the audience for reports of settlements and trials matched the audience for *60 Minutes*. Thus, inputs and even preinputs (that is, happenings prior to formal commencements of cases or events that precipitated litigation by inducing Audi owners to sue) dominated coverage as cases and outputs and outcomes never did.

An Exception to Our Tentative Hypothesis

The Audi affair poses an exception to our tentative contention that most civil litigation does not emerge before formal inputs such as the formal filings of cases and the opening statements of trials. "Sudden acceleration" surfaced before the stage that I have labeled "inputs." From this episode I conclude that organized and organizing interests may make the news before inputs. More, Audi litigation indicates that individual verdicts may be covered less than preinput activities when national television enters a fray. *60 Minutes* cranked up the volume, in my view, because the organizing and organized litigants had arresting stories: dramatized, personalized, and morselized. However, the key sources—Audi owners irate at out-of-control products—had to be normalized. Tales of cars crashing through walls while the driver floored her or his brakes might create great skepticism without apparently credible sources such as a reverend's spouse and seemingly expert explanations from organized entities. Even such source-ery might have proved inadequate to normalize the dispute, however, without a quarter-century of recalls and complaints.

Although I want to draw attention to the specifics of the Audi cases, I do not mean to suggest that these cases are unique. Indeed, proponents of reform of civil litigation, such as Huber, would insist that spasms of ill-informed coverage of pseudoscientific claims that cannot stand rational scrutiny are far too common. We cannot be certain, for example, whether silicone breast implants will turn out to have been perfectly innocent of the various malfunctions attributed to them.[32]

Instead, my point is that organized litigants and stories suited to mass media news angles provide an exception to the tentative hypothesis that this chapter has advanced. Almost all cases and disputes will not make the news during inputs let alone before that stage. However, groups that know how to make the news can achieve notoriety and even, as in the case of Audi, create a boomlet if national television takes up the cause.

Coverage of Outrageous Outputs— Stella Liebeck's Java

Have you slandered Stella Liebeck? Do not answer before you read this news capsule:

> An 81-year-old woman has won a $2.9 million lawsuit against McDonalds Corp. after she suffered third-degree burns from coffee from the fast-food chain that spilled on her lap, her attorney, Ken Wagner, said.
>
> A jury in Albuquerque Wednesday awarded Stella Liebeck $2.7 million in punitive damages and $200,000 in compensatory damages from McDonalds, he said.
>
> In 1992, Liebeck bought coffee from a drive-through

McDonalds near her home, and it spilled as she tried to remove the cap from a Styrofoam cup.

Wagner said McDonalds serves its coffee at 180 to 190 degrees, compared with coffee made at home, which has a temperature of 135 to 140 degrees.[33]

Do you now recognize Stella Liebeck? Liebeck's victory made an episode of *Seinfeld*, Jay Leno's nightly monologue, a commercial for a long distance company, and countless conversations. You may still hear jokes about spilling coffee on yourself for profit on the Internet and the World Wide Web, on talk radio, and among colleagues and coworkers.

At least two features of the verdict and award made the Liebeck-McDonald's case newsworthy. First, the size of the award marked Liebeck as a winner of a litigational lottery. When someone wins millions for an accident that likely has befallen every viewer or reader, that is news. Second, the apparent frivolousness of the lawsuit reminded many viewers and readers of claims that Americans were lawsuit crazy and that jurors were soft touches for plaintiffs' attorneys.[34] It seemed that a clumsy woman had spilled coffee on herself while driving and then collected from McDonald's because the spilled coffee burned her.

"The Case of the Scalding Coffee" seemed to many Americans so scandalous and so frivolous that Stella Liebeck became an icon[35] both for those who would reform civil litigation in the United States and for those who lamented the decline of personal responsibility. We will look at five phases of the Liebeck coverage for what we can learn from this story. In general, cases about civil litigation do not have multiple phases. It is difficult enough for most cases to make the papers once!

Lucky Liebeck (August 18 to September 2, 1994)

After the jury's award was announced on August 18, 1994, many newspapers dispatched immediately a story that they had not previously covered. This first stage reiterates the perils of cases that surface at their conclusions, for news reporters and editors seized their readers' attention at the expense of accuracy and perspective. In this largest wave of stories (see figure 5.1), jurors seemed to have awarded Liebeck nearly $3 million for spilling coffee on herself while driving away from a drive-through window. Readers could easily have concluded that Liebeck not only scalded herself through her own clumsiness but also that she then got greedy and with the help of lawyers and jurors ripped off a blameless McDonald's franchise. Little wonder that initial reactions evinced sympathy for McDonald's, anger with Liebeck and her attorneys, and disdain for the jury!

Libeled Liebeck (September 3 to September 14, 1994)

Many of the inadequacies of the initial wave of coverage were addressed two weeks later when a reporter for the *Wall Street Journal*, Andrea Gerlin, returned to the story and corrected some of the media's misapprehensions.[36] While this second phase of coverage was carried by a fraction of the newspapers that covered the disgraceful "Lucky Liebeck" story (see figure 5.1), those who read it got a very different view of the matter. Your sympathies might change a little if you were aware that:

- Liebeck was riding in the car, *not* driving.
- The car was parked to the side of the lot before Liebeck opened her coffee.
- Liebeck took the lid off her coffee to add cream and sugar.
- McDonald's had had more than seven hundred complaints about the temperature of its coffee but continued in its manual to recommend that coffee be served at or above 175 degrees Fahrenheit.
- Albuquerque, where Liebeck purchased the coffee, is so high that the coffee might have been near boiling.
- Liebeck originally sought only compensatory damages for her third-degree burns on her legs and lap and pursued punitive damages when McDonald's refused to pay her hospital bills.
- The jurors awarded $2.7 million against the McDonald's corporation because that sum represented two days' coffee sales and would induce McDonald's to serve safer coffee.

Liebeck Loses (September 14 to December 1, 1994)

Stage 3 started on September 14, 1994, when the judge at the trial reduced punitive damages to $480,000 to go with $160,000 compensation for medical bills, pain, and permanent scarring. Such reductions are hardly unusual but are usually covered less than the original outrages. Thus, even attentive readers and especially viewers may miss the reductions and other adjustments of civil awards. If, for example, a huge punitive award gets the attention of the defendant but the defendant does not have to pay the award, citizens might conclude that the civil courts punish malingering and malfeasance without costing businesses, insurers, and consumers a bundle. If, in contrast, citizens do not know about adjustments, they proceed with faulty information. This phase also reminds us that the jury's award does not end the case but reports of postverdict developments may not be as copious as reports of attention grabbing awards. Thus, some quite public outputs may never surface.

Stella Settles (December 2 to December 5, 1994)

The settlement between Liebeck and McDonald's was covered even less than the third phase. This fourth stage of the Stella Liebeck saga was the actual end of this episode of litigation. Relative to the outrageous verdict, however, this report was undercovered. Indeed, coverage of the fourth stage was about one-third that of the first. This alerts us to the fact that posttrial settlements may be barely more noticeable than pretrial negotiations. They often are just as secret. While Liebeck got far less from the settlement than the millions she had been awarded, we must imagine that few citizens were attentive enough to the news to learn that her award had shrunk by perhaps an order of magnitude.

Symbolic Stella (December 5, 1994)

Once her case settled amid little fanfare, a fifth phase began. Figure 5.2 reveals longer-term coverage. Long before this fifth stage, proponents of tort-reform and wags had appropriated the coffee verdict to support their claims and cause. Once Liebeck settled, she ceased to exist for most of us and became a symbol. I suspect that because coverage of the verdict itself dwarfed subsequent developments, Stella Liebeck now represents a tort system out of control. People who no longer associate her name with her case believe that they possess an important piece of evidence in a policy debate. To the extent that Liebeck is now a captive of the first stage of her story that the media covered, the real Stella Liebeck has been supplanted by the symbolic. Since McDonald's announced the settlement on December 1, 1994, symbolic Stella Liebeck has starred in discussions of the "Contract with America," in articles about a second McDonald's suit involving hot coffee, and in the Ann Landers advice column. These political and cultural dialogues keep a myth of Stella Liebeck, as opposed to her story, before people attentive to newspapers.

Figure 5.1 Number of Articles per Date, Liebeck vs. McDonald's

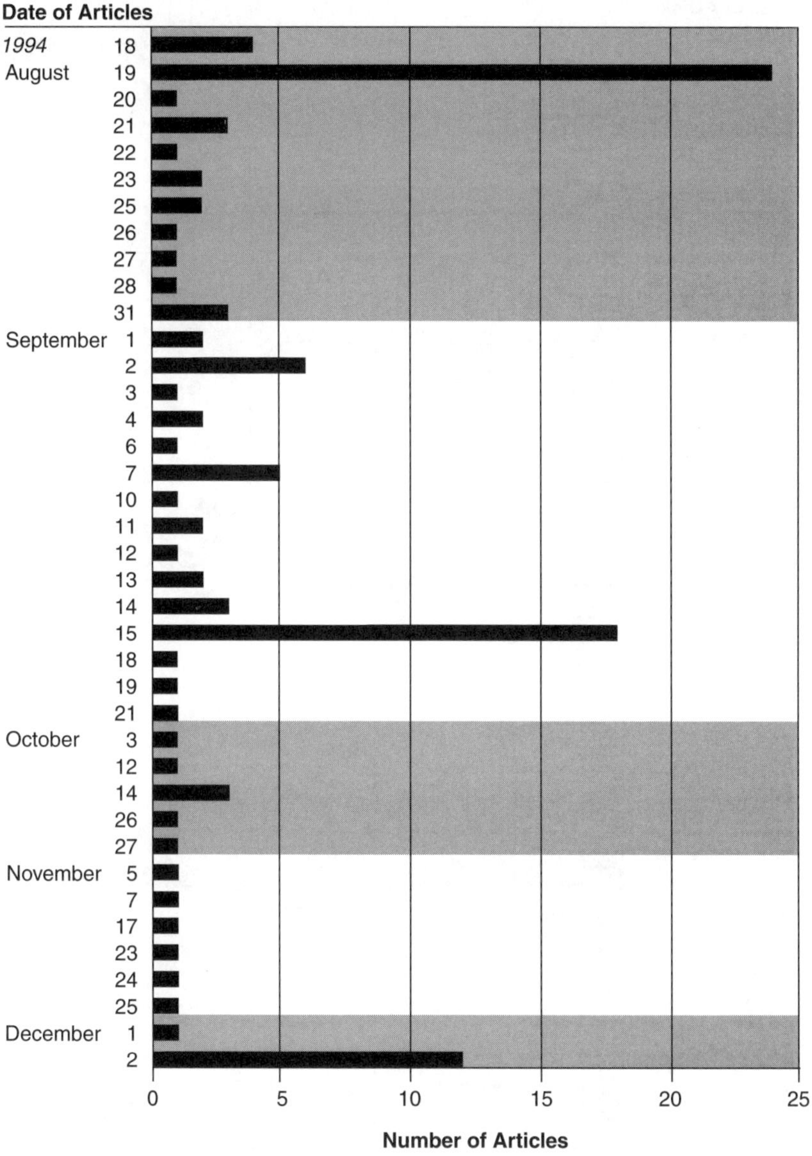

Date of Articles

Number of Articles

Figure 5.2 Number of Articles per Date, Stella Liebeck

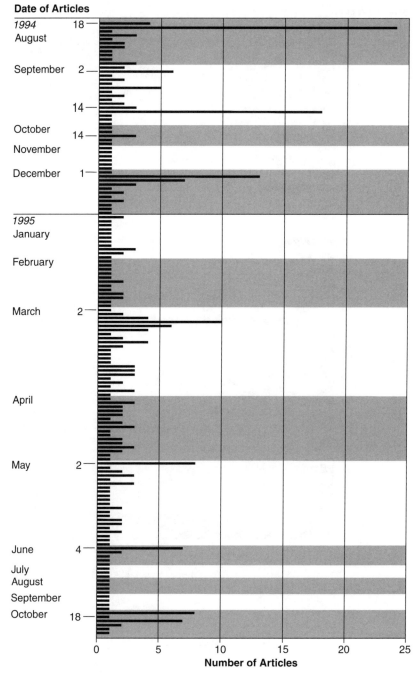

Another Exception to Our Tentative Hypothesis

This cultural kidnapping of Stella Liebeck qualifies, it seems to me, the tentative hypothesis that this chapter has presented. Even the formal institution of the Liebeck case made little news. However, an output of that case—that is, the $3 million verdict—dominated coverage initially. Adjustments, corrections, and subsequent events never caught up with these initial, flawed reports. When the Liebeck case submerged in later stages, the public outcome of her litigation disappeared. Now a mythic outcome endures. Had Stella Liebeck's story arrested attention before or during the trial of her complaint, some or many misconceptions about the nature of her litigation might have been avoided.

Most such reports glimmer in mass media but fade quickly. These cases seem to conform to my hypothesis because they surface at their conclusions and then dive back into obscurity. Like Stella Liebeck's case, many cases did not surface before verdicts. However, the case of Stella Liebeck's coffee resurfaces often, I have observed, in mass media, in legislative debates, in entertainment, on the Internet, and in conversation. If cases symbolize some social trend, it seems, they can emerge and not submerge.

Liebeck's case has persisted as an object lesson against frivolous lawsuits despite mass-media efforts to debunk errant reports of the case, despite the severe "downsizing" of the damages, and despite the efforts of many restaurants to reduce the temperature of coffee and especially hot chocolate. This persistence suggests that *we must qualify our expectation that cases only briefly surface. Most do; but some newsworthy cases surface and linger.*

Cigarette Wars—Newsworthy Throughputs

I have hypothesized that most civil trials get no coverage and that the few trials that do tend to be covered at their inceptions and conclusions but seldom otherwise. Next, we examine lawsuits against tobacco companies to remind ourselves that many cases can sustain coverage between inception and conclusion. As with our review of litigation about Audis and coffee, our survey of tobacco cases will be brief. As with the previous case studies, I am trying only to show that our hypothesis admits of exceptions.

Cipollone v. Liggett Group, Philip Morris, and Loews

Cipollone has drawn more extensive coverage than other tobacco cases, so we will examine that coverage to expose another exception to our tentative hypothesis. That exception concerns news-worthy evidence and testimony. I have speculated that most civil cases submerge during technical, tedious, and inconclusive testimony and evidence, and so that throughputs should be expected to draw little coverage even for the minority of cases that elicit any notice from mass media. Some throughputs are newsworthy intrinsically and other throughputs may be made newsworthy. When testimony, motions, evidence, judges' rulings, and other ordinary features of civil procedure feature angles that are dramatic, personalized, morselized, and normalized, coverage is likely.

Rose Cipollone had averaged more than a pack of cigarettes per day for decades and expired from lung cancer before her day in court.[37] Cipollone knew about the warnings on the sides of packs of cigarettes but had difficulty quitting. Her lawyer, Marc Edell, alleged that the tobacco companies deprived Cipollone of information by contesting findings concerning cancer and tobacco. To support claims that tobacco corporations had conspired to suppress information that might have scared smokers off, Edell got more than half a million documents from the companies. These documents may best explain the extensive coverage of the Cipollone litigation, for the promise of revelations and the claim of conspiracy presented far more news-worth than another round of dueling doctors and paid experts.

Table 5.3 shows us that we should not exaggerate the coverage that even this most publicized case received.[38] Major newspapers in table 5.3 typically featured few articles over the almost five months between the beginning and the ending of the formal trial. Perhaps the dearth of articles in newsmagazines is understandable. Why the *Wall Street Journal, Boston Globe, Miami Herald,* and *San Diego Union-Tribune* managed less than an article per month is less clear. The *St. Petersburg Times, Chicago Tribune,* and *Christian Science Monitor* averaged about two articles per month. Only the top five dailies in table 5.3 covered *Cipollone* in a manner that one might call extensive. The skimpy coverage that most newspapers in the sample afforded Cipollone reminds us that landmarks get little coverage from even prestigious papers, and so we should expect less momentous cases to secure even less coverage, especially from less resourceful news gatherers.

I do not mean to attack newspapers that modestly covered *Cipollone.* Tobacco corporations had never lost a case or settled a civil claim, so editors might have chosen not to devote much space or many resources to what could become tobacco litigation as usual. On the

Table 5.3   Mentions of *Cipollone v. Liggett Group,*
Philip Morris, and Loews (1988)

	Pretrial	Opening Statements	Plaintiff's Case	Defense's Case	Closing Statements	Deliberations	Verdict	Posttrial[a]
Bergen Record	14	1	16	3	0	2	0	7
Newsday	2	1	10	2	2	4	15	4
Washington Post	4	1	19	12	2	2	4	1
New York Times	9	0	7	7	2	4	8	3
Los Angeles Times	7	0	0	4	2	2	5	3
Christian Science Monitor	0	0	2	1	1	0	2	0
Chicago Tribune	1	0	0	1	0	0	5	1
St. Petersburg Times	1	0	1	1	1	1	4	1[b]
San Diego Union-Tribune	0	0	0	3	0	0	0	0
Miami Herald	0	0	0	0	0	0	1	0
Boston Globe	0	0	0	0	0	0	0	1
Wall Street Journal	0	0	0	0	1	0	2	1
U. S. News & World Report	0	0	0	0	0	0	1	0
Time	0	0	0	1	0	0	1	0
Newsweek	0	0	0	1	0	0	1	0
Total Mentions	38	3	55	36	11	15	49	22
Percent of 229 Mentions	17%	1%	24%	16%	5%	7%	21%	10%

a. Articles more than two weeks after the verdict (June 13, 1988) until the end of 1988.
b. This article is a book review.

other hand, the cache of documents that Cipollone's attorneys had obtained promised startling testimony and damaging evidence, so I might have expected more newspapers to be more interested than they appear to have been.

Print-media[39] removed from the Newark courtroom appear to have relied on four nearby dailies—the *Record* of Bergen, New Jersey; *Newsday* of Garden City, Long Island; the *New York Times*; and the *Washington Post*—for coverage. Ease of coverage and lack of expenses may explain why those four papers accounted for three quarters of the coverage.

The exceptional coverage by those four papers, however, thunders that throughputs will be covered by some news organs if commercial biases and angle biases favor such coverage. The four covered the plaintiff's revelations and the defendants' replies in addition to extensive coverage of outputs and inputs. Over the months of the trial, these papers featured more articles on throughputs than outputs or inputs. The *New York Times* balanced plaintiff and defendant equally. Recall that the tobacco companies' publicist protested the imbalance in the *Washington Post* (nineteen articles while the plaintiff presented evidence, and a dozen while the defendant responded). If the *Record* or *Newsday* had wider readership or national prominence, perhaps their far higher ratios of stories about the plaintiff to stories about the defendants' cases would have attracted attacks as well.

What might account for the preponderance of throughputs in this instance? Most antitobacco suits feature gut-wrenching testimony from dying plaintiffs and their relatives, so the presence of dramatic, personal morsels in *Cipollone* is hardly distinctive. Rather, *Cipollone* was distinctively convenient for the four newspapers to cover and featured internal memoranda from tobacco companies. The revelatory documents were authoritative because they came from the defendants. The plaintiff relied not on testimony from witnesses and experts who might be thought to be self-serving but on defendants' own paper trail. Civil cases are often convenient and cheap to cover (commercial biases) and occasionally are endowed with obvious angles (angle biases), but seldom are plaintiffs able to, in effect, make the defendants condemn themselves.

How often tobacco cases generate relatively or absolutely extensive coverage of throughputs may be gathered from table 5.4. Three other cases featured coverage in which weeks or months of throughputs were covered more than the months leading up to the trial and the days on which trials begin and end. In *Galbraith v. R. J. Reynolds* (1985), the plaintiff and defendant arrayed experts against one another and the experts' testimony made news in what was then a novel sort of civil action.[40] Over an eight-week period eight years later, lawyers for Charles H. Kueper squared off against R. J. Reynolds in a similar bout of expert witness versus expert witness. Kueper's case in Belleville, Illinois, got prominent play in nearby papers such as the *St. Louis Post-Dispatch* and *Chicago Tribune*. In *Haines v. the Liggett Group*, nine years of legal maneuvering generated a smattering of articles when trial and appellate rulings appeared to favor the plaintiff's case, which otherwise drew little or no attention as this case slowly proceeded.[41]

Table 5.4   **Stages Covered in Civil Trials**

	Inputs		Throughputs		Outputs		Posttrial	
	In-State	Out-of-State	In-State	Out-of-State	In-State	Out-of-State	In-State	Out-of-State
Roysdon (1985)	0[a]	1	0[a]	3	0[a]	8	0[a]	0
Galbraith (1985)	4	8	10	13	10	14	4	2
Marsee (1986)	0[b]	7	0[b]	4	0[b]	11	0[b]	2
Cipollone (1988)	25[c]	16	45	46	37	38	14	8
Kyte (1988)	2	1	0	0	0	2	0	0
Horton 1 (1988)	0[d]	10	0[d]	5	0[d]	15	0[d]	5
Kotler (1990)	4	5	5	0	5	4	1	1
Horton 2 (1990)	3[e]	7	3	1	2	10	2	1
Kueper (1991)	4[f]	7	27[f]	9	4[f]	16	5[f]	7
Ierardi (1991)	0	8	0	1	1[g]	14	0	0
Haines (1993)	0	1	0	18	0	0	0	0
Wilks (1993)	0	0	3	1	1	5	0	0

a. No Tennessee newspapers in sample.
b. No Oklahoma newspapers in sample.
c. The *New York Times* and the *Garden City Newsday* were treated as in-state for Newark's *Cipollone* case.
d. No Mississippi newspapers in sample.
e. The *Memphis Commercial Appeal* was available for the second Horton trial and treated as an in-state newspaper.
f. *St. Louis Post-Dispatch* treated as an in-state daily for this downstate Illinois case.
g. The *Record* of Bergen, New Jersey, was treated as an in-state paper for this Philadelphia case.

Even if we dismiss *Haines* as an aberration, *Kueper* and *Galbraith* reiterate the prominence of throughputs, especially when we examine local media. Local media can cover in-town or in-state trials cheaply and suits by neighbors are far easier to personalize and to morselize than distant cases. If locality *may* entice coverage of throughputs, national significance may do so as well. Out-of-state coverage of battling witnesses and telling documents in *Galbraith*, in *Cipollone*, and in *Kueper* matched out-of-state coverage of decisions and exceeded out-of-state coverage of inputs.

More Prominent Exceptions to Our Hypothesis

While a majority of the newspapers in table 5.4 featured minimal coverage of throughputs, three or four landmarks showed that not all cases submerge between formal inputs and official outputs. I have suggested why throughputs generally should not be newsworthy, but these data suggest that such an expectation should not be taken for an invariant rule. Furthermore, this brief survey has shown that throughputs will, in complicated, hard-fought cases, occupy weeks or months. If a typical case opens and closes within a week or a month, mass media may cover the case with articles about pretrial maneuvers, opening salvos, closing shots, and verdicts with little loss. Extraordinary cases offer weeks of potentially newsworthy developments, and diligent media may report this or that morselized or dramatic moment as a pretext for bringing those interested in the trial up to speed. Last, this survey reminds us that research will have to include local newspapers and perhaps even neighborhood papers and weeklies if even tentative hypotheses are to survive exceptions.

Restating the Hypothesis

These brief case studies suggest the need for systematic studies of civil coverage. Our tentative generalizations may be reasonable starting points for conjecture and study, but they are bereft of much evidence. We barely needed to consider product-liability litigation to spot one reason why research in this area may be lagging: exceptions threaten to swallow rules! Still, our tentative hypothesis may serve us *if* we attend to the commercial biases, angle biases, and source-ery on which it was based. The exceptions, I believe, make sense in terms of one or more of these three tendencies established in the literature about mass media. All we need to do—about all we can do until methodical studies come forth—is keep our minds open and our expectations flexible and contextual. This chapter's organizing hypothesis can be rephrased to show what I mean by flexibility and contextuality.

Our tentative hypothesis was that *the minimal coverage of civil cases will emphasize inputs (official, public filings of cases and dramatic, public opening statements) and outputs (official, public, and often dramatic decisions) over almost everything else.*

The Minimal Coverage of Civil Cases

The vast majority of civil cases, which do not go to trial, go unreported because they present no news pegs to offset costs of coverage. Most civil disputes that are not formulated as legal cases will not make the press. While many newspapers routinely feature disputes and civil cases, and while large newspapers may feature multiple civil matters, cases covered constitute a small fraction of cases and disputes ongoing. *Hence, our first expectation for routine cases, built into our hypothesis, is no coverage.* Even most ordinary cases tried will present too few authoritative, credible sources and too few news angles to justify costly coverage. Indeed, we might embellish this expectation to predict that even when cases meet some minimal thresholds for source-ery and angles, they are likely to create only news capsules or filler. Phrased in the opposite: *few cases match the needs and habits of mass media, so commercial biases, angle biases, and source-ery will make mass media most selective in their reports of civil matters.*

Still, cases *will* be covered. Cases are far more likely to draw reportage when they present conflict and struggle (dramatization), when litigating parties or third parties interest viewers and readers (personalization), when episodes in cases are discrete and well defined (morselization), and, perhaps most crucial, when procedures and stakes are explicable to laypeople (normalization).

As noted throughout this chapter, developments that seem perverse or unjust to ordinary observers will tend to outdraw mundane occurrences that correspond to common sense. Injustice and perversity virtually bring with them dramatization and personalization and, by definition, they elicit from readers and viewers angry, anguished, or anxious reaffirmations of norms. Whether these events or stories are constructed as isolated incidents (morselized) or fitted into some trend is a matter of journalistic discretion. Either way, the extraordinary tends to supplant the ordinary in the few civil disputes covered.

... Will Emphasize Inputs ...

We expect some newspapers and perhaps local electronic media to cover two sorts of kickoffs to civil cases. Filings of cases and opening statements are cheap to cover and easy to source. If cases promise or can be portrayed to promise angles or other enticements, even bombast and puffery can make the news. I have noted that modern media tend to like the predictability of performative events, events in which some verbal action carries political force. Filing a case is such a performative verbal act that, if predigested skillfully by attorneys, it can furnish mass media with angles and sources at minimal expense.

I have no expectations about patterns of surfacing and submerging prior to trials. Such patterns depend on context so much that the best procedure is to observe patterns in various sorts of mass and specialized media and only then to posit some tendencies. Between the filing of a case and the official beginning of the trial, we may expect most disputes to submerge and to remain beneath most notice forever because most such cases will settle. However, strategies and tactics of negotiation include prodding the opposing party through hurtful publicity, so we should expect some prelitigation coverage if sources make angles cheap to cover. Preliminary rulings about the kinds of information each side owes the other side, motions about procedures, and wrangling over the law as it will apply to this or that set of facts all may make news.

... and Outputs ...

We have hypothesized that many resolutions of civil cases yield public, accessible, authoritative and credible sources in predictable places saying predictable words organized for reporters' routines and thus that, if any part of a case gets covered, its conclusion should. Perhaps the chief advantage of outputs over inputs and throughputs lies in clarity. Inputs may promise great legal stories but many highly anticipated cases go off track before news-worth fulfills their promise. Throughputs are often more or less significant in retrospect than they seemed when they occurred, so reporting this case or that rebuttal can be dicey. Outputs are not always perfectly clear, but winners and losers usually can be distinguished. The contributions of tactics and the vagaries of chance are both easier to assess at the end of the trial than they are as the trial proceeds.

As a result of such reasoning, we expect outputs to be reported more often than inputs or throughputs. Indeed, we might formulate a simple generalization: *if any aspect of a civil case is reported, it will probably be its verdict or result.* Again, this is particularly the case if reporters can depict a miscarriage of justice. Parties done wrong or laws misapplied might be newsworthy at all times, but the consequences of legal errors are most stark and arresting at an apparent end of proceedings. Before outputs, errors may be overcome. At outputs, errors seem likely to endure. More, at the stage of outputs injustices are usually easier to explain even if the medium has room for but a capsule. At other stages, give and take over issues will probably consume far more space or air time.

. . . Over Most Everything Else

Chastened by exceptional coverage of evidence and testimony in some tobacco cases, we must refine our expectations about aspects of disputes and cases other than outputs and inputs. We have just rehearsed why filing, jury selection, opening statements, closing statements, and verdicts occasionally tend toward news-worth. Another reason that such inputs and outputs get covered now and then is that they provide discrete, concentrated contexts for coverage. News media usually need wager no more than a column or a few seconds of air time on the news-worth of an opening or closing incident. In contrast, rendering testimony or evidence in representative, balanced, and accurate paragraphs may compel journalists to shoehorn days or weeks into a story or to lavish scarce space and sparse time on multiple stories.

If throughputs and other usually submerged aspects of cases tend to be relatively costly to cover, commercial biases lead us to expect that they will seldom be covered. However, we must remember what the tobacco cases showed us. The parts of cases that are usually submerged are the parts of cases that extend over days, weeks, or months. This means that media will have more opportunities to cover aspects of cases, to check in with an ongoing case. Thus, we should not be surprised to see coverage of cases that take a while to get started or a while to get over or both. Most inputs and outputs become stale news quickly. The expiration dates for other aspects of litigation are more variable. A startling admission by a witness or a medical emergency for a juror will tend to be relatively perishable news. The cumulative effects of memoranda revealed or rippling consequences of a landmark verdict, in contrast, may be assessed in features that may wait for time or space.

Thus, we should expect that most phases of civil litigation will be covered even less than inputs and outputs, but we should not be surprised to see some coverage of some cases.

Conclusion—
An Atheoretical Scorecard

Since most of this chapter is so exploratory and preliminary, we might conclude that we have too little information for any perspective to explain. Still, the case studies and skimpy literature do suggest some insights from which further inquiry might proceed.

What the Inside-Out Perspective Accounts For

Our limited information has suggested that civil cases surface in news media at the beginnings and ends of formal proceedings. In this respect, civil cases seem to resemble criminal cases. However, there are important differences. In criminal cases, crime reporters will survey many of the developments of cases before and, to a lesser degree, after formal courtroom actions and decisions. In civil cases, most of the negotiations and actions that precede trial are kept from reporters, deliberately and assiduously. Thus, civil cases achieve far less visibility on average than criminal cases. Civil cases spend far more of their "tours of duty" submerged and many never surface in the media.

I do not intend this generalization as criticism, and I urge you not to take it as such. Lawyers and judges have specialized media to cover civil cases and developments, so mass media restrict themselves to civil cases that will interest viewers and readers. I do not believe that a glut of largely unread news capsules about civil cases would improve public awareness. Indeed, the persistence of *Reader's Digest*, *USA Today*, *Cliffs Notes*, and newsmagazines leads me to assume that selective, concise coverage may induce ordinary citizens to read more than more extensive coverage.[42]

We have seen that the modest coverage may follow from concerns for accuracy and objectivity, the Inside-Out mission for news media. In journalistic practice under demands of deadlines, editors, and libel lawyers, accuracy and objectivity dictate limited coverage of civil suits. Accuracy in journalistic practice, we have now seen repeatedly, compels reporters to authenticate their copy by citations to officials who may be presumed to know or at least to be in the best position to know. Without the time and resources to verify most details, reporters must achieve acceptable accuracy by quoting and paraphrasing official pronouncements with fidelity. Reporters achieve acceptable objectivity by emphasizing and balancing accounts that will be familiar to readers, viewers, or listeners. The more novel, controversial, and enlightening an event or case is, the more difficulty reporters and editors will have cramming it into a story that fits the news hole and strikes litigants as balanced.

In short, the very pursuit of accuracy and objectivity may foredoom much coverage of civil litigation. Relative to criminal cases, civil cases feature fewer officials and authorities because civil cases are predominately private. Given the secrecy of pretrial negotiations and maneuvering, those who know may not tell and those who tell may not know. Comments by litigants and their lawyers are presumably tactical, neither accurate nor objective but simply their side of the story. If we then compare civil cases to competing stories outside the courts, we appreciate why news media would usually prefer news that they can predict, process, and document far more easily and efficiently.

If the Inside-Out mission of the press seems to account for minuscule or modest coverage of almost all civil cases, the mission of courts prescribed by the Inside-Out Perspective might explain the dearth of coverage as well. That mission was craft and candor. The more straightforward and adept the legal participants (that is, the judge and the lawyers) are, the harder they may make things for reporters. It is ironic that histrionics and miscarriages of justice will often be far easier for reporters to report. Routine civil procedures, in contrast, may defy coverage.

What Our Outside-In Perspective Accounts For

Still, I am somewhat concerned to have found that "Mainstream Standards" prevail mainly through noncoverage and distortions. If the objective accuracy that the Inside-Out Perspective presumes for news media entails coverage that is morselized and minimal in the minority of civil cases covered at all, observers schooled in our Outside-In Perspective are likely to note noncoverage and distorted coverage as justifications for a second look from outside the usual viewpoint.

At the beginning of this chapter I took some pains to differentiate coverage of civil courts from coverage of criminal courts. The first set of differences that I mentioned may accord with the Inside-Out Perspective. Insiders may excuse skimpy coverage of civil litigation by the private nature of many civil cases, by the relative technicality of issues and proceedings, and by the fact that civil cases that do not result in trials are settled out of court while criminal cases that do not result in trials usually end in court. These causes of skimpy coverage and noncoverage, it seems to me, are realities that reporters and their critics must acknowledge.

However, angle biases, commercial biases, and barriers to symbiosis and source-ery constituted a second set of differences that weigh against objective accuracy among reporters. Let us begin with angle biases. If civil cases have less news-worth because they do not suit angles that news media prefer, then noncoverage follows from expediency and the absence of hype rather than objectivity or accuracy. In addition, the little coverage that civil cases receive is likely to ensue from ease of coverage and susceptibility to hype at least as much as from objectivity, accuracy, and other journalistic ideals. If "law-worth" translates to "news-worth" only when cases are dramatized, morselized, personalized, and normalized, then decisions to cover and not to cover are neither objective nor accurate. From our Outside-In Perspective, coverage and noncoverage seem regularly to evince the distortions expected in the upper right corner of table 1.1.

If angle biases account for much of the coverage of civil matters, that would seem to support our Outside-In Perspective's conception of the flow of information about civil cases. That is, civil cases appear to be more newsworthy as drama and spectacle than as the two-step flow idealized by the Inside-Out Perspective. I have paraded examples of the rare instances in which civil disputes draw coverage. These examples almost always evinced exactly the drama that students of mass media and our Outside-In Perspective describe. I have wondered but I do not know the extent to which advocates of tort reform rely on this skewed, hyped version of civil litigation. Thus, angle biases play into an Outside-In account.

If angle biases impart more than a modicum of expediency and hyperbole to coverage of civil cases, commercial biases impart even more. I have cited from the few works on civil court reporting ample authority for the notion that reporters and editors shape coverage to the interests and tastes that they attribute to their audiences. The more news-worth is determined by the market for reports about civil courts, the more objectivity and accuracy are routinely subordinated to profitability: minimized costs and maximized sales. An Outside-In observer need not sniff that such mercenary considerations are beneath journalism. However, the Inside-Out observer should not object to the clear bias of news media in favor of commercial advantage. Plainly, commercial biases exacerbate angle biases and the two together compromise accuracy, objectivity, and perhaps even expansion of popular interest in and knowledge about the civil courts.

Worse, barriers to symbiosis and source-ery mean that civil

cases feature fewer experts and authorities to impart objectivity and accuracy to reports than in criminal cases, further constricting and compromising the two-step flow of information. What Outside-In critics should not decry Inside-Out defenders should not deny: mass media *cannot* cover civil cases as well as they cover criminal cases. Even if angle and commercial biases did not constrict such coverage, reporters and editors would need routine recourse to legal experts to convey coverage as accurate and objective as coverage of criminal courts. Criminal court reporting habitually relies on knowledgeable personnel (many of the commentators on the Simpson trials excepted). Civil court reporting has fewer such sources and relationships on which to draw.

Angle biases and commercial biases, if I am correct, reveal the judgment of news professionals that the audience for civil case coverage is far from extensive or attentive (the prescription of the Inside-Out Perspective) and at least resembles the inadvertent, occasional audience described by our Outside-In Perspective. Citizens drawn from the pages of civics texts might want to know what goes on in routine lawsuits; citizens constructed by news decisions may be eager to learn about the outrageous or the bizarre but are decidedly uninterested in the routine.

What Neither Perspective Accounts For

The secret life of most of the civil law implies that only specialized media are likely to inform readers and viewers about civil litigation. Almost all lawyering and negotiation, and most civil cases, will escape the notice of mainstream media. While the Inside-Out Perspective prepared us for rather idealized intersections of courts and press and our Outside-In Perspective anticipated commercialized expediences, neither perspective hinted that coverage might accentuate and perpetuate the chasm between the legal mind and the lay mind. Let us briefly examine this perspective.

While intimations of a lawyerly aristocracy have come down from de Tocqueville and Dickens if not from Shakespeare and More, civics texts insist that the law ultimately derives its content from democratically elected representatives. If this insistence is to be anything more than legitimating myth, attentive citizens must have some notions of the laws that govern their lives. Laypersons, it is true, do not know the intricacies of the criminal codes, but most of them easily avoid the clutches of the criminal justice system by normal, moral living. Ordinary morality and common sense, however, will not suffice in civil disputes. Property, inheritance, insurance, contracts, discrimination, institutionalization, and taxes all surpass lay understanding and implicate attorneys almost inevitably.

Laypersons usually know very little about the civil law and civil litigation, despite the fact that they are much more likely to need some knowledge of civil law than of criminal law. As we have seen, criminal cases are far more titillating than civil cases, so more criminal cases (in raw numbers but not in percentages) appear in news media. News media's preferences for the violent, the prurient, and the bizarre squeeze out more normal, more useful news about civil cases. The press may protest that readers want the titillating more than the informative, but that excuse cannot gainsay the fact that mass media currently provide little coverage of civil law and litigation for consumers who would pay for it.

It is bad enough, from this third perspective, that energetic readers and dedicated viewers get so little from news media. A worse consequence of minuscule coverage of civil law is that the systematic preferences of the legal system in favor of the socially, politically, and economically advantaged are understated or unremarked. In a previous chapter we reviewed Black's conclusion that the law serves elites far more than masses. Certainly such is the case in civil litigation, where the ability to secure and remunerate counsel is a key hurdle to be overcome. The late former judge, Lois G. Forer, has documented other civil obstacles to the disadvantaged in *Unequal Protection: Women, Children, and the Elderly in Court*.[43]

In sum, a useful third perspective might stress a two-tiered system of information and advantage in civil law. That third perspective might recast table I.1 in terms reminiscent of Justice Scalia's model (table I.2). Recall that Justice Scalia despaired of mass media's ever passing along legal results and reasoning without distortions. He then opined that media stick to what they are good at—diverting the citizenry—and leave the law to the professionals. A proponent of the third perspective could adopt most of Justice Scalia's premises but reach a different conclusion by being critical rather than cynical or supercilious. That is why I provide dual valuative criteria in table 5.5. This perspective will usually be forwarded by anti-elitist critics. Still, as Justice Scalia has shown, it can be wielded by those eager to point out how they outstrip other humans.

Table 5.5   **An Above and Below Perspective**

	The Aware Above and the Unaware Below
Primary Audience	While lawyers "above" use specialized media to obtain useful information, laypersons "below" are entertained with minimal information in mass media.
Information Flow	Law goes from courts to Bench and Bar "above," while diverting myths go through journalistic intermediaries to mass publics "below."
Media Mission	Legal media inform and educate those "above" with technical, comprehensive coverage; Mass media amuse or titillate with "info-tainment" the popular audiences "below."
Judge's Job	Judges formulate law for Bench and Bar "on high," explain a little to reassure the press, and ignore the lowly public.
Valuative Criteria	On the part of those who define themselves "above," Elitist Self-Congratulation and Cynicism; for those more sympathetic to underlings, Anti-Aristocratic Critique.

CHAPTER 6

Judicial Selection

This chapter surveys how mass media cover routes by which judicial personnel reach courts. I begin by defining *judicial selection* as the set of ways in which states and the United States choose judges. Then I sing my familiar refrain: research in this area remains underdeveloped. Nevertheless, this underdevelopment need not slow us. Certain generalizations may guide students of the courts and consumers of mass media to expectations about coverage. Because knowledge has not been developed, insights abound but are not yet organized. Because even commonsense expectations improve on this disorder, the few generalizations that follow can make sense of what must be, for most readers of this book, unfamiliar territory.

What Is Judicial Selection?

Judicial Selection is an imposing term for a simple necessity: societies that maintain courts must designate judges. A similar concept, *judicial recruitment*, encompasses all procedures (explicit rules and standards for identifying, screening, and selecting judges) and practices (actual behavior, including conduct that violates rules and standards) by which courts acquire and retain judges. Judicial recruitment goes on all the time, even when there are no openings on courts. Every time a well-wisher mentions that someone would make a great judge, whenever a politician sees a way to discharge a political debt through a judicial appointment, and while would-be judicial candidates assess their chances in an upcoming campaign, judicial recruitment may be said to be in progress. Only when judicial office is officially up for grabs does the public process of judicial selection commence.[1]

Most judicial recruitment occurs behind closed doors and thus is seldom available to news reporters. Judicial selection is much more accessible to mass media on occasion. The scholarly literature on judicial recruitment is but embryonic; scholarly literature on news coverage of judicial recruitment has yet to be conceived. Therefore, coverage of judicial selection, rather than recruitment, is the subject of this chapter.

Judicial selection seems simple. All judges arrive at courts through appointment or election. Legislators or voters elect some judges. Executives or sitting judges appoint other judges. In merit systems, commissions and executives collaborate in appointments and appointees may then stand for reelection.[2] One might even consider impeachment, resignation, and retirement as means of "de-selecting" judicial personnel. If that capsulized survey seemed complicated, fasten your safety belt for the bumpy details to follow.

Number and Variety of Judges

Among the greatest challenges both to coverage of the staffing of courts and to understanding that coverage are the *number of judges* and the *variety of routes to judgeships*. United States judges number more than one thousand and states' judges more than thirty-five thousand.[3] So numerous and various are judges and their positions that we are unreasonable if we expect media even to list all the sorts of judges. In this respect, judges may not differ much from other elected officials who attract little or no attention.[4]

Judges assume their offices in such different ways that only experienced observers can keep many aspects straight, so the complexity of selection challenges the press as well. Indeed, one specialist in the study of judicial selection advised fellow specialists not to attribute to his conclusions too much certainty, for "a particular system may vary in its working not only among states but within them. . . ."[5]

Selection for National Courts

For national courts, selection is uniform: all judges exercising authority under the United States of America are nominated by the president and serve if a majority of the U. S. Senate consents to the nomination. Judges on the U. S. Supreme Court, the courts of appeals (intermediaries between the Supreme Court and U. S. trial courts), and U. S. district courts (courts that first hear most federal cases) serve for life. In other words, most U. S. judicial appointees stay in office until they retire, resign, or are removed.

While I use *appointment* to cover U. S. judges, appointments vary. Almost all national appointments of judges are low-key matters on which most senators expend little attention. That is the sort of process that the term *appointment* calls to my mind. However, some appointments are anything but automatic, as disappointed nominees to U. S. courts could testify.[6] To the degree that presidential appointments are contested, U. S. judicial selection can involve nominations by presidents, confirmations by senators, and campaigning, advertising, polling, and lobbying by a host of others. Thus, do not let my casual use of the word *appointment* mask the array of activities that national judicial selection occasionally involves. In addition, please do not forget the host of actions that contribute to judicial recruitment and that precondition national judicial selection.

Selection in the States

Once we turn to state courts, judicial selection gets complicated. Let's simplify matters a little. States secure judges in one of three ways: by appointment, by election, or by a combination of appointment and election. We may say judges are "appointed," as with U. S. judges, if an official or officials name judges. We may call judges "elected" if some institution (such as a state legislature) or constituency votes for them. Many judges are appointed and then must stand for election and perhaps even reelection, so we may say that those judges are both appointed and elected. In addition, some states employ different methods for different levels of courts. As of 1992, for example, Alabama elected all of its judges on partisan ballots except municipal judges, who were appointed by the officials in charge of the city or town.[7] Such a variety can bewilder students of state courts.

As of 1992, at least twenty-four states selected the members of their highest courts (usually, but not always, called a "supreme court") by appointment, at least thirteen by nonpartisan elections, and at least eight by partisan elections.[8] In partisan elections, candidates for the peak of the state judiciary stand before voters as nominees or members of a political party. In nonpartisan elections, the party label is not on the ballot. Ohio splits the difference: candidates survive party primary elections and then appear on the general election ballot without partisan designation.

Notice that I left five states out of my tally. You may wonder why I kept using "at least" in front of the numbers I reported. Five states defied easy categorization in my threefold scheme (appointment; partisan election; nonpartisan election). In Rhode Island and Virginia, Supreme Court personnel are elected by the state legislature. Is that the equivalent of being appointed or elected by partisan ballot? Connecticut's legislators appoint Supreme Court judges from a list of nominees forwarded by the governor from a larger list approved by the

Judicial Selection Commission. That sounds like appointment, but I am not certain. South Carolina's legislature elects its highest court from a list of names submitted by a nonpartisan committee of the legislature. Is that the equivalent of nonpartisan election? Finally, in Pennsylvania, all judges except Pittsburgh's traffic court judges and magistrates are elected on a partisan ballot but reelected on a nonpartisan ballot![9]

We have covered only the highest state courts and already we are enmeshed. Imagine the rigors of informing citizens about judicial selection in more than one state or more than one system!

Beyond states' highest courts, appointment is less commonly the mode of selection. In 1991, only eight states purely appointed lower court judges.[10] Some states demand that governors secure legislative approval of appointees. Some states permit some courts to appoint judges. Massachusetts permits governors to appoint many judges for life, while New Jersey allows governors to appoint judges for seven-year terms after which judges may be reappointed for life.

Such surveys convince many that media should not cover judicial selection because viewers and readers would be more confused by information than by its absence. I have one more complication to add.

About half of the states use some form of merit selection for their trial or appeals courts or both. Merit selection is usually a hybrid of appointment and election. In the appointment phase of merit selection, governors and special commissions agree on whom to appoint. Under the California Plan, the governor names a judge whom a three-member commission must approve. The Missouri Plan, in contrast, mandates the governor to choose his or her appointee from among a few names forwarded by a commission. Under both plans, appointees then must stand for election. In such retention elections, the judge's name is on the ballot without partisan or other designation and *without any other named opponent*. In retention elections, incumbents are the only individuals named on the ballot. Voters assent to the continuation of the appointee in office or vote not to retain the appointed incumbent.

The multiplicity of judges and complexity of judgeships, in sum, should lead us to expect little coverage. Merely to explain the various judges, levels, and procedures for selection is the stuff of textbooks. We read textbooks because instructors compel us to do so. Media other than textbooks succeed or fail on the intelligibility of their material and the interest that material engenders in audiences. Judicial selection is hard to understand, hard to interpret, hard to convey, and hard to care about. Despite the manifest importance of judges to society, under most circumstances and to most citizens judges and especially their selection are not newsworthy, not news, not understood, and not interesting. While I cannot make most judicial selections newsworthy or news, let me now try to make judicial selection more understandable and more interesting.

A Continuum of Coverage and Contexts

Judges are so numerous and their routes to office so various that we must simplify the most important aspects of judicial selection. I know of no research or theory that tells us how or even if we ought to expect news media to handle judicial selection. Still underdeveloped research on mass media again leaves us on our own.

We may simplify selection a bit by assuming that journalists suit their coverage to the contexts of selection. While there will be exceptions, defining a few recurring contexts will allow us to formulate expectations about coverage. Let us imagine four such contexts, each based on the degree to which selection is contested.

A Continuum of Conflict and Coverage

Let us begin by placing the four contexts for mass media coverage of judicial selection on a *continuum*,[11] a segment between endpoints or poles. Between any two points of that continuum we may imagine an intermediate point. Using a continuum permits us to reduce the varieties of judicial selection to a single dimension.

One Endpoint—Utterly Closed Selection

At one endpoint of this continuum, let us imagine judicial selection that presents no conflict of appreciable scope or intensity, "Utterly Closed Selection." This endpoint contains disagreements within the walls—some physical, some social—of organizations or groups and preserves cooperative relations among all involved in selection. Any conflict over the choice of judges is severely circumscribed and assiduously moderated.

An easy example of utterly closed selection would be uncontested elections. Whatever voters may think of a judge running without an opponent on the ballot, chances of beating the incumbent with a write-in campaign are remote. Such an election is unlikely to have broad conflict, intense conflict, or any conflict at all.

A more contestable example would be merit selection systems. Under the California Plan, governors appoint judges to the state supreme court and courts of appeals but must secure the assent of the Commission on Judicial Appointments. Since only one nominee of one governor had been disapproved by that commission as of 1991,[12] the California Plan seems to have resulted almost always in utterly closed selection. While the retention elections to which the appointee is subject may one day open up selection, at first the appointment is almost always a matter resolved harmoniously by governors and commissioners.

Selections are often utterly closed because processes of judicial recruitment that preceded public selections have reconciled many parties and potentates to the selected jurist. For judicial elections, raising funds and becoming recognized may give some candidates an air of inevitability that closes off conflict long before any campaigning is evident. Governors may not make appointments until they have assurances that appointees will not be opposed. President Clinton, to cite a third example, seems to have delayed his choices for the U. S. Supreme Court until he could be confident that whomever he named would incite no great opposition.[13]

An Opposite Endpoint—Wide-Open Selection

As an opposite endpoint of the continuum that we are creating, let us conceive of judicial recruits who inspire such opposition that the scope of conflict expands and the intensity of conflict escalates to make selection unmanageable. If the first endpoint represented the absence of conflict, this opposite represents absolute conflict, "Wide-Open Selection."

The confirmations of Judges Robert H. Bork and Clarence Thomas in the U. S. Senate exemplify such conflicts.[14] In addition, the rejection of Chief Justice Rose Elizabeth Bird of California in a 1986 retention election may qualify. (These incidents are discussed later.)

Ranges of Conflict—
Largely Closed and Largely Open Contests

Between these extremes I shall focus on two ranges of conflict. "Largely Closed Contests" includes any selection that a given official or group of officials controls with little interference or influence from outside forces. Such largely closed contests include elections in which incumbents face opponents with little chance of winning and states in which legislatures elect judges. A second range, "Largely Open

Contests," includes most appointments to the U. S. Supreme Court since 1954 and fiercely contested judicial elections. In this range, contests are genuine, and conflict is liable to be broad and deep.

Mark Silverstein's book *Judicious Choices: The New Politics of Supreme Court Confirmations*[15] suggests examples of both ranges from different eras of the Supreme Court. For the majority of the present century, selection of justices for the U. S. Supreme Court was a matter between presidents and the Senate. Indeed, even the Senate consented to almost all nominations to the highest court with so little evident concern that nomination by a president was tantamount to confirmation. Between 1901 and 1967, only one nominee was rejected, and fewer than a dozen nominees were subjected to any review that might be called open. In this first era, nominations to the Court were largely closed.

Amid the Warren Court (1953–1969), the process of advice and consent opened up. Senators began to pay more attention to nominations. Even a nonmember of the Senate Judiciary Committee grilled nominees. Nominees now routinely appeared before the committee. Pressure groups began to interest and then to involve themselves more and more often. Presidential and congressional campaigners began to posture regarding the Court.

By 1967[16] or 1968,[17] Supreme Court appointments were open, though not "largely" open. In several cases confirmations opened wide.[18] In all other cases, I regard nominations as largely open. Presidents in this modern era must sell their nominees.[19] Senators are more likely to devote some of their valuable time and energy to scoring nominees or otherwise scoring points. Interest groups and ideologues are involved more often, so executives and solons cannot rely on inside politics and must anticipate pressure from outside.

Other examples of largely closed and largely open selection follow. For now, it is enough if you can imagine the endpoints and the ranges that I have delineated. Now we will examine what this continuum tells us about coverage of recruitment.

The Continuum
Guides Expectations

While we may imagine other contexts of conflict along this continuum, the four contexts identified earlier furnish some simple expectations to guide our survey. I expect utterly closed judicial selection to yield minimal coverage in mass media because "recruiters,"[20] by closing off selection, leave reporters little or nothing to report. I expect the most common context, largely closed selection, to yield coverage only slightly more extensive, perhaps on days that have little other news of great interest. The more recruiters close appointments to influence from others, for example, the less they leave reporters to discover and commentators to discuss. The range in which selection is largely open will produce more stories, because open contests tend to proliferate intrigue, posturing, and, most important, sources. Wide-open selection promotes the most copy and air time as reporters and editorialists, sources and spin artists, proponents and opponents squabble and battle.

Of course, conflicts about judicial selection are more than one dimensional. Even along the single dimension I assumed earlier, conflicts may occupy different contexts at different times. Judge Clarence Thomas's largely open confirmation, for example, gaped wide once Anita Hill was introduced to the media. I have said little about the cusp between largely closed and largely open contexts. This continuum of conflicts and contexts was devised merely to simplify the welter of appointments, elections, and other selection into four contexts for which we can anticipate coverage.

If we agree that this continuum of contexts is a reasonable assumption from which to proceed, and if we further assume that coverage almost always conforms to such contexts, we should expect judicial selection seldom to achieve news-worth. After all, many appointments, nominations, and elections are wholly or largely uncontested, especially if appointers have skillfully practiced recruitment prior to announcing their selections. Even the minority of selection that is open to any substantial degree may yield too few news values to justify prominent or prolonged play in mass media. Episodes of wide-open selection will elicit ink both from mass media and from scholars but they are exceptions, not the rule.

To understand both the rule and the exceptions, we now reconsider each context in turn and in detail. Let's move from the Utterly Closed pole through the two ranges to the Wide Open pole.

Expectation One— No Contest, No Coverage

I expect very little coverage when selection is utterly uncontested. When judges stand for reelection without opponents, for instance, what need they provide news reporters to cover other than announcements of candidacies and election returns?

I expect utterly closed selection to create little news, because no one has an incentive to make news in such circumstances. The will-be jurist has an interest in appearing judicious, which means that she or he will welcome a smattering of praise but not so much notice as to arouse suspicions that this clique, that party, or those ideologues are too pleased by the ascension to the bench. Executives or legislators who appoint judges may delight in reports on the merit of an inevitable appointee, but they too must fear that too much praise from certain partisans or interests will make of a silk purse a sow's ear. For candidates without opponents, free media would be gratuitous and paid media wasteful, so no news is good news to judges in uncontested elections.

Journalists and editors will almost always be able to construct better news more easily and inexpensively elsewhere, especially amid nonjudicial campaigns designed to draw coverage. Even insiders and sources who bear the recruited jurist a grudge have little interest in prosecuting their prejudices lest they seem malicious. Why risk angering a decision maker who may be able to harm them?

Expectation Two—
Closed Contests, Stifled Coverage

I would expect largely closed selection, the most common context for coverage, to draw only a little more coverage than utterly closed selection draws. Appointments and elections that are ritually conducted or barely contested usually provide predictable outcomes and sheltered processes, so judicial selection creates little or no news beyond announcements and other events created for safe spot-news.[21] We expect news media routinely to find themselves excluded from the inner processes of judicial recruitment. News media are more likely to be included when judicial selection begins, but that inclusion can be distinctly bounded. For exclusion from recruitment and limited inclusion during selection, we expect journalists to be grateful when potential news would not justify expenses.

When nominations and elections are utterly closed (the first context discussed) or largely closed (the second context discussed), mass media may perform their most undisputed role—notifying citizens of choices—in a perfunctory and inexpensive manner. As a result, we expect even attentive, concerned citizens who rely on television, radio, news magazines, and newspapers to learn little or nothing about almost all appointments. Many meekly contested judicial elections will get minimal notice from news media, again to the detriment of voters' knowledge, interest, and involvement. Judicial elections, then, may promise open selection but may remain largely closed.

Like utterly closed selection, largely closed selection deprives most actors of much incentive to create news. What journalists are unable to cover when selection is utterly closed, they are unwilling to cover when selection is largely closed. To the degree that selection is confined and controlled, there is little news to cover. Consider one expert's observation about Senate confirmations: "The vast majority of hearings on lower-court judges last less than five minutes, with only the presiding senator and the nominee present."[22]

Elections and rituals of selection automatically confer on recruits most desired qualities, provided that recruits and supporters know what to say. Indications of less desirable qualities will be unavailable to news media without costly investigation. Those who strive to keep selection closed will construct a coherent, positive storyline out of information already in the public domain. If appointing authorities anticipate that they will not be able to close off the appointment, they may ponder whether the appointee justifies what may become an open process.

Rubber-Stamping Clinton's Nominees

A recent example may clarify the connection between largely closed selection and passive, paltry press coverage. Most nominees to United States courts are confirmed with such modest interaction among executive and legislative officials that not only mass media but almost everyone fails to notice. Consider the following complaint from Thomas L. Jipping, a prominent conservative deputized to keep President Clinton from loading the federal benches with liberals:

> [T]he Republican Senate has been handling lifetime appointments to the judicial branch in the same routine way it handles temporary appointments to the executive branch. It considers nearly all nominees without any floor debate and without a roll-call vote. On August 11, 1995, for example, minutes before the Senate adjourned for a recess, Majority Leader Dole, in a nearly empty chamber, asked for "unanimous consent" confirmation of a list of nominees. In less than a minute, the Senate confirmed 53 presidential nominees. Most of these were to patronage posi-

tions such as the Marine Mammal Commission, but 11 of them were federal judges.[23]

We may explain why advice and consent to U. S. judicial appointees is often largely closed if we understand that President Clinton, former Senator Dole, the nominees, and the press have little interest in opening up confirmations or creating news in this instance. We may assume that President Clinton wanted to expend as little of his political capital, energy, and time on judicial appointments as he could both to save resources for his reelection campaign and to overcome his administration's early bumbling on appointments.[24] We may further presume that Senator Dole had some interest in Clinton's reelection campaign as well and may have wanted to clear the Senate's business expeditiously to free himself to campaign against the incumbent (among other grounds, on the basis of the unsuitability of Clinton's judicial appointees!). Third, we suspect that the eleven nominees liked their confirmations as automatic as practicable. From the viewpoint of the press, nominations concerning which activists such as Jipping have uncovered no substantial weaknesses can have no debilitating problems and thus are not very newsworthy. While we cannot be certain how each actor regarded each nomination, we can safely predict that most nominations will lead to little conflict, little drama, little interest among insiders, and, hence, little news.

We may even generalize that: *advice and consent will tend to be closed because senators seldom have much interest in opening up judicial selection.* Impressive as the Senate's constitutional authority to confer or withhold consent may seem, cursory consent is usually the course of least resistance for busy solons who do not want to squander their staff and embroil their colleagues. Watson and Stookey have developed an imposing argument that searching confirmation hearings and debates are so much more demanding than ordinary Senate routines that senators usually invest their time and effort in goals other than examining nominees.[25] Remember that important senators may have participated in recruitment long before a nomination was made public and selection began.

If my generalization has merit, we may now answer Jipping. Senators probably provided reporters little inexpensive information because senators had quickly satisfied themselves that there would not be much trouble about these nominees and, thus, that the expense and bother of heightened scrutiny were not justified. They thereby deprived reporters of authoritative sources with which to counter President Clinton's prerogative. As a result, standard, largely closed procedures enshrouded the nominees. We regret to inform Jipping that importance is a poor substitute for source-ery.

Other Largely Closed Selection

Let us further generalize these insights about advice and consent in the United States Senate to include appointments confirmed by state legislatures. If governors and their allies keep the apparent stakes of a nomination low, they may prevent intensified inquiry and may reduce patent opposition to prevent expansion of the scope of conflict.

Let us predict little coverage in the many judicial elections that are not utterly closed but are largely closed. Elections may seem to open up judicial selection but often provide no contest and pose no threat to incumbents and those who put incumbents in office. These elections epitomize largely closed selection.

A most common example of apparently open but actually closed elections involves judges appointed to their offices in states that feature elected judiciaries. Because governors are often authorized to fill vacancies between elections, many judges are appointed to office and then seek election (not reelection, for they were not elected) as incumbents.[26] Such judges need never have stood for election as little-known challengers.[27] Even if challenged, these appointees and their allies may be able to use judicial robes and roles to fend off a genuine campaign and to garner campaign contributions that frighten off genuine challengers.

Other devices tend to close judicial elections by reducing the scope and intensity of conflict. Many judicial campaigns are sharply circumscribed by canons of legal ethics, election laws, and traditions. Nonpartisan elections deprive the vast majority of voters of the party label, the only cue on which many could have relied.

Retention elections, virtually designed to insulate the judiciary from mundane influences that might open up selection, likewise discourage coverage. I described retention elections above as part of merit selection. Merit plans aim to keep out of judicial selection the very partisan and ideological influences that might increase the scope and intensity of conflict. True to the designs of merit selection, retention elections are seldom even close,[28] owing to the absence of named competition and party labels and, in most cases, information. Evaluations of candidates for retention by state bar associations appear to make little difference,[29] so legal experts are unlikely to redress mass ignorance and indifference even if it is in their interest to do so.

Most judicial selection is closed to one degree or another. If our continuum aptly represents the fit of context and coverage at all, *expect almost all judicial selection to go almost uncovered*. Modest coverage characterizes many local and state races and most appointments, so we should not expect judges to get more coverage than comparable officials in other areas of government. Nonetheless, I have listed reasons why we should not expect utterly closed or largely closed judicial selection to exceed that low threshold of coverage.

Open Selection

Even open selection may lead to coverage not much deeper or more extensive than closed selection unless selection is not merely open but largely open. That is why I have not drawn attention to "somewhat closed" or "sort of open" conflicts and contexts. Experienced, competent professionals will seldom let appointments or elections get out of their control. When they do, they will get negative reinforcement that induces them to maintain control over selection as much as they may. Incumbent judges who must face reelection may undertake to close their elections as much as possible, even if they would seem to have little to fear.[30]

When contests are open but not largely open, procedures and rituals of judicial selection tend to contain conflict lest judicial independence be publicly and chronically compromised. As appointments to the U. S. Supreme Court, for example, have evolved from mostly closed exercises into usually open selection, participants such as nominees, their nominators, and their supporters have adapted to the open contexts by trying to limit the scope and intensity of hearings and floor fights. When Judge Antonin Scalia refused during his confirmation to discuss even the most sacrosanct precedent in U. S. constitutional law, *Marbury v. Madison* (1803), he may have been upholding judicial independence and personal integrity. Certainly, he was also delimiting the extent and intensity of disagreement possible at the hearing.

A Quick Glance at Coverage of Open Selections

Table 6.1 shows how little coverage many open selections receive.[31] Table 6.1 reports coverage in mass media of recent, openly controversial nominations to U. S. courts of the Bush and Clinton presidencies.[32] This table features counts of every mention of controversial judicial candidates. Thus, a passing reference is counted alongside a lengthy analysis.[33] Because even references to the necessity of filling the office formerly held by the confirmed candidates were counted, this table may overcount. Sparse as mere mentions are, in-depth coverage may be even rarer.

To scan the counts of mentions in national electronic media and news magazines is to be stunned by controversial candidates' invisibility to common media. Every reference to the candidates on ABC's news shows, CNN's news shows (I even counted *Capital Gang*), PBS's *Newshour*, and National Public Radio's *Morning Edition* and *All Things Considered* should have been detected. The three leading news magazines, *Time, Newsweek,* and *U. S. News and World Report* might have been expected to cover controversial nominations. They did not. Three of the controversial candidates surfaced (Ryskamp twice; Carnes and Sarokin once) on ABC, CNN, or PBS, but the rest went unnoticed. Only Carnes made National Public Radio. Edelman and Carnes drew a notice from a newsmagazine, while Ryskamp dominated that medium with six mentions in the three news magazines combined. To the extent that ordinary citizens use national media to keep up with U. S. judges, they had better make time to read national newspapers or more specialized media.

Newspapers seem to have the only coverage that might even be called modest: President Bush's two nominees, Judge Kenneth L. Ryskamp and Edward E. Carnes, and one of President Clinton's nominees, Chief Justice Rosemary Barkett, received some coverage, even if in-state newspapers' coverage of local celebrities (the nominees) is discounted. These nominees had found their candidacies sharply contested by interest groups within and without the Senate and coverage followed a predictable sequence. Appointments were announced to some notices; opposition developed and opponents voiced doubts striking enough to garner press; pithy charges and outraged defenses shaped point-counterpoint stories; Judge Ryskamp was denied access to the floor of the Senate by a straight party-line vote of the committee (8–6) that made the news as the first rejected Bush nominee after seventy-six confirmed; and senators staked out positions leading up to a floor debate with quotable hyperbole before confirming Chief Justice Barkett (61–37) and Carnes (62–36).

Other nominees in table 6.1 and one prominent non-nominee, Peter Edelman, drew faint notice. Judge H. Lee Sarokin was so controversial that he was attacked in the 1996 presidential campaign and dismissed from the Cipollone cigarette case for judicial bias, but his nomination got coverage in but fifty-eight articles, of which eleven were coverage of attacks in Senate campaigns on Democrats who voted for Sarokin. Chief Justice James L. Dennis of the Louisiana Supreme Court

Table 6.1   Stories in Which Controversial Judicial Candidates Were Mentioned

Recruit	Office	Named	Decided	All Newspapers	Newspapers In-State	Newspapers National	News Magazines	TV and Radio	Total
Kenneth Ryskamp	11th Circuit	4/26/90	NO,[1] 4/11/91	147	46	68	6	2	155
Edward E. Carnes	11th Circuit	1/27/92	OK, 9/9/92	95	—	43	1	6	102
Alexander Williams	District Court MD	8/7/93	OK, 8/18/94	24	24[2]	15	0	0	24
Rosemary Barkett	11th Circuit	9/24/93	OK, 4/14/94	190	99	39	0	0	190
H. Lee Sarokin	3rd Circuit	5/5/94	OK, 10/4/94	58	10	20	0	1	58
David F. Hamilton	District Court IN	6/8/94	OK, 10/7/94	2	2[3]	0	0	0	2
James L. Dennis	5th Circuit	6/8/94	OK, 9/28/95	39	32	2	0	0	39
Judith McConnell	District Court CA	8/5/94	NO, 1/20/95	19	11	6	0	0	19
R. Samuel Paz	District Court CA	8/5/94	NO, 1/20/95	21	10	10	0	0	21
David A. Katz	District Court OH	8/12/94	OK, 10/7/94	9	5	3	0	0	9
Peter Edelman	U. S. Court	Never	NO, 9/1/95	54	14[4]	20	1	0	55

1. Rejected by Senate Judiciary Committee, which did not report nomination to the Senate.
2. *Washington Post* and *Washington Times* counted as in-state newspapers for Judge Williams.
3. The *Cincinnati Enquirer* treated as an in-state newspaper in this instance.
4. The *Baltimore Sun*, *Washington Post*, and *Washington Times* were counted as in-state for Edelman.

was opposed by Mississippi's powerful Republican senators and was linked to a scholarship scandal at Tulane University while he was seeking the Senate's advice and consent, but barely made the news outside Louisiana.

Alexander Williams, David A. Katz, and David F. Hamilton were the only three Clinton nominees rated "not qualified" by the Standing Committee on the Federal Judiciary of the American Bar Association, but Senate Republicans chose not to make an issue of that shortfall. Their nominations were thus largely closed and minimally noticed.

The nominations of Judge McConnell, Paz, and Edelman were scuttled. McConnell and Paz were not renominated by President Clinton after the Republicans regained the Senate in 1994 and made it clear that they thought very little of the California pair. Edelman's non-candidacy elicited fifty-four articles, which sounds like an impressive figure until one realizes that fully twenty-two of those articles (41 percent) were widely reprinted columns (one each) by pundits George F. Will (n=13), Anthony Lewis (n=5), and Jeffrey Rosen (n=4).

While more systematic studies of coverage will be necessary before we can say just how modest coverage of controversial federal judicial nominations may be, the small sample of the most controversial nominations 1989–1995 in table 6.1 suggests that coverage of most nominations must be minuscule. Some of these nominations may not quite have been largely open, although I would thus classify them. Even if they were merely open, however, I am impressed by how limited the coverage was. If this is how controversial nominations to U. S. courts are treated, how much coverage should we expect for noncontroversial nominees?

Expectation Three—Largely Open Contests, Largely Controlled Coverage

Still, some selection opens up, especially when activists and politicians undertake to load courts with members of their parties or factions too obviously[34] and when judges diverge from safe, settled norms and traditional values and policies.[35] The availability of embarrassing information, innuendo, and invective from credible sources creates drama and other news hooks, a horse race, competing quotes, and intelligibility—all cheaply and conveniently. If the stakes of a selection can be made to appear to be high enough, the scope of the conflict widens and its intensity deepens.

As processes of selection become accessible, news media may

increase their coverage of newsworthy aspects. While news-worth is situational, we have already reviewed chronic patterns of press coverage.[36] Stories are more likely to be covered (and covered more) whenever they can be shaped into reports that are dramatized, personalized, morselized, and normalized.

Increasing the scope and intensity of conflict augments each inducement to cover selection. As disagreements escape the control of those who would prefer that selection be more closed, the potential for dramatization increases. Widening and intensifying conflict tends to personalize stories around the recruit at the center of the controversy and sometimes the recruiters. Discrete stages in the process—campaign statements, debates, hearings, evaluations by the bar, votes—morselize immediate happenings into clusters that are understandable (and more dramatic and more personal) that news media may easily convey and news consumers easily appreciate. Finally, open conflicts will tend to be interpretable in terms of rituals, customs, and habits as well as partisanship, ideology, or other enduring cleavages, so journalists will be able to normalize events.

Controlling Largely Open Supreme Court Nominations

The most obvious reason that even selection to the Supreme Court so seldom becomes wide open is that nominating presidents and their staffs and supporters in the Senate understand and accommodate the biases of mass media. That is, *recruiters control coverage by controlling conflict and control conflict by controlling coverage.* There are at least three general strategies of media control in this context: avoid nominees likely to engender conflict; accentuate the positive by giving the press biographical and legal information tailored to the media's preferences for normalized, morselized, and personalized drama; or suppress negative characterizations before they supplant or undermine the positive drama and data. Let us briefly consider each strategy in turn to illustrate how recruits and their teams may control coverage.

Risk-averse executive teams may minimize the openness of confirmations by grading potential nominees on their potential for positive image control and their vulnerability to attacks on their images. Presidents and their allies must anticipate great returns from a selection before they will risk wide-open selection.[37] Senator Warren B. Rudman said of President George Bush's nomination of Judge David Hackett Souter that "I suspected that the president was less concerned with how his nominee eventually voted on *Roe* [the landmark abortion ruling, *Roe v. Wade* (1973)] than that he or she be nominated without a fight. . . . His priority was to find a nominee who could be confirmed without harming his party's congressional prospects that year or his own in 1992."[38] One scholar has suggested that President Clinton learned from his predecessor, who enjoyed one open contest and endured one that was wide open. He has opted for techno-judges, jural technicians notable more for their absence of disqualifications than for their distinction.[39]

To accentuate the positives that lead them to select nominees (strategy two), presidents propagate storylines. Storylines may supply dramatized, personalized, morselized, and normalized angles for which reporters and editors are looking. To control coverage, however, such positive angles must be credible as well as expedient. President Reagan's people portrayed Judge Bork as a judicial moderate in the mold of Justice Powell and a brilliant legal technician. The first characterization was not plausible and, had it been plausible, would have infuriated Bork's strongest supporters.[40] The second characterization fell apart during the hearings when Bork's opponents orchestrated sound bites and news morsels that made Bork seem abstruse and heartless. Simply, Bork's opponents wrested control of coverage by supplying mass media with more news in a form that mass media could use.

To be credible and expedient, positive storylines should be hard to check. President Bush and his staff secured great coverage with their storyline about Clarence Thomas pulling himself up from dire circumstances in Pin Point, Georgia[41] but weathered ridicule for the president's claim that Thomas was the best person for the job.[42] The latter claim was far easier for opponents and reporters to question and contradict with minimal research, while the former claim suited Horatio Alger myths and the memories of those likely to support Judge Thomas. President Clinton had great success in claiming that Judge Ruth Bader Ginsburg was "the Thurgood Marshall of the women's movement,"[43] perhaps because reporters and scholars would find it difficult even to begin to argue with the claim. How does one measure "Thurgood Marshall-ness" or critique a metaphor?

As challenges to a nomination arise, supporters must quickly neutralize negative imagery or lose media control and conflict containment. This is the third strategy I listed earlier. If journalists can be persuaded early that opposition is unfair, nominees may even gain from the challenges. Suspicions about Judge Souter's sexual preference were quickly turned against those spreading innuendo.[44] In the case of

Judge Thomas, even members of the Senate Judiciary Committee who were prepared to oppose Thomas did not want to raise sexual harassment as a reason lest they seem unfair and desperate.[45]

Expectation Four—Wide-Open Selection, Extensive Coverage

Usually, only the fourth context of selection inspires the sort of coverage that most academics have considered in print. We have too little literature on the first three contexts, the contexts in which almost all judicial selection occurs. We have dozens of books and thousands of articles, however, on the few contests in which selection was wide open. What has been said of so many areas of intellectual life is assuredly true of the study of coverage of judicial selection: we know the most about the least and the least about the most.

When selection is wide open to contending interests and investigating reporters, I am unsure what to expect. True, hype and histrionics *may* drive coverage. Unlike uncontested and closed contexts, wide-open contests provide high stakes and dramas, titillation and news hooks that mass media seek. More important, cracking open selection supplies reporters with authoritative spokespeople and other sources to contradict or to question nominees and their supporters. Ordinary proceedings and ritualized contests cannot constrain opposition and prevent escalation of both the scope and intensity of conflict, as they might even for largely open contests. I concede that wide-open selection offers news reporters what they want and presents journalists with many points of access.

However, I do not want to overgeneralize. Not every wide-open contest will lead to a feeding frenzy.[46] As we regain perspective after the retention election of Chief Justice Bird and the confirmations of Judges Robert Bork and Clarence Thomas, we must reflect on the rarity of raucous, outrageous coverage sustained in the news media. Instances of riotous journalism may be sufficiently rare that we cannot predict or explain news riots. For now, the safer expectation is that *news media will feature plenty of probing reportage and provocative commentary amid wide-open selections but seldom otherwise.*

One example of an extraordinary, wide-open contest—the California retention elections of 1986—aptly demonstrates what so many have to lose when judicial selection gapes. While six of the seven justices of the California Supreme Court stood for retention that year, Chief Justice Rose Bird attracted the most attention.[47] The campaign drew more than three thousand articles in print media alone.[48] California's governor opposed three candidates for retention, pressure groups raised $5 million to $10 million for the campaign,[49] and voters turned out for the judicial election in great numbers and with great interest.[50] As should be expected, such a wide-open affair deprived Chief Justice Bird of control of her image, although Bird's image had not been typically judicious before.[51] Bird's image was created largely by news coverage and paid media during the campaign. Concerning the paid media, even an academic critic of Bird conceded that television ads were scurrilous.[52] Once her retention election became wide open, the chief justice had no chance of victory.

To see why Bird had no chance is to understand why few incumbents permit elections to become wide open and why contests such as those in California are so rare. Justice Joseph R. Grodin, who lost his seat on the same court the same day as Bird, has detailed the severe disadvantages under which judicial candidates labor.[53]

First, unpopular decisions that imperil judicial incumbents challenge audiences and media. Judicial decisions challenge audiences because voters need not be familiar with legal reasoning and need not discipline their thinking by such reasoning. Decisions challenge media and, through media, audiences because most mass media are much better at conveying outcomes than processes by which outcomes were obtained, as we have seen in previous chapters of this book. Grodin graphically makes the point:

> [I]magine the power of the 30-second television spot: here was a stomach-turning crime, committed by a person whose humanity was cloaked in blood; here is the mother, or the grandmother, or the daughter of the victim lamenting her loss, and suggesting, or implying, that the California Supreme Court, in its unalterable opposition to the death penalty, and in defiance of the public will, had in reliance upon some unidentified technicality set the defendant loose on the streets. Of course, it was no technicality, it was a matter of constitutional or statutory right, and of course the defendant was not turned loose, but returned for retrial—in fact by the time the opposition ran the principal ad I have described, the defendant in the case had already been retried, reconvicted, and resentenced to death. *But try explaining all of that effectively in 30 seconds on television, or in any manner sufficient to offset the emotional impact of the opponents' appeal.*[54]

Grodin reminds us that, second, most judges are anonymous: "very few voters knew either of us [Grodin or Justice Cruz Reynoso] from Colonel Sanders."[55] Starting with almost no image, most elected jurists concede image control to detractors on those rare occasions when detractors break open judicial elections.

Third, many judges are inexperienced and even inept campaigners.[56] Particularly difficult given modern media campaigns, judges will probably be outspent.[57]

Fourth, detractors may say almost anything; judicial candidates must abide by canons of ethics:

> Unlike most political candidates, I could make no campaign promises, nor could I state my position on any legal issue pending or likely to be pending before the court, unless I had already done so in an opinion. If I knew of cases in the court's pipeline that would be decided in a way pleasing to a majority of the voters, I could not talk about them. I could say very little about the cases that had already been decided, by way of defending them, for fear of saying things that would be viewed as providing an interpretation of the opinions themselves. . . . I felt constrained not to attack the motives or tactics of the officials and politicians who opposed me, out of a concern that in doing so I would further politicize the court.[58]

Justice Grodin provides eloquent testimony concerning the travails of judges entangled in wide-open elections. It is easy to see why judicial candidates would avoid such contests if they could. What may be less obvious is that those who opposed Bird, Grodin, and Reynoso in 1986 expended vast sums and wearied themselves. Wide-open electoral contests tax voters and news media as well, although perhaps not enough to deter opening elections. Wide-open contests alarm the legal and lay observers who wonder about the independence of the judiciary and democracy run amok.

Conflict, Context, and Coverage

As hypotheses or mere conjectures, the four contexts examined explain why most coverage of judicial selection is minimal. By minimal, I mean that news media announce candidacies, report nominations, and acknowledge appointments, confirmations, and election returns. Announcements, reports, and acknowledgements are brief, superficial spot news. For judicial selection, little or no coverage is the norm.

While coverage of judicial selection occasionally exceeds this norm, extensive coverage is exceptional. Between announcements of openings, nominations, and candidacies and reports of completed appointments and elections, mass media sometimes feature stories on candidates for judgeships and descriptions or analyses of selection. News media report statements of concern or murmurings of opposition as harbingers of more open selection, but such reports will almost always be brief and the conflicts and concerns transitory. Such modest coverage outstrips the minimal coverage that is the mode but falls far short of the media spectacles that dominate the literature.

Coverage of Selection for the Supreme Court

While I hope that examination of the contexts of coverage scaled back your expectations regarding the depth and breadth of coverage of most judicial selection in most mass media, I realize that to an extent most judicial selection will seem trivial to many readers. What you hear about, you are more likely to think important; what you never hear about, you are likely to think unimportant. In addition, many will believe that selection of justices for the U. S. Supreme Court is where most of the action is. As we turn to expectations about coverage of Supreme Court nominations, I hope to advance some useful propositions that follow from my continuum.

Most Supreme Court Selection Gets Stylized Coverage

Nominations to the U. S. Supreme Court, as we saw earlier, were more open in the latter half of the twentieth century than they generally were in the first half. As interest in Supreme Court appointments broadened and intensified, so did coverage in mass media. Such coverage, however, falls far short of the frenzied spectacles of which critics have complained. That is, *even when we look at selection to the U. S. Supreme Court alone, wide-open selection and concomitant press overload are still exceptions rather than the rule!*

Indeed, a large majority of Supreme Court nominees have been confirmed even in the most recent period because they and their allies have kept largely open processes from breaking wide open.[59] As long as confirmations are open but not wide open, ordinary procedures will generate coverage that can largely be controlled. I dub such coverage "stylized" because most reports will conform to patterns dictated by those ordinary procedures and the predilections of news media. Ordinarily, nominations to the High Court traverse four stages for confirmation and, in my observation, almost always get coverage suited to each stage. Let us examine each stage in turn to see why this expectation makes sense.

Coverage of Stage One Almost Always Flatters the Nominee

The first stage is announcement of the president's nominee.[60] Modern presidents use the nomination as an opportunity to dominate first impressions with releases of information and imagery that flatter the nominee. Mass media disseminate this flattery because presidential releases are authoritative, inexpensive to gather, and fashioned for journalistic biases (such as the four discussed earlier) and public tastes. Only in the opening stages of the nomination of Judge Bork has an opponent of the nomination managed to compromise this first spin with a countermessage.[61]

Coverage of Stage Two Is Usually Courteous and Supportive

The second stage—the long period during which the Senate Judiciary Committee prepares for hearings—can be perilous but usually is not. Before potential opponents ascertain weaknesses, nominees usually make courtesy calls on senators.[62] Because these visits are mostly opportunities to be photographed in polite poses that are supposed to dramatize seriousness and mutual respect, they do not threaten to contradict the image of the nominee. Supportive senators all but commit themselves to vote for the nominee, while senators troubled by the nomination usually indicate that they will wait and see. Opportunities for inexpensive coverage, then, will usually be lopsided in the nominee's favor. Unless, as was the case with Judge Bork, groups have already done their homework on the nominee,[63] they will not be well positioned to counter the still authoritative, still inexpensive, and still predigested plaudits for the nominee. Most nominees have avoided the spotlight outside the legal community and thus challenge the resources of would-be detractors. As a result, the press will ordinarily have few sources of conflict on which to rely.[64]

Coverage of Stage Three Usually
Conveys More Calm than Acrimony

Once hearings before the Judiciary Committee (stage three) commence, coverage increases but seldom endangers the nominee. Most confirmations, even for the high court, are not very conflictual because most nominees were prescreened for acceptability and have been prepared to finesse questions and issues that threaten them. Nominees' handlers may even stage mock hearings in which nominees practice avoiding difficulties and scoring positive points. If concerns have arisen, nominators and handlers have cultivated support among friendly members of the committee to remedy vulnerabilities. Nominees may expect such friends to ask easy, anticipated questions the answers to which will reiterate the virtues of the would-be justice and rehearse the storyline created in the first two stages. Friendly senators also spell the nominee after less friendly questioners because questioning usually alternates between the members of the majority party and the minority.

Even unfriendly questioners need not be problems. Hearings allow nominees many ways in which to stonewall senators and stymie news stories. Nominees almost always proclaim themselves unwilling to answer questions about how they will rule in cases that may come before them if they are confirmed. Judge Bork again excepted,[65] nominees may claim that they have never considered divisive issues, have yet to take a position on such dangerous matters, and must not commit themselves prior to pondering the specific facts of specific cases. Since this tactic denies both opponents and reporters the information they most need to maintain conflict and drama, coverage of committee hearings ordinarily reinforces the nominee's acceptability by the sheer absence of drama or conflict.

Coverage of Stage Four Usually
Characterizes Victory

By the final stage, debate and vote on the floor of the Senate, the absence of debilitating disqualifications will have made the nomination uninteresting and the vote a foregone conclusion. Nominees, for the Court or for other offices, seldom persevere to the floor vote absent a chance of confirmation. Consequently, the debate is almost always desultory and the confirmation anticlimactic. While nominees have, of late, survived floor votes closer than most in previous decades, even tight squeezes may generate little news.

Stages Stylize Coverage

In sum, Supreme Court nominations do make news but seldom in the manner that infuriates critics of the modern process. Confirmation is almost always a sure thing, so senators are disinclined to expend scarce resources to no material end. Indeed, senators drained by previous fights may tend to underestimate their odds of denying confirmation, as was the case with Judge Harrold Carswell.[66] Because skillful selection and early management will usually preclude denial of confirmation, senators will usually adopt roles at worst passively opposed.[67] When opponents default, coverage should be expected to mirror the rituals by which Supreme Court nominations are legitimized.

Aberrant Nominations, Abhorrent Coverage

Most selection, even at the level of the United States Supreme Court, is stylized and safe; therefore, I have glided over the exceptions to the rule. Now we will consider the exceptions. Selection to the U. S. Supreme Court has lately featured wide-open contests that have appalled practitioners and observers alike. Wide-open selection is judicial selection out of control as nominees career from innuendo to fiasco to farce. Victors may salute popular democracy and losers may lament the decline of jural independence and civility, but everyone loses when triumph and disaster march arm in arm.

One reason that wide-open selection is so rare is that few participants gain from such escalation. Fights over Carswell, Bork, and Thomas exposed many participants to ridicule and animosity. The wide-open efforts against Bork created a perhaps Pyrrhic victory when spent Democrats acceded to Judge Anthony Kennedy.[68] I do not know whether news media in the long run gain more in profits than they lose in good will from feeding frenzies over wide-open contests, but I am certain that such coverage costs media and polity plenty.

There is not enough space here in which to recall all the excesses of coverage of Judge Bork's and Judge Thomas's nominations. Most observers agree that many of the press, like other participants, went too far. An ample literature documents those excesses well—too well in the view of those who agree that wide-open conflict and frenzied coverage are abominations. As past excesses beget present, many retrospectives and memoirs exude rationalization, spin, and folderol[69] from which few reliable propositions may be derived.

Borking

When President Reagan nominated Robert H. Bork of the Circuit Court of Appeals for the District of Columbia to the U.S. Supreme Court, he fulfilled conservatives' dreams and caused liberals nightmares. Judge Bork had long been touted for the Court. Admirers saw him as the most qualified nominee in decades and a man who would bring to the Court consistent, cogent arguments for judicial restraint. Detractors saw Bork as an ideologue who had campaigned for the Court in right-wing circles and a threat to years of expanding rights and equality. If Bork had been either deliverer or destroyer, his confirmation might have been largely open but successful. Because Judge Bork was both deliverance for the right and destruction for the left, it seems to me, his confirmation was wide open and, from his point of view, unsuccessful.

While much of the confirmation was within the bounds of democratic fair play, Judge Bork's treatment gave rise to the infinitive "to bork." To bork a nominee is to take her or his virtues and distort them into vices. Once antagonists have "borked" a candidate for high office, mass media will tend to spread distortions to every hamlet in the land. Even if the nominee survives borking, his or her reputation has been thoroughly besmirched and the process of selection has been fouled.

Judge Bork had barely been named and praised by President Reagan when Senator Edward M. Kennedy took to the floor:

> Robert Bork's America is a land in which women would be forced into back alley abortions, blacks would sit at segregated lunch counters, rogue policemen could break down citizens' doors in midnight raids, school children could not be taught about evolution, writers and artists could be censured at the whim of government.[70]

Scholars score this characterization of Judge Bork's record, but my concern here is that Senator Kennedy's broadside was reported widely without critical scrutiny from the press. If Kennedy slandered Bork, media were derelict in relaying those slanders without assessments.

Of course, assessments of claims in the media are themselves dangerous, for they can spread slander. When Senator Orrin Hatch attacked the accuracy of a television advertisement created by People for the American Way, for example, he publicized an ad that had run a few times in a few markets and made it a story in far more markets.

Perhaps most disgusting to Bork's supporters were reports from the Senate Judiciary Committee. Some of Bork's backers expected the judge to have his way with senators in the hearings. When Bork proved far less astute at television than the senators, his supporters began to decry oversimplified, superficial coverage of the hearings. The coverage they abhorred most made Bork look like a droning, heartless intellectual without an ounce of compassion and humanity. Bork's supporters found Bork's opponents mendacious and mean and believed that coverage purveyed this meanness into Americans' homes.[71]

To most of these charges of abhorrent coverage and abusive conduct, reporters and Bork's opponents (to many disappointed supporters of Judge Bork, those groups greatly overlap) plead not guilty. Since charges, countercharges, and pleadings have now endured for a number of years, we will not resolve the matter here and now. My point in recounting Judge Bork's experience is to illustrate the odious reporting that has moved commentators and scholars to advocate screening nominations from television or closing off the process in other ways.

The Bork nomination in particular may reveal much about modern selection if that fight is viewed in the broader context of wide-open selection. Judge Bork's nomination ignited news media as judicial selection never had and, excepting Judge Thomas's October surprise four years later, likely never would again. However, every prognostication or generalization that takes Bork's immolation for a norm misleads us. We must not form expectations from a unique case. Hypotheses forged in such a fire emit ideological, partisan, and jurisprudential heat but very little light.

Lynching

While we must never forget that Judge Clarence Thomas got fairly (detractors would say "unfairly") flattering coverage during most of his confirmation, before his ordeal was over Thomas would be vilified, mocked, pitied, and scorned. I doubt that anyone who paid any attention to the Clarence Thomas–Anita Hill hearings in October 1991 recalls the events without shock and anger. Perhaps Phelps and Winternitz captured the episode best:

> The ceremony was performed in secret at high noon. . . .
> "I, Clarence Thomas, do solemnly swear that I will administer justice without respect to persons, and do equal right to the poor and to the rich, and that I will faithfully and impartially discharge and perform all the duties incumbent on

me as an associate justice of the Supreme Court of the United States. . . . "

Watching in the oak-paneled conference room, the Court's inner sanctum, were only his wife, Virginia, and his very best man, U. S. Senator Jack Danforth. Senator Danforth took pictures with Mrs. Thomas's camera. Clarence Thomas had leaped aboard the Court with the hounds of the press nipping at his heels amid rumors about pornographic video tapes. . . .[72]

Judge Thomas became Justice Thomas in the first private swearing-in in fifty years because he and his supporters feared the next revelation of a scandal-filled fall. Television viewers had heard Professor Anita Hill charge Thomas with sexual harassment. Hearings had disclosed more than most people wanted to know about pornographic media and Long Dong Silver, about pubic hairs on cans of Coke, about perjury and erotic fantasizing, and about keeping independent African Americans from thinking for themselves. Now the Bush administration and Judge Thomas intended to force opponents to impeach Thomas if they wanted to keep him off the Court.

For our purposes, the important point often lost amid these lurid details is that Thomas's hearings were largely open at first but not very problematic. Before Hill's charges, Thomas had the votes to be confirmed. It seems to me, then, that ordinary aspects of the Thomas nomination reiterate the norm: *largely open Supreme Court selections lead to extensive but stylized and "safe" coverage.*

Although Thomas had an extensive record of problematic pronouncements that he could not or would not defend,[73] the Senate was poised to confirm when new charges made the papers and airwaves. Thomas and his handlers had controlled his image and his press. Judge Thomas and his allies emphasized his lowly start and vaulting accomplishments. This was "the Pin Point strategy." Chronicling his rise from tiny Pin Point, Georgia, to the zenith of the U. S. judicial system dramatized and personalized Thomas's selection and immunized him to much criticism from senators of far more privileged backgrounds.

In addition, Thomas's team had learned from Bork's debacle. Reporters addicted to instant interpretations and catchy characterizations were only too happy to pass along inexpensive, preformulated impressions of Thomas's testimony, so Thomas's team took up positions during breaks to praise their nominee and attack his detractors.[74] Thomas cleverly evaded dangerous questions and calmly ignored provocations.[75]

Even when Hill's charges scrambled Thomas's image control,

Thomas was able to regain the advantage through his sound bite at the Senate Judiciary Committee after Hill had electrified the nation:

> This is a circus. It's a national disgrace. And from my standpoint as a black American, as far as I'm concerned, it is a high-tech lynching for uppity blacks who in any way deign to think for themselves, to do for themselves, to have different ideas, and it is a message that unless you kowtow to an old order, this is what will happen to you. You will be lynched, destroyed, caricatured, by a committee of the U. S. Senate rather than hung from a tree.[76]

Thomas managed to claim the mantle of the victim and to paint his interrogators as a lynch mob. Democrats were immobilized and mostly mute; Republicans were energized and nearly manic. From this stunning turning point, Thomas and his supporters took the offensive and won the confirmation.

Thomas's nomination rewards serious scrutiny as a wonderful example of selection out of control. Indeed, I cannot imagine a more powerful lesson regarding the necessity of maintaining image control or a more arresting illustration of regaining control over a situation.

My major conclusion from Clarence Thomas's unique path to the high bench, however, is that *this aberration proves too much to support those who would reform confirmations!* For all the disgusting stories with which the second round of hearings on Judge Thomas littered mass media, Thomas rather quickly and easily regained the seat that seemed to have been denied him. The charges against Thomas were far more salacious and devastating than any others leveled at a Supreme Court nominee. That such a mediocre nominee so damaged by charges and doubts could survive the October ordeal seems to me powerful evidence that nominators and nominees may anticipate little trouble in almost every other circumstance.

Abhorrent Coverage Is an Aberration

At the least, we may fashion from the agonies of Judge Bork and Judge Thomas a generalization that abhorrent coverage is aberrant coverage. Do not forget how rare "borking" is.[77] Although we will consider some contentions about modern, wide-open confirmations almost all deductions from the Bork and Thomas tragedies will mislead you. Paid and free media handled Judge Bork, by his own account, in a manner utterly unprecedented. Judge Thomas's tribulation was unique. As I now attempt to reformulate case-specific points into broader conjectures that may inform citizens and researchers, do not forget that I must reformulate those points because most of them do not apply beyond one or another celebrated incident or nominee.

Hypothesis One—News Media Abet Desperate Efforts to Pack or Hold Courts

Less compelling once a Democrat won the White House and the Republicans seized the Senate, this hypothesis nonetheless connects the confirmation fights of Judges Bork and Thomas with broader cultural and intellectual wars. Judge Bork,[78] Suzanne Garment,[79] and David Brock[80] have each advanced the claim that judicial selection represents a last gasp of the losing left as conservatives sweep the field in every other arena of democratic competition. Opponents of conservative jurisprudence have claimed that conservatives took over the White House and the Senate in 1981 determined to ensconce their ideology in the third branch but have not, to my knowledge, suggested that mass media participate in the process.

Without a general understanding, such propositions profit students of selection coverage too little and partisans and ideologues too much. I do not question that news media purveyed rumor and distortion in Judge Bork's case as in others. I wonder whether sources will ever again oppose a nominee as violently as in Bork's case and on what grounds mass media might refuse to carry opponents' claims if a Bork-like case were to occur.

Hypothesis Two—Television-Dominated News Distorts Selection

Hypotheses about televised confirmations may be informative if we can formulate them to account for more than one or two recent, wild contests. To understand what television has changed, as opposed to distorted, is difficult because television has dominated the news roughly in the same age as largely open or wide-open modern confirmations. To avoid overgeneralization is difficult when radio and television coverage is so new that only since 1981 has the Senate allowed electronic coverage of the nominees' testimony before the Judiciary Committee.[81]

Professor Stephen Carter has added nonjudicial confirmation hearings to his study and has articulated what may be useful admonitions. Carter attributes "confirmation messes" to two related problems: *the sound-bite problem* and *the disqualification problem*.[82] The sound-bite problem, as its name implies, follows from the propensity of news media to report events in morsels suitable for superficial reactions but not thoughtful contemplation. I have called this the tendency to morselize. Mass media, especially television, are not adept at conveying complexity and nuance but are excellent at purveying spin and applause lines. The disqualification problem always looms because qualification is an intricate, subtle judgment while this or that disqualification can be simple and lurid. Because sound bites are so amenable to broadcast journalism and putative disqualifications are so much more accessible to mass audiences than true qualifications, confirmations become ordeals that, even if nominees survive, cheapen the appointment and coarsen the polity.

Carter self-consciously abstracted these problems from recent nonconfirmations because he was interested in reforming the process to prevent "messes." One easily spots the paper trails of Judge Bork and Professor Lani Guinier[83] and "gotcha" sound bites unrelated to scholarship in the nanny imbroglio that afflicted Zoë Baird, whom President Clinton nominated to be his attorney general.[84] To build on Carter's work, scholars must reformulate the sound bite and disqualification problems if they are to assess the culpability of television or television-dominated media for creating or perpetuating each problem.

The sound-bite problem seems to me to be an important insight because it dovetails with criticisms of news in many other contexts and studies. We have already relied on such studies above to postulate a propensity in modern mass media for expedient angles and inexpensive articles. To blame sound bites for modern confirmation messes, however, we must establish what coverage would or might be like were our media not "sound-bite mad."[85]

One option would be careful historical work. Consider the disqualification problem. Carter likens vilification of Judge Thurgood Marshall to that of Judge Clarence Thomas,[86] a chilling parallel if the likeness can be sustained. Such parallels invite scholarship to show if and how the relative preeminence of print or other media in similar situations—nonconfirmations of Justice Fortas, Judge Haynsworth and Judge Carswell suggest themselves—led to different and better processes or outcomes. One might compare and contrast William Rehnquist's two confirmations to see what difference the increased dominance of television in the 1980s made. One might stretch one's imagination to compare nominations across media regimes. My reading of studies of advice and consent in the cases of Louis Brandeis, Pierce

Butler, John Parker, and Hugo L. Black leads me to conclude that the disqualification problem long predated the reign of television, but I should welcome creative work to establish that the absence of sound bites might have been a boon.

Students of media might appraise the sound bite problem as well. If television culture has exacerbated the disqualification problem because television is so superficial and sensational, media that do not emulate television should improve on mass media coverage. That Carter cites distortions of Guinier's work from the *Legal Times* does not make me optimistic that the sound bite problem is limited to mass media, but it would profit scholars to ponder the degree to which even specialized and sophisticated media help to create disqualifying sound bites.

Even if Carter is correct about television, we must acknowledge that television-driven coverage cuts both ways. Some nominees may be confirmable precisely because they or their handlers effectively use sound bites. We have seen that Judge Clarence Thomas may have become Justice Clarence Thomas due to sound bites more than any other single factor. Over the summer of 1991, his detractors could not convey their deprecations of his scholarship and alarums about his views in terms that resonated as broadly as the "Pin Point" and other anecdotes. More to the point, Judge Thomas's October sound bite attacking "high-tech lynching" may have decided his fate.

Until scholars have clearer ideas about the kinds of coverage that might prevail in media less tyrannized by television, hypotheses concerning television provoke concern but provide too little evidence and inference. With Carter, we doubt that television has made matters better. However, our doubts and his do not substitute for findings and informed speculation.

Hypothesis Three—Mass-Mediated Selection Reduces Merit

Many commentators have expressed the fear that the greater the role of mass media in selection, the lower the quality of judges is likely to sink. Perhaps Ronald Rotunda has put this contention best:

> The increased public scrutiny may encourage the nomination of relative unknowns to the Court because there is less of a paper trail that might draw questions. Although weak presidents have always found it politic to nominate compromise or unknown

candidates, the creation of a confirmation hearing as a media event may encourage such action. In addition, some first-class nominees may refuse to be considered because they do not wish to endure the gauntlet of being subjected to unfair fly-specking of one's career. And a president, particularly a weak one, may refuse to nominate some candidates because that president does not wish to take a risk with those who may be the object of various rumors of long past events. That the rumors may prove to be false is relevant but not conclusive.[87]

Most members of the Twentieth Century Fund Task Force on Judicial Selection appear to have agreed with this assessment.[88] Reporting immediately after Senate action regarding Bork and Douglas Ginsburg, the Task Force accepted most features of appointing federal judges but objected that "several recent developments threaten the efficiency, stature, and independence of the federal judiciary."[89] The Task Force recommended that the Senate depoliticize Supreme Court confirmations by reducing visibility and publicity and by minimizing incentives and opportunities for posturing and distortion.[90] One Bork supporter on the Task Force suggested that television cameras be banned from the hearings.[91] The Task Force concluded that hearings need to be restrained so that merit, temperament, experience, and integrity could triumph.

Judge Bork's experience justifies the claim that visibility and boldness can target nominees. Even if mass media and largely open, openly ideological confirmations more generally bar some meritorious appointees, we resist generalizing this drawback into a systemic verity. That Bork and some other brilliant thinkers on the bench and in the bar (Judges Epstein and Posner and Professors Tribe[92] and Dworkin come immediately to mind) risk wide-open selection implies neither that all terrific appointments are now impossible nor that all justices confirmed in the modern era are unworthy. Unless carefully qualified, then, this "least common denominator" hypothesis may be an outright fallacy.

Indeed, the "stealth strategy" (David Souter's obscurity deprived critics of grounds for guessing his views) and the "Pin Point strategy" of Judge Clarence Thomas assisted President Bush's Supreme Court nominees in sidestepping pitfalls of mass-mediated confirmations. For Justice Souter and Justice Thomas alike, initial impressions of mediocrity have given way to some respectful notices, although it is still too early to tell. Likewise, Justice Ruth Bader Ginsburg and Justice Stephen Breyer seem at least comparable to most justices and markedly superior to some whose selection was screened from the media (President Harry S Truman's nominees come to mind).

Even though the least common denominator hypothesis is specific to Senate confirmations and, usually, to nominations to the U. S. Supreme Court, and even though this hypothesis often amounts to little more than a dirge for the defeated Judge Bork, this overgeneralization may nonetheless have utility. If the hypothesis were retooled to express a more general, inverse relationship between jural quality and inoffensiveness to mass media and to the officials and interest groups whom media cover, it might reveal important features about differences between legal logic and media logic. Such an onerous undertaking is a primary prerequisite for use of this hypothesis.

If one considers the broad sweep of judicial selection, this least common denominator hypothesis is not very helpful. Were one first to establish that the quality of judges had declined,[93] he or she would next have to show some relationship between such decline and mass media. I noted earlier that media coverage of almost all elections and almost all appointments is so sparse that coverage cannot account for much. In sum, if the glare of the media spotlight leads to mediocre judges, Rotunda and others should rejoice that the lights are so seldom even on.

Comfortable Coverage and Judicial Independence

Scholars interested in the role of media in selection must appreciate a possibility that disappointed nominees, political operatives, spin artists, pundits, and other participants seldom state: most mass media coverage of decisions regarding judicial staffing is comfortable and convenient for most recruits and recruiters. I advance this thesis neither as a scientific law nor as an empirical hypothesis. Rather, I offer it as a general perspective that throws into clearer relief the role that news media play in judicial selection almost to the exclusion of other roles. Appropriating terms crafted by Watson and Stookey to categorize senators, I assert that reporters almost always serve as passive validators rather than active participants or even critical observers. Let us see how journalistic silence becomes assent.

Joys of Controlled Selection

Ample evidence warrants the claim that knowledge of judicial recruitment seldom extends beyond political and legal insiders. Even easily available information about judicial selection is newsworthy neither to most journalists nor to almost all of their readers and viewers. Our continuum of conflict and coverage presumes not just that awareness of judicial selection is quite limited but also that insiders want to keep awareness limited to preserve their own prerogatives. The staffing of courts may be obscure because judgeships are so numerous and systems of courts so complex, but it is obscured by insiders who keep outsiders (such as ordinary citizens of the republic) from learning much about judicial personnel.

I do not suggest that insiders guard their walls against impassioned villagers demanding to know what has been going on in the capital castle. Most citizens and—truth be told—most political scientists and lawyers have neither time nor interest to monitor most judicial selection. However, strategic incumbents and insiders likely prefer controlled news. One way to control news is to insure that there is little or no news. Most judicial selection is not very newsworthy, and most judicial recruits and recruiters profit from keeping it that way.

At least in the short run, the contracted scope and moderated intensity of most judicial selections benefit or would seem to benefit press, politicians, and voters. The press, free to cover rare open episodes and freed from covering common closed selection, may turn from barren to fertile news environs. Politicians outside the judiciary face less competition for attention, both when electioneering (significant attention to judicial races would reduce the news hole for other races) and when governing (judicial decisions and behavior can seldom help appointers and can often embarrass them). Voters may ration their limited attention and interest to contested races and issues concerning which they have at least marginally more knowledge.

Closed Selection Inverts
Common Sense

To the degree that minimal coverage usually benefits political activists, journalists, and voters, common observations about judicial elections invert matters. Judicial elections generate little interest and less knowledge among voters not because they are inherently uneventful but because quiet campaigns let sleeping adversaries lie. Many students of judicial selection have found the paucity of public awareness undemocratic. Viewed from the standpoint of politicians and journalists, however, external pressures on decision makers are choked off and noncoverage of noncampaigns is welcomed by recruiters and recruited, while the press is spared any insistence that selection be covered beyond public notices in news capsules and filler. If voters or critics deplore the losses in accountability, champions of incumbents may cite gains in judicial independence.

Many selection systems were designed to dilute democratic accountability in favor of judicial independence or merit or both, so politicians and press may find nothing amiss in closed and controlled selection. Nonpartisan elections undermine the cue most useful for ordinary voters. Retention elections deprive voters of flesh-and-blood competitors, so it cannot surprise us that so few incumbents have been spurned. Commissions and other merit-based selection are supposed to reduce the spoils system, but they reduce as well accountability and awareness. Such systems close selection and contain conflict by design.

Indeed, many intellectuals and pundits have reacted to wide-open selection with calls to circumscribe conflict and keep outsiders outside. The battle over Bork so annoyed some advocates that they argued for sharply limiting the Senate's role in consenting to nominees,[94] for getting cameras out of the Judiciary Committee, and for eliminating electioneering, advertising, lobbying, and other means by which Supreme Court nominations have been opened. The wild contest over Chief Justice Bird and two of her colleagues hardly imbued academic observers with reverence for plebiscitary control over the judiciary, despite the fact that the California retention campaign of 1986 was unique or nearly so.

If constraints on the scope and intensity of conflict are not only expedients for politicians but prophylactics against excess, desultory campaigns and covert appointments may be salutary both for political and judicial strategists managing selection in the short run and for a republic of laws and reason in the longer run. Scholars have found that extensive knowledge of courts and judges often correlates with opposition to judges, if not courts.[95] One need not be an aristocratic snob to argue that the polity profits when popular intensity is arrested and moderated, particularly when the most passionate are misinformed.

Beyond expedience and prophylaxis, closing off the scope and intensity of conflict is central to the construction of legality and courts. Popular images of courts as passive resolvers of conflicts and judges as neutral arbiters demand suspended disbelief. Open selections make the politics of selection obvious. Closed selection assists recruiters in emulating Claude Rains in the film *Casablanca*: they profess to be "Shocked! Shocked!" that politics should enter into the selection of judges.[96] Contrary to experience as such shock may be, expressions of shock recapitulate the social logic underlying adjudication and autonomy in a legal order, as we saw in chapter 1.

A Concluding Metahypothesis

To the difficulties of overgeneralization from anomalous wide-open selection mentioned, let me add one more. Recruiters have changed tactics to gain control over the selection process and to co-opt coverage.

The nominations of Justices Ginsburg and Breyer present obvious examples in which the Clinton administration permitted friend and foe a veto over potential nominees at the *selection* stage and in so doing guaranteed smooth sailing at the *confirmation* stage. Commentators may have battered the administration on the extraordinary lag between vacancy and nomination, but conflict at this earliest stage of the selection process presented mass media and pressure groups with far fewer opportunities to crack the process wide open.

Indeed, confirmations following the defeat of Judge Bork may be best understood as recruiters' strategies to frustrate opponents and the media in their efforts to break judicial selection wide open. In securing confirmation of Judge David Souter, the Bush White House easily circumvented a key predictor of wide-open proceedings. Many observers traced Judge Bork's difficulties to his lengthy paper trail and predicted that any nominee with extensive public remarks on complex issues would find confirmation difficult because senators could transform even respectable academic arguments into extreme positions. Judge Souter's nonexistent public record on divisive issues coupled with a steadfast refusal to engage the Senate Judiciary Committee in meaningful discussion of his position on controversial issues inured him to most attacks. When experts predicted that a continued policy of refusing to answer controversial questions might pose difficulties for future nominees, the Bush administration countered by nominating Clarence Thomas, whose race and Horatio Alger story undercut opposition based on limited qualifications and evasive responses to Senate inquiries.

Politicians, pundits, and practitioners of judicial selection, if I am correct in my assessment, have combined—which is not to say colluded—to create a system in which even attentive, involved citizens have few means by which they may interfere with the staffing of their own courts. To defend this system, which often resembles the Jacksonian spoils system in that those who win elections tend to get to preserve their mandates and their preferences in courts far longer than anywhere else, officials and journalists alike rail against the few anomalies of democratic exertion.

I understand why elites try to defend their advantages, but I am puzzled by the manner in which scholars abet these insiders. Adapting a verse from poet Robinson Jeffers, "Who would have thought this incredibly little democracy to be too much?"[97] My answer to this question: academics!

I have singled out the Twentieth Century Fund and Carter and Rotunda for scrutiny because they exemplify the best scholarship that bears on coverage of judicial selection. They are favorably representative of scholarship that seems to me to concentrate so on the occasionally baying press that they overlook the significance of the fact that most of the press most of the time is not baying at all.

With respect for the scholarly accomplishments of my betters, I advance an hypothesis that I hope that we all can soon disprove: *Participants in judicial selection processes—executives, legislators, interest-group leaders, and journalists—understand the relationship of coverage to judicial selection, but scholars as yet do not.*

Conclusion—A Theoretical Scorecard

What the Inside-Out Perspective Accounts For

To the extent that the number, variety, and complexity of venues for judicial selection explain paltry coverage, an idealistic but practical view of media would appear to be satisfied by routine coverage of judicial appointments and elections. Coverage, when it comes, is as objective and accurate as one could expect (refer to the Media Mission in table I.1). Judicial candidates are reasonably candid in dealing with reporters who cover their campaigns (Court Mission in table I.1). We cannot be certain how well the dual missions of the Inside-Out Perspective might be fulfilled, for coverage is far too occasional. More, that perspective was developed for adjudication, not judicial selection.

If the Inside-Out view were to be adapted to judicial selection, its prescriptions for media and judges might be met, but its prescriptions for audiences would need adjustment. The primary audience for judicial selection is attentive only if we look at insiders. The exten-

sively attentive audience too often presumed by Inside-Outers is neither very extensive nor very attentive with regard to judicial selection.
Table I.1 refers to a two-step flow of information. With regard to judicial selection, that flow is at best a trickle.

What Our Outside-In Perspective Accounts For

In still another demonstration that our Outside-In Perspective
is *an* and not *the* opposite of the mainstream view, that skeptical alternative matches judicial selection in but one respect. Audiences for
judicial selection are mostly inadvertent—indeed, mostly nonexistent
would be closer to the mark.

Every other Outside-In description of coverage of adjudication
badly misstates coverage of selection. To be sure, mass media will
likely go with inexpensive hype when it is available, but any hype,
cheap or dear, seldom attaches to judicial selection. Despite an extensive literature covering aberrant selection, almost all judges secure
appointment, election, and reelection without a scintilla of scandal and
without a single item of interest to the most desperate tabloid. Perhaps
the imagery of judicial candidates is strategic (the Outside-In
Perspective mission statement for courts), but the predominate strategy by far is anonymity. While I have shown the utility of that strategy,
that is not what I take imagery to denote. The drama and spectacle on
which the Outside-In Perspective fastens is virtually always absent
from judicial selection.

What Neither Perspective Accounts For

Since neither perspective was designed to cover judicial
selection, we should not be too surprised that they apply poorly.
Justice Scalia's and Davis's alternatives are also inapposite. What
should we do?

I recommend that we "get real." The continuum of coverage and
contexts that I introduce in this chapter suggests that mass media cover
judicial selection in a manner quite different from any sort of coverage of
adjudication. This makes some sense, if we think about it. Adjudicators
purport to be engaged in a mostly nonpolitical endeavor. Judicial recruitment and judicial selection, in contrast, are much more political. Indeed,
practitioners of judicial recruitment and judicial selection often write of
their political campaigns; few judges acknowledge that they ever practice politics behind the bench and behind their robes.

Table 6.2   **A Perspective on Judicial Selection**

	A Continuum of Coverage *A Strategic, Realistic View*
Media Mission	Objective accuracy: media cover the little news that comes from campaigns and are not self-serving.
Judges' Mission	Maximize judiciality: incumbents rely on name-recognition and anonymity; challengers must remain judicious while attacking.
Audience	Barely cognizant: most constituents are barely aware of judicial selection.
Information Flow	Carefully constricted: insiders control recruitment as long as outsiders are unaware.
Stance	Primarily descriptive

If we acknowledge the position of judicial selection at a cusp between law and politics, the continuum makes sense. That continuum presumes that recruiters and selectors want to preserve their room to maneuver. This they do by keeping selection as covert as possible. The more patent the process of selection, the more peril for decision makers. As conflict expands, appointing executives and incumbent judges may lose control of processes. To fend off such peril, they engage in activities hypothesized in table 6.2.

Table 6.2 presents the continuum in terms that match table I.1 at least to a degree. However, this ad hoc table reconsiders most entries from table I.1. The media, we may hypothesize, are accurate and objective in their coverage, but their coverage is much more occasional even than coverage of court decisions. Sources usually will not want to part with any information that reporters truly desire, so reporters will generally ignore self-serving electoral and executive campaigns and will report events elsewhere. The information of greatest interest, as Carter told us, is disqualifying information. News media may seek disqualifying information if such information is cheap. However, hiding such information will be a major aim of judicial candidates and their supporters, so expect disqualifying data to be dear.

Judicial candidates are severely circumscribed because they must avoid injudicious remarks. Canons of legal ethics prohibit them from discussing most of the pressing judicial, legal, and political issues, so candidates have little to say that anyone would want to hear. Judiciousness is mostly a matter, it seems, of holding one's tongue.

Audiences seem to have adapted well to judicious noncampaigns and journalistic noncoverage. Most voters, for example, know very little about judges whom they elect. This makes voters ripe for being stampeded and thus must incline sitting judges to circumspection and perhaps even to capitulation from time to time. Most citizens know even less about appointed judges than they do about elected. Judicial selection plays out before a very select audience of insiders.

Perhaps the most crucial aspect of this chapter is my insistence that most judicial selection is closed. I have posited as the prime directive for recruiters and candidates that the scope and intensity of conflict over appointments and elections be minimized. This prime directive seems to account for the noncoverage and noncampaigning that are the rule. Insiders, especially recruiters and candidates for the bench, prosper from keeping others outside.

While the continuum and the representation in table 6.2 need refinement and testing, they represent my best account of scholarly findings to date.

CONCLUSION

Before we may say more about coverage of courts, we need much more research. Time and again I have tried your patience by my tentative language and my inconclusive endings of sections and chapters. You may wonder if we have learned anything about courts. The foregoing chapters show that we have learned some things. In this concluding chapter, we will review, briefly and summarily, what we have learned.

We have learned enough to be confident that the intersections of courts and news media demand more study and greater insight. Our insights and our studies must be *critical* and *perspectivist*. Our work must be critical lest we overlook alternatives to the mainstream standards that journalistic and legal practitioners invoke. We must acknowledge what these professionals show us, but we must look for what they themselves do not acknowledge or need not know. We need to be perspectivists, because in order to be critical we require at least one sophisticated framework to tell us what to look for. A single perspective will not long suffice to provide the insights and context that will lead to new knowledge. We need to see matters from more than one point of view. We need to triangulate, be critical, and look at the familiar askew and anew!

Supreme Court Coverage

Refer to table 2.3, which represents the four major perspectives that warred in chapter 2. Table 2.3 depicts four possibilities for critical curiosity and skeptical study. Each possibility is linked to an authoritative source—my own source-ery?

I argued in chapter 2 that we must defer to the views of Linda Greenhouse and her peers on the Supreme Court beat. While their coverage is far more selective than we may have assumed, their coverage tends to meet mainstream standards most of the time. If a few critics lament a "Greenhouse effect"[1] and legal specialists lament misstatements of technicalities, *we have every reason to conclude that major newspapers cover many, if not most, High Court opinions fairly and accurately.* Lesser newspapers, weekly newsmagazines, and broadcast media tend toward less coverage, but *I found no evidence that these media failed of reasonable fairness and accuracy.* I concluded that the Public Court, the Supreme Court self-consciously on display for oral arguments and in opinions, will ordinarily match standards for adjudication both in fact and in news media.

However, I also agreed with some critics of coverage. In table

2.3, we considered frameworks advanced by two observers in positions to know: Justice Antonin Scalia of the U. S. Supreme Court and Richard Davis, perhaps the leading academic student of Supreme Court reporting. Each asserted that *either* the news media *or* the Court satisfied mainstream standards. Each then insisted that the other institution did not.

Justice Scalia (table 2.3, upper-right cell) presumed that he and his fellows habitually emulated the highest standards but that mass media too often failed of even competence. Now, Scalia often plays the wag and the scold. In some of his dissents, he has been less generous in his appraisal of majority and individual opinions. Nonetheless, he has a point. Even national newspapers of record can render complex, difficult opinions of the justices only superficially. The more popular news source—television—seldom can even match the superficial coverage of the flimsiest national newspaper. While Justice Scalia has overstated his case and surrendered too quickly and too conveniently a role for the press, he is undoubtedly correct that the well-informed participant in democratic governance will need to exploit more specialized and more sophisticated media. Even if you are optimistic about the possibility that coverage in the *Washington Post* or the *Wall Street Journal* will spur *you* to find out more for yourself, most citizens will go with the overview and will have no time to strike out on their own. President Truman feared for citizens who believed that the papers told them what was going on[2]; Justice Scalia has repeated that fear with regard to the High Court. Presuming media distortion, Scalia's Court must be private and secretive to preserve itself. Even the Court's public outputs surpass ordinary understanding.

In the most recent book-length investigation of Supreme Court coverage, Davis identified an opposite, if not equal, deviation from mainstream standards and located the problem a bit closer to Justice Scalia. Davis suggested that the Supreme Court is private *not* because it is intrinsically incomprehensible to mass media *but* because the justices bewilder most observers by secrecy and chicanery. In Davis's view, Scalia and colleagues could come down from their clouds and guide the press and reach the citizenry. If the justices did so, however, they might expose their own authority to question. The Court keeps the secrets, in sum, to preserve its authority and to baffle the credulous.

The fourth position that I auditioned in chapter 2 conformed nicely to my preference for "both/and" thinking. Suppose, two other critics theorized, *both* that the Court mystifies *and* that mass media distort. Although their study is dated, David Paletz and Robert Entman have offered the most systematic critique of Supreme Court coverage of which I know. I suggested that the most fascinating insight they offered us was that noncoverage serves the majesty of the Court and the profitability of media. This possibility I labeled Dual Pragmatism in table 1.1. Throughout chapter 2, I found it remarkably coincidental that the High Court was as public and private and secret as suited the justices, the press, or both. Paletz and Entman hypothesized that the Court is publicized, privatized, and secretive *strategically*. They concluded that news coverage tended to distort in favor of the Court's outputs and imagery, so we must remember that they drew from the simplicity and brevity of coverage a conclusion quite different from that of Justice Scalia.

Chapter 2 concluded that the prevalence and importance of noncoverage must be acknowledged. We may reassess the relative prevalence empirically, but the importance of the aspects not covered cannot be measured. *We are likely to attribute importance to suit the perspective foremost in our minds.* If we take the mainstream view, we probably assume that the newsworthy gets covered and what is not covered is not newsworthy. At the least, chapter 2 should suggest some alternative views of the meaning of noncoverage.

If we try to winnow the number of plausible perspectives on noncoverage and on coverage, we shall probably start by establishing how often and under what conditions the High Court is relatively public, relatively private, or utterly secret. Davis and others have explored the conditions that shape coverage of the Court. I am not satisfied that they or we know very much about the qualities or sufficiency of the coverage. I conclude that the most basic, most rewarding next step is to analyze empirically and to assess normatively the quantity and quality of coverage and noncoverage that the Court receives in various mass media. If we had better notions of what specialists select and what they reject, we might begin to fathom news-worth. Any gains in understanding news-worth might incline us toward one or another perspective. Such gains might suggest when this perspective applies and when that perspective would do better.

Until we take a closer look at the outputs, the inputs that the perspectives presume will all remain possible and even plausible.

Appellate Courts Other Than the U. S. Supreme Court

Research about appeals courts other than the U. S. Supreme Court was both dated and depressing. I know of so few studies of coverage of lower appeals courts that I reached my most tentative, most qualified conclusions in chapter 3. I noted the glaring absence of coverage as a signal datum, but I cannot be certain that coverage of, say, state supreme courts has not improved. For that matter, I cannot be sure whether it has gotten worse since the few fledgling studies.

From those sparse pioneering efforts, it seemed to me that *coverage, while scant, met mainstream standards presumed by the Inside-Out Perspective.* This led me to conclude that, with respect to appellate courts, the media watchdog displayed highly selective acuity. Most of the time, it barked seldom and seemed to notice little. What the watchdog chose to notice, however, it inspected reasonably well.

While that conclusion, too, is better than nothing, beyond that pittance of understanding I cannot go. In table 3.1, I speculated regarding symbiotic relations between mass media and appellate courts. I adapted the imposing theoretical understanding of Professors Paletz and Entman to these appeals courts. Indeed, it seemed to me that their Outside-In Perspective suited lower appellate courts even better than the Supreme Court for which Paletz and Entman had developed their ideas. Since new research into various appeals courts is beyond the scope of this book, I noted that we needed more and more recent studies of appeals courts. I left the matter there.

Further studies may question the symbioses posited in chapter 3. Perhaps the most useful next step would be for scholars to interview reporters and editors for news organs that purport to track appeals courts. These news professionals might be able to explain their selections in ways that would suggest alternatives to the symbiotic hypothesis. Until such studies are done, the best that I can do is to notice that noncoverage may serve judicial and journalistic professionals well, if citizens poorly.

Coverage of Criminal Trial Courts

Chapter 4 concerned two ironies. The first irony was that *most stories matched mainstream standards for journalism and adjudication but cases covered most tended to match those standards least.* While the infamous murder trial of O. J. Simpson provided an extreme example of this irony, much research to date seemed to support it as well. The second irony was that *ordinary coverage tended to trumpet crime control, while extraordinary coverage emphasized due process.* That is, to the extent that mainstream expectations would dictate that mass media should educate the citizenry about legal ideals and constitutional rights, such topics would arise most likely in sensationalized reporting of unrepresentative, notorious cases.

I attempted to account for these ironies by source-ery and by symbiosis, two phenomena more consonant with Outside-In Perspectives than with the Inside-Out Perspective. I likened criminal coverage to voyages of submarines: criminal cases begin as crime coverage, are submerged most of the time (absolutely or relatively), and resurface when jurors or judges reach decisions. Since procedures and rights (that is, due process) tend to dominate during trials, submersion tends to hide due process, and surfacing tends to highlight parts of trials that more concern crime control. This "submarine hypothesis" thus explains (at least partially) the second irony. More, it conforms to the first irony; that is, the tendency of criminal trials to submerge except at their beginnings and endings parallels conventional coverage. *Most coverage of most trials will concern parts of cases most conducive to spot coverage that is fair and accurate. The more challenging parts of trials (such as witnesses, motions, rulings, cross-examination, and evidence) will be submerged except during more notorious, sensationalized trials.*

Still, my "submarine hypothesis" is conjecture, not fact. The patterns of coverage may be established empirically but such findings were beyond the scope of this book. I hope that such studies lie in our near future.

My final conjecture in chapter 4 was an Outside-Out hypothesis. This hypothesis does not, to the best of my knowledge, inform studies of court coverage, although similar views animate studies of coverage of crime. An unabashed critic of reporting of criminal courts might look for coverage that alternately agitates and soothes. Mass media can guarantee themselves attention and audience by dramatizing threats to crime control. If these threats are allayed by due process that appears to protect the innocent and the rights-sensitive but seldom jeopardizes convictions and punishments, then criminal court productions maximize the interconnected missions of courts and media. Naturally, such a system depends on audiences' being unaware of the actual workings of courts but thoroughly aware of trials presented by popular culture. If rights and judicial fairness obstruct the criminal justice conveyor belt, especially when those who tune in only now and then happen to be watching, courts may expect pressure to get the conveyor belt moving again. If crime control seems to be going well, the occasional observer may be disposed to generous allotments of rights and process. In sum, coverage of criminal courts may wax and wane as audiences become agitated or acquiescent.[3]

We have seen that this outside-out framework easily accounts for the twin ironies of chapter 4. However, I know of no efforts to apply any similar framework to journalism about courts. The next step for those impressed by this perspective, then, will be to use it to explain what other views explain less well or not at all.

Coverage of Civil Litigation

We discovered why *most phases of civil litigation are covered even less than prosecutions*. While the dominance of noncoverage again impressed me, I explored some patterns of surfacing and submersion in coverage. Reports of many civil cases seemed to conform to my submarine hypothesis, but I exposed some very prominent exceptions as well. My next step will be to confirm both the rule and the exceptions to the rule in civil cases.

Chapter 5 provided tentative explanations for the relative paucity of coverage of civil suits. I wondered if lawsuits that do not involve the state may alternatively feature too little or too much source-ery. The more that parties and attorneys keep their own counsel, the less access reporters have to leads and sources. (No sources, no source-ery, no news?) If both parties are working the press, every factoid and every interpretation is liable to spin. (A surfeit of sources equals no authoritative sources equals no objectivity?) Even if one side plays to the media and the other side does not, the disadvantaged are likely to score news media for unfair coverage. Thus, I have speculated that reporters luxuriate in authoritative, credible sources less often when covering civil matters than when covering prosecutions. *When sources are too few or too many and when sources and reporters have little to exchange, coverage will be scarce.*

In chapter 5 angle biases and commercial biases account for relative undercoverage of civil courts. While I found those biases revelatory, so little work has been done on civil coverage that I cannot place much faith in my tentative, perhaps fanciful account. This appealing explanation needs support.

Still, angle biases and commercial biases are important. Criminal courts would seem to feature more opportunities for dramatization, personalization, morselization, and normalization than civil cases simply because there are so many more criminal court cases that are, at least, processed in a courtroom. I rehearsed reasons to suppose that a greater proportion of criminal cases may be newsworthy, both in terms of angles and in terms of enticing viewers and readers. I speculated that criminal cases are easier to render in spots or briefs. I also noted that, given crime control propensities and indifference to defendants presumed guilty, criminal cases permit reporters and editors to see matters mostly through the eyes of the state: the government's prosecutors, the government's police, the government's forensics experts, and the government's judge. Governments supply judges for civil cases, but everyone else involved will be presumed to have a private interest, even in public interest cases. Attorneys for the damned and advocates for the accused will often possess little or no retaliatory capacity, unlike many participants in civil cases.

This role for angles and commercial concerns remains merely a possibility until enterprising researchers interview and monitor reporters and editors. We need a better sense of news-worth in practice before we can be confident that the general patterns established in study after study of modern news media explain civil coverage as well as criminal.

At the end of chapter 5, I offered a critical perspective that resembled Justice Scalia's view of coverage of the U. S. Supreme Court. Table 5.5 depicted a two-tiered model. This model presupposes that coverage of civil courts should be viewed from above and from below. From above, civil court coverage in specialized media can handle issues and decisions technically and comprehensively in reportage that would baffle the few nonlawyers who would persist in viewing or reading. Seen from below, coverage of civil suits is spotty except when suits feature titillation or other sorts of "info-tainment" fit for nonlawyers and mass media. This model locates reporters and editors as key intermediaries who direct the best information to the higher strata and the best entertainment to the lower reaches.

This "above and below model" may have promise but has to my knowledge never informed studies. For now, then, I can only report this model as a suspicion: I suspect that Justice Scalia was correct about courts defying lay understanding; he and I just disagree about *which* courts do this.

Coverage of Judicial Recruitment and Selection

The appointment and election of judges induced us to go outside the courtroom and into a community. Here, too, we found that *coverage is ordinarily minuscule.* However, I was able to infer from an extensive literature a continuum that *might* account for coverage of appointments and elections. At one pole, recruitment and selection are latent. By definition, latent events are hard to cover. Only when selections open up do mass media have much to cover. In such open contexts, judicial selection may supply the angles that make coverage profitable. Knowing this, those who recruit judges and would like to control selection strive to minimize any angles other than positive. Reporters seldom have the resources to investigate recruitment or selection unless they sense some opportunity.

This "continuum of coverage and contexts" promises to bring more order to studies of judicial selection if it conforms to evidence past and future. Further study will be necessary to understand how and how often selection gets opened. I do not know, for example, whether selection is more often obscured by an absence of information or by an avalanche of positive storylines. Do recruiters more often value silence or a positive hard sell? We could also use historical surveys to see how often we might justifiably pronounce recruitment even modestly open. Have, as many observers suspect, nominations for high judicial office become more open more often in the last decade or so, or is that perception the product of overestimating the trials of Justice Thomas, Judge Bork, and Chief Justice Bird? These and other questions await critical examination from multiple perspectives.

Toward Critical, Perspectivist Inquiry

While the research that I have summarized has led us to few conclusions, studies have justified *critical, perspectivist* inquiries. I have encouraged you to undertake such inquiries, challenge conventional thinking, and ponder phenomena in more than one way. Each chapter has shown that we know too little. Each chapter has shown that we assume or accept too much of the professional self-images of adjudicators and journalists. Each chapter has shown that features of court coverage may with profit be conceived from multiple viewpoints. The Inside-Out Perspective and one or more Outside-In Perspectives have illuminated studies of the United States Supreme Court, other appellate courts, criminal trial courts, and civil trial courts. Even our sole excursion outside courtrooms (chapter 6) demonstrated that contexts for understanding are various.

Indeed, it seems to me that we found the most perspectives and more alternatives to self-congratulatory perspectives in those areas in which the scholarly literature is most extensive and most developed. Regarding the Supreme Court of the United States and judicial selection, we had sufficient studies to array contrasting perspectives and critical alternatives. For court coverage, we constructed a fourfold scheme of possibilities. Based on literature on judicial recruitment and selection, we conceived a continuum of contexts and contests. Research remains insufficient and inchoate concerning lower appeals courts and trial courts, but even in those domains alternatives at least as plausible as the Inside-Out Perspective arose. Coverage of appeals courts suggested a symbiotic hypothesis. Criminal court coverage inspired an Outside-Out Perspective. For civil courts, I proposed an "above and below" model that combined mainstream and alternative perspectives.

Thus, I can end this book with more than an admonition that we need more studies. We *do* need more studies. More than that, we need to study noncoverage perhaps even more than coverage. What we do *not* learn about courts, cases, and judges may be as significant as what is covered. Still more, we need to be skeptical, especially when judges, lawyers, reporters, editors, and other professionals justify their products and processes. I have directed your attention to incentives and disincentives, to interests and indifference: symbioses, source-ery, angle biases, commercial biases, and other strategic relations are examples.

Throughout, I have insisted that the additional, critical work that we need will likely not be forthcoming without attention to perspectives. What perspectives disguise, contrasting perspectives reveal. Too much of what I have reviewed and you might read is written from the mainstream view, from insiders to those on the outside. I have demonstrated how to remain outside and to penetrate the Inside-Out Perspective. You may prefer to go inside and tend to that mainstream view. That is fine, provided that you do so self-consciously. Before you read this book, you might have been innocent of the presumptions that underlie conventional thinking about coverage of courts; now you should see those presumptions. Defend them if you can, but acknowledge them as you must. Get skeptical! Be critical! See matters afresh!

notes

INTRODUCTION

Getting Courts and Media in Perspective

1. Bob Baum, "Tonya: I'm Guilty—Skater Signs Plea on Conspiracy Charge," *Burlington Free Press*, March 17, 1994, p.1A.

2. Notice that the Inside-Out Perspective, at least as I define here, need not involve presumptions about the conduct of lawyers, jurors, police, or others in the legal system. While a thorough representation of legal journalism must include such participants, those who use the Inside-Out Perspective need not. Rather, they may (and, according to my observation, do) restrict their presumptions to the two sets of participants bound by standards of formal objectivity.

3. For disparate examples of this tendency, see Robert H. Bork, *The Tempting of America* (New York: Free Press, 1990), and Jeffrey A. Segal and Harold J. Spaeth, *The Supreme Court and the Attitudinal Model* (New York: Cambridge University Press, 1993).

4. Elihu Katz, "Two Step Flow of Communication," *Public Opinion Quarterly* 21 (1957): 61–78. On television as a medium that modifies this flow, see Robert Shelby Frank, *Message Dimension of Television News* (Lexington, KY: Lexington Books, 1973), and David Morgan, *The Capitol Press Corps: Newsmen and the Governing of New York State* (Westport, CT: Greenwood Press, 1978), ch. 1.

5. Depending on their estimation of the size of the attentive public, insiders may then posit a third step: the attentive public tutors and tempers reactions among a largely inert and usually malleable mass public. The smaller one assumes the attentive public to be, the greater the role the attentive public must play to make the resulting model even appear democratic.

6. Lyle Denniston, *The Reporter and the Law: Techniques of Covering the Courts* (New York: Hastings House, 1980), p. xvii.

7. Such odic idealism prepares us for the rest of Mr. Denniston's introduction. Mr. Denniston states that his book aims to acquaint journalists with the law as part of a larger effort "to achieve a workable, mutual understanding among lawyers and journalists" (*The Reporter and the Law*, p. xvii). Mr. Denniston's sponsors expound that purpose in a very *inside-out* statement: ". . . the aim of the book is to bring the highest possible quality of information to a citizenry which bears the ultimate responsibility for maintenance of an effective judicial system within our democratic society" (*The Reporter and the Law*, p. xxiii). This traditional view implicitly presumes an extensive attentive audience and a mediated two-step flow of information.

8. Richard Davis, *Decisions and Images: The Supreme Court and the Press* (Englewood Cliffs, NJ: Prentice-Hall, 1994), pp. 42, 65.

9. Denniston, *The Reporter and the Law*, p. xvii.

10. Ibid., p. xix; emphasis added.

11. Ibid., p. xx.

12. J. Edward Gerald, *News of Crime: Courts and Press in Conflict,* Contributions to the Study of Mass Media and Communications, Number 1 (Westport, CT: Greenwood Press, 1983), pp. vii–viii.

13. It is interesting to notice that Gerald presumes an extensive attentive public and a two-step flow of information just one paragraph before admitting that "[t]he general reader cannot translate the language of the courts without taking the time to become a specialist, . . ." See Gerald, *News of Crime*, p. vii.

14. Chester A. Newland, "Press Coverage of the United States Supreme Court," *Western Political Quarterly* 17 (March 1964): 15. Readers who take Newland to mean that public opinion of judicial behavior and public opinion of law are vital will regard the use of "are" in the quoted language as a solecism. I have not inserted a damning "sic" because I suppose it possible that Newland meant that public opinion and law are important to the legal system.

15. "The Myth of Mechanical Jurisprudence" is a belief usually constructed by those who do not hold it. This allusion to machines is intended to be derisive and dismissive, since all-too-human justices will obviously not decide any case as if they were machines programmed by law alone.

16. Newland, "Press Coverage of the United States Supreme Court," p. 15.

17. So common is the Inside-Out Perspective in the literature that virtually any scholarship on legal reporting will invoke one or more elements of the perspective as it was defined earlier. Let me regale you with just a few more examples, element by element. Authors regularly cite an expectation that reporters strive for accuracy and objectivity and often or usually achieve those lofty goals. For an example, see Robert Drechsel, *News Making in the Trial Courts* (New York: Longman, 1983), pp. 2–4. Authors also tend to expect judicial candor and craft to predominate in practice. For an example, see Tim O'Brien, "Best Kept Secrets of the Judiciary," *Judicature* 73 (April–May 1990): 342. Those who study legal reporting routinely assume an extensive attentive public and a mediated two-step flow of information; see Jack C. Doppelt, "Strained Relations: How Judges and Lawyers Perceive the Coverage of Legal Affairs," *The Justice System Journal* 14 (1991): 420. Finally, much of the literature on legal reporting is explicitly prescriptive. See, for examples, David L. Grey, *The Supreme Court and the News Media* (Evanston, IL: Northwestern University Press, 1968) and Tim O'Brien, "Best Kept Secrets of the Judiciary."

18. Because the coherence of the representation and not the order in table I.1 is the crucial consideration, I could begin with any element and see how adjusting any assumption forces adjustments in the others. Skeptical and enterprising readers should test other starting points to assure themselves that the coherence of both perspectives is as constraining as I have argued.

19. Charles H. Franklin and Liane Kosaki, "Media, Knowledge, and Public Evaluations of the Supreme Court," in Lee Epstein (ed.), *Contemplating Courts* (Washington: C Q Press, 1995), pp. 352–75; Lionel S. Sobel, "News Coverage of the Supreme Court," *American Bar Association Journal* 56 (June 1970): 548.

20. The reader should not assume from this sentence that even audiences aware of and outraged by judicial malfeasance or nonfeasance will have much power to sanction judges. Judicial independence, the improbability of appeal, and the modesty of electoral discipline combine to insulate judges.

21. For the deeper meaning and functions of such political dramaturgy, see Murray Edelman, *Constructing the Political Spectacle* (Chicago: University of Chicago Press, 1988).

22. The attentive reader will notice at this point that our budding Outside-In Perspective accommodates actors in the legal system, while, as mentioned in note

2, the Inside-Out Perspective cannot incorporate them as readily.

23. Some such chronic tendencies of mass media will be defined in chapter 1 as journalistic biases.

24. David L. Paletz and Robert M. Entman, *Media Power Politics* (New York: Free Press, 1981), ch. 6.

25. Ibid.

26. Ibid., pp. 101–4.

27. M. L. Stein, "Scalia Discusses the Press," *Editor & Publisher* 123 (Sept. 8, 1990): 16.

28. Ibid.

29. G. Alan Tarr and Mary Cornelia Aldis Porter, *State Supreme Courts in State and Nation* (New Haven, CT: Yale University Press, 1988), pp. 180–81.

30. Paletz and Entman, *Media Power Politics*, p. ix.

31. Gerald, *News of Crime*, p. viii.

CHAPTER 1

Construction of Judicial and Journalistic Authority

1. See David V. J. Bell, *Power, Influence, and Authority: An Essay in Political Linguistics* (New York: Oxford University Press, 1975).

2. A classic account of the bases of legitimate authority is Max Weber, *Economy and Society*, edited by Guenter Roth and Claus Wittich (Berkeley: University of California Press, 1978), pp. 212–16. To begin to understand Weber's trichotomy, see Reinhard Bendix, *Max Weber: An Intellectual Portrait* (Berkeley: University of California Press, 1977), pp. 298–457. I have substituted "standards" for Weber's "rational grounds" because the former term accentuates the rhetorical construction of judicial and journalistic authority.

3. Martin Shapiro, *Courts: A Comparative and Political Analysis* (Chicago: University of Chicago Press, 1981), pp. 1–2.

4. Phillip M. Gollner, "Consulting by Peering into Minds of Jurors," *New York Times,* Jan. 7, 1994, p. A23.

5. Lief H. Carter, *Reason in Law,* 3d ed. (Boston: Little Brown, 1988).

6. Robert Cover, *Justice Accused* (New Haven, CT: Yale University Press, 1975).

7. Shapiro, *Courts,* p. 1.

8. *The Behavior of Law* (New York: Academic Press, 1976), pp. 11–121. See also Donald Black, *Sociological Justice* (New York: Oxford University Press, 1989), in which Black makes similar points amid some "both/and" thinking:

> The two models are not simply different versions of legal reality with different assumptions about how law works. They arise from different perspectives and have different purposes and goals. The jurisprudential model is a participant's view, employed by practicing lawyers who seek to show how the rules of law lead logically to a particular decision. Judges routinely employ the jurisprudential model as well, since they frame their decisions in terms of how the rules logically apply to the facts. . . . Contrariwise, the sociological model entails an observer's perspective. It draws attention to the social characteristics of the partici-

pants while ignoring the matters emphasized by lawyers and judges. But this is not because any sociologist regards the rules as entirely irrelevant. Every case has a technical core—the rules in the face of the evidence—that can be meaningfully analyzed in the jurisprudential tradition. And, other things being equal—including the social characteristics of all concerned—this technical core is important in the handling of cases.

Black here complements the Jurisprudential Model's "ought" with the Sociological Model's "is" to understand better the legal system.

9. W. Lance Bennett and Martha S. Feldman, *Reconstructing Reality in the Courtroom: Justice and Judgment in American Culture* (New Brunswick, NJ: Rutgers University Press, 1981).

10. Abraham S. Blumberg, "The Practice of Law as a Confidence Game," *Law and Society Review* 1 (June 1967):15–39.

11. Such organizational biases are not limited to the criminal justice system. See, for example, Herbert M. Kritzer, *Let's Make a Deal: Understanding the Negotiation Process in Ordinary Litigation* (Madison: University of Wisconsin Press, 1991), and Sheldon Engelmayer and Robert Wagman, *Lord's Justice: One Judge's Battle to Expose the Deadly Dalkon Shield I.U.D.* (Garden City, NY: Anchor Press/Doubleday, 1985).

12. Gene Gilmore, *Modern Newspaper Editing,* 4th ed. (Ames: Iowa State University Press, 1990), pp. 225–27.

13. Sol Robinson, *Guidelines For News Reporters* (Blue Ridge Summit, PA: Tab Books, 1971), p. 25: "Irrespective of the quality or tone of the newscaster's voice, his technique or style, nothing, and I repeat, nothing, can or will ever replace *accuracy*" (emphasis in original).

14. See, for example, Fred Graham, *Happy Talk: Confessions of a TV Newsman* (New York: Norton, 1990), pp. 74–75:

> The secret for the broadcaster was to decide which information, at a bare minimum, must be reported in order to tell the story and then rate the other facts according to their importance. . . . That meant sacrificing some information to make the central point. But because we were reaching as many people as we were, and with the additional visual impact that television could deliver, there was very little frustration in the brevity of our reports.
>
> The hazard was that, in selecting the crucial points to be made and those to be sacrificed, the broadcast journalist would sometimes miss the important point and not get around to reporting that at all. . . .

Mr. Graham seems to argue that the size of his audience and the visual impact of television somehow atoned for brevity, superficiality, and inaccuracy.

15. Kenneth Burke, *A Grammar of Motives* (Berkeley: University of California Press, 1969), Part 1.

16. Gilmore, *Modern Newspaper Editing*, p. 226: "Human limitations may prevent a paper's being really accurate and truly objective, but readers know whether the editors try to be fair. They treat everybody alike."

17. "Our reporters do not cover stories from their point of view. They are present-

ing them from *nobody's* point of view." Richard S. Salant, president of CBS News, in *TV Guide*, quoted in the front of Edward Jay Epstein, *News From Nowhere: Television and the News* (New York: Random House, 1973), italics in original.

18. Ibid., pp. 14–16.

19. Gaye Tuchman, *Making News: A Study of the Construction of Reality* (New York: Free Press, 1978); Mark Fishman, *Manufacturing the News* (Austin: University of Texas Press, 1980); David L. Altheide, *Creating Reality: How TV News Distorts Events* (Beverly Hills: Sage, 1976). "The news is an account of the event, not something intrinsic in the event itself"—Curtis MacDougall, *Interpretive Reporting*, 5th ed. (New York: Macmillan, 1968), p. 12.

20. More, the mirror metaphor need not be an excuse but can serve as a criterion for critical analysis of mass media. See Doris A. Graber, *Crime News and the Public* (New York: Praeger, 1980), p. 28.

21. Epstein is correct about the ubiquity of the mirror metaphor. Who would have believed that Bob Woodward would call television a mirror? "[TV] is at best a mirror, albeit a large and glorious mirror," from "Mike Wallace: Grand Inquisitor of '60 Minutes,' " *TV Guide*, Nov. 6–12, 1993, p. 16.

22. See Graber, *Crime News and the Public*: "Nonfiction crime news is fiction, to a certain degree. It does not depict crime in the United States as it really is. The pictures in the minds of media audiences are, in many significant respects, even more remote from reality than the media images. The public lives in a world of unreality when it comes to criminals, victims, and the criminal justice system" (p. vii). See also Inez Dussuyer, *Crime News: A Study of 40 Ontario Newspapers* (Toronto: University of Toronto Centre of Criminology, 1979), pp. 13–15.

23. Anthony Lewis, *Gideon's Trumpet* (New York: Random House, 1964).

24. Bob Woodward and Scott Armstrong, *The Brethren: Inside the Supreme Court* (New York: Simon and Schuster, 1979).

25. Kurt Luedtke, *Absence of Malice*, Columbia Pictures, 1981. When reporter Megan Carter (Sally Field) is asked whether a statement is true, she responds, "No, but it's accurate." In context, I take her to observe that it is sufficient for journalists to get what sources said verbatim. Whether that statement is true is another matter.

26. Lawrence C. Soley, *The News Shapers: The Sources Who Explain the News* (New York: Praeger, 1992), pp. 15–27. Indeed, routine use of biased sources unbalances coverage and transforms journalism into propaganda. Martin A. Lee and Norman Solomon analyze specific abuses of "source-ery" in *Unreliable Sources: A Guide to Detecting Bias in the News Media* (Secaucus, NJ: Lyle Stuart, 1990), ch. 2. On the central role of "the usual sources" in modern U. S. politics, see Robert Parry, *Fooling America: How Washington Insiders Twist the Truth and Manufacture the Conventional Wisdom* (New York: William Morrow, 1992).

27. Soley, *The News Shapers*; Eric Alterman, *Sound and Fury: The Washington Punditocracy and the Collapse of American Politics* (New York: HarperCollins, 1992).

28. Lee and Solomon, *Unreliable Sources*, ch. 2; Parry, *Fooling America*.

29. David S. Broder, *Behind the Front Page: A Candid Look at How the News Is Made* (New York: Simon and Schuster, 1987), p. 18.

30. Fishman, *Manufacturing the News*, p. 27: " . . . the beat system of news cover-

age is so widespread among established newspapers that *not* using beats is a distinctive feature of being an experimental, alternative, or underground newspaper" (italics in original).

31. Kathleen Hall Jamieson and Karlyn Kohrs Campbell, *The Interplay of Influence: Mass Media and Their Publics in News, Advertising, Politics,* 2d ed. (Belmont, CA: Wadsworth, 1988), pp. 31–32:

> News organizations struggle to impose order in the midst of chaos. Reporters often have little or no idea when or where the news will break: when or where a crime will be committed, a riot will break out, one country will attack another. Thus, reporters are assigned to beats so they can monitor the goings-on in places where newsworthy events often occur—the police station, city hall, the State Department, the House of Representatives, the Supreme Court.

32. See Fishman, *Manufacturing the News*, pp. 33–53 and, more generally, chs. 2–5.

33. Ibid.; Leon V. Sigal, *Reporters and Officials: The Organization and Politics of Newsmaking* (Lexington, MA: Heath, 1973); Tuchman, *Making News.*

34. W. Lance Bennett, *News—The Politics of Illusion,* 2d ed. (New York: Longman, 1988), pp. 21–67. There are, of course, many other ways to conceive of biases in the media. Refer to Stephen Chibnall, *Law-and-Order News: An Analysis of Crime Reporting in the British Press* (London: Tavistock, 1977), p. 23, where the list of news values includes immediacy, dramatization, personalization, simplification, titillation, conventionalism, "structured access" (that is, those with greater status, expertise, and wealth are more likely to be in or on the news than those with less), and novelty. See also Richard Davis, *Decisions and Images: The Supreme Court and the Press* (Englewood Cliffs, NJ: Prentice-Hall, 1993), p. 22: "The preponderant professional criterion is newsworthiness. . . . These values include event-orientation, conflict, drama, timeliness, proximity, and unusualness."

35. Chibnall, *Law-and-Order News*, pp. 23–25. Chibnall notes on pp. 24–25: "The event-orientation of news is reinforced by an emphasis on the dramatic. News is commercial knowledge designed in a situation of competition with profit in mind. Its purveyors are concerned with grabbing the attention of prospective audiences by making an 'impact.' This stress on impact contributes towards the predisposition to communicate concrete happenings and to neglect underlying patterns of motivation and belief."

36. Ibid, p. xi: "The reason . . . why deviant behaviour occupies so much media space is not because it is intrinsically interesting, but because it is intrinsically instructive. It serves to reinforce the world-taken-for-granted by restating social rules and warning subjects that violators will not be tolerated. In this way, the wayward are cautioned and the righteous are comforted." Chibnall quoted from S. Box, *Deviance, Reality, and Society,* (New York: Holt, Rinehart and Winston, 1971), p. 40.

37. Bennett, *News*, p. 52.

38. Chibnall, *Law-and-Order News*, p. 33.

39. Ibid., p. 35.

40. Ibid.

41. See Doug Underwood, *When MBAs Rule The Newsroom: How the Marketers and Managers Are Reshaping Today's Media* (New York: Columbia University Press, 1993); James D. Squires, *Read All About It! The Corporate Takeover of America's Newspapers* (New York: Random House/Times Books, 1993); and Ben H. Bagdikian, *The Media Monopoly*, 4th ed. (Boston: Beacon Press, 1992).

42. Solomon and Lee, *Unreliable Sources.*

43. Or, as George Orwell put it about an earlier, somewhat different power:

> One of the most extraordinary things about England is that there is almost no official censorship, and yet nothing that is actually offensive to the governing class gets into print, at least in any place where large numbers of people are likely to read it. If it is "not done" to mention something or other, it just doesn't get mentioned. The position is summed up in the lines by (I think) Hilaire Belloc:
>
> You cannot hope to bribe or twist
> Thank God! the English journalist:
> But seeing what the man will do
> Unbribed, there is no reason to.
>
> No bribes, no threats, no penalties — just a nod and a wink and the thing is done.

In Sonia Orwell and Ian Angus, eds., *The Collected Essays, Journalism, and Letters of George Orwell*, Vol. 3, *As I Please* (London: Secker and Warburg, 1968), p. 180.

44. David Morgan notes, for example, that many legislators and public servants in New York state decried "the preference of publishers and station managers for heavy reliance on national and international news that comes in over the wire services and is, thus, already paid for. Since most of their remaining news space is given over to dense local cover, journalists assert, it is little wonder that State political news receives coverage that is episodic and, above all, marked by a tendentious, pervasive *local* perspective" (*The Capitol Press Corps*, p. xii).

45. See Phyllis Kaniss, *Making Local News* (Chicago: University of Chicago Press, 1991), ch. 2.

46. Robert M. Entman, *Democracy Without Citizens: Media and the Decay of American Politics* (New York: Oxford University Press, 1989), p. 17.

47. To read why and how Democrats and liberals control mass media, see Edith Efron, *The News Twisters* (New York: Manor Books, 1971), and Robert S. Lichter, Stanley Rothman, and Linda S. Lichter, *The Media Elite* (Bethesda, MD: Adler and Adler, 1986). That Republicans and conservatives control mass media, see Lee and Solomon, *Unreliable Sources,* and Edward S. Herman and Noam Chomsky, *Manufacturing Consent: The Political Economy of the Mass Media* (New York: Pantheon Books, 1988). That the major bias is mainstream is the contention of John Corry, *TV News and the Dominant Culture* (Washington, DC: Media Institute, 1986).

48. Even if some substantial, "net" bias(es) were demonstrated, Professor Entman has argued that partisan and ideological tendencies would matter less than content and commercial biases. "News slant" is inevitable due to journalists'

choices, but most "slant" is a consequence of journalistic norms, not individuals' biases. Content and commercial biases count for far more than the personal beliefs of reporters because the norms of modern journalism make it easier for astute insiders to predict news angles and content. "Objectivity" and other canons facilitate the manipulation of news slant. In other words, "source-ery" by itself is a far more substantial influence than ideological bias. See Entman, *Democracy Without Citizens*, pp. 36–38.

49. Jerome O'Callaghan and James O. Dukes, "Media Coverage of the Supreme Court's Caseload," *Journalism Quarterly* 69 (Spring 1992): 195–203.

50. To understand more generally how less useful news crowds more useful news out of the mass media, see James Fallows, *Breaking the News: How the Media Undermine American Democracy* (New York: Pantheon Books, 1996).

51. Oliver Wendell Holmes, Jr., *Northern Securities Company v. United States* 193 U. S. 197, at 400 (1904): "Great cases like hard cases make bad law."

52. Davis, *Decisions and Images*.

53. Cover, *Justice Accused*.

54. And, of course, the more that one moves away from the Inside-Out Perspective on Media Mission the more that this mystification hypothesis becomes a corollary of my Outside-In Perspective.

55. Justice Antonin Scalia, Francis Boyer Lecture, December 6, 1989, as quoted in Elliot E. Slotnick, "Media Coverage of Supreme Court Decision Making: Problems and Prospects," *Judicature* 75 (Oct.–Nov. 1991):130.

CHAPTER 2

The Supreme Court of the United States: Very Public But Very Private

1. Linda Greenhouse, "Press Coverage," *The Oxford Companion to the Supreme Court of the United States*, Kermit L. Hall, Jr., ed. (New York: Oxford University Press, 1992), pp. 666–67.

2. Richard Davis, *Decisions and Images: The Supreme Court and the Press* (Englewood Cliffs, NJ: Prentice-Hall, 1994).

3. Anthony Lewis, "Problems of a Washington Correspondent," *Connecticut Bar Journal* 33 (1959):365.

4. Lewis wrote *Gideon's Trumpet* (New York: Vintage, 1964), which detailed how the justices abandoned precedent to force states to provide attorneys for non-capital defendants too poor to afford representation. Lewis, then on the Supreme Court beat for the *New York Times*, thus reported judicial politicking and judicious imagery that belied his claim that the justices are indifferent to public relations. So did his colleague, James E. Clayton, who wrote about the Court for the *Washington Post* and who published his own book on the Court the same year: *The Making of Justice: The Supreme Court in Action* (New York: Dutton, 1964). Clayton deftly explores the public and private imagery of the Warren Court on pages 36–37, for example.

5. Chester A. Newland, "Press Coverage of the United States Supreme Court," *Western Political Quarterly* 17 (1964):15–36.

6. Fred Graham, *Happy Talk: Confessions of a TV Newsman* (New York: Norton, 1990), pp. 119–20.

7. Davis, *Decisions and Images*, p. 131.

8. For expanded treatment of this point, refer to Richard Davis's *Decisions and Images*, passim.

9. Richard Davis, "Lifting the Shroud: News Media Portrayal of the U. S. Supreme Court," *Communication and Law* 9 (Oct. 1987):52.

10. Doug Underwood, *When MBAs Rule the Newsroom: How the Marketers and Managers Are Reshaping Today's Media* (New York: Columbia University Press, 1993); James D. Squires, *Read All About It! The Corporate Takeover of America's Newspapers* (New York: Random House, 1993).

11. For further insights about the economics of covering the Court, refer to Elliot Slotnick, "Media Coverage of Supreme Court Decision Making: Problems and Prospects," *Judicature* 75 (Oct.–Nov. 1991):138.

12. David L. Altheide and Robert P. Snow, *Media Logic* (Beverly Hills, CA: Sage, 1979).

13. James E. Clayton, "Interpreting the Court," *Columbia Journalism Review* 7 (Summer 1968):49.

14. M. L. Stein, "Scalia discusses the press," *Editor & Publisher* 123 (Sept. 8, 1990):16.

15. Ibid.

16. For three examples of angle biases' distortions, see Wallace Carroll, "Essence, Not Angle," *Columbia Journalism Review* 4 (Summer 1965):5–6.

17. Davis, *Decisions and Images*, p. 22.

18. Tim O'Brien, "Best Kept Secrets of the Judiciary," *Judicature* 73 (April–May 1990):341–42.

19. Bennett used the term *fragmented* to describe news that I call *morselized*.

20. Lyle Denniston, *The Reporter and the Law: Techniques of Covering the Courts* (New York: Hastings House, 1980), p.14.

21. "Each Court decision, regardless of how important it may be in its own right, is only a part of a chain of decisions that began years ago and will end God knows when. A story that fails to make this clear often shortchanges the reader" (James E. Clayton, "Interpreting the Court," p. 49). See also Everette Dennis, "Another Look at Press Coverage of the Supreme Court," *Villanova Law Review* 20 (March 1975):772; and John P. MacKenzie, "The Warren Court and the Press," *Michigan Law Review* 67 (1968):304.

22. David L. Paletz and Robert M. Entman, *Media Power Politics* (New York: Free Press, 1981), p. 104.

23. David L. Grey, *The Supreme Court and the News Media* (Evanston, IL: Northwestern University Press, 1968), p. 78.

24. Carroll, "Essence, Not Angle," pp. 5–6.

25. David Shaw, *Press Watch: A Provocative Look at How Newspapers Report the News* (New York: Macmillan, 1984), p. 116. See also Davis, *Decisions and Images*, p. 73.

26. Davis, "Lifting the Shroud," p. 48.

27. Tim O'Brien of ABC News is an example. Slotnick, "Media Coverage of Supreme Court Decision Making," p. 136.

28. Stephanie Greco Larson, "How the *New York Times* Covered the Discrimination Cases," *Journalism Quarterly* 62 (1985):894–96.

29. Lionel S. Sobel, "News Coverage of the Supreme Court," *American Bar Association Journal* 56 (June 1970):547–50.

30. Davis, "Lifting the Shroud," p. 45.

31. For figures on docketing decisions and other actions at the High Court, see Stephen L. Wasby, *The Supreme Court in the Federal Judicial System* 4th ed. (Chicago: Nelson-Hall, 1993), chs. 6–7.

32. See, for example, David Ericson, "Newspaper Coverage of the Supreme Court: A Case Study," *Journalism Quarterly* 54 (1977):605–7, and Davis, "Lifting the Shroud," p. 44.

33. Davis, "Lifting the Shroud," p. 43. Davis here reiterates a most common theme in the literature. See Grey, *The Supreme Court and the News Media*, pp. 49–50; Gilbert Cranberg, "What Did the Supreme Court Say?" *Saturday Review*, (April 8, 1967), p. 92; and Carroll, "Essence, Not Angle," p. 5.

34. Stephanie Greco Larson and Bryan Tramont, "The Supreme Court and Television: Predicting Case Coverage," paper presented at the Midwest Political Science Association meeting, Chicago, 1993.

35. Cranberg, "What Did the Supreme Court Say?" p. 91.

36. *ABC Evening News,* June 29, 1995. I added ellipsis to eliminate a transitional clause.

37. Denniston, *The Reporter and the Law*, p. 51.

38. Richard Davis, *Decisions and Images*, p. 21; Ericson, "Newspaper Coverage of the Supreme Court: A Case Study," p. 607; and MacKenzie, "The Warren Court and the Press," p. 303.

39. Grey, *The Supreme Court and the News Media*, p. 2.

40. Carroll, "Essence, Not Angle," p. 6.

41. See Newland, "Press Coverage of the United States Supreme Court," p. 31, on hazards of wire service reporting in early 1960s.

42. Slotnick, "Media Coverage of Supreme Court Decision Making," p. 133.

43. Dennis, "Another Look at Press Coverage of the Supreme Court," p. 784.

44. Ericson, "Newspaper Coverage of the Supreme Court: A Case Study," pp. 605–7.

45. MacKenzie, "The Warren Court and the Press," p. 306.

46. O'Brien, "Best Kept Secrets of the Judiciary," p. 342; Tim O'Brien, "Yes, But . . . ," *Judicature* 67 (June–July):14. On the other hand, O'Brien informed Elliot Slotnick that the problems were not incapacitating under most conditions. Slotnick, "Media Coverage of Supreme Court Decision Making," p. 133.

47. For example, see Grey, *The Supreme Court and the News Media*, p. 72.

48. Davis, *Decisions and Images*, p. 67.

49. Tony Mauro, "Debate Widens Over Religion in Public Life," *USA Today* (June 30, 1995), p. 8A.

50. Linda Greenhouse, "The Supreme Court: Church-State Relations—Ruling on Religion," *New York Times,* June 30, 1995, Section A, p. 1.

51. Davis, "Lifting the Shroud," p. 48.

52. Ibid., p.49.

53. Ibid., pp. 50–51.

54. Grey, *The Supreme Court and the News Media,* p. 66.

55. Davis, "Lifting the Shroud," p. 48.

56. Ibid.

57. Slotnick, "Media Coverage of Supreme Court Decision Making," p. 137.

58. For a contention slightly to the contrary of my supposition, see Slotnick, "Media

Coverage of Supreme Court Decision-Making," p. 138. Slotnick contends that newspapers may increase sales by adding references of interest to groups of readers. I concede that newspapers may do so but suspect that the economics of the business will seldom incline them to do so.

59. David M. O'Brien, *Storm Center: The Supreme Court in American Politics,* 3d ed. (New York: Norton, 1993), p. 353.

60. Dennis, "Another Look at Press Coverage of the Supreme Court," p. 790.

61. Ibid., p. 798.

62. Davis, *Decisions and Images,* passim.

63. 448 U. S. 297 (1980).

64. 432 U.S. 464.

65. Syllabus for *Harris v. McRae,* 448 U. S. 297 (1980) at 298. Emphasis added.

66. Most editorialists cannot afford to read the Court's opinions. Cranberg, "What Did the Supreme Court Say?" p. 90.

67. Warren G. Bovée, "Court Comment," *The Masthead,* Spring 1981, p. 28.

68. Norman Provizer, "A Case Study," *The Masthead,* Spring 1981, p. 26.

69. Ibid.

70. Ibid.

71. MacKenzie, "The Warren Court and the Press," pp. 304–5, n.21.

72. Ibid., p. 305.

73. Michael Solimine, "Newsmagazine Coverage of the Supreme Court," *Journalism Quarterly* 57 (Winter 1980):661–63; Davis, *Decisions and Images,* p. 114.

74. Eldon Knoche, "A Reporter's View of Relations with Judges," *Judicature* 70 (1987):268.

75. Davis, "Lifting the Shroud," p. 53.

76. Ibid., pp. 53–54.

77. Ibid., p. 54.

78. Ibid., p. 54.

79. For example, see Newland, "Press Coverage of the United States Supreme Court," pp. 23–31.

80. Davis, "Lifting the Shroud," 54–55.

81. MacKenzie, "The Warren Court and the Press," p. 309.

82. Stein, "Scalia Discusses the Press," p. 16.

83. Davis, "Lifting the Shroud," 50-51

84. Grey, *The Supreme Court and the News Media,* p. 67.

85. Clayton, *The Making of Justice,* pp. 17–22.

86. MacKenzie, "The Warren Court and the Press," pp. 310–13; and William A. Hachten, "Journalism and the Prayer Decision," *Columbia Journalism Review* 1 (Fall 1962):4–5.

87. Hachten, "Journalism and the Prayer Decision," p. 5.

88. Newland, "Press Coverage of the United States Supreme Court," pp. 15, 23–31.

89. Clayton, "Interpreting the Court," p. 49.

90. Dennis, "Another Look at Press Coverage of the Supreme Court," p. 780.

91. Sobel, "News Coverage of the Supreme Court," p. 548.

92. Edward J. Cleary, *Beyond the Burning Cross: The First Amendment and the Landmark R.A.V. Case* (New York: Random House, 1994), p. 191.

93. Grey, *The Supreme Court and the News Media,* p. 48.

94. Jerome O'Callaghan and James O. Dukes, "Media Coverage of the Supreme Court's Caseload," *Journalism Quarterly,* 69 (Spring 1992):195–203.

95. F. Dennis Hale, "A Comparison of Coverage of Speech and Press Verdicts of Supreme Court," *Journalism Quarterly,* 56 (1979):43–47.

96. Slotnick, "Media Coverage of Supreme Court Decision-Making," p. 136.

97. Mary Ann Glendon, *Rights Talk: The Impoverishment of Political Discourse* (New York: Free Press, 1991).

98. Davis, *Decisions and Images*, pp. 22–23.

99. O'Brien, "Yes, But . . . ," p. 14.

100. Davis, *Decisions and Images*, pp. 22–23; Davis, "Lifting the Shroud," p. 52.

101. "The Greenhouse Effect," *Wall Street Journal* (March 8, 1994), p. A10.

102. Davis, *Decisions and Images,* pp. 16-20.

103. MacKenzie, "The Warren Court and the Press," p. 304.

104. Richard Davis, "Lifting the Shroud," p. 43.

105. Stein, "Scalia Discusses the Press," p. 16.

106. A writ of *certiorari* orders the entire record of a case to be sent from a court that has already decided on the case to a higher court to which that decision has been appealed. In theory, the Supreme Court *must* hear *appeals* but may reject petitions for a writ of *certiorari* at its whim. In practice, the justices are quite adept at avoiding any cases that six or more of them want *not* to hear.

107. Davis, "Lifting the Shroud," p. 44.

108. *The Washington Reporters* (Washington, DC: The Brookings Institution, 1981) p. 110, n. 38.

109. Grey, *The Supreme Court and the News Media*, p. 67.

110. For trends in reports on the Supreme Court, see Charles H. Franklin and Liane Kosaki, "Media, Knowledge, and Public Evaluations of the Supreme Court," in Lee Epstein, ed., *Contemplating Courts* (Washington, DC: CQ Press, 1995), pp. 356–357.

111. Dennis, "Another Look at Press Coverage of the Supreme Court," p. 784.

112. Ibid., pp. 790–94.

113. Paletz and Entman, *Media Power Politics,* pp. 104–5.

114. Ibid., p. 105.

115. Dennis, "Another Look at Press Coverage of the Supreme Court," pp. 777–78

116. Stephen L. Wasby, *The Impact of the United States Supreme Court* (Homewood, IL: Dorsey Press, 1970), ch. 2.

117. MacKenzie, "The Warren Court and the Press," p. 305.

118. Slotnick, "Media Coverage of Supreme Court Decision-Making" p. 136.

119. Ibid.

120. See Saul Brenner and John F. Krol, "Strategies in Certiorari Voting on the United States Supreme Court," *Journal of Politics,* 51 (Nov. 1989):828–40; Gregory A. Caldeira and John R. Wright, "Organized Interests and Agenda-Setting in the U. S. Supreme Court," *American Political Science Review,* 82 (Dec. 1988): 1109–1128; and H. W. Perry, Jr., *Deciding to Decide: Agenda-Setting in the U. S. Supreme Court* (Cambridge, MA: Harvard University Press, 1992).

121. Dennis, "Another Look at Press Coverage of the Supreme Court," pp. 790–94.

122. Ibid., p. 775, n. 48.

123. Ibid., p. 766.

124. MacKenzie, "The Warren Court and the Press," p. 304.

125. Davis, Decisions and Images, pp. 6–8; Davis, "Lifting the Shroud," p. 45.

126. Paul Duke, "The U. S. Supreme Court: A Journalist's View," *Washburn Law Journal*, 28 (Spring 1989):343.

127. Graham, *Happy Talk*, pp. 119–20.

128. Davis, "Lifting the Shroud," p. 45.

129. Graham, *Happy Talk*, p. 119.

130. Davis, *Decisions and Images*, pp. 119–20; Grey, *The Supreme Court and the News Media*, pp. 50–51.

131. Davis, "Lifting the Shroud," p. 46.

132. Dennis, "Another Look at Press Coverage of the Supreme Court," p. 777.

133. Davis, *Decisions and Images,* p. 23.

134. Ibid., pp. 46, 48.

135. Davis, "Lifting the Shroud," p. 45.

136. Grey, *The Supreme Court and the News Media*, p. 55.

137. Ibid., pp. 48–56.

138. Dennis, "Another Look at Press Coverage of the Supreme Court," p. 777; Slotnick, "Media Coverage of Supreme Court Decision-Making," p. 134. On the habits of nonjudicial actors in mass mediated democracy, see Michael Schudson, *The Power of News* (Cambridge, MA: Harvard University Press, 1995), ch. 3.

139. Davis, "Lifting the Shroud," p. 47.

140. Dennis, "Another Look at Press Coverage of the Supreme Court," p. 773.

141. For examples of justices getting "burned," refer to Clayton, *The Making of Justice*, pp. 21–22; Hachten, "Journalism and the Prayer Decision"; Alpheus T. Mason, *Harlan Fiske Stone, Pillar of the Law* (New York: Viking Press, 1956), pp. 626, 699–700; and Alpheus T. Mason, *William Howard Taft: Chief Justice* (New York: Simon and Schuster, 1965), pp. 278–79.

142. Dennis, "Another Look at Press Coverage of the Supreme Court," p. 772.

143. Davis, *Decisions and Images*, pp. 8-10.

144. See Grey, *The Supreme Court and the News Media*, p. 4.

145. Paletz and Entman, *Media Power Politics*, p. 104

146. O'Brien, "Best Kept Secrets of the Judiciary," p. 343.

147. Davis, *Decisions and Images*, p. 136; Slotnick, "Media Coverage of Supreme Court Decision-Making," p. 132; Shaw, *Press Watch*, p. 120.

148. Davis, *Decisions and Images*, p. 138.

149. Ibid., pp. 136–38.

150. Ibid., p. 70.

151. Ibid., p. 129.

152. Shaw, *Press Watch*, p. 116.

153. Ibid., pp. 42–43.

154. Ibid., pp. 102–10.

155. Grey, *The Supreme Court and the News Media*, p. 22 (italics in original).

156. Solimine, "Newsmagazine Coverage of the Supreme Court," pp. 661–63; J. Douglas Tarpley, "American Newsmagazine Coverage of the Supreme Court, 1978-1981," *Journalism Quarterly,* 61 (Winter 1984):801–4.

157. Dorothy A. Bowles and Rebekah V. Bromley, "Newsmagazine Coverage of the Supreme Court During the Reagan Administration," *Journalism Quarterly*, 69 (Winter 1992):948–59.

158. Ericson, "Newspaper Coverage of the Supreme Court: A Case Study," pp. 605–7.

159. Slotnick, "Media Coverage of Supreme Court Decision-Making," p. 138.

160. O'Brien, "Best Kept Secrets of the Judiciary," pp. 341–42.

161. Slotnick, "Media Coverage of Supreme Court Decision-Making," p. 138.

162. Ibid., pp. 138–39.

163. Ibid., p. 139.

164. O'Brien, "Best Kept Secrets of the Judiciary," p. 341.

165. Slotnick, "Media Coverage of Supreme Court Decision-Making," p. 133.

166. Paletz and Entman, *Media Power Politics*, p. 104.

167. Contrast Dennis, "Another Look at Press Coverage of the Supreme Court," p. 775, note 49 with Ethan Katsh, "The Supreme Court Beat: How Television Covers the U. S. Supreme Court," *Judicature*, 67 (1983):8.

168. Franklin and Kosaki, "Media, Knowledge, and Public Evaluations of the Supreme Court," p. 369.

169. Slotnick, "Media Coverage of Supreme Court Decision-Making," pp. 129–30.

170. W. Russell Neuman, Marion R. Just, and Ann N. Crigler, *Common Knowledge: News and the Construction of Meaning* (Chicago: University of Chicago Press, 1992).

171. Slotnick, "Media Coverage of Supreme Court Decision-Making," p. 130.

172. The work of Bernard Schwartz is a happy exception. See *Behind Bakke: Affirmative Action and the Supreme Court* (New York: New York University Press, 1988), for example.

173. Clayton, "Interpreting the Court," p. 48.

174. Paletz and Entman, *Media Power Politics*, pp. 100–4.

175. Graham, *Happy Talk*, pp. 100–102.

CHAPTER 3

Modest Coverage of Appellate Courts

1. Max Freedman, "Worst Reported Institution," *Nieman Reports*, 10 (April 1956):2.

2. See Frank X. Gordon, "The Judicial Image: Is a Facelift Necessary?" *Justice System Journal*, 10 (March 1985):315; Hearst Corporation, *The American Public, the Media, and the Judicial System: A National Survey on Public Awareness and Personal Experience* (New York: Hearst Corp., 1983).

3. On this "watchdog" role, see F. Dennis Hale, "The Press and a State Appellate Court: News Coverage by Six Dailies of Forty Decisions by the Washington State Supreme Court," master's thesis, University of Oregon, 1973, pp. 2–3 and Timothy W. Gleason, *The Watchdog Concept* (Ames: Iowa State University Press, 1990).

4. See Franklin Dennis Hale, "Variables Associated with Newspaper Coverage of California Supreme Court Decisions: A Multivariate Analysis," Ph. D. dissertation, Southern Illinois University, 1977, pp. 3–4.

5. Ibid., p. 26, and F. Dennis Hale, "The Court's Perception of the Press," *Judica-*

ture, 57 (Dec. 1973):183.

6. G. Alan Tarr and Mary Cornelia Aldis Porter, *State Supreme Courts in State and Nation* (New Haven, CT: Yale University Press, 1998), p.150, emphasis added.

7. Hale, "Variables," pp. 10–11.

8. F. Dennis Hale, "How Reporters and Justices View Coverage of a State Appellate Court," *Journalism Quarterly,* 52 (1975):106–10.

9. Jack C. Doppelt, "Strained Relations: How Judges and Lawyers Perceive the Coverage of Legal Affairs," *Justice System Journal,* 14 (March 1991):424.

10. Tarr and Porter, *State Supreme Courts in State and Nation,* p. 180.

11. Hale, "Variables," p. 85.

12. Ibid., pp. 86–88.

13. Hale, "The Press," p. 76.

14. Robert E. Drechsel, *News Making in the Trial Courts* (New York: Longman, 1983), p. 79.

15. M. Marvin Berger, "Do the Courts Communicate?" *Judicature,* 57 (April 1972):318–23.

16. Hale, "Variables," p. 10.

17. Ibid., p. 11.

18. David L. Grey, "Covering the Courts," *Nieman Reports,* 26 (March 1972):18, cited in Hale, "Variables," p. 29.

19. Hale, "How Reporters and Justices View Coverage of a State Appellate Court," p. 108.

20. Ibid.

21. Ibid., p. 109.

22. Hale, "The Press," p. 80.

23. Hale, "Variables," pp. 86–87.

24. Hale, "How Reporters and Justices View Coverage of a State Appellate Court," pp. 108–10.

25. Cynthia Gorney, "Guam Antiabortion Law Contested in U.S. Court," *Washington Post* (Nov. 5, 1991), p. A4.

26. Hale, "How Reporters and Justices View Coverage of a State Appellate Court," p. 109.

27. Tarr and Porter, *State Supreme Courts in State and Nation.*

28. Hale, ""How Reporters and Justices View Coverage of a State Appellate Court," p. 108.

29. Reported in "Demystifying the Judicial Process: How Can Judges and Journalists Really Help?" *Judicature,* 67 (April 1984):450.

30. Hale, "How Reporters and Justices View Coverage of a State Appellate Court," p. 108.

31. "Often the critics are more interested in dissenting opinions where the logic is clearer because there were no compromises" (Shirley S. Abrahamson, Justice of Wisconsin Supreme Court, in "Demystifying the Judicial Process," p. 450).

32. Hale, "The Court's Perception of the Press," p. 188.

33. W. Russell Neuman, Marion R. Just, and Ann N. Crigler, *Common Knowledge: News and the Construction of Personal Meaning* (Chicago: University of Chicago Press, 1992).

34. M. L. Stein, "Scalia Discusses the Press," *Editor & Publisher,* 123, (Sept. 8, 1990):16.

35. On symbiosis, see W. Lance Bennett, Lynne A. Gressett, and William Haltom, "Repairing the News: A Case Study of the News Paradigm," *Journal of Communication,* 35 (Spring 1985):50–68; Susan Heilmann Miller, "Reporters and Congressmen: Living in Symbiosis," *Journalism Monographs,* 53 (1978), pp. 1–25.

36. F. Dennis Hale, "Press Releases vs. Newspaper Coverage of California Supreme Court Decisions," *Journalism Quarterly,* 55 (Winter 1978), pp. 696–702, 710.

37. *Textile Mills Securities Corporation v. Commissioner* 314 U.S. 326 (1941). Cf. Public Law Number 88–176, 77 Stat. 331, 28 U.S.C. 46(c) (1982).

38. *Mary Bartlett, o/b/o Josephine Neuman v. Otis R. Bowen, Secretary, Health and Human Services* 824 F.2d 1240.

39. Ibid., at 1243.

40. Ibid.

41. Ibid., pp. 1243–44.

42. Ibid., at 1253.

43. I searched indices for major newspapers, *Newspaper Abstracts,* and NEXIS, an electronic, full-text data base of newspapers and even transcripts of ABC News.

44. Nancy Lewis, "Factions' Squabbling Rocks U.S. Court of Appeals Here," *Washington Post* (Aug. 1, 1987), p. A1.

45. Stephen Wermiel, "Appeals Court Reverses Itself in 3 Cases, Spotlighting Partisan Splits Nationwide," *Wall Street Journal,* (Aug. 3, 1987), p. 7. See also Wermiel, "Full-Court Review of Panel Rulings Becomes Tool Often Used by Reagan Judges Aiming to Mold Law," *Wall Street Journal,* (Mar. 22, 1988), p. 70.

46. See "NOTE: The Politics of En Banc Review," *Harvard Law Review,* 102 (Feb. 1989) pp. 864–84; Michael Solimine, "Ideology and En Banc Review," *North Carolina Law Review,* 67 (Nov. 1988), pp. 29–71; Wermiel, "Full-Court Review," p. 70; and Herman Schwartz, *Packing the Courts: The Conservative Campaign to Rewrite the Constitution* (New York: Simon and Schuster, 1988), p. 155.

47. Stuart Taylor, Jr., "Ideological Feud Erupts in a Key Appeals Court," *New York Times,* (Aug. 15, 1987) p. 7.

48. See n. 46 for sources.

49. Michael Hedges, "A Long-Shot Liberal Sweep: 3 Key Cases, Same 3 Judges," *Washington Times* (Dec. 3, 1993), p. A1.

50. Ibid.

CHAPTER 4

Covering Criminal Justice

1. On reciprocation between sources who define events and news media, see Stuart Hall, Chas Critcher, Tony Jefferson, John Clarke, and Brian Roberts, *Policing the Crisis: Mugging, the State, and Law and Order* (London: Macmillan Education, 1978), pp. 74–77. For the view of the reciprocation from news sources, see Philip Schlesinger and Howard Tumber, *Reporting Crime: The Media Politics of Criminal Justice* (Oxford: Clarendon Press, 1994), pp. 6–34.

2.   Garth Crandon, *The Police and the Media: Information Management and the Construction of Crime News* (Bradford, West Yorkshire: Horton Publishing Ltd., 1992), p. 4.

3.   Robert Drechsel, *News Making in the Trial Courts* (New York: Longman, 1983) p. 80; Larry Berkson and Steven Hays, "The Forgotten Politicians: Court Clerks," *University of Miami Law Review*, 30 (Spring 1976):499–516.

4.   Donald R. Fretz, *Courts and the Community* (Reno, NV: National College of the State Judiciary, 1973), p. 9.

5.   Lyle Denniston, *The Reporter and the Law: Techniques of Covering the Courts* (New York: Hastings House, 1980), pp. 60–65.

6.   Ibid., p. 9.

7.   Nancy Boles and Katherine Heaviside, "When a Reporter Calls," *American Bar Association Journal*, 73 (June 1, 1987):90–92.

8.   Mark Fishman, *Manufacturing the News* (Austin: University of Texas Press, 1980), pp. 44–45.

9.   Ibid., pp. 46–74; Drechsel, *News Making in the Trial Courts*, pp. 78–79.

10.   Charles Sevilla, *Wilkes: His Life and Crimes* (New York: Ballantine, 1991), p. 117.

11.   For a fuller discussion, see Martin A. Lee and Norman Solomon, *Unreliable Sources: A Guide to Detecting Bias in News Media* (New York: Lyle Stuart, 1990), ch. 2, and Robert Parry, *Fooling America: How Washington Insiders Twist the Truth and Manufacture the Conventional Wisdom* (New York: William Morrow, 1992).

12.   Drechsel, *News Making in the Trial Courts*, p. 81.

13.   Denniston, *The Reporter and the Law*, p. 53.

14.   Ibid., pp. 56, 59.

15.   Fishman, *Manufacturing the News*, ch. 3, esp. pp. 54–71.

16.   Fishman calls these interpretations *phase-structures*, a better term than *phases* if readers are well acquainted with the concept of structure in sociology and ethnography. Since I do not assume such acquaintance here, I have chosen what I regard as the more accessible if less fecund term.

17.   Ibid., p. 62.

18.   Ibid.

19.   Ibid.

20.   Herbert L. Packer, *The Limits of the Criminal Sanction* (Stanford: Stanford University Press, 1968), pp. 153–73.

21.   Almost all criminal suspects and convicts are male, so I consistently refer to criminal suspects in the masculine.

22.   Packer, *The Limits of the Criminal Sanction*, pp. 153–63.

23.   Susan Janelle Helling, Police and the News Media: An Analysis of Perceived Patterns of Interaction, Master's Thesis, University of Colorado, 1990.

24.   Ibid., pp. 45–69.

25.   Graber, *Crime News and the Public* (New York: Praeger, 1980), p. 28.

26.   Personalization suits stories about both crime control and due process, but not in equal measure. Crime control coverage focuses on sympathetic victims, dastardly perpetrators, heroic cops, and fearless prosecutors and so easily personalizes arrests and trials. On the other hand, due process coverage can personalize the struggle of individuals against police or prosecutorial misconduct and

indifference. *Gideon's Trumpet* by Anthont Lewis (New York: Random House, 1964), for example, attributed an expansion of the right to counsel to a few colorful persons. Lewis's book shows, however, that it is far more manageable to personalize the struggle of the wrongly accused for the due process that will exonerate the accused than it would be to take the part of a guilty party, insisting that the rules be followed even if the guilty go free. Since most due process claimants will in fact be guilty of some serious offense(s), personalized coverage of due process matters will usually lack sympathetic figures aside from crime victims who stir crime control sentiments.

27.   Examples abound. The press overreports black men preying on white women and white perceptions match media more than reality. Please refer to my discussion of dramatized normality later in this chapter. See Daniel Abbott and James Calonico, "Black Man, White Woman—The Maintenance of a Myth: Rape and the Press in New Orleans," *Crime and Delinquency: Dimensions of Deviance*, M. Reidel and T. Thornberry, eds. (New York: Praeger, 1974), pp. 141–53. Stephen Chibnall, *Law and Order News: An Analysis of Crime Reporting in the British Press* (London: Tavistock, 1977), p. xi, quoting S. Box, *Deviance, Reality, and Society* (New York: Holt, Rinehart and Winston, 1971), 1971, p. 40:

> The reason . . . why deviant behaviour occupies so much media space is not because it is intrinsically interesting, but because it is intrinsically instructive. It serves to reinforce the world-taken-for-granted by restating social rules and warning subjects that violators will not be tolerated. In this way, the wayward are cautioned and the righteous are comforted.

See also Margaret T. Gordon and Stephanie Riger, *The Female Fear* (New York: Free Press, 1989) p. 69:

> [A]lthough three rapes are reported to the police for every murder, the papers report only one rape for every eleven murders. Editors have decided that almost every murder is news and most rapes are not. In deciding which rapes are newsworthy, newspapers distort their presentation, avoiding the representative rape in favor of the most lurid, in order to capture their readers' attention.

Gordon and Riger go on (pp. 69–70) to note that there are far more attempts than completed rapes and many attempters get away, but newspapers reported thirteen completed rapes for every one attempt reported, and reports of attempts tend to concern the bizarre. This may lead women to believe that most rapes are completed and women seldom get away.

28.   Graber, *Crime News and the Public*, pp. 39–41; George E. Antunes and Patricia A. Hurley, "The Representation of Criminal Events in Houston's Two Daily Newspapers," *Journalism Quarterly*, 54 (1977):756–757; Inez Dussuyer, *Crime News: A Study of Forty Ontario Newspapers* (Toronto: University of Toronto Centre of Criminology), p. 48; Jason Ditton and James Duffy, "Bias in the Newspaper Reporting of Crime News," *British Journal of Criminology*, 23 (April 1983):162.

29. Dussuyer, *Crime News,* p. 46; Drechsel, *News Making in the Trial Courts,* pp. 135–37; Shanto Iyengar, *Is Anyone Responsible?* (Chicago: University of Chicago, 1991), ch. 4.
30. See, as examples, Graber, *Crime News,* pp. 32–35; Bernard Roshco, *Newsmaking* (Chicago: University of Chicago Press, 1975); Leon V. Sigal, *Reporters and Officials* (Lexington, MA: D. C. Heath, 1973); Fishman, *Manufacturing the News.*
31. Denniston, *The Reporter and the Law,* p. 57. The line is shifting, however. Today, "full-service" lawyering may include considerable attention to public relations. See Robert L. Shapiro, "Secrets of a Celebrity Lawyer: How O.J.'s Chief Strategist Works the Press," *Columbia Journalism Review,* 33 (Sept.-Oct. 1994:25.
    Consider Standard 8-1.1 "Extrajudicial statements by attorneys," of the *ABA Standards for Criminal Justice Fair Trial and Free Press,* 3rd ed., (Washington, DC: American Bar Association, 1992), p. 1.

    > (a) A lawyer should not make or authorize the making of an extrajudicial statement that a reasonable person would expect to be disseminated by means of public communication if the lawyer knows or reasonably should know that it will have a substantial likelihood of prejudicing a criminal proceeding.

32. Drechsel, *News Making in the Trial Courts,* pp. 80–81.
33. Ibid., pp. 87–88.
34. Denniston, *The Reporter and the Law,* p. 59.
35. Drechsel, *News Making in the Trial Courts,* p. 115.
36. Fishman, *Manufacturing the News,* pp. 85–92.
37. Drechsel, *News Making in the Trial Courts,* pp. 118–31.
38. Ibid., p. 80.
39. Denniston, *The Reporter and the Law,* pp. 60–61.
40. Drechsel, *News Making in the Trial Courts,* pp. 88–89.
41. Ibid., pp. 90–95.
42. Fretz, *Courts and the Community,* p. 60: "The foundation for such cooperation must be laid long before the need for it arises. In major metropolitan areas, there may be a frequent need for such help and a tradition and working relationship. . . . The bar association should have a committee with this duty."
43. Ibid.
44. Drechsel, *News Making in the Trial Courts,* p. 88
45. Jack C. Doppelt, "Strained Relations: How Judges and Lawyers Perceive the Coverage of Legal Affairs," *Justice System Journal,* 14 (March 1991):419–44.
46. Drechsel, *News Making in the Trial Courts,* pp. 135–137.
47. Dussuyer, *Crime News,* p. 46.
48. Drechsel, *News Making in the Trial Courts,* p. 115.
49. Denniston, *The Reporter and the Law,* p. 57.
50. Drechsel, *News Making in the Trial Courts,* pp. 78-79, 84; Fretz, *Courts and the Community,* p. 12. Drechsel reports (p. 115) that, in addition to the justice beat, almost all reporters had other responsibilities and spent 75% or more of their time on noncourt duties, such as government reporting and general assignment.

51.   Drechsel, *News Making in the Trial Courts*, pp. 98–99.

52.   Ibid., pp. 88, 114; Boles and Heaviside, "When A Reporter Calls," pp. 90–94.

53.   Edna Buchanan, *The Corpse Had a Familiar Face: Covering Miami, America's Hottest Beat* (New York: Random House, 1987).

54.   "Louisville Crime Court Reports," *Louisville Courier-Journal*, Feb. 6, 1991, Metro Edition, p. 2B. I have altered the names and addresses of defendants.

55.   "Africa: Third Group on Trial in Egyptian Plot Case," *San Francisco Chronicle*, Sept. 13, 1993, Three star edition, p. A14.

56.   J. L. Austen, *How to Do Things with Words* (New York: Oxford University Press, 1962).

57.   "Kerrigan Attacker and Accomplice Sent to Jail," *New York Times*, May 17, 1994, p. B13.

58.   "Two Start Sentences in Kerrigan Case," *St. Petersburg Times*, May 17, 1994, p.2C

59.   For examples, see "Al Unser Sr. Announces He's Retiring as Driver," *San Diego Union Tribune*, May 17, 1994, Editions 8 and 9, p. D2 (76 words); "Two Sentenced in Assault on Kerrigan," *Los Angeles Times*, May 17, 1994, Home Edition, p. 3, col. 4 (124 words); and "Kerrigan attacker, accomplice sentenced to prison," *Dallas Morning News*, May 17, 1994, Home Final Edition, p. 3A (100 words).

60.   Denniston, *The Reporter and the Law*, p. 54.

61.   Milton Heumann, *Plea Bargaining: The Experience of Prosecutors, Judges, and Defense Attorneys* (University of Chicago Press, 1977), pp. 27–33; Peter F. Nardulli, James Eisenstein, and Roy B. Flemming, *The Tenor of Justice: Criminal Courts and the Guilty Plea Process* (Urbana: University of Illinois Press, 1988), pp. 203–4.

62.   Heumann, *Plea Bargaining*, p. 1.

63.   Fishman, *Manufacturing the News*, pp. 70-71.

64.   For example, David Johnston, "Overtures Begun for Plea Bargain on Rostenkowski," *New York Times*, May 19, 1994, p. A1, col. 6.

65.   Fishman, *Manufacturing the News*, p. 65.

66.   Ibid., p. 64.

67.   To create table 4.2, my student, Jeffrey Schaus, coded news stories about courts for four randomly chosen dates in 1993. I had used Mead Data Central's Lexis/Nexis Service to retrieve articles from twenty-eight newspapers. Schaus read the complete text of every article that contained the words *court, courts, trial, trials, lawsuit, lawsuits, jury, juries,* or *jurors*. For each article related to a litigation, Schaus then determined whether the trial was criminal, civil, or appellate and what stage or stages of the trial were covered.

68.   Consider the priority given to dramatization and personalization in Denniston's advice to reporters on the court beat: " . . . it is the daily or periodic task of legal reporting to tell who won or lost. Of course, it is also part of the task to describe how the process went, and—if at all possible—how the ultimate result was reached" (Denniston, *The Reporter and the Law*, p. 51).

69.   In *Manufacturing the News*, Fishman argues (p. 71) that the official bureaucratic disposition of the case dominates coverage, while all other aspects are secondary and less likely to be covered. Official decisions are foreground, ren-

dering all else background. They become features or "soft news" but never "hard news."

70. Drechsel, *News Making in the Trial Courts*, pp. 102–8.

71. Ibid., pp. 118–23.

72. Drechsel, *News Making in the Trial Courts*, p. 102.

73. Ibid., p. 13; Doppelt, "Strained Relations," p. 440.

74. Alan M. Dershowitz, *Reasonable Doubts: The O. J. Simpson Case and the Criminal Justice System* (New York: Simon and Schuster, 1996) pp. 142–44.

75. Donald Black, *The Behavior of Law* (New York: Academic Press, 1976); Donald Black, Sociological Justice (New York: Oxford University Press, 1989).

76. See, for storied examples, E. P. Thompson, *Whigs and Hunters* (London: Allen Lane, 1975) and Douglas Hay, Peter Linebaugh, John G. Rule, E. P. Thompson, and Cal Winslow, *Albion's Fatal Tree: Crime and Society in Eighteenth-Century England* (New York: Pantheon, 1975).

77. "The Practice of Law as a Confidence Game," *Law and Society Review,* 1 (June 1967):15–39.

78. Drechsel, *News Making in the Trial Courts*, pp. 110–11; Jeremy Harris Lipschultz, "A Comparison of Trial Lawyer and News Reporter Attitudes about Courthouse Communication," *Journalism Quarterly,* 68 (Winter 1991):760.

79. Drechsel, *News Making in the Trial Courts*, pp. 111–12; Doppelt, "Strained Relations," pp. 433, 440–41.

80. The data reported in table 4.3 were drawn from the same survey of four days' coverage in twenty-eight newspapers that led to table 4.2.

81. Excellent examples of how dramatization distorts criminal trials festoon *Popular Trials: Rhetoric, Mass Media, and the Law*, edited by Robert Hariman (Tuscaloosa: University of Alabama Press, 1990), and Paul Thaler, *The Watchful Eye: American Justice in the Age of the Televised Trial,* (Westport, CT: Praeger, 1994).

82. My best guess here is informed by David L. Altheide, "TV News and the Social Construction of Justice," in *Justice and the Media*, Ray Surette, ed., (Springfield, IL: Charles C. Thomas, 1984), pp. 292–304.

83. Refer to Thomas J. Harris, *Courtroom's Finest Hour in American Cinema* (Metuchen, NJ: Scarecrow Press, 1987), for more recent examples.

84. (New York: Addison-Wesley, 1996). I am guided in my critique by the persuasive criticisms of Robert P. Mosteller in "Book Review: Popular Justice," *Harvard Law Review* 109 (Dec. 1995): 487–517.

85. Ibid., p. 489.

86. Alan M. Dershowitz, *The Abuse Excuse—And Other Cop-Outs, Sob Stories, and Evasions of Responsibility* (Boston: Little, Brown, 1994).

87. Gerald F. Uelmen, *Lessons from the Trial: The People v. O. J. Simpson* (Kansas City, MO: Andrews and McMeel, 1996), p. 54.

88. Harold J. Rothwax, *Guilty: The Collapse of Criminal Justice* (New York: Random House, 1996).

89. Michael L. Radelet, Hugo Adam Bedau, and Constance E. Putnam, *In Spite of Innocence: The Ordeal of Four Hundred Americans Wrongly Convicted of Crimes Punishable by Death* (Boston: Northeastern University Press, 1992).

90. "Book Review: Defender of the Faith in the Midst of the Simpson Circus," *Southwestern University Law Review* 24 (1995): 1215–16.

91. See Uelmen, *Lessons from the Trial*, pp. 92–101, for telling examples of biases and errors.

92. This is my own observation. See also Lincoln Caplan, "The Failure (and Promise) of Legal Journalism," in Jeffrey Abramson, ed., *Postmortem: The O.J. Simpson Case* (New York: Basic Books, 1996), pp. 199–200.

93. Ibid., p. 200.

94. Ibid., p. 94.

95. Ibid., p. 200.

96. Ibid.

97. Jeffrey Toobin, "Asking for It: O. J. Simpson's New Defense Strategy Is as Audacious as the Last," *New Yorker*, Dec. 9, 1996, pp. 56–60.

98. Jeffery Abramson, "The Pros and Cons of Televising Trials," in Abramson, ed., *Postmortem*, pp. 195–198.

99. Hank M. Goldberg, *The Prosecution Responds: An O. J. Simpson Prosecutor Reveals What Really Happened* (Secaucus, N J: Carol Pub. Group, 1996), p. 360.

100. Betsy Streisand, "And Justice For All?" *U. S. News and World Report*, Oct. 9, 1995, p. 46.

101. Drechsel, *News Making in the Trial Courts*, pp. 102, 113; Doppelt, "Strained Relations," p. 440.

102. Jonathan Rabinovitz, "Gag Order Sought for Lawyers in Long Island Train Shootings," *New York Times*, April 2, 1994, p. 25, cols. 3-6. I have omitted three paragraphs discussing a 1991 U. S. Supreme Court ruling on the matter, both for simplicity and because the original story separated the paragraphs on the Supreme Court ruling (paragraphs four, eleven, and twelve) that my readers might have as much difficulty piecing together the story as the readers of the original must have. I also omitted paragraphs seven through ten because they were largely redundant, which may explain why "news holes" shrink relative to copy?

103. Denniston, *The Reporter and the Law*, p. 111.

104. For an example, see Hall and others, *Policing the Crisis*.

105. Murray Edelman, *Politics as Symbolic Action: Mass Arousal and Quiescence* (New York: Academic Press, 1971).

106. Alan M. Dershowitz, *The Best Defense* (New York: Vintage, 1982) pp. xiii-xxii.

107. See Chibnall, *Law and Order News*, and Hall and coauthors, *Policing the Crisis*.

108. On how the news media manage this task, see W. Lance Bennett, Lynne A. Gressett, and William Haltom, "Repairing the News: A Case Study of the News Paradigm," *Journal of Communication*, 35 (Spring 1985):50–68.

CHAPTER 5

Covering Civil Litigation

1. For examples, see Neil Vidmar, *Medical Malpractice and the American Jury* (Ann Arbor: University of Michigan Press, 1996), which refutes many canards and slanders about the competence and reasonableness of juries in malpractice cases and calls into question the cherished beliefs of tort reformers; Stephen

Daniels and Joanne Martin, *Civil Juries and the Politics of Reform* (Evanston. IL: Northwestern University Press, 1995), which likewise focuses on juries but comments on suggested problems and remedies; Michael Rustad, "In Defense of Punitive Damages in Products Liability: Testing Tort Anecdotes with Empirical Data," *Iowa Law Review* 78 (October 1992):1–78; and Michael Rustad and Thomas Koenig, "The Historical Continuity of Punitive Damages Awards: Reforming the Tort Reformers," *American University Law Review* 42 (1993):1269–1333. Of course, not every criticism of civil litigation is specious. See Dan Quayle, "Civil Justice Reform," *American University Law Review* 41 (1992):559–69; President's Council on Competitiveness, *Agenda for Civil Justice Reform in America* (1991); Walter K. Olson, *The Litigation Explosion: What Happened When America Unleashed the Lawsuit* (New York: Thomas Talley Books—Dutton, 1991); Peter W. Huber, *The Liability Maze: The Impact of Liability Law on Safety and Innovation* (Washington, DC: Brookings, 1991); and Peter W. Huber, *Liability: The Legal Revolution and Its Consequences* (New York: Basic Books, 1988).

2. Lyle Denniston, *The Reporter and the Law* (New York: Hastings House, 1980), p. 167.

3. Ibid., p. 169.

4. Ibid.

5. To create table 5.1, my student, Jeffrey Schaus, coded news stories about courts for four randomly chosen dates in 1993. I had used Mead Data Central's Lexis/Nexis Service to retrieve articles from twenty-eight newspapers. Mr. Schaus read the complete text of every article that contained the words *court, courts, trial, trials, lawsuit, lawsuits, jury, juries,* or *jurors.* For each article related to a litigation, Schaus then determined whether the trial was criminal, civil, or appellate and what stage or stages of the trial were covered.

     I have eliminated from Table Twelve all stories of fewer than forty words. This removed from the table mere compendia of "notices." Some newspapers listed filings of bankruptcies, for example. To treat notices of a dozen or so words as an article would skew counts and overestimate coverage.

6. Jack C. Doppelt, "Strained Relations: How Judges and Lawyers Perceive the Coverage of Legal Affairs," *Justice System Journal,* 14 (March 1991):426.

7. Denniston, *The Reporter and the Law,* p. 16.

8. Ibid., p. 83.

9. Robert E. Drechsel, *Newsmaking in the Trial Courts* (New York: Longman, 1983), p. 88.

10. Doppelt, "Strained Relations," p. 427.

11. David Shaw, *Press Watch: A Provocative Look at How Newspapers Report the News* (New York: Longman, 1984), p. 116.

12. Ibid., p. 115.

13. Ibid., p. 119.

14. Drechsel, *Newsmaking in the Trial Courts,* p. 88.

15. Ibid.

16. Mark Fishman, *Manufacturing the News* (Austin: University of Texas Press, 1980), pp. 94–100.

17. Denniston, *The Reporter and the Law,* p. 168.

18. As was table 5.1, table 5.2 is based on four random dates in 1993.

19. Norimitsu Onishi, "The Courts, and Not Grades, May Decide a High School's Valedictorian," *New York Times*, June 12, 1996, p. A5.

20. "Man Sues State: Not Enough Hot Air in Capitol," *Tacoma Morning News Tribune,* Nov. 15, 1996, p. A9.

21. "Sleeping Pills in Asia and Milwaukee, Etc.," *Washington Times,* Feb. 8, 1992, p. B2.

22. Let us review the previous chapter briefly here. To secure much coverage, criminal cases usually must feature pathetic victims (the more victims, the more news-worth) dastardly deeds (the more deeds and the more dastardly and hence atypical, the more coverage), and/or remorseless perpetrators. Herbert Gans put the matter well: ". . . for the most part, news reports on those at or near the top of the hierarchies and on those, particularly at the bottom, who threaten them, to an audience, most of whom are located in the vast middle range between top and bottom." Herbert Gans, *Deciding What's News: A Study of CBS Evening News, NBC Nightly News, Newsweek, and Time* (New York: Pantheon, 1979), p. 284.

23. Richard Kluger, *Ashes to Ashes: America's Hundred-Year Cigarette War, the Public Health, and the Unabashed Triumph of Philip Morris* (New York: Knopf, 1996), pp. 663–64, 669–70.

24. Ibid., pp. 669–70.

25. For an example, see Arlen J. Large, "My Brother the Car: Public Irritation at Auto Defects Smooths Way for New Law," *Wall Street Journal,* April 27, 1966, p. 16.

26. Ralph Nader, *Unsafe at Any Speed: The Designed-In Dangers of the American Automobile,* Expanded ed. (New York: Grossman, 1972). Nader's book originally appeared in 1965.

27. Mark Dowie, "Pinto Madness," *Mother Jones* (Sept./Oct. 1977) pp. 18–32.

28. Peter W. Huber, *Galileo's Revenge: Junk Science in the Courtroom* (New York: Basic Books, 1991), ch. 4.

29. Ibid., pp. 58, 61.

30. Ibid., p. 62; italics in original.

31. Bradley A. Stertz, "Jury Clears Audi of Auto Defect Causing Death," *Wall Street Journal,* June 15, 1988, Section 1, p. 4.

32. For opposing views, consult John A. Byrne, *Informed Consent* (New York: McGraw-Hill, 1995), and Marcia Angell, *Science on Trial: The Clash of Medical Evidence and the Law in the Breast Implant Case* (New York: Norton, 1996).

33. "McDonalds Cup of Scalding Coffee: $2.9 Million Award," *Chicago Tribune*, Aug. 18, 1994, p. 1.

34. Philip K. Howard, *The Death of Common Sense—How Law Is Suffocating America* (New York: Random House, 1994).

35. W. Lance Bennett and Regina Lawrence, "News Icons and the Mainstreaming of Social Change," *Journal of Communication,* 45 (Summer 1995):20–39.

36. "A Matter of Degree," *Wall Street Journal*, September 1, 1994, p. A1.

37. I draw this summary of Ms. Cipollone's case from Kluger, *Ashes to Ashes*, pp. 639–77.

38. Kluger notes "Because media attention had been lavished on the *Horton* trial, . . . the press by and large gave slim coverage to *Cipollone* until its final stages."

(*Ashes to Ashes*, p. 663). Kluger looked at coverage in the Jackson Clarion Ledger and Greenwood (Mississippi) Commonwealth [please see pp. 786–87], so he means that local media covered the trial. Table 5.4 shows that my data did not confirm Mr. Kluger's claims for the *Horton* case, so I have examined *Cipollone*. Subsequent cases may yet draw more attention, for they involve sovereign states suing tobacco corporations.

39. The data I used afforded me only one broadcast source, National Public Radio. While I could have checked electronic coverage through other sources, I could not insure comparability to the full-text source. Hence, tables 5.3 and 5.4 omit electronic media.

40. The most extensive coverage of *Galbraith* was in the *Santa Barbara News-Press*, consistent with commercial biases. See Kluger, *Ashes to Ashes*, pp. 786–87.

41. As of spring of 1996, discovery issues were still being ironed out before the case could be tried.

42. See W. Russell Neuman, Marion R. Just, and Ann N. Crigler, *Common Knowledge* (Chicago: University of Chicago Press, 1992).

43. Lois G. Forer, *Unequal Protection: Women, Children and the Elderly in Court* (New York: Norton, 1991).

CHAPTER 6

Judicial Selection

1. I thank Professor Charles H. Sheldon for suggesting how I might clarify my thinking in this paragraph.

2. To understand the intricacies of systems for recruitment of judicial personnel, see Henry J. Abraham, *The Judicial Process: An Introductory Analysis of the Courts of the United States, England, and France*, 6th ed. (New York: Oxford University Press, 1993), pp. 21–51. The best surveys of research are now getting dated but still reward readers: Elliot E. Slotnick, "Federal judicial recruitment and selection research: A review essay," *Judicature* 71 (April–May 1988):317–24, and Slotnick, "Review Essay on Judicial Recruitment and Selection," *Justice System Journal* 13 (Spring 1988):109–24.

3. Abraham, *The Judicial Process*, p. 22.

4. Again, I thank Professor Sheldon for suggesting this reminder.

5. Lawrence Baum, "The Electoral Fate of Incumbent Judges in the Ohio Court of Common Pleas," *Judicature* 66 (April 1983): 420–30.

6. See, for example, Robert H. Bork, *The Tempting of America: The Political Seduction of the Law* (New York: Free Press, 1990).

7. Council of State Governments, *The Book of the States 1992–1993* (Lexington, KY: Council of State Governments, 1992), p. 233.

8. Ibid., pp. 233–35. For a slightly different tally, consult Abraham, *The Judicial Process*, p. 22.

9. Readers may check on states' practices by referring to the most recent copy of *The Book of the States*. Issued annually by The Council of State Governments, this reference is authoritative and current. I garnered the information in the preceding paragraph from *The Book of the States 1992–1993* and from David

B. Rottman, Carol R. Flango, and R. Sheldine Lockley, *State Court Organiza-tion 1993* (Washington, DC: Bureau of Justice Statistics, 1995), Table 4.

10. Abraham, *The Judicial Process*, p. 34.

11. This continuum is similar to the dimension of articulation conceived by Profes-sors Nicholas Lovrich and Charles H. Sheldon. Please see "Assessing Judicial Elections: Effects upon the Electorate of High and Low Articulation Systems," *Western Political Quarterly* 38 (June 1985):276–93.

12. Abraham, *The Judicial Process*, p. 36.

13. Mark Silverstein and William Haltom, "You Can't Always Get What You Want," *The Journal of Law and Politics* 12 (Sept. 1996): 459–79.

14. See, for example, Ethan Bronner, *Battle for Justice: How the Bork Nomina-tion Shook America* (New York: Norton, 1989), and Timothy M. Phelps and Helen Winternitz, *Capitol Games: Clarence Thomas, Anita Hill, and the Story of a Supreme Court Nomination* (New York: Hyperion, 1992).

15. Mark Silverstein, *Judicious Choices: The New Politics of Supreme Court Confirmations* (New York: Norton, 1994).

16. Stephen L. Carter, *The Confirmation Mess* (New York: Basic Books, 1994) pp. 3–5.

17. Silverstein, *Judicious Choices*, pp. 10-32.

18. I should count the nominations of Abe Fortas and William Rehnquist to be Chief Justice and of Clement Haynsworth, G. Harrold Carswell, William Rehnquist, Robert Bork, and Clarence Thomas to be Associate Justice. Reasonable stu-dents of the Court might disagree with my choices, however.

19. Regarding the buying and selling of justices, see John Anthony Maltese, *The Selling of Supreme Court Nominees* (Baltimore, MD: Johns Hopkins Univer-sity Press, 1995), and John Massaro, *Supremely Political: The Role of Ideol-ogy and Presidential Management in Unsuccessful Supreme Court Nomi-nations* (Albany: State University of New York Press, 1990). Regarding a recent transaction, see Jane Mayer and Jill Abramson, *Strange Justice: The Selling of Clarence Thomas* (Boston: Houghton Mifflin, 1994).

20. By "recruiters," I mean officials with a formal role in the selection of judges. In the case of U. S. appointees, the president and the Senate are primary recruiters, although interest groups, other public officials, and advisors and handlers certainly play major roles. For elected judges, those with major, public roles in the nomination process are primary recruiters, although many others will have secondary or less formal roles.

21. I mean by spot news a journalistic report of a discrete event. Such reports tend to be brief. In such reports, journalists answer traditional questions ("Who?" "What?" "When?" and so on) specifically and concretely, as opposed to features, investigative journalism, and "running stories."

22. David M. O'Brien, *Judicial Roulette: Report of the Twentieth Century Fund Task Force on Judicial Selection* (New York: Priority Press, 1988) p. 21.

23. Thomas L. Jipping, "Judging Clinton," *National Review* 48 (May 20, 1996):24.

24. To refresh your memory regarding President Clinton's early travails, consult Carter, *The Confirmation Mess*.

25. George L. Watson and John A. Stookey, *Shaping America: The Politics of Supreme Court Appointments* (New York: HarperCollins, 1995) pp. 148–64.

26. Glenn R. Winters, "One-Man Judicial Selection," in Glenn R. Winters, ed.

Selected Readings—Judicial Selection and Tenure (Chicago: American Judicature Society, 1967), pp. 120–25.

27. Philip L. Dubois has shown that Winters's thesis obtains most in states with nonpartisan elections. *From Ballot to Bench: Judicial Elections and the Quest for Accountability* (Austin: University of Texas Press, 1980), pp. 139–43.

28. William K. Hall and Larry T. Aspin, in "What Twenty Years of Judicial Retention Elections Have Told Us," *Judicature* 70 (April–May 1987):340–47, reported that incumbents received more than three-quarters of the votes in retention elections in ten states examined over twenty years.

29. Kenyon N. Griffin and Margaret Maier Murdock, "Practicing Attorneys and Judicial Retention Decisions: Judging the Judges in Wyoming," *Judicature* 69 (June–July 1985):36–42; John M. Scheb, Jr., "Is Anyone Listening? Assessing Bar Influence in Merit Retention Elections in Florida," *Judicature* 67 (Sept. 1983): 113–19.

30. Studies demonstrate that judicial incumbents have been and still are usually electorally secure. See Kermit L. Hall, "Progressive Reform and the Decline of Democratic Accountability: The Popular Election of State Supreme Court Judges, 1850–1920," *American Bar Foundation Research Journal* 1984 (Spring 1984): 345–69, especially at p. 363, for one historical overview. More recent results in Ohio reiterate incumbents' safety, see Baum, "The Electoral Fate of Incumbent Judges in the Ohio Court of Common Pleas," p. 429.

31. I draw table 6.1 from table 1 in "Judicial Recruitment: An Inventory of Hypotheses," a paper delivered to the American Political Science Association on August 29, 1996, at the San Francisco Hilton. I thank Mark Silverstein, my coauthor, for permission to use this table here.

32. To create table 6.1, my colleague and I relied on the research of Sheldon Goldman: "Judicial selection under Clinton: A Midterm Examination," *Judicature* 78 (May–June, 1995):276–91; "Bush's Judicial Legacy: The Final Imprint," *Judicature* 76 (April–May, 1993):282–97. Goldman's lists yielded ten names, to which we added Judge James L. Dennis as the only contested nomination after Goldman's article was published. We compiled every mention of the eleven names in newspapers, news magazines, and electronic media collected on Lexis/Nexis. We traced each name back from two weeks after a resolution of the candidacy to the earliest mention of the candidacy that we could find.

33. Counting words would not, in my judgment, materially alter my contentions or substantially qualify Hypothesis Five. I decided that counting mentions, if anything, overestimated coverage and thus provided a challenge to the hypothesis being considered.

34. Stephen L. Carter summarizes the changes wrought by modern presidencies: "The Reagan and Bush administrations, by most accounts, raised what had been occasional habit to a science, for they were less interested in party labels as such than in structuring the membership of courts in ways that would turn back what was seen as a rolling tide of liberal activism." *The Confirmation Mess*, p. 71. Elliot E. Slotnick includes President Carter among the executives with rich opportunities to remake the U. S. district courts by filling newly authorized openings. See his "Review Essay on Judicial Recruitment and Selection," p. 110. Refer as well to O'Brien, "Judicial Roulette," pp. 25–27, 50–64, and, generally, Herman Schwartz, *Packing the Courts: The Conservative Campaign to Rewrite the Constitution* (New York: Scribner, 1988).

35. Slotnick, "Review Essay on Judicial Recruitment and Selection," p. 111.

36. Please review W. Lance Bennett, *News — The Politics of Illusion,* 2nd ed. (New York: Longman, 1988), pp. 21–67; Stephen Chibnall, *Law-and-Order News: An Analysis of Crime Reporting in the British Press* (London: Tavistock, 1977), p. 23; and Richard Davis, *Decisions and Images: The Supreme Court and the Press* (Englewood Cliffs, NJ: Prentice-Hall, 1993), p. 22.

37. Many of President Reagan's aides and allies, for example, thought Judge Robert H. Bork well worth the risks that they anticipated his nomination would entail. See Patrick McGuigan and Dawn Weyrich, *Ninth Justice: The Fight for Bork* (Washington, DC: Free Congress, 1990). While scholars have often noted that lame-duck presidents lose their potency and may have to settle for safe nominees, the Bork nomination showed that the absence of a future election may also liberate a president. President Reagan was past re-election in 1984 and congressional elections in 1986 when he risked appointing Judge Bork.

38. Warren B. Rudman, *Combat: Twelve Years in the U. S. Senate* (New York: Random House, 1996), p. 167.

39. Mark Silverstein, "Special Interests Produce Dull Court Nominees," *National Law Journal,* July 11, 1994, p. A21.

40. O'Brien, *Judicial Roulette,* p. 100.

41. See Mayer and Abramson, *Strange Justice.*

42. Even Republicans who voted for Judge Thomas could not agree with President Bush on Thomas's merit. See Rudman, *Combat,* p. 251.

43. Goldman, "Judicial Selection under Clinton: A Midterm Examination," p. 277.

44. Rudman, *Combat,* pp. 178–79.

45. See Phelps and Winternitz, *Capitol Games.*

46. Larry J. Sabato, *Feeding Frenzy: How Attack Journalism Has Transformed American Politics* (New York: Free Press, 1991).

47. On this campaign, please see John T. Wold and John H. Culver, "The defeat of the California justices: the campaign, the electorate, and the issue of judicial accountability," *Judicature* 70 (April–May 1987):348–55; "After California, what's next for judicial elections?" *Judicature* 70 (April–May 1987):356–64; Joseph R. Grodin, "Judicial elections: the California experience," *Judicature* 70 (April–May 1987):365–69; Joseph R. Grodin, *In Pursuit of Justice: Reflections of a State Supreme Court Justice* (Berkeley: University of California Press, 1989), pp. 169–77; and Paul Reidinger, "The Politics of Judging," *ABA Journal* (April 1, 1987):52–58.

    While Associate Justices Joseph R. Grodin and Cruz Reynoso also met rejection in this election, I focus on Chief Justice Bird as the central figure in making a largely open retention election become wide open.

48. National Center for State Courts, cited by Ted Gest in "After California, What's Next for Judicial Elections?" p. 358, col. 1.

49. Wold and Culver "The Defeat of the California Justices," p. 350, col. 3, put the figure at more than $5 million; Grodin ("Judicial Elections," p. 368) at $7 million; and Reidinger, citing the *Los Angeles Times,* at more than $10 million ("The Politics of Judging," p. 54, col. 1).

50. Wold and Culver, "The Defeat of the California Justices," p. 351, col. 3.

51. Ted Gest cited the following lead paragraph from "Lone Justice in Search of the Real Rose Bird," an article from the *Los Angeles Times* ("After California, What's Next for Judicial Elections?" p. 364, col. 1) that Gest characterizes as

among the more responsible pieces: "Rose Bird is a character, sipping carrot juice, talking to the animals at the city's zoo, discussing meditation and her search for an inner sea of calm, asking the beleaguered chief of Sydney, Australia's highest court if his scalp itched, lecturing a cab diver on the dangers of cocaine, denouncing the political system as "bankrupt" and then insisting after the 59th consecutive time she overturned a death penalty that her personal views on capital punishment do not affect her opinions."

52. Reidinger, "The Politics of Judging," p. 56, col. 1.

53. Grodin, "Judicial Elections," pp. 366–69.

54. Ibid., p. 566, col. 3 to p. 567, col. 1, emphasis added.

55. Ibid., p. 367, col. 3.

56. Ibid., p. 367, col. 3.

57. Ibid., p. 368, cols. 1–2.

58. Ibid., p. 368, col. 2.

59. By my count, the Senate has rejected but four of seventeen nominees (23.5%) on which it acted since 1968. The rate of confirmation would, of course, skyrocket if one started to count before President Lyndon Johnson's filibustered nomination of Justice Abe Fortas to succeed Chief Justice Earl Warren. I do not count Homer Thornberry and Douglas H. Ginsburg as rejected nominations, for both exited the confirmation process early for highly unusual reasons. Others would count Thornberry and Ginsburg. Please see Watson and Stookey, *Shaping America*, pp. 241-243, and Massaro, *Supremely Political*, for contrary views. Were one to count those two, 68.4% of those nominated would have been confirmed.

60. President Clinton has deviated from this pattern by extending the time between public awareness of an opening on the Court and public announcement of his nominee. I do not dwell on this recent exception because, if anything, President Clinton's practice prescreens nominees and permits his administration to side-step potentially wide-open confirmation. After the "great wait," President Clinton nominated two judges virtually assured of controlled, predictable, safe, and stylized coverage.

61. See Bronner, *Battle for Justice*, pp. 98–99, on Senator Edward M. Kennedy's immediate reaction to the nomination of Judge Bork. I discuss this in greater detail later in the chapter and so do not belabor the matter here.

62. See Ronald D. Rotunda, "Innovations Disguised as Traditions: A Historical Review of the Supreme Court Nominations Process," *University of Illinois Law Review* 1995 (1995):123-31, p. 129.

63. Michael Pertschuk and Wendy Schaetzel, *The People Rising: The Campaign against the Bork Nomination* (New York: Thunder's Mouth Press, 1989), pp. 62–92.

64. Even a prominent exception proves this rule: Nina Totenberg could scuttle the nomination of Judge Douglas H. Ginsburg on his pot-smoking only because the Reagan Administration had botched the preliminary investigation of its successor to the failed Bork nomination—Bronner, *Battle for Justice*, pp. 328–36. When administrations vet potential recruits thoroughly, the press seldom will have access to information with which to balance, let alone contradict, the nominee's image.

65. Bork, *The Tempting of America*, p. 279: "A nominee who has not written on the relevant subjects can decline discussion. I could not."

66. Richard Harris, *Decision* (New York: Dutton, 1971), p. 20.
67. Refer to Watson and Stookey, Shaping America, pp. 148-155.
68. On the other hand, Justice Kennedy's differences from Judge Bork are not inconsequential. Justice Kennedy wrote the majority opinion in *Romer v. Evans* (1996), the decision by which the Court invalidated Colorado's Amendment 2 and extended to gays and lesbians the same rights as others. Judge Bork crafted a brief explaining why states could disadvantage homosexuals. See Jeffrey Toobin, "Supreme Sacrifice: Laurence Tribe may never be on the Supreme Court, but then he really doesn't need to be." *New Yorker*, July 8 1996, pp. 43–47.
69. For example, Judge Bork in *The Tempting of America*, p. 273, assures readers that "President Reagan has been accused of appointing judges with a political agenda, but that is almost certainly not the case. He was committed to the idea that judges should not make up law but should interpret law." I leave it to you to decide which is worse: Bork believes both that the Reagan administration did not select judges who would advance the administration's values and that the distinction between making up law and interpreting law is tenable or Bork is being disingenuous or intellectually expedient.
70. Henry J. Abraham, *Justices and Presidents: A Political History of Appointments to the Supreme Court,* 3rd ed. (New York: Oxford University Press, 1992), p. 357.
71. Bronner, *Battle for Justice*, pp. 208-276.
72. Phelps and Winternitz, *Capitol Games*, pp. xiii-xvii.
73. Ibid., pp. 167–210.
74. Ibid., pp. 181–82.
75. Ibid., p. 197.
76. Ibid., p. 332.
77. I acknowledge that some scholars would argue that borking is not that rare and that, among others, Justice Rutledge, Justice Brandeis, Judge Parker, Justice Thurgood Marshall, Justice Fortas, and Judge Haynsworth were borked before Bork was borked.
78. Bork, *The Tempting of America*, chs. 14–16.
79. Suzanne Garment, "The War Against Robert Bork," *Commentary*, Jan. 1988, pp. 17–26.
80. David Brock, *The Real Anita Hill: The Untold Story* (New York: Free Press, 1993).
81. Nina Totenberg, "The Confirmation Process and the Public: To Know or Not to Know," *Harvard Law Review* 101 (April 1988): 1213; O'Brien, *Judicial Roulette*, p. 21.
82. Carter, *The Confirmation Mess*, pp. 10, 23.
83. Ibid., p. 10: "The trouble is that scholarship, when at all complex, is easily chopped up into smaller bits, just the right size for our sound-bite-mad media to digest and spit out again in a form even more garbled and out of context than when one's opponents first set out to distort the work."
84. Ibid., p. 23: "Baird broke the law in a rather mundane way and was pilloried for it, the punishment in media humiliation far outweighing the crime. As for Guinier, the matter is a good deal simpler: she was railroaded. In both cases, a moderate, thoughtful dialogue would have served the nation well. In neither

case was it allowed to happen, for simple sound-bites beat complex explanations every time."

85. Ibid., p. 10.

86. Ibid., pp. 3–5.

87. Rotunda, "Innovations Disguised as Traditions," p. 131. A trenchant if qualified version of the same fear was offered by the late Max Lerner in an essay included in *Nine Scorpions in a Bottle: Great Judges, Great Cases of the Supreme Court* (New York: Arcade, 1994), p. 284: "The fact is that if the fate of future nominees is decided by pressure groups, on TV, this will have a devastating effect on the available talent for the federal courts. Constitutional scholars and sitting judges will begin to tailor their public views or decisions to the interest groups sitting in judgment on them."

88. O'Brien, *Judicial Roulette*, pp. 3–12.

89. Ibid., p. 4.

90. Ibid., pp. 8–10.

91. Ibid., p. 10. This position was attributed to Professor Walter Berns.

92. Laurence Tribe presents a fascinating counterpart to Judge Bork. Tribe has established a far more extensive scholarly record in constitutional law than Judge Bork. His record as an advocate before the Supreme Court might rival Judge Bork's experience as solicitor general. However, Tribe's longer "paper trail" is perhaps as "left" as Judge Bork's was "right." Worse, Tribe assisted Democrats in defeating Judge Bork in 1987, diminishing his own chances to be a justice. See Toobin, "Supreme Sacrifice," pp. 43–47.

93. Establishing quality would be daunting. "Senatorial courtesy" and "blue slips," for example, allowed senators to operate such a judicial spoils system that U. S. judges historically have been appointed more for whom they knew than for what they knew. See O'Brien, *Judicial Roulette*, pp. 70–72.

94. Bruce Fein, "Commentary: A Circumscribed Senate Role," *Harvard Law Review* 102 (Jan. 1989):672–87.

95. Review Slotnick, "Review Essay on Judicial Recruitment and Selection."

96. So prevalent has closed recruitment been that, in many cases, professions of shock are genuine. Recruiters know that politics has influenced judicial selection in the United States all along, but they had not expected "outside" interference.

97. "A little knowledge, a pebble from a shingle,
A drop from the oceans: who would have
dreamed this infinitely little too much?"
Robinson Jeffers, "Science," in *Robinson Jeffers—Selected Poems* (New York: Vintage, 1965), p.39.

Conclusion

1. Thomas Sowell, "The Greenhouse Effect," *Wall Street Journal,* March 8, 1994, p. A10.

2. "I really look with commiseration over the great body of my fellow citizens who, reading newspapers, live and die in the belief that they have known something

of what has been passing in the world in their time." President Harry S Truman quoted by W. Lance Bennett in *News—The Politics of Illusion,* 2nd ed. (New York: Longman, 1988), p. xi.

3.   Murray Edelman, *Politics as Symbolic Action: Mass Arousal and Quiescence* (New York: Academic Press, 1971).

bibliography

Abbott, Daniel, and James Calonico. 1974. "Black Man, White Woman—The Maintenance of a Myth: Rape and the Press in New Orleans." In *Crime and Delinquency: Dimensions of Deviance*, M. Reidel and T. Thornberry, eds., pp. 141–153. New York: Praeger.

Abraham, Henry J. 1992. *Justices and Presidents: A Political History of Appointments to the Supreme Court.* 3rd ed. New York: Oxford University Press.

Abraham, Henry J. 1993. *The Judicial Process: An Introductory Analysis of the Courts of the United States, England, and France.* 6th ed. New York: Oxford University Press.

Abramson, Jeffrey. 1996. "The Pros and Cons of Televising Trials." In *Postmortem: The O.J. Simpson Case,* J. Abramson, ed., pp. 195–98. New York: Basic Books.

Alterman, Eric. 1992. *Sound and Fury: The Washington Punditocracy and the Collapse of American Politics.* New York: HarperCollins.

Altheide, David L. 1976. *Creating Reality: How TV News Distorts Events.* Beverly Hills, CA: Sage.

Altheide, David L. 1984. "TV News and the Social Construction of Justice." In *Justice and the Media*, Ray Surette, ed., pp. 292–304. Springfield, IL: Charles C. Thomas.

Altheide, David L., and Robert P. Snow. 1979. *Media Logic.* Beverly Hills, CA: Sage.

American Bar Association. 1992. *ABA Standards for Criminal Justice Fair Trial and Free Press.* 3d ed. Washington, DC: American Bar Association.

Angell, Marcia. 1996. *Science on Trial: The Clash of Medical Evidence and the Law in the Breast Implant Case.* New York: Norton.

Antunes, George E., and Patricia A. Hurley. 1977. "The Representation of Criminal Events in Houston's Two Daily Newspapers." *Journalism Quarterly* 54 (Winter): 756–60.

Austen, J. L. 1962. *How to Do Things with Words.* New York: Oxford University Press.

Bagdikian, Ben H. 1992. *The Media Monopoly.* 4th ed. Boston: Beacon Press.

Baum, Bob. 1994. "Tonya: I'm Guilty—Skater Signs Plea on Conspiracy Charge." *Burlington Free Press,* March 17, p. 1A.

Baum, Lawrence. 1983. "The Electoral Fates of Incumbent Judges in the Ohio Court of Common Pleas." *Judicature* 66 (April):420–30.

Bell, David V. J. 1975. *Power, Influence, and Authority: An Essay in Political Linguistics.* New York: Oxford University Press.

Bendix, Reinhard. 1977. *Max Weber: An Intellectual Portrait.* Berkeley: University of California Press.

Bennett, W. Lance. 1988. *News—The Politics of Illusion.* 2d ed. New York: Longman.

Bennett, W. Lance, and Martha S. Feldman. 1981. *Reconstructing Reality in the Court-*

room: Justice and Judgment in American Culture. New Brunswick, NJ: Rutgers University Press.

Bennett, W. Lance, Lynne A. Gressett, and William Haltom. 1985. "Repairing the News: A Case Study of the News Paradigm." *Journal of Communication* 35 (Spring): 50–68.

Bennett, W. Lance, and Regina Lawrence. 1995. "News Icons and the Mainstreaming of Social Change." *Journal of Communication* 45 (Summer): 20–39.

Berger, M. Marvin. 1972. "Do the Courts Communicate?" *Judicature* 57 (April): 318–23.

Berkson, Larry, and Steven Hays. 1976. "The Forgotten Politicians: Court Clerks." *University of Miami Law Review* 30 (Spring): 449–516.

Black, Donald. 1976. *The Behavior of Law.* New York: Academic Press.

Black, Donald. 1989. *Sociological Justice.* New York: Oxford University Press.

Blumberg, Abraham S. 1967. "The Practice of Law as a Confidence Game." *Law and Society Review* 1 (June): 15–39.

Boles, Nancy, and Katherine Heaviside. 1987. "When a Reporter Calls." *American Bar Association Journal* 73 (June 1): 90–92.

Bork, Robert H. 1990. *The Tempting of America: The Political Seduction of the Law.* New York: Free Press.

Bovée, Warren G. 1981. "Court Comment." *Masthead* (Spring): 18–30.

Bowles, Dorothy A., and Rebekah Bromley. 1992. "Newsmagazine Coverage of the Supreme Court During the Reagan Administration." *Journalism Quarterly* 69 (Winter): 948–59.

Brenner, Saul, and John F. Krol. 1989. "Strategies in Certiorari Voting on the United States Supreme Court." *Journal of Politics* 51 (Nov.): 828–40.

Brock, David. 1993. *The Real Anita Hill: The Untold Story.* New York: Free Press.

Broder, David S. 1987. *Behind the Front Page: A Candid Look at How the News Is Made.* New York: Simon and Schuster.

Buchanan, Edna. 1987. *The Corpse Had a Familiar Face: Covering Miami, America's Hottest Beat.* New York: Random House.

Burke, Kenneth. 1969. *A Grammar of Motives.* Berkeley: University of California Press.

Byrne, John A. 1995. *Informed Consent.* New York: McGraw-Hill.

Caldeira, Gregory A., and John R. Wright. 1988. "Organized Interests and Agenda-Setting in the U. S. Supreme Court." *American Political Science Review* 82 (Dec.): 1109–28.

Caplan, Lincoln. 1996. "The Failure (and Promise) of Legal Journalism." In *Postmortem: The O.J. Simpson Case,* J. Abramson, ed., pp. 199-200. New York: Basic Books.

Carroll, Wallace. 1965. "Essence, Not Angle." *Columbia Journalism Review* 4 (Summer): 4–6.

Carter, Lief H. 1988. *Reason in Law*. 3d ed. Boston: Little, Brown.

Carter, Stephen L. 1994. *The Confirmation Mess: Cleaning Up the Federal Appointment Process*. New York: Basic Books.

Chibnall, Steve. 1977. *Law-and-Order News: An Analysis of Crime Reporting in the British Press*. London, U.K.: Tavistock.

Clayton, James E. 1964. *The Making of Justice: The Supreme Court in Action.* New York: Dutton.

Clayton, James E. 1968. "Interpreting the Court." *Columbia Journalism Review* 7 (Summer): 48–49.

Cleary, Edward J. 1994. *Beyond the Burning Cross: The First Amendment and the Landmark* R. A. V. *Case.* New York: Random House.

Corry, John. 1986. *TV News and the Dominant Culture.* Washington, DC: Media Institute.

Council of State Governments. 1992. *Book of the States, 1992–1993.* Lexington, KY: Council of State Governments.

Cover, Robert M. 1975. *Justice Accused: Antislavery and the Judicial Process.* New Haven, CT: Yale University Press.

Cranberg, Gilbert. 1967. "What Did the Supreme Court Say?" *Saturday Review* 60 (April 8): 90–92.

Crandon, Garth. 1992. *The Police and the Media: Information Management and the Construction of Crime News.* Bradford, West Yorkshire: Horton Publishing Ltd.

Daniels, Stephen, and Joanne Martin. 1995. *Civil Juries and the Politics of Reform.* Evanston, IL: Northwestern University Press.

Davis, Richard. 1987. "Lifting the Shroud: News Media Portrayal of the U. S. Supreme Court." *Communication and Law* 9 (Oct.): 43–59.

Davis, Richard. 1994. *Decisions and Images: The Supreme Court and the Press.* Englewood Cliffs, NJ: Prentice-Hall.

Dennis, Everette E. 1975. "Another Look at Press Coverage of the Supreme Court." *Villanova Law Review* 20 (March): 765–99.

Denniston, Lyle. 1980. *The Reporter and the Law: Techniques of Covering the Courts*. New York: Hastings House.

Dershowitz, Alan M. 1982. *The Best Defense.* New York: Vintage.

Dershowitz, Alan M. 1994. *The Abuse Excuse—And Other Cop-Outs, Sob Stories, and Evasions of Responsibility.* Boston: Little, Brown.

Dershowitz, Alan M. 1996. *Reasonable Doubts: The O.J. Simpson Case and the Criminal Justice System.* New York: Simon and Schuster.

Ditton, Jason, and James Duffy. 1983. "Bias in the Newspaper Reporting of Crime News." *British Journal of Criminology* 23 (April): 159–65.

Doppelt, Jack C. 1991. "Strained Relations: How Judges and Lawyers Perceive the Coverage of Legal Affairs." *Justice System Journal* 14 (March): 419–44.

Dowie, Mark. 1977. "Pinto Madness." *Mother Jones* (Sept.-Oct.): 18–32.

Drechsel, Robert. 1983. *News Making in the Trial Courts.* New York: Longman.

Drechsel, Robert E. 1987. "Uncertain Dancers: Judges and the News Media." *Judicature* 70 (Feb.-March): 264–72.

Dubois, Phillip L. 1980. *From Ballot to Bench: Judicial Elections and the Quest for Accountability.* Austin: University of Texas Press.

Duke, Paul. 1989. "The U. S. Supreme Court: A Journalist's View." *Washburn Law Journal* 28 (Spring): 343–56.

Dussuyer, Inez. 1979. *Crime News: A Study of 40 Ontario Newspapers.* Toronto: University of Toronto Centre of Criminology.

Edelman, Murray. 1971. *Politics as Symbolic Action: Mass Arousal and Quiescence.* New York: Academic Press.

Edelman, Murray. 1988. *Constructing the Political Spectacle.* Chicago: University of Chicago Press.

Efron, Edith. 1971. *The News Twisters.* New York: Manor Books.

Engelmayer, Sheldon, and Robert Wagman. 1985. *Lord's Justice: One Judge's Battle to Expose the Deadly Dalkon Shield I.U.D.* Garden City, NY: Anchor/ Doubleday.

Entman, Robert M. 1989. *Democracy Without Citizens: Media and the Decay of American Politics.* New York: Oxford University Press.

Epstein, Edward Jay. 1973. *News from Nowhere: Television and the News.* New York: Random House.

Ericson, David. 1977. "Newspaper Coverage of the Supreme Court: A Case Study." *Journalism Quarterly* 54 (Autumn): 605–7.

Fallows, James. 1996. *Breaking the News: How the Media Undermine American Democracy.* New York: Pantheon Books.

Fein, Bruce. 1989. "Commentary: A Circumscribed Senate Role." *Harvard Law Review* 102 (Jan.): 672–87.

Fishman, Mark. 1980. *Manufacturing the News.* Austin: University of Texas Press.

Fletcher, George P. 1996. *With Justice for Some: Protecting Victims' Rights in Criminal Trials.* New York: Addison-Wesley.

Forer, Lois G. 1991. *Unequal Protection: Women, Children, and the Elderly in Court.* New York: Norton.

Frank, Robert Shelby. 1973. *Message Dimension of Television News.* Lexington. KY: Lexington Books.

Franklin, Charles H., and Liane Kosaki. 1995. "Media, Knowledge, and Public Evaluations of the Supreme Court." In *Contemplating Courts,* Lee Epstein, ed., pp. 352–375. Washington, DC: CQ Press.

Freedman, Max. 1956. "Worst Reported Institution," *Nieman Reports* 10 (April): 2.

Fretz, Donald R. 1973. *Courts and the Community.* Reno, NV: National College of the State Judiciary.

Gans, Herbert. 1979. *Deciding What's News: A Study of CBS Evening News, NBC Nightly News, Newsweek, and Time.* New York: Pantheon.

Garment, Suzanne. 1988. "The War Against Robert Bork." *Commentary,* Jan., pp. 17–26.

Gerald, J. Edward. 1983. *News of Crime: Courts and Press in Conflict.* Contributions to the Study of Mass Media and Communications, No. 1. Westport, CT: Greenwood Press.

Gerlin, Andrea. 1994. "A Matter of Degree." *Wall Street Journal,* Sept. 1, p. A1.

Gilmore, Gene. 1990. *Modern Newspaper Editing.* 4th ed. Ames: Iowa State University Press.

Gleason, Timothy W. 1990. *The Watchdog Concept.* Ames: Iowa State University Press.

Glendon, Mary Ann. 1991. *Rights Talk: The Impoverishment of Political Discourse.* New York: Free Press.

Goldberg, Hank M. 1996. *The Prosecution Responds: An O. J. Simpson Prosecutor Reveals What Really Happened.* Secaucus, NJ: Carol Publishing Group.

Goldman, Sheldon. 1993. "Bush's Judicial Legacy: The Final Imprint." *Judicature* 76 (April-May): 282–97.

Goldman, Sheldon. 1995. "Judicial Selection under Clinton: A Midterm Examination." *Judicature* 78 (May-June): 276–91.

Gollner, Philip M. 1994. "Consulting by Peering into Minds of Jurors." *New York Times,* Jan. 7, p. A23.

Gordon, Frank X., Jr. 1985. "The Judicial Image: Is a Facelift Necessary?" *Justice System Journal* 10 (March): 315–24.

Gordon, Margaret T., and Stephanie Riger. 1989. *The Female Fear.* New York: Free Press.

Gorney, Cynthia. 1991. "Guam Antiabortion Law Contested in U.S. Court." *Washington Post,* Nov. 5, p. A4.

Graber, Doris A. 1980. *Crime News and the Public.* New York: Praeger.

Graham, Fred. 1990. *Happy Talk: Confessions of a TV Newsman.* New York: Norton.

Greenhouse, Linda. 1992. "Press Coverage." In *The Oxford Companion to the Supreme Court of the United States,* Kermit L. Hall, Jr. , ed., pp. 666–67. New York: Oxford University Press.

Greenhouse, Linda. 1995. "The Supreme Court: Church-State Relations—Ruling on Religion." *New York Times,* June 30, p. A1.

Grey, David L. 1968. *The Supreme Court and the News Media.* Evanston, IL: Northwestern University Press.

Grey, David L. 1972. "Covering the Courts: Problems of Specialization." *Nieman Reports* 26 (March): 17–19.

Griffin, Kenyon N., and Margaret M. Murdock. 1985. "Practicing Attorneys and Judicial Retention Decisions: Judging the Judges in Wyoming." *Judicature* 69 (June-July): 36–42.

Grodin, Joseph R. 1987. "Judicial Elections: the California Experience." *Judicature* 70 (April-May): 365–69.

Grodin, Joseph R. 1989. *In Pursuit of Justice: Reflections of a State Supreme Court Justice,* pp. 169–77. Berkeley: University of California Press.

Hachten, William A. 1962. "Journalism and the Prayer Decision." *Columbia Journalism Review* 1 (Fall): 4–9.

Hale, F. Dennis. 1973. "The Court's Perception of the Press," *Judicature* 57 (Dec.): 183–89.

Hale, F. Dennis. 1973. The Press and a State Appellate Court: News Coverage by Six Dailies of Forty Decisions by the Washington State Supreme Court. Master's thesis, University of Oregon.

Hale, F. Dennis. 1975. "How Reporters and Justices View Coverage of a State Appellate Court." *Journalism Quarterly* 52 (Spring):106–10.

Hale, F. Dennis. 1977. Variables Associated with Newspaper Coverage of California Supreme Court Decisions: A Multivariate Analysis. Ph. D. diss., Southern Illinois University.

Hale, F. Dennis. 1978. "Press Releases vs. Newspaper Coverage of California Supreme Court Decisions." *Journalism Quarterly* 55 (Winter): 696–702, 710.

Hale, F. Dennis. 1979. "A Comparison of Coverage of Speech and Press Verdicts of Supreme Court." *Journalism Quarterly* 56 (Spring): 43–47.

Hall, Kermit L. 1984. "Progressive Reform and the Decline of Democratic Accountability: The Popular Election of State Supreme Court Judges, 1850-1920." *American Bar Foundation Research Journal* (Spring): 345–69.

Hall, Stuart, Chas Critcher, Tony Jefferson, John Clarke, and Brian Roberts. 1978. *Policing the Crisis: Mugging, the State, and Law and Order.* London, U.K.: Macmillan Education.

Hall, William K. and Larry T. Aspin. 1987. "What Twenty Years of Judicial Retention Elections Have Told Us." *Judicature* 70 (April-May): 340–47.

Hariman, Robert, ed. 1990. *Popular Trials: Rhetoric, Mass Media, and the Law.* Tuscaloosa: University of Alabama Press.

Harris, Richard. 1971. *Decision.* New York: Dutton.

Harris, Thomas J. 1987. *Courtroom's Finest Hour in American Cinema.* Metuchen, NJ: Scarecrow Press.

Hay, Douglas, Peter Linebaugh, John G. Rule, E. P. Thompson, and Cal Winslow. 1975. *Albion's Fatal Tree: Crime and Society in Eighteenth-Century England.* New York: Pantheon.

Hearst Corporation. 1983. *The American Public, the Media and the Judicial System: A National Survey on Public Awareness and Personal Experience.* New York: Hearst Corp.

Hedges, Michael. 1993. "A Long-Shot Liberal Sweep: 3 Key Cases, Same 3 Judges." *Washington Times*, Dec. 3, p. A1.

Helling, Susan. 1990. Police and the News Media: An Analysis of Perceived Patterns of Interaction. Master's thesis, University of Colorado.

Herman, Edward S., and Noam Chomsky. 1988. *Manufacturing Consent: The Political Economy of the Mass Media.* New York: Pantheon.

Hess, Stephen. 1981. *The Washington Reporters.* Washington, DC: Brookings Institution.

Heumann, Milton. 1977. *Plea Bargaining: The Experience of Prosecutors, Judges, and Defense Attorneys.* Chicago: University of Chicago Press.

Howard, Philip K. 1994. *The Death of Common Sense—How Law Is Suffocating America.* New York: Random House.

Huber, Peter W. 1988. *Liability: The Legal Revolution and Its Consequences.* New York: Basic Books.

Huber, Peter W. 1991. *Galileo's Revenge: Junk Science in the Courtroom.* New York: Basic Books.

Huber, Peter W. 1991. *The Liability Maze: The Impact of Liability Law on Safety and Innovation.* Washington, DC: Brookings Institution.

Iyengar, Shanto. 1991. *Is Anyone Responsible?* Chicago: University of Chicago Press.

Jamieson, Kathleen H., and Karlyn K. Campbell. 1988. *The Interplay of Influence: Mass Media and Their Publics in News, Advertising, Politics.* 2nd ed. Belmont, CA: Wadsworth.

Jeffers, Robinson. 1965. "Science." *Robinson Jeffers—Selected Poems.* New York: Vintage Books.

Jipping, Thomas L. 1996. "Judging Clinton. (Pres. Clinton's Judicial Selections)." *National Review* 48 (May 20): 24.

Johnston, David. 1994. "Overtures Begun for Plea Bargain on Rostenkowski." *New York Times*, May 19, p. A1.

Kaniss, Phyllis. 1991. *Making Local News.* Chicago: University of Chicago Press.

Katsh, Ethan. 1983. "The Supreme Court Beat: How Television Covers the U. S. Supreme Court." *Judicature* 67 (June-July): 6–15.

Katz, Elihu. 1957. "Two Step Flow of Communication." *Public Opinion Quarterly* 21 (Summer): 61–78.

Kluger, Richard. 1996. *Ashes to Ashes: America's Hundred-Year Cigarette War, the*

Public Health, and the Unabashed Triumph of Philip Morris. New York: Knopf.

Knoche, Eldon. 1987. "A Reporter's View of Relations with Judges." *Judicature* 70 (Feb.-March): 268–69.

Kritzer, Herbert M. 1991. *Let's Make a Deal: Understanding the Negotiation Process in Ordinary Litigation.* Madison: University of Wisconsin Press.

Large, Arlen J. 1966. "My Brother the Car: Public Irritation at Auto Defects Smooths Way for New Law." *Wall Street Journal*, April 27, p. 16.

Larson, Stephanie G. 1985. "How the *New York Times* Covered the Discrimination Cases," *Journalism Quarterly* 62 (Winter): 894–96.

Larson, Stephanie G., and Bryan Tramont. 1993. "The Supreme Court and Television: Predicting Case Coverage." Paper presented at the meeting of the Midwest Political Science Association, Chicago.

Lee, Martin A., and Norman Solomon. 1990. *Unreliable Sources: A Guide to Detecting Bias in the News Media.* Secaucus, NJ: Lyle Stuart.

Lerner, Max. 1994. *Nine Scorpions in a Bottle: Great Judges and Cases of the Supreme Court.* New York: Arcade.

Lewis, Anthony. 1959. "Problems of a Washington Correspondent," *Connecticut Bar Journal* 33: 363–71.

Lewis, Anthony. 1964. *Gideon's Trumpet.* New York: Vintage.

Lewis, Nancy. 1987. "Factions' Squabbling Rocks U.S. Court of Appeals Here." *Washington Post*, Aug. 1, 1987, p. A1.

Lichter, S. Robert, Stanley Rothman, and Linda S. Lichter. 1986. *The Media Elite.* Bethesda, MD: Adler and Adler.

Lind, Robert C. 1995. "Book Review: Defender of the Faith in the Midst of the Simpson Circus." *Southwestern University Law Review* 24 (Dec.): 1215–16.

Lipschultz, Jeremy H. 1991. "A Comparison of Trial Lawyer and News Reporter Attitudes about Courthouse Communication," *Journalism Quarterly* 68 (Winter): 750–63.

Lovrich, Nicholas P., John C. Pierce, and Charles H. Sheldon. 1989. "Citizen Knowledge and Voting in Judicial Elections," *Judicature* 73 (June-July): 28–42.

Lovrich, Nicholas P. and Charles H. Sheldon. 1985. "Assessing Judicial Elections: Effects upon the Electorate of High and Low Articulation Systems." *Western Political Quarterly* 38 (June): 276–93.

Luedtke, Kurt. 1981. *Absence of Malice.* Los Angeles, CA: Columbia Pictures.

MacDougall, Curtis. 1968. *Interpretive Reporting.* 5th ed. New York: Macmillan.

MacKenzie, John P. 1968. "The Warren Court and the Press." *Michigan Law Review* 67 (Nov.): 303–16.

Maltese, John A. 1995. *The Selling of Supreme Court Nominees.* Baltimore, MD: Johns Hopkins University Press.

Mason, Alpheus T. 1956. *Harlan Fiske Stone, Pillar of the Law*. New York: Viking.

Mason, Alpheus T. 1965. *William Howard Taft: Chief Justice*. New York: Simon and Schuster.

Massaro, John. 1990. *Supremely Political: The Role of Ideology and Presidential Management in Unsuccessful Supreme Court Nominations*. Albany: State University of New York Press.

Mauro, Tony. 1995. "Debate Widens over Religion in Public Life." *USA Today*, June 30, p. 8A.

Mayer, Jane, and Jill Abramson. 1994. *Strange Justice: The Selling of Clarence Thomas*. Boston: Houghton Mifflin.

McGuigan, Patrick, and Dawn Weyrich. 1990. *Ninth Justice: The Fight for Bork*. Washington, DC: Free Congress.

Miller, Susan H. 1978. "Reporters and Congressmen: Living in Symbiosis." *Journalism Monographs*, No. 53, pp. 1–25.

Morgan, David. 1978. *The Capitol Press Corps: Newsmen and the Governing of New York State*. Westport, CT: Greenwood Press.

Mosteller, Robert P. 1995. "Book Review: Popular Justice," *Harvard Law Review* 109 (Dec.): 487–517.

Nader, Ralph. 1972. *Unsafe at Any Speed: The Designed-In Dangers of the American Automobile*. Expanded ed. New York: Grossman.

Nardulli, Peter F., James Eisenstein, and Roy B. Flemming. 1988. *The Tenor of Justice: Criminal Courts and the Guilty Plea Process.* Urbana: University of Illinois Press.

Neuman, W. Russell, Marion R. Just, and Ann N. Crigler. 1992. *Common Knowledge: News and the Construction of Political Meaning*. Chicago: University of Chicago Press.

Newland, Chester A. 1964. "Press Coverage of the United States Supreme Court." *Western Political Quarterly* 17 (March): 15–36.

O'Brien, David M. 1988. *Judicial Roulette: Report of the Twentieth Century Fund Task Force on Judicial Selection*. New York: Priority Press.

O'Brien, David M. 1993. *Storm Center: The Supreme Court in American Politics*. 3rd. ed. New York: Norton.

O'Brien, Tim. 1983. "Yes, But . . . ." *Judicature* 67 (June-July): 12–15.

O'Brien, Tim. 1990. "Best Kept Secrets of the Judiciary." *Judicature* 73 (April-May): 341–43.

O'Callaghan, Jerome, and James O. Dukes. 1992. "Media Coverage of the Supreme Court's Caseload." *Journalism Quarterly* 69 (Spring): 195–203.

Olson, Walter K. 1991. *The Litigation Explosion: What Happened When America Unleashed the Lawsuit*. New York: Thomas Talley Books/Dutton.

Onishi, Norimitsu. 1996. "The Courts, and Not Grades, May Decide a High School's Vale-dictorian." *New York Times*, June 12, p. A5.

Orwell, Sonia, and Ian Angus, eds. 1968. T*he Collected Essays, Journalism, and Let-ters of George Orwell.* London, U.K.: Secker and Warburg.

Packer, Herbert L. 1968. *The Limits of the Criminal Sanction.* Stanford, CA: Stanford University Press.

Paletz, David L., and Robert M. Entman. 1981. *Media Power Politics.* New York: Free Press.

Parry, Robert. 1992. *Fooling America: How Washington Insiders Twist the Truth and Manufacture the Conventional Wisdom.* New York: William Morrow.

Patrinos, D. 1993. "Cameras in the Dahmer Courtroom: The Media Circus That Wasn't." *Wisconsin Lawyer* 66 (March): 10–13.

Perry, H. W. Jr. 1992. *Deciding to Decide: Agenda-Setting in the U. S. Supreme Court.* Cambridge, MA: Harvard University Press.

Pertschuk, Michael, and Wendy Schaetzel. 1989. *The People Rising: The Campaign against the Bork Nomination.* New York: Thunder's Mouth Press.

Phelps, Timothy M., and Helen Winternitz. 1992. *Capitol Games: Clarence Thomas, Anita Hill, and the Story of a Supreme Court Nomination.* New York: Hyperion.

President's Council on Competitiveness. 1981. *Agenda for Civil Justice Reform in America.* Washington, DC: U. S. Government Printing Office.

Provizer, Norman. 1981. "A Case Study." *Masthead* 33 (Spring): 26.

Quayle, Dan. 1992. "Civil Justice Reform" *American University Law Review* 41 (Spring): 559–69.

Rabinovitz, Jonathan. 1994. "Gag Order Sought for Lawyers in Long Island Train Shoot-ings." *New York Times*, April 2, p. 25.

Radelet, Michael L., Hugo A. Bedau, and Constance E. Putnam. 1992. *In Spite of Inno-cence: The Ordeal of 400 Americans Wrongly Convicted of Crimes Punish-able by Death.* Boston: Northeastern University Press.

Reidinger, Paul. 1987. "The Politics of Judging." *ABA Journal* (April 1): 52–58.

Robinson, Sol. 1971. *Guidelines for News Reporters*, p. 25. Blue Ridge Summit, PA: Tab Books.

Roshco, Bernard. 1975. *Newsmaking.* Chicago: University of Chicago Press.

Rothwax, Harold J. 1996. *Guilty: The Collapse of Criminal Justice.* New York: Random House.

Rottman, David B., Carol R. Flango, and R. Sheldine Lockley. 1995. *State Court Organi-zation 1993.* Washington, DC: Bureau of Justice Statistics.

Rotunda, Ronald D. 1995. "Innovations Disguised as Traditions: A Historical Review of the Supreme Court Nominations Process." *University of Illinois Law Review* 1995: 123–31.

Rudman, Warren B. 1996. *Combat: Twelve Years in the U. S. Senate*. New York: Random House.

Rustad, Michael. 1992. "In Defense of Punitive Damages in Products Liability: Testing Tort Anecdotes with Empirical Data." *Iowa Law Review* 78 (Oct.): 1–78.

Rustad, Michael, and Thomas Koenig. 1993. "The Historical Continuity of Punitive Damages Awards: Reforming the Tort Reformers." *American University Law Review* 42 (Summer): 1269–1333.

Sabato, Larry J. 1991. *Feeding Frenzy: How Attack Journalism Has Transformed American Politics*. New York: Free Press.

Scheb, John M., Jr. 1983. "Is Anyone Listening? Assessing Bar Influence in Merit Retention Elections in Florida." *Judicature* 67 (Sept.): 113–19.

Schlesinger, Philip, and Howard Tumber. 1994. *Reporting Crime: The Media Politics of Criminal Justice*. Oxford: Clarendon Press.

Schudson, Michael. 1995. *The Power of News*. Cambridge, MA: Harvard University Press.

Schwartz, Bernard. 1988. *Behind Bakke: Affirmative Action and the Supreme Court*. New York: New York University Press.

Schwartz, Herman. 1988. *Packing the Courts: The Conservative Campaign to Rewrite the Constitution*. New York: Simon and Schuster.

Segal, Jeffrey A., and Harold J. Spaeth. 1993. *The Supreme Court and the Attitudinal Model*. New York: Cambridge University Press.

Sevilla, Charles. 1991. *Wilkes: His Life and Crimes*. New York: Ballantine.

Shapiro, Martin. 1981. *Courts: A Comparative and Political Analysis*. Chicago: University of Chicago Press.

Shapiro, Robert. 1994. "Secrets of a Celebrity Lawyer: How O.J.'s Chief Strategist Works the Press." *Columbia Journalism Review* 33 (Sept.-Oct.): 25.

Shaw, David. 1981. "Media Coverage of the Courts: Improving But Still Not Adequate." *Judicature* 65 (June-July): 18–24.

Shaw, David. 1984. *Press Watch: A Provocative Look at How Newspapers Report the News*. New York: Macmillan.

Sigal, Leon V. 1973. *Reporters and Officials*. Lexington, MA: Heath.

Silverstein, Mark. 1994. *Judicious Choices: The New Politics of Supreme Court Confirmations*. New York: Norton.

Silverstein, Mark. 1994. "Special Interests Produce Dull Court Nominees." *National Law Journal* 16 (July 11): A21.

Silverstein, Mark, and William Haltom. 1996. "You Can't Always Get What You Want: Reflections on the Ginsburg and Breyer Nominations." *Journal of Law & Politics* 12 (Summer): 459–79.

Slotnick, Elliot E. 1988. "Federal Judicial Recruitment and Selection Research: A Review Essay," *Judicature* 71 (April-May): 317–24.

Slotnick, Elliot E. 1988. "Review Essay on Judicial Recruitment and Selection," *Justice System Journal* 13 (Spring): 109–24.

Slotnick, Elliot E. 1991. "Media Coverage of Supreme Court Decision-Making: Problems and Prospects," *Judicature* 75 (Oct.-Nov.): 128–31.

Sobel, Lionel S. 1970. "News Coverage of the Supreme Court." *American Bar Association Journal* 56 (June): 547–50.

Soley, Lawrence C. 1992. *The News Shapers: The Sources Who Explain the News.* New York: Praeger.

Solimine, Michael E. 1980. "Newsmagazine Coverage of the Supreme Court." *Journalism Quarterly* 57 (Winter): 661–63.

Solimine, Michael E. 1988. "Ideology and En Banc Review." *North Carolina Law Review* 69 (Nov.): 29–71.

Sowell, Thomas. 1994. "The Greenhouse Effect." *Wall Street Journal,* March 8, p. A10.

Squires, James D. 1993. *Read All About It! The Corporate Takeover of America's Newspapers.* New York: Random House/Times Books.

Stein, M. L. 1990. "Scalia Discusses the Press." *Editor & Publisher* 123 (Sept. 8): 16.

Stertz, Bradley A. 1988. "Jury Clears Audi of Auto Defect Causing Death." *Wall Street Journal,* June 15, p. 4.

Streisand, Betsy. 1995. "And Justice for All?" *U. S. News & World Report,* Oct. 9, p. 46.

Tarpley, J. Douglas. 1984. "American Newsmagazine Coverage of the Supreme Court, 1978–81." *Journalism Quarterly* 61 (Winter): 801–4.

Tarr, G. Alan, and Mary C. A. Porter. 1988. *State Supreme Courts in State and Nation.* New Haven, CT: Yale University Press.

Taylor, Stuart, Jr. 1987. "Ideological Feud Erupts in a Key Appeals Court." *New York Times,* Aug. 15, p. 7.

Thaler, Paul. 1994. *The Watchful Eye: American Justice in the Age of the Television Trial.* Westport, CT: Praeger.

Thompson, E. P. 1975. *Whigs and Hunters: The Origin of the Black Act.* London, U.K.: Allen Lane.

Toobin, Jeffrey. 1996. "Asking for It: O. J. Simpson's New Defense Strategy Is as Audacious as the Last." *New Yorker,* Dec. 9: 56–60.

Toobin, Jeffrey. 1996. "Supreme Sacrifice: Laurence Tribe May Never Be on the Supreme Court, But Then He Really Doesn't Need to Be." *New Yorker,* July 8, pp. 43–47.

Totenberg, Nina. 1988. "The Confirmation Process and the Public: To Know or Not to Know." *Harvard Law Review* 101 (April):1213–29.

Tuchman, Gaye. 1978. *Making News: A Study in the Construction of Reality.* New York: Free Press.

Uelmen, Gerald F. 1996. *Lessons from the Trial: The People v. O. J. Simpson.* Kansas City, MO: Andrews and McMeel.

Underwood, Doug. 1993. *When MBAs Rule the Newsroom: How the Marketers and Managers Are Reshaping Today's Media.* New York: Columbia University Press.

Vidmar, Neil. 1996. *Medical Malpractice and the American Jury.* Ann Arbor: University of Michigan Press.

Wasby, Stephen L. 1970. *The Impact of the United States Supreme Court.* Homewood, IL: Dorsey Press.

Wasby, Stephen L. 1993. *The Supreme Court in the Federal Judicial System.* 4th ed. Chicago: Nelson-Hall.

Watson, George L., and John A. Stookey. 1995. *Shaping America: The Politics of Supreme Court Appointments.* New York: HarperCollins.

Weber, Max. 1978. *Economy and Society.* Edited by Guenter Roth and Claus Wittich. Berkeley: University of California Press.

Wermiel, Stephen. 1987. "Appeals Court Reverses Itself in 3 Cases, Spotlighting Partisan Splits Nationwide." *Wall Street Journal,* Aug. 3, 1987, p. 7.

Wermiel, Stephen. 1988. "Full-Court Review of Panel Rulings Becomes Tool Often Used by Reagan Judges Aiming to Mold Law." *Wall Street Journal,* March 22, p. 70.

Winters, Glenn R. 1967. "One-Man Judicial Selection." In *Selected Readings — Judicial Selection and Tenure,* Glenn R. Winters, ed., pp. 120–25. Chicago: American Judicature Society

Wold, John T., and John H. Culver. 1987. "The Defeat of the California Justices: The Campaign, The Electorate, and the Issue of Judicial Accountability," *Judicature* 70 (April–May): 348–55.

Woodward, Bob. 1993. "Mike Wallace: Grand Inquisitor of *60 Minutes.*" *TV Guide,* Nov. 6-12, 1993, p. 16.

Woodward, Bob, and Scott Armstrong. 1979. *The Brethren: Inside the Supreme Court.* New York: Simon and Schuster.

Articles

"Africa: Third Group on Trial in Egyptian Plot Case." 1993. *San Francisco Chronicle,* Sept. 13, three star ed., p. A14.

"After California, What's Next for Judicial Elections?" 1987. *Judicature* 70 (April–May): 356–64.

"Al Unser Sr. Announces He's Retiring as Driver." 1994. *San Diego Union Tribune,* May 17, 8th and 9th eds., p. D2.

"Demystifying the Judicial Process: How Can Judges and Journalists Really Help?" 1984. *Judicature* 67 (April): 448–57.

"Kerrigan Attacker and Accomplice Sent to Jail." 1994. *New York Times,* May 17, p. B13.

"Kerrigan Attacker, Accomplice Sentenced to Prison." 1994. *Dallas Morning News*, May 17, Home Final ed., p. 3A.

"Louisville Crime Court Reports." 1991. *Louisville Courier-Journal,* Feb. 6, metro ed., p. 2B.

"Man Sues State: Not Enough Hot Air in Capitol." 1996. *Tacoma Morning News Tribune*, Nov. 15, p. A9.

"McDonalds Cup of Scalding Coffee: $2.9 Million Award." 1994. *Chicago Tribune*, Aug. 18, p. 1.

"Note: The Politics of En Banc Review." 1989. *Harvard Law Review* 102 (Feb.):864–84.

"Sleeping Pills in Asia and Milwaukee, Etc." 1992. *Washington Times,* Feb. 8, p. B2.

"Two Sentenced in Assault on Kerrigan." 1994. *Los Angeles Times*, May 17, Home ed., p. 3.

"Two Start Sentences in Kerrigan Case." 1994. *St. Petersburg Times,* May 17, p. 2C.

index